教育部、国家语委重大文化工程

　　"中华思想文化术语传播工程"成果

国家社会科学基金重大项目

　　"中华思想文化术语的整理、传播与数据库建设"（15ZDB003）

"十三五"国家重点出版物出版规划项目

获评第二届向全国推荐中华优秀传统文化普及图书

Key Concepts in Chinese
Thought and Culture :
Literature and Art
|Chinese-English|

中华思想文化术语

|中英对照|

文艺卷

《中华思想文化术语》编委会 编

外语教学与研究出版社
FOREIGN LANGUAGE TEACHING AND RESEARCH PRESS
北京 BEIJING

"中华思想文化术语传播工程"
专家团队
（按音序 In Alphabetical Order）

Scholars Participating in the Project "Key Concepts in Chinese Thought and Culture: Communication Through Translation"

顾问（Advisors）

李学勤（Li Xueqin） 林戊荪（Lin Wusun）

叶嘉莹（Florence Chia-ying Yeh） 张岂之（Zhang Qizhi）

专家委员会（Committee of Scholars）

主任（Director）

韩　震（Han Zhen）

委员（Members）

晁福林（Chao Fulin） 陈德彰（Chen Dezhang）

陈明明（Chen Mingming） 冯志伟（Feng Zhiwei）

韩经太（Han Jingtai） 黄友义（Huang Youyi）

金元浦（Jin Yuanpu） 李建中（Li Jianzhong）

李照国（Li Zhaoguo） 楼宇烈（Lou Yulie）

马箭飞（Ma Jianfei） 聂长顺（Nie Changshun）

潘公凯（Pan Gongkai） 王　博（Wang Bo）

王　宁（Wang Ning）　　　　叶　朗（Ye Lang）

袁济喜（Yuan Jixi）　　　　袁行霈（Yuan Xingpei）

张立文（Zhang Liwen）　　　张西平（Zhang Xiping）

郑述谱（Zheng Shupu）

特邀汉学家（Scholars of China Studies）

艾　恺（Guy Salvatore Alitto）　　安乐哲（Roger T. Ames）

包华石（Martin Joseph Powers）　狄伯杰（B. R. Deepak）

顾　彬（Wolfgang Kubin）　　　韩安德（Harry Anders Hansson）

柯鸿冈（Paul Crook）　　　　　柯马凯（Michael Crook）

司马麟（Don Starr）　　　　　王　健、李　盈（Jan & Yvonne Walls）

魏查理（Charles Willemen）

学术委员会（Academic Committee）

安　瑞（Andrea M. Harwell）　　白振奎（Bai Zhenkui）

蔡力坚（Cai Lijian）　　　　　陈海燕（Chen Haiyan）

陈少明（Chen Shaoming）　　　戴斯客（Lawrence Scott Davis）

付志斌（Fu Zhibin）　　　　　郭晓东（Guo Xiaodong）

郝任德（Michael Hoare）　　　何世剑（He Shijian）

胡　海（Hu Hai）　　　　　　胡智锋（Hu Zhifeng）

黄春艳（Huang Chunyan）　　　贾德忠（Jia Dezhong）

姜海龙（Jiang Hailong）　　　　蒋好书（Jiang Haoshu）

李存山（Li Cunshan）　　　　　李景林（Li Jinglin）

李雪涛（Li Xuetao）　　　　林满秋（Lin Man-Chiu）

刘　青（Liu Qing）　　　　　柳　拯（Liu Zheng）

吕玉华（Lü Yuhua）　　　　　满兴远（Man Xingyuan）

梅缵月（Mei Zuanyue）　　　孟庆楠（Meng Qingnan）

裴德思（Thorsten Pattberg）　乔　希（Joshua Mason）

乔　永（Qiao Yong）　　　　任大援（Ren Dayuan）

沈卫星（Shen Weixing）　　　施晓菁（Lynette Shi）

孙艺风（Sun Yifeng）　　　　陶黎庆（Tao Liqing）

童孝华（Tong Xiaohua）　　　王刚毅（Wang Gangyi）

王柯平（Wang Keping）　　　王丽丽（Wang Lili）

王　琳（Wang Lin）　　　　　王明杰（Wang Mingjie）

王维东（Wang Weidong）　　　魏玉山（Wei Yushan）

温海明（Wen Haiming）　　　吴根友（Wu Genyou）

徐明强（Xu Mingqiang）　　　徐亚男（Xu Yanan）

徐　英（Xu Ying）　　　　　严文斌（Yan Wenbin）

严学军（Yan Xuejun）　　　　杨雪冬（Yang Xuedong）

杨义瑞（Yang Yirui）　　　　于文涛（Yu Wentao）

余来明（Yu Laiming）　　　　张建敏（Zhang Jianmin）

张　静（Zhang Jing）　　　　章思英（Zhang Siying）

赵　桐（Zhao Tong）　　　　赵　悠（Zhao You）

郑　开（Zheng Kai）　　　　周云帆（Zhou Yunfan）

朱绩崧（Zhu Jisong）　　　　朱良志（Zhu Liangzhi）

朱　渊（Zhu Yuan）　　　　左　励（Zuo Li）

前言

韩震

作为莎士比亚所说的"万物的灵长",人与其他动物的区别,也许就在于思想的有无。人也是一个物种、一种动物,但却是一种有思想的动物。当然,从动物意识发展到人的思想,之间肯定不是没有丝毫联系的绝对鸿沟。但是,在漫长的进化史中,人类意识逐步符号化,让人的情感、欲望、冲动、想象获得了标识,有了这些标识,人们就可以把零碎的意识形成某种系统的思想。

在动物那里,如鹿的眼中看到的是作为食物的各种草本身,而老虎眼里看到的是作为猎物的鹿本身,但人则变得越来越经过"草"这个词语来理解草本身,经过"鹿"这个词语来理解鹿本身,经过"虎"这个词语来理解虎本身。人在思想意识中失去了与世界的直接性,但却获得了超越具体性的抽象能力。正是这种抽象能力让人获得了越来越宽广的思想空间。

最初的思想空间是靠声音符号构筑的。代际之间的口口相传就成为思想延续的途径。再加上远古时代人的寿命的短暂,因而思想与知识的积累非常缓慢,甚至许多知识和思想往往因为有思想的个体生命的消失而消失。

有了文字之后,人类思想的发展呈现出一个不断加速的过程。这是因为有了文字对思想与知识的标识性固化:一方面有了文字的标识,人相对容易思想了。就像行路者有了地图,更容易理解自己在什么方位上，应该朝什么地方走。正如维特根斯坦所说的，文字表达的命题图示着世界。另一方面，即使掌握思想与知识的某个人因其生命的结束在肉体上消失了，但有了文字的记叙，思想仍然可能被其他人激活。只要这种文字仍然被使用，后人就可以通过阅读来激活这种知识与思想，甚至不再被使用的死语言也可以破解，古代许多文明的成就就是通过这种方式被重新认识的。在人类语言中，那些最重要的概念就是我们所说的"思想文化术语"。

有了对文字的阅读，我们不仅可以理解几千年前先辈们的智慧结晶，如《道德经》《论语》《庄子》《孟子》《韩非子》，而且可以理解地球对面我们从未谋面的欧美人的思想。这就是阅读的力量，人们通过阅读在不断拓展着思想的空间。一个人阅读的空间，就是这个人思想的空间，而这个空间是由许许多多的思想文化术语支撑起来的。显然，正是这些思想文化术语引导着人们的思想运思，支撑着越来越广阔的思想空间。在欧洲文化中，像德谟克利特的"原子"、柏拉图的"理念"、亚里士多德的"形式"、孟德斯鸠的"法的精神"、康德的"先验理念"、黑格尔的"绝对精神"……就是支撑西方思想文化运思的术语。

同世界上其他民族的思想文化和知识体系一样，中国的思想文化和知识体系也有自己的特殊的术语。正是这些术语构成中国特色的思想文化和知识体系。在历史上，中国的先贤一直通过基于中国时空体系下的学术话语表达中国人对世界的认识，因此就有了源远流长、博大精深的中国思想文化和知识体系。今天，任何人要理解中国学术思想的文脉，理清中国学术演化的谱系，就会迎面碰到许多特殊的或非常具有中国特色的术语，如"阴阳""中道""和""义礼""厚德载物""自强不息""知行合一"……只有理解了这些术语，才能正确地把握中国的思想文化。

在漫长的中华文明演进历史中形成的中国传统思想文化术语，

对于理解当代中国思想文化、知识体系和中国的现实具有基础性的意义。

首先，中华思想文化术语蕴含着中国文化传统和思想意识的精髓。面对不同时空体系下的挑战，不同的民族在生产方式和生活方式上就有了特定的差异。譬如，在人们生产活动和生活样式上，热带和温带肯定不同，平原为主的地域和山峦为主的地域当然有差异，沙漠地带和沿海地区显然有别，牧区和农耕区也会有许多迥异之处。这些生产活动和生活样式的特点逐渐积淀凝结，就必然影响到民族的文化样式、行为习惯和精神特质。民族的文化样式、行为习惯和精神特质反过来又阐释、维护和强化着其赖以出现和发展的特定生产方式和生活方式。例如，作为以农业为主的古代中国，必须靠一定规模的水利工程才能保证民众的安全和生产，因此，中国自古以来就强调人际关系之间的和谐与秩序，所以就有了具备中国特点的思想文化术语，譬如，"家国天下"之中的"家"和"国"就有了特定的精神内涵。英语中的国家有nation、country、state等表达，但nation更倾向于以国民、民族的角度谈国家，country则倾向于从国土的视角去看国家，state是从制度的侧面看国家，所有这些表达都与"家"没有半点关系，但中国一提到"国家"就会想象到家庭的温暖，国家与作为社会细胞的家庭之间的内在联系就得到了很好的确证。

其次，中华思想文化术语体现着中国人特有的文化传统、思维方式和理解结构。中国的"中道"概念与中国人的理智密切相关，这有效地消解了时常出现的思想极端化的倾向；"和而不同"在理性处理人际关系方面有明显的中国特色。实际上，即使中国人在学习外来的理论和思想时，也是按照中国人的理解结构和文化想象力来理解外来的东西的。譬如，中国人民在进行中国特色社会主义市场改革时，就不搞什么"休克疗法"，而是摸着作为中国社会现实问题的"石头"过河，这种中道、理智的方式保证了改革开放和经济发展沿着稳妥的道路高速前进，从而取得了举世瞩目的成就。另外，在科学技术和人文社科学术方面中国也有新的进展，在世界学术界的影响开始提升，这就说明中国有自己特殊的文化传统和学术理解结构，这种结构把外来的思想和理论进行消化、转化，从而有利于学术上的自主创新。显然，中国是根据中华民族长期认识世界、改造世界过程中形成的"理解结构"，自主地、有选择地汲取和消化外来学术成果的。

最后，中华思想文化术语是构成中国特色学术体系和话语体系的基本表达方式或特定符号，或者说，是构成中国话语体系中链接思想观念的关节点。很多思想文化的学术理论或学说，都有普遍的世界意义。但是，不同的理论或学说却各有自己的表达方式，理论的独特性往往是由不同的术语或概念来体现的。譬如，约瑟夫·奈提出所谓"软实力"和"硬实力"的区分，但在中国，几千年前就有了"王道"和"霸道"的分野。所谓"王道"，就是统治者要按照当时通行的人性理解、价值观念和社会道德标准进行治理；反之，如果统治阶级依靠武力、蛮横无礼、颐指气使、巧取豪夺，就表现为"霸道"。另外，像处理相辅相成的事物或关系时，各国都有保持某种平衡的观点，但中国阴阳平衡的思想就更加积极，中国认为阴柔胜过刚强，"阴"不仅不是消极的，而是在特定条件下更加积极的力量。西方在看待竞争时，往往采取的是"零和思维"方式；而中国人持有关于阴阳之间你中有我、我中有你及二者相互转化的思维方式，因而更加愿意采取双赢、多赢、共赢的方法。由于同样的原因，中国的术语"礼"就包含有英语propriety等词语所无法表达的文化及人际关系制度性的内容。

总之，在漫长的历史中，中国形成了自己的文化传统和学术理解结构，中华思想文化术语就是这种传统和思想结构的结晶，这些术语蕴含着中国文化传统和思想意识的精髓，体现着中国人特有的思维方式和理解结构，并且构成中国话语体系和思想表达方式。只有准确理解这些术语的微妙内涵，才能真正在深层意义上理解中国的社会和文化，理解中国人的思维方式和行为。因此，在考察、思考和理解中国问题时，必须理解中国本身的概念和术语，弄清楚这些概念和术语的特殊内涵和规定性。鉴于此，对内涵丰富、多姿多彩的思想文化术语进行整理、研究和翻译，就成为特别有意义的工作。

为做好中华思想文化术语的整理和传播工作，2014年经国务院批准，设立"中华思想文化术语传播工程"（以下简称"工程"），并建立了由教育部、国家语委作为召集单位，多个部委（单位）为成员的部际联席会议机制，负责统筹协调中华思想文化术语传播工作。教育部、国家语委委托北京外国语大学和外语教学与研究出版社具体承担项目的推进。奉献给读者的《中华思想文化术语》（哲学卷、历史卷、文艺卷）就是这些研究工程的成果，图书的出版必将有利于中外文化的交流互鉴，促进中外人民之间的相互理解，推动世界更好地走和平与发展之路。

Foreword

Han Zhen

Human beings, described by William Shakespeare as "the paragon of animals," probably differ from other species in that they are able to think. Yet there can be no absolute gulf between animal consciousness and human thought; it is certainly not true that nothing connects them. However, in the long history of evolution, human consciousness has gradually evolved a system of symbols, so that emotions, desires, impulses, and imaginations have acquired markers, and with these markers people can form fragmentary consciousness into systematic thought.

In the eyes of animals, such as the deer, grass is seen as food, while to the tiger the deer is identified as prey. Humans, however, increasingly understand the word "grass" as an identifier of the plant itself, and the word "deer" as identifying the deer itself, and ditto for the word "tiger." Through their thought process humans have lost their sense of immediacy in relation to the world, but they have gained the ability to abstract beyond the concrete. It is this ability that allows humans to obtain an ever-widening space of thought.

Initially the space of thought was constructed by sound symbols. Therefore oral transmission between generations was the main means by which ideas were passed on. This, plus the short lifespan of the ancients, slowed the accumulation of ideas and knowledge. Indeed, knowledge and ideas often got lost upon the death of the individuals who held them.

With the advent of written language, the development of human thought has become an ever-accelerating process. This is because written language makes solid records of ideas and knowledge possible. With the help of written language, people find it easier to think, just as a traveler with a map finds it easier to understand where he is and where he should be heading. As Ludwig Wittgenstein put it, the propositions expressed in words map the world.

In addition, with written language, even if someone who holds ideas and knowledge disappears physically at the end of his life, his ideas may still be accessible to others. As long as that written language remains in use, future generations can access his knowledge and ideas by reading his works. Even if a language is no longer in use, it can still be deciphered, and this has made it possible to recapture the achievements of many ancient civilizations. The most important conceptualizations in human language are what we call "key concepts in thought and culture."

With the ability to read words, the Chinese people could not only come to fathom the wisdom of their forefathers going back thousands of years, expressed in works such as *Dao De Jing*, *The Analects*, *Zhuangzi*, *Mencius*, and *Hanfeizi*, but also gain an understanding of the thoughts of Europeans and Americans across the oceans, whom they may have never encountered. This is the power of reading, through which people are constantly expanding the space of their thought.

The space in which one reads is the space in which one thinks, and this space is supported by many concepts in thought and culture.

Obviously, it is these concepts that guide people's thinking and support their ever-widening space of thought.

In European culture, concepts such as Democritus' "atom," Plato's "doctrine of ideas," Aristotle's "form," Montesquieu's "spirit of laws," Kant's "*a priori* knowledge," and Hegel's "absolute spirit" are what underpins Western thought and culture.

As is the case with other nations in the world, China's system of thought, culture, and knowledge possesses its own distinct concepts. It is these concepts that constitute the knowledge, culture and thought with Chinese characteristics. Throughout history, Chinese scholars expressed their understanding of the world through academic discourse based on the Chinese system of time and space, thus giving rise to the longstanding and profound Chinese thought.

Today, anyone who wishes to understand Chinese academic thought and gain insight into the genealogy of Chinese academic evolution will be confronted with many concepts specific to Chinese culture, such as yin and yang, the middle way, harmony, righteousness and propriety, having ample virtue and carrying all things, striving continuously to strengthen oneself, or unity of knowledge and action. Only by understanding such very Chinese concepts can one correctly grasp the essence of Chinese thought and culture.

The concepts in traditional Chinese thought and culture formed during the long evolution of Chinese civilization are of fundamental significance for understanding contemporary Chinese thought, culture, knowledge, and indeed China itself.

First of all, such concepts contain the essence of Chinese cultural traditions and thought. Faced with the challenges of different systems of time and space, different peoples have different modes of production and lifestyles. For example, in terms of people's production activities and lifestyles, there are different characteristics between tropical and temperate zones; between the plains and mountainous regions; between deserts and coastal areas; and between pastoral and agricultural areas. These characteristics of production activities and lifestyles gradually accumulate and coalesce. They inevitably affect people's culture, behavioral habits, and spirit which, in turn, explain, maintain, and strengthen the specific modes of production and lifestyles on the basis of which they have emerged and developed.

For example, in ancient China, where agriculture was the mainstay, a certain scale of irrigation works was necessary to ensure the safety and production of the population. Therefore, harmony and order in interpersonal relations has always been paramount, which has found expression in the language. For instance, the words "family" and "state" are brought together in the concept "family, state, and all under heaven," and imbued with a specific cultural connotation.

In English, the Chinese word *guojia* (国家) can be rendered variously as nation, country, or state. "Nation" generally denotes the people, "country" denotes its land mass, and "state" emphasizes the administration system. None of them has anything to do with family. However, the Chinese term *guojia* (literally national family) reminds people of the warmth of a family and proves the intrinsic link between the country and the family, a cell of society.

Secondly, concepts in Chinese thought and culture reflect the unique cultural traditions, ways of thinking and structures of understanding of the Chinese people. The Chinese concept "the middle way" is closely related to the Chinese people's reasoning, which effectively dissipates the tendency of extreme ways of thinking that occurs from time to time. The concept "harmony but not uniformity" has distinctive Chinese characteristics in the rational handling of interpersonal relations.

In fact, even when the Chinese people learn foreign theories and ideas, they understand them according to their own structure of understanding and cultural imagination. For example, when the Chinese people carried out socialist market reforms, they did not engage in shock therapy, but rather solved problems in a manner of "crossing the river by feeling the stones." Such a balanced and rational approach ensured proper and rapid reform, opening up, and economic development, with impressive achievements.

In addition, China has made new advances in science and technology and in the humanities and social sciences, and has begun to increase its influence in the world academic community. This shows that China uses its own special cultural traditions and academic understanding structure to digest and transform foreign ideas and theories, in a manner conducive to taking ownership of such academic innovation. Thus China independently and selectively absorbs and digests foreign academic achievements, utilizing the "structure of understanding" evolved by the Chinese people in the long process of understanding and transforming their world.

Finally, concepts in Chinese thought and culture are the basic expressions or specific symbols that constitute the academic system and discourse system with Chinese characteristics. In other words, they are the joints that link thoughts and ideas in the Chinese discourse system.

Many academic theories or doctrines of thought have universal significance. However, different theories or doctrines have their own ways of expression, and the uniqueness of theories is often reflected in different terms or concepts. For example, Joseph Nye coined the terms "soft power" and "hard power," while thousands of years ago in China, the concepts "kingly way" and "despotic governance" were created. The "kingly way" means that the ruler governs according to the prevailing understanding of human nature, values, and social moral standards; on the other hand, if the ruling class relies on ruthless, arbitrary, and oppressive force, then it is deemed to be "despotic."

When dealing with complementary things or relationships, all countries hold to the idea of maintaining a certain balance, but in China, the pursuit of balancing yin and yang is more active. The Chinese believe that femininity surpasses masculinity, and that yin is not only non-negative, but is a more positive force under certain conditions. The West tends to adopt zero-sum thinking toward competition, whereas the Chinese hold the idea that yin and yang are interwoven and can be transformed into each other, thus they are more willing to adopt a win-win approach. For the same reason, the Chinese term *li* (礼 rites/social norms/propriety) encompasses cultural and interpersonal institutional content beyond what is expressed in English by words such as "propriety."

In short, over its long history, China has developed its own cultural traditions and structures of academic understanding, and concepts in Chinese thought and culture are the crystallization of such traditions and structures of thought. These concepts embody the essence of China's cultural traditions and ideas, reflect the unique Chinese way of thinking and structure of understanding, and constitute the Chinese discourse system and the way of expressing ideas. Only by accurately understanding the subtle connotations of these concepts can one truly appreciate Chinese society and culture, and comprehend the thinking and behavior of the Chinese people in a deeper sense. It is therefore important to understand these concepts and terms and learn their special connotations and prescriptive nature, when examining, thinking about and understanding China. And it is this that has made the collating, studying, and translating of the concepts in Chinese thought and culture a particularly meaningful task.

In order to collate and better share these concepts with international audiences, the project "Key Concepts in Chinese Thought and Culture: Communication Through Translation" was established with the approval of the State Council in 2014. In addition, an inter-ministerial joint meeting involving many diverse institutions was established under the leadership of the Ministry of Education and the State Language Affairs Commission to coordinate the dissemination of concepts in Chinese thought and culture, who commissioned Beijing Foreign Studies University and Foreign Language Teaching and Research Press to push forward this project. The present three volumes of *Key Concepts in Chinese Thought and Culture* (i.e., *Philosophy*, *History*, and *Literature and Art*) are the result of these endeavors, and are published to promote the exchange between Chinese and other cultures, enhance the mutual understanding between the Chinese and other people, and help the world move along the path of peace and development.

出版说明

　　"中华思想文化术语"是由中华民族所创造或构建，凝聚、浓缩了中华哲学思想、人文精神、思维方式、价值观念，以词或短语形式固化的概念和核心词。中华文明素以历史悠久、博大精深闻名世界。由于特殊的地理环境和历史发展，中华民族孕育繁衍了独特的社会构造、历史形态、政治伦理、学术思想、人文精神等，经孔、墨、老、庄、孟、荀等许多思想家的浓缩提纯和历代学者的推阐增益，凝练形成了数以千计的蕴含丰富且充满理性特征的范畴、概念和核心词，并由此支撑起辉煌宏富的中华思想文化大厦。它是中华民族千百年来对宇宙万物、社会伦常、人与自然关系进行独立探索与理性思考的智慧结晶，代表了中华民族的思想基因、精神追求、文明标识。这些历千百年而弥新的思想文化术语至今仍在人类文明的天空熠熠生辉，它们是中华先哲留给今人的伟大精神遗产，也是中华民族贡献给世界的珍贵精神财富。

　　然而，在很长一段时期，我们对中华传统思想文化术语研究不够，在与世界其他文明特别是与西方文明的对话中，难免袭用西方话语，或者按西方话语标准解读中华传统思想文化术语的内容，造成语义的错置和误读；在引用这些术语时，外国受众也时常因为不了解术语的确切含义或深层意蕴而感到困惑甚而出现误读、误译、误解的情况。究其原因，是我们没有注重中华思想文化术语的系统整理、诠释、翻译和传播，更没有以此为依托去构建能够反映和代表中华民族哲学思想、人文精神、价值观念、思维方式、文化特征的核心话语体系。

基于这样的背景，北京外国语大学、外语教学与研究出版社在教育部及国家语委的指导下，于2014年正式启动了"中华思想文化术语传播工程"（以下简称"工程"）。"工程"聘请著名学者叶嘉莹、李学勤、张岂之、林戊荪担任顾问，聘请韩震教授担任专家委员会主任；成立了由哲学、文学艺术、历史等学科以及翻译、传播、海外汉学等领域上百位专家学者组成的团队，聚焦中华思想文化术语的整理、诠释、翻译、传播与学术研究；在外语教学与研究出版社设立秘书处，具体落实、推进"工程"各项工作并出版相关成果。"工程"的目标是：立足于中华传统思想文化，深度挖掘那些包含中华思想基因、精神追求、文明标识，在中华思想文化史上具有开创意义或承先启后作用，在国际文化交流与传播中有较高使用频度，具有超越时空的普遍意义与当代价值的思想文化术语，用通俗易懂的语言进行诠释，并将其译成英语和其他外语，以便世界更准确地了解中华传统思想文化，进而更全面地了解中国，了解中华民族的过去、现在和未来，了解中国人及海外华人的精神世界，促进中外文明之间的平等对话和互学互鉴。

"工程"迄今7年，共整理、出版了9辑中英对照"中华思想文化术语"系列图书，还衍生了若干系列产品，深受学界与广大读者的好评。"中华思想文化术语"系列图书已授权30种语言在国外出版发行。2020年11月，我们将900条术语以"合订本"形式出版，现在又将其按哲学、历史、文艺学科分类，辑为三卷本，即"哲学卷""历史卷""文艺卷"。各卷术语数量不尽相同；还有少量基础性术语是各学科共通共用的，因而同时收录进不同学科卷。借此次"三卷本"出版之机，我们对参与"工程"的各位专家学者致以最诚挚的谢意！同时对术语的整理、诠释和翻译等情况略作介绍：

1. **术语整理**。由于"中华思想文化术语"的概念是首次提出，首先需要科学界定"术语"含义、确定遴选范围与释义原则等。专家学者们经过若干次研讨，广泛征求各方意见，初步提出了"中华思想文化术语"的定义，确定术语整理范围暂限于人文社科领域，以辛亥革命之前的传统思想文化术语为主，分别从文、史、哲三个学科入手进行遴选。术语的遴选须体现以下原则：（1）由中华民族创造构建并构成中华传统思想文化的基础概念。（2）已经融入中华思想文化并且由中华民族赋予了新的含义或理解的外来术语，也是中华思想文化术语的有机组成部分。（3）体现中华传统的哲学思想、人文精神、思维方式和价值观念。（4）形式上已经凝固成词或已经短语化，考虑到中华思想文化的特殊性，少数结构定型的思想命题也可作为术语。（5）在中华思想文化史上具有一定的开创意义或承先启后作用。（6）在文化交流与传播中使用频度较高并符合人类的共同价值。（7）对构建当代中国话语体系有重要的参考价值。

2. **术语诠释**。毋庸讳言，用二三百字的语言既准确又通俗地讲清楚中华思想文化术语的内涵，难度远大于撰写一篇五六千字的学术文章。因为每一条术语都连接着中华思想文化的整座大厦，对具体条目的诠释关乎对中华思想文化整座大厦的理解与把握，也关乎在现代语境下对传统思想文化术语的重新定位与构建。并且，中国古代没有类似现代的学科分界，一些核心术语几乎通用于现代多个学科，而对于今天的研究者来说，只能从某些方面去认识、诠释这些跨多学科的术语，因此我们所做的诠释不可避免地会带有一定的学科局限。为了尽可能准确呈现术语的丰富内涵，专家团队达成以下共识：术语诠释不可能回答中华思想文化史上的所有问题，不应当也不可能对学术上的不同看法做出定论，更不可能同时满足所有层次的读者需求。我们的目的是梳理、归纳并传达中华思想文化术语的核心含义和主要内容，考辨、还原术语的历史源流与本来面貌不是我们这个基础性文化工程应当承担的任务。在尊重思想史、文化史、学术史研究成果的前提下，也应当根据当今中国实际与新的时代要求，根据世界文明的发展趋势与人类共同的价值观念，重点挖掘、阐发那些最能体现中华民族人文精神、思维方式、价值观念、文化特征，对人类文明建设具有普遍价值与借鉴意义的内容和含义，舍弃其糟粕或与当今社会几无关联的成分。

3. **术语引例**。术语的释义多在二三百字，简要诠释其核心或主要含义，很难将其丰富的思想蕴含讲深说透，为了弥补这一不足，我们吸收了专科辞书和语文辞书的长处，专门设计了"引例"。每条术语的"引例"数量1—3个，引例的选取主要遵循四个原则：（1）原初性：能够说明术语的源头或流变。（2）普遍性：具有超越时空的普遍意义。（3）差异性：可以展示术语的不同语义或思想内涵。（4）积极性：对今天的读者具有正面引导价值。

4. **术语翻译**。为了方便外国受众了解中华思想文化术语，所有术语条目的释义与引例都配有英文翻译。过去，术语翻译仅散见于少量古籍的外译本，且大多是对译词，没有释义，对译词淹没于全书的译文中；另外，不同的译者在对术语内涵的理解上有差异，所以同一个术语往往有二三种甚至更多译法，这极大地影响了外国受众对中华思想文化术语的准确理解，也影响了术语国际传播的质量。因此，术语翻译工作的重要性是不言而喻的。可是，无论在学界还是在译界，这都是一项史无前例的开创性工作，而且数量多达900条，既无过往经验借鉴，又无现成作品参考，不难想象在翻译过程中会遇到怎样的困难。经过一段时间的摸索，译审专家最终确定了以下原则：（1）忠实原文文本：翻译之前先要充分理解中文文本的意思，译文力求准确传达中华思想文化术语的核心含义。（2）贴近目标语：尽可能符合目标语的表达习惯以及外国普通受众的认知水平。（3）力求达意，适当音译：当外文翻译作为对译词不能涵盖或无法传达一个术语的主要含义时，可选择音译。（4）规范流程：严格遵循中国译界近70年实践总结的中译外翻译经验，即译者翻译，经汉学家/目标语母语专家润色，最后由中国资深外语专家定稿。实践证明，这几条原则不仅切实可行，也确保了译文的质量。需要说明的是，我们对术语条目的翻译，并不表示其适用于该术语在不同语境中的所有含义。对广大读者而言，这是最贴近原文的翻译；对研究者、翻译者而言，意味着多了一种选择和参考。

相对于中华传统思想文化术语的总量而言，已经整理翻译的900条只是其中的核心术语或基础性术语，哲学、文艺、历史、政治、法律、教育、经济、军事、科技等领域还有数量众多的思想文化术语等待我们深入整理发掘。我们热切希望业界专家和广大读者能够参考、应用我们的释义和译文，也恳切希望业界专家和广大读者给我们提出改进建议，以助力我们将这项工作做得更好。

"中华思想文化术语传播工程"秘书处

外语教学与研究出版社

2021年1月

Publisher's Note

Solidified in the form of words or phrases, the key concepts in Chinese thought and culture collected here comprise the core beliefs and expressions of the Chinese people. They can be seen as crystallizations of Chinese philosophy, humanistic spirit, way of thinking, and values.

Chinese civilization is world-renowned for its long history and its extensive and profound nature. Due to their particular geographical environment and historical development, the Chinese people have nurtured and developed unique social structures, historical forms, political ethics, academic beliefs, and humanistic spirit. These have been refined by the great philosophers Confucius, Mozi, Laozi, Zhuangzi, Mencius, Xunzi and many others, and elaborated by scholars throughout the ages, resulting in the formation of thousands of concepts and core words that are rich in content, the magnificent outcome of independent inquiry into and rational contemplation of the universe, social ethics and the relationship between human beings and nature.

The key concepts in Chinese thought and culture represent the intellectual tradition, cultural pursuit, and civilizational identity of the Chinese people. These centuries-old concepts, strongly-rooted and ever enlightening, are like stars still shining brightly in the sky of human civilization. They are the great cultural legacy of Chinese philosophers, as well as the precious cultural wealth contributed by the Chinese nation to the world.

However, for a long period of time, Chinese scholars have not conducted enough research on concepts in traditional Chinese thought and culture. In dialogue with other civilizations in the world, especially with Western civilizations, they have unavoidably adopted Western discourse or interpreted the content of these concepts according to Western standards, resulting in misplaced semantics and even misinterpretation. When these concepts are quoted, foreign audiences often find it difficult to grasp their exact meaning or profound implications, often leading to misunderstanding, mistranslation, and misinterpretation. The reason for this is that as Chinese scholars we have failed to work on the systematic interpretation, translation and dissemination of these concepts, nor have we built up a core discourse system that reflects and represents the philosophy, humanistic spirit, values, ways of thinking, and culture of the Chinese people.

Against this backdrop, Beijing Foreign Studies University and Foreign Language Teaching and Research Press, under the auspices of the Ministry of Education and the State Language Commission, officially launched the project "Key Concepts in Chinese Thought and Culture: Communication Through Translation" (hereinafter "the Project") in 2014.

The Project invited famous scholars Florence Chia-ying Yeh, Li Xueqin, Zhang Qizhi, and Lin Wusun to serve as advisors, and appointed Professor Han Zhen as the head of the Committee of Scholars. It is supported by a team of more than one hundred experts and scholars specializing in philosophy, literature and art, history, as well as in translation, communication and sinology. These experts and scholars select, explain, translate, share and research key concepts in Chinese thought and culture.

The secretariat of the Project at Foreign Language Teaching and Research Press has been responsible for the implementation and promotion of the Project, and the publication of its results.

The goals of the Project are as follows:

(1) Explore in-depth the key concepts that contain the essence of Chinese thought, Chinese spiritual pursuits, and symbols of Chinese civilization, that have pioneering significance and form a bridge between earlier and later stages in the history of Chinese thought and culture, that have a high frequency of use in international cultural exchange and communication, and that have universal significance and contemporary value beyond time and national boundaries;

(2) Interpret these concepts in easy-to-understand language;

(3) Translate the concepts into English and other languages;

(4) Help the world acquire a more accurate understanding of traditional Chinese thought and culture, and thus gain a more comprehensive understanding of China, of the past, present and future of the Chinese nation, and of the cultural life of the Chinese people, including overseas Chinese; and

(5) Promote dialogue and mutual learning between Chinese and other civilizations.

So far, during a period of seven years, nine Chinese-English bilingual volumes of *Key Concepts in Chinese Thought and Culture* have been produced, along with a number of other research results, which have been well received by academics and general readers. Outside China the book series has been published in 30 languages.

In November 2020, we published the 900 concepts as a bound volume. Now these concepts are categorized into three separate volumes: *Philosophy*, *History*, and *Literature and Art*. The number of concepts in each volume is not exactly the same, and a few basic concepts shared by more than one category can be found in different volumes.

Taking the opportunity of the publication of these three volumes, we'd like to express our sincere gratitude to the experts and scholars taking part in the Project. At the same time, we would like to give a brief account of the selection, explanation, and translation of the concepts.

1. Selection

Since this is the first time the idea of "key concepts in Chinese thought and culture" has been proposed, it is necessary to define the concepts, and determine where they came from and how they should be explained. Following a number of discussions and an extensive solicitation of opinions, experts and scholars made preliminary proposals regarding the selection of the concepts. It was decided, for the time being, to focus on the realms of humanities and social sciences, and confine the scope largely to concepts that appeared before the Revolution of 1911, in the three categories of literature and art, history, and philosophy.

It was thus decided that the following concepts should be selected:

(1) The basic concepts that constitute traditional Chinese thought and culture;

(2) External concepts that have been integrated into Chinese thought and culture and given new meaning or understanding by the Chinese people and have become an organic part of concepts in Chinese thought and culture;

(3) Concepts that embody traditional Chinese philosophy, humanistic spirit, ways of thinking, and values;

(4) Concepts that have been solidified into the form of words or expressions, and (considering the unique feature of Chinese thought and culture) some intellectual propositions with established structures;

(5) Concepts that have seminal significance in the history of Chinese thought and culture or form a bridge between earlier and later stages in the history of Chinese thought;

(6) Concepts that are frequently used in cultural communication and are consistent with the common values of humankind; and

(7) Concepts that have important reference value for the construction of a contemporary Chinese discourse system.

2. Explanations

Needless to say, it is much more difficult to explain the connotation of a concept in Chinese thought and culture accurately and in easy-to-understand language in 200 - 300 words than to write an academic article of 5,000 - 6,000 words. This is because each concept is an integral part of Chinese thought and culture, and explaining it requires a comprehensive understanding of Chinese thought and culture, as well as a familiarity with the reorientation and reconstruction of ancient concepts in the modern context.

In addition, ancient China had no disciplinary boundaries similar to those of modern times, and some core concepts straddle a variety of modern disciplines. We as modern-day researchers are keenly aware that we may only understand and explain these interdisciplinary concepts from a certain perspective, and are subject to disciplinary limitations in our explanation.

In order to explain concepts with rich connotations as accurately as possible, the experts and scholars working on the Project therefore reached the following consensus:

In explaining concepts, the Project is unable to answer all the questions in the history of Chinese thought and culture. The Project should not and cannot aspire to be conclusive about different academic views, nor can it meet the needs of readers at all levels at the same time. The Project should aim to tease out, summarize and convey the core meanings and main contents of key concepts in Chinese thought and culture. As a basic cultural project, the Project should not attempt to identify and restore the historical origin and all the original features of concepts. On the premise of respecting the research results in the intellectual, cultural and academic history, the Project should furthermore focus on identifying and explaining those contents and meanings that best embody the humanistic spirit, ways of thinking, values, and culture of the Chinese nation and have general value and reference significance for the development of human civilization, in accordance with the actual situation in China today and the requirements of the new era, as well as the development trend of world civilization and the common values of humanity, discarding any dross or components that have little or no relevance to today's society.

3. Citations

The 200-300 words used to explain the core or main meaning of each concept can hardly explain in full its rich thought content. In order to remedy this deficiency, on the strength of specialist dictionaries and language dictionaries, the Project specially uses "citations." The number of citations for each concept ranges from one to three, and the selection of citations is based on four principles:

(1) Originality: being able to explain the origin or change of the concept;

(2) Universality: having universal meaning beyond time and national boundaries;

(3) Differentiation: being able to show the different semantic or intellectual connotations of the concept; and

(4) Positivity: having a positive guiding value for today's readers.

4. Translation

In order to facilitate international readers' understanding of the concepts, all concepts and their accompanying citations are translated into English.

Until this Project, translations of concepts were only found in a few English translations of ancient books, and most of them were direct word for word translations without further elaboration. The translated words were also submerged in the body of the whole book. In addition, different translators had different understanding of the meaning of concepts, so there are often two or three or even more varying translations of the same concept. This greatly affects international readers' accurate understanding of the concepts, as well as the quality of international communication of the concepts. The importance of translation, therefore, is self-evident. The present endeavor has been an unprecedented and groundbreaking mission in both academic and translation circles. In the translation of the 900 concepts, there was no past experience or ready references to draw on, so it is not difficult to imagine the challenges encountered in the translation process. After a period of exploration, our translators finally decided on the following principles:

(1) Be faithful to the original text: The meaning of the Chinese text should be fully understood before being translated, and the translation should accurately convey the core meaning of the concepts;

(2) Stick closely to the target language: As much as possible, the translation should be in line with the habits of expression of the target language and the cognitive level of foreign readers;

(3) Aspire to be comprehensible in explanation, using transliteration where appropriate: When the English translation cannot cover or convey the full meaning of a concept, transliteration can be used; and

(4) Follow standard procedures: The Project should strictly follow the Chinese-English translation experience accumulated over the past almost 70 years of practice by Chinese translators, i.e., translators translate, and the translation is polished by scholars of China studies or native English language experts, and is finalized by experienced English experts in China.

These principles have proved not only practical, but also served to ensure the quality of the translation. It should be noted that the translation of a concept does not imply that it applies to all the meanings of the concept in different contexts. For general readers, we have aimed to provide a translation as close as possible to the original text; for researchers and translators, we have striven to provide additional choice and sources of reference.

Compared to the total number of key concepts in Chinese thought and culture, the 900 translated expressions represent only the core or fundamental ones. There are many more concepts in philosophy, literature, art, history, politics, law, education, economics, military affairs, science, and technology to be explored.

We earnestly hope that scholars and readers will be able to refer to and make use of our explanations and translations, and can give us suggestions for future improvement.

Secretariat of the Project "Key Concepts in Chinese Thought
and Culture: Communication Through Translation,"
Foreign Language Teaching and Research Press
January 2021

目录

Contents

Key Concepts in Chinese
Thought and Culture

中华思想文化术语

哀吊 /āidiào/

Essay of Mourning and Essay of Memory

　　古代文体名称，用于哀悼死者或对遭遇不幸者表示慰问。"哀"的意思是哀悼、哀悯，最早用于哀悼夭折短寿的人，后也用于哀悯身遭不幸的人或不幸的事；"吊"的意思是凭吊，是对逝者表达追思或对遭遇不幸之事的人、国家等表示慰问。从哀吊对象说，"哀"一般用于当下的人或事，而"吊"常用于古人。从文体上说两者区别不大，略相当于今天的悼词，属于应用文，有些可以视为悼亡、怀古类的抒情散文。刘勰（465？—520？或532？）在《文心雕龙》中指出，哀辞重在表达对未及立德建功者的痛惜之情，因此不必追求辞藻；吊文多用于缅怀古人，因此常寓一定褒贬评价，具有反思和感怀的特点。这些见解对于今天的散文写作仍有指导意义。

Ai (哀) and *diao* (吊) essays were written in ancient times to express mourning for someone who had died a natural death or from an extreme misfortune. *Ai*, or an essay of mourning, was written to express grief or compassion. It was originally written for someone who died young; later, it was written to mourn a person's miserable life or unfortunate encounters. *Diao*, or an essay of memory, was intended to express one's deep affection for a long-deceased person or to offer his sincere condolences to the fatal misfortune suffered by a particular country or an individual. An essay of mourning was usually written for a recently deceased person, whereas an essay of memory showed one's abiding love for someone who died long ago. Stylistically, there is much resemblance between these two types of writing. They were like today's condolence speeches delivered at funerals, and some may be characterized as mourning or nostalgic lyrical essays. As Liu Xie (465 ?-520 ? or 532 ?) put it in his literary critique *The Literary Mind and the Carving of Dragons*, *ai*, or an essay of mourning, expresses sorrow for the deceased person's yet unaccomplished merits, so it need not be excessively rhetorical in style. *Diao*, or an essay of memory, on the other hand, often shows one's love for someone who died long ago, so it may contain an evaluation of his life tinged with sentimental attachment. Liu's views still influence prose writing today.

引例 Citations：

◎奢体为辞，则虽丽不衰；必使情往会悲，文来引泣，乃其贵耳。（刘勰《文心雕龙·哀吊》）

（以浮夸文风写作哀辞，虽然华丽却不会使人哀伤；一定要让所抒之情出于内心悲痛，写出的文辞使人悲泣，这才是可贵的作品。）

Ai, an essay of mourning, written in a pompous style, beautiful as it may sound, will not really arouse a sense of grief among its readers. Only an essay which expresses one's deeply felt emotions and moves readers to tears can be regarded as a truly remarkable essay. (Liu Xie: *The Literary Mind and the Carving of Dragons*)

◎夫吊虽古义，而华辞未造；华过韵缓，则化而为赋。固宜正义以绳理，昭德而塞违，割析褒贬，哀而有正，则无夺伦矣。（刘勰《文心雕龙·哀吊》）

（"吊"的意义虽然很古，但写得华丽则是后来的事情；华丽过分而节奏弛缓，就演变为"赋"了。应该端正意义而斟酌事理，彰显美德而防范过失，辨析善恶而加以褒贬，表达哀情而内容纯正，这样就不会违背吊文的写作原则了。）

Although the meaning of *diao*, or an essay of memory can be traced a long way back, it was much later that an essay of memory became excessively rhetorical in style. If such an essay is written in a flowery style and drags on, it would look more like *fu* or rhapsodic prose. In writing an essay of memory, one should focus on a key message and explains its relevance, extol virtue and warn against errors, distinguish right from wrong and make evaluation accordingly, and express grief without distracting from the core message. These are rules to be observed in writing essays of memory. (Liu Xie: *The Literary Mind and the Carving of Dragons*)

哀景写乐 /āijǐng-xiělè/

Depict Sorrowful Scenery to Express Happiness

　　以哀伤的景致描写愉快的情绪。属于情景相衬、对面落笔的描写手法。以乐景写哀伤比较常见，以哀景写快乐却不常见。因此，对"哀景写乐"的理解可以与"乐景写哀"综合起来，它们都是指言情而不直露，借用景物描写抒发情致，情与景互相映衬，彼此交融，作品的审美效果含蓄婉转，别有韵味。

Depicting sorrowful scenery to express happiness is a technique which integrates sentiment and scenery and indirectly expresses sentiment through describing scenery. Although it is quite common to express sadness through joyful scenes, artists rarely describe sorrowful scenery to express joy. Thus, we can better understand the latter technique by comparing it with the former. Both are techniques of expressing sentiment implicitly by describing scenery. Sentiment and scenery set each other off beautifully and are well integrated, thus giving works an aesthetic elegance and a unique and lingering charm.

引例 Citations：

◎ "昔我往矣，杨柳依依；今我来思，雨雪霏霏。"以乐景写哀，以哀景写乐，一倍增其哀乐。（王夫之《姜斋诗话》卷一）

（"以前我离开，杨柳枝条轻柔飘拂；现在我归来，大雪纷纷漫天飞舞。"以快乐的景物写哀伤，以悲哀的景物写快乐，更加重了哀伤与快乐的气氛。）

"When I left here, willows were gently swaying in the wind. Now I'm back, snow flakes are in the air." This poet describes happy scenery to express sadness and sorrowful scenery to express happiness, thus intensifying both sentiments. (Wang Fuzhi: *Desultory Remarks on Poetry from Ginger Studio*)

◎ 情、景名为二，而实不可离。神于诗者，妙合无垠。巧者则有情中景、景中情。（王夫之《姜斋诗话》卷二）

（情与景虽然名称上为二，但实际上不可分离。善于作诗的人，二者融合巧妙，看不出界限。构思精巧的则会情中有景、景中有情。）

Sentiment and scenery seem to be distinct from each other, but in fact they cannot be separated. A good poet knows how to integrate them seamlessly. An ingenious combination of sentiment and scene means scenery embedded in sentiment and vice versa. (Wang Fuzhi: *Desultory Remarks on Poetry from Ginger Studio*)

八音克谐 /bāyīn-kèxié/
Harmonious Combination of Eight Sounds

八类乐器所演奏的声音能够协调配合，在整体上达到和谐。"八音"指由金、石、土、革、丝、木、匏、竹等八种材质制成的乐器所演奏出的不同声音。"八音克谐"的说法出自《尚书》。它强调发挥八音各自的长处，在整体协调、多样统一中臻于化境，体现了中国古典音乐及词曲创作中以"和"为美的审美追求。而音乐又与人的心灵相通，"八音"能够呈现或感动不同的心灵状态，故而它也成为古代教化的一种方式。其意在于使人心在不同乐声的影响下达到同样和谐的状态，以符合礼乐对于人的心灵与行为的要求；同时它也蕴含不同的人或群体都能发声，但须遵守共同规范、相互配合而能和谐共处之意。

Different sounds produced when eight musical instruments made of gold, stone, earth, leather, silk, wood, gourd and bamboo are played together create harmonious music. This term comes from *The Book of History*. The term, which stresses that different tunes produced by the eight musical instruments should be blended in a harmonious way to create beautiful melody, epitomizes the pursuit of harmony of ancient Chinese music. Music gives expression to people's sentiments; the eight different sounds relate to people's different frames of mind, and can become a way of enlightenment. The term means that people can achieve peace of mind by listening to different kinds of music and should think and act in keeping with what the rites and music require of them. The phrase also implies that different people and groups can all voice their views, but should abide by common rules so as to maintain harmonious ties among them.

引例 Citation：

◎诗言志，歌永言，声依永，律和声。八音克谐，无相夺伦，神人以和。(《尚书·舜典》)

(诗是表达内心志向的，歌是用语言吟唱的，五音（宫、商、角、徵、羽）的高低变化要随吟唱而定，音律则要与五音谐和。八类乐器所演奏的音乐能够和谐配合，不要相互扰乱彼此的秩序，那么神与人都能依此进入和谐的状态。)

Poems express aspirations deep in one's heart, whereas songs are verses for chanting. Undulation of tunes of five notes depends on chanting, and meter and melody must be in harmony with the five notes. If the sounds from the eight different music instruments create harmonious music without interfering with each other, such music enables both gods and man to enter a state of harmony. (*The Book of History*)

白描 /báimiáo/
Plain Line Drawing

中国画的表现手法之一。用墨线勾勒描摹物象的轮廓，不设颜色。白描多用于画人物、花卉，着墨不多，气韵生动。白描源于古代的"白画"。一般运用同一墨色，通过线条的长短、粗细、轻重、转折等表现物象的质感和动势。白描流行于晋唐时期，宋代以后自成一格。晋代顾恺之（345？—409）、北宋李公麟（1049—1106）、元代赵孟頫（1254—1322）等擅长铁线描，唐代吴道子、南宋马和之等擅长兰叶描。白描也是文学创作中非常重要的表现手法，主要指用朴素简练的笔墨，不加烘托渲染，描绘出鲜明生动的形象。古典小说《水浒传》《三国演义》等多有高超的白描手法。

Plain line drawing is one of the traditional Chinese styles of artistic presentation. It features the contours of images sketched in black ink lines. This style of painting is mostly used in painting human figures and flowers. Although not much ink is applied, this technique can achieve a very lively effect. Plain line drawing originated from the plain drawing of earlier times; through variations in lines' length, thickness, pressure, and changes in trajectory, the artist can portray the texture and motion of images. Plain line drawing was prevalent from the Jin Dynasty through the Tang Dynasty. During the Song Dynasty, it formed a distinctive style of its own. Gu Kaizhi (345?-409) of the Jin Dynasty, Li Gonglin (1049-1106) of the Northern Song Dynasty, and Zhao Mengfu (1254-1322) of the Yuan Dynasty specialized in painting lines of perfectly even width like iron wire, while Wu Daozi of the Tang Dynasty and Ma Hezhi of the Southern Song Dynasty were renowned for their skill in drawing thick, wavy lines resembling orchid leaves. Plain drawing is also a very important style of expression in narrative literature. In this context it refers to a simple and concise style of writing, without embellishment, so as to produce fresh, lively images. In classic novels such as *Outlaws of the Marsh* or *Romance of the Three Kingdoms*, one finds abundant instances of a plain drawing style of writing.

引例 Citation：

◎ 白描画易纤弱柔媚，最难遒劲高逸，今观此图如屈铁丝，唐有阎令，宋有伯时，元有赵文敏，可称鼎足矣。（王穉登《题李龙眠〈维摩演教图〉》）

（白描所描摹出的画作容易流于纤细瘦弱、阴柔妩媚，最难表现遒劲有力、高古飘逸的感觉，而今观赏此画，用笔好似弯曲铁丝一般

[刚劲有力]，唐代的阎立本、北宋的李公麟、元代的赵孟頫可称得上三足鼎立。）

Paintings drawn with plain lines are prone to being overly fine or weak, often lacking a soaring spirit and vigor despite a feminine beauty. But today, after admiring this particular painting, I have found its strokes to be vigorous like bent wire. (When it comes to vigorous brushwork,) Yan Liben of the Tang Dynasty, Li Gonglin of the Northern Song Dynasty, and Zhao Mengfu of the Yuan Dynasty were three eminent figures. (Wang Zhideng: Postscript to Li Longmian's "Korimaro Preaches a Sermon")

百戏 /bǎixì/
Baixi (All Performing Arts)

中国古代歌舞杂技表演的总称。包括武术、魔术、驯兽、歌舞、滑稽戏表演，及空中走绳、吞刀、踏火等各种杂技，内容丰富，形式多样，表演比较自由而随意，追求娱乐效果，具有民间性和通俗性。汉代开始流行，随着各民族的文化交流与融汇，乐舞杂技表演形式也不断融合、丰富，"百"是表示其种类繁多。南北朝以后其义同于"散乐"。唐代进一步盛行。宋代以后，散乐侧重指文人创作、艺人表演的歌舞、戏剧，百戏则相当于民间杂技。有时，统治者会因为百戏耽误正业甚至影响风气而颁布禁令。总的来说，百戏孕育了歌舞、戏剧等高雅艺术，留下了中国杂技这一非物质文化遗产，丰富了人们的精神文化生活。

It's a generic term in history for performing arts, including martial arts, magic, taming animals, song and dance, farce, tightrope walking, knife swallowing, walking on fire, and other acrobatic performances. Such performing arts were diverse in both form and content and the performance could easily take place, the only criterion being to entertain the popular audience. Such performances began in Han times, and as culture and art forms from different ethnic groups were slowly integrated into local practice, performing arts and acrobatics came to be increasingly diversified. The term *baixi* (百戏) literally means "a hundred forms of performances," and suggests, different kinds of performing arts. After the Southern and Northern Dynasties another term, *sanyue* (散乐), became synonymous with *baixi*. During the Tang Dynasty the performing arts became even more popular. In Song times *sanyue* came to refer mainly to song and dance performances or operas created by men of letters; while *baixi* came to mean principally acrobatic shows by folk artists. At times the authorities would impose a ban on *baixi*, believing that such performing arts exerted a bad influence on social customs. Still it is fair to say that *baixi* gave birth to high-brow song and dance as well as operas. It turned acrobatics into a form of intangible cultural heritage, enriching the cultural life of the people.

引例 Citation：

◎秦汉已来，又有杂伎，其变非一，名为百戏，亦总谓之散乐。(郭茂倩《乐府诗集》卷五十六引《唐书·乐志》)

(自秦汉以后，又加入了各种杂技，演变出的种类很多，总称为"百戏"，也总称为"散乐"。)

From the Qin and Han dynasties onward, there appeared different kinds of acrobatic shows and a great variety of performing arts, which were referred to as *baixi*, and were also called *sanyue*. (*The History of the Tang Dynasty*, as cited in Guo Maoqian: *Collection of Yuefu Poems*)

悲慨 /bēikǎi/

Depressed and Enraged

悲伤愤慨。慨，感慨，愤慨。是晚唐诗人司空图 (837—908) 所概括的诗歌的二十四种风格之一。主要指诗作中所表现出的悲剧性情结。当诗人命途多舛或身处困境，或面对壮阔景观或大的事件而自觉力量渺小，会产生忧愁、悲哀、感伤、激愤的情绪，投射到诗歌创作中则形成"悲慨"风格。这一术语看似近于西方文学理论的"悲剧"范畴，实质上受道家思想影响较大，而最后往往或趋于无奈或趋于旷达。

Feeling depressed and enraged, which here refers to a sense of helplessness found in poems, is one of the 24 poetic styles summarized by Sikong Tu (837 - 908), a poet in the late Tang Dynasty. Faced with frustrations and tough challenges in life, or overwhelmed by the immensity of nature or major events, poets were often seized by dejection, grief, sadness, and anger, which gave rise to a "depressed and enraged" style in poetry writing. While the style bears similarity with the genre of tragedy in Western literary tradition, it is more influenced by Daoism, often featuring a sense of resignation or stoic optimism.

引例 **Citations**：

◎大风卷水，林木为摧。适苦欲死，招憩不来。百岁如流，富贵冷灰。大道日丧，若为雄才。壮士拂剑，浩然弥哀。萧萧落叶，漏雨苍苔。（司空图《二十四诗品·悲慨》）

（大风卷起狂澜，树木遭受摧折。心中悲苦痛不欲生，想休憩片刻亦不可得。百年岁月像流水永逝，富贵繁华都化作冷寂尘埃。大道日益不行，谁才是当世雄才？壮士拔剑仰天叹，凝望苍穹愈悲哀。好比落叶萧萧下，且听漏雨滴苍苔。）

Winds are howling, waves raging, and tree branches breaking. Gripped by an agonizing pain at my heart, I yearn for a spell of peace but only in vain. As time slips by, year after year, decade after decade, all the riches, fame, and splendor are but nothing. Facing moral degeneration, who will rise and salvage the world? With sword in hand, I heave a deep sigh and stare intensely at the sky. Overwhelmed with sorrow, all I can do is to watch leaves falling and hear rain beating against the moss. (Sikong Tu: Twenty-four Styles of Poetry)

◎感叹之余，作诗相属，托物悲慨，厄穷而不怨，泰而不骄。（苏轼《和王晋卿［并叙］》）

（在感叹之余，蒙其作诗劝慰嘱咐，借景物抒发内心悲伤愤慨的情绪，虽遇困厄而不怨恨，命运通达也不骄狂。）

After a deep sigh, he wrote a poem to admonish and comfort me, in which he expressed his indignation and resentment by making an analogy with imagery. He advised me not to grudge about tough times or be complacent when everything goes well in life. (Su Shi: A Poem in Reply to Wang Jinqing with a Preface)

北曲 /běiqǔ/

Northern Opera

起源于北方的戏剧。北曲的源头是北宋甚至更早时期流行于北方民间的曲子，配合曲子的词多滑稽浅俗。南宋以后，北方地区在金、元统治之下，女真、蒙古等族的歌舞与音乐元素被大量引入，逐渐形成了独特的北曲体系，同时逐渐吸引了文人加入创作队伍，从而产生了大量优秀作品。与宋代文人词相比，北曲朴素率真，多用口语，格律调式更加自由。其主要演唱形式为小令和套数。用北曲演唱的戏曲形式为杂剧。元代文人社会地位低下，借助北曲抒情寄意，创作盛况空前，代表人物有关汉卿、马致远（1251？—1321后）、白朴（1226—1306后）、郑光祖（？—1324前），被称为"元曲四大家"。

Beiqu (北曲), the Northern Opera, originated in northern China. It was based on northern folk songs that were popular in the Northern Song Dynasty or earlier, and its lyrics were often funny and simple. After the Southern Song Dynasty, northern China fell under the rule of the Jin and Yuan dynasties. As a result, songs, dances, and musical elements of Nüzhen, Mongolian and other ethnic groups were widely incorporated into the Northern Opera, making it a unique form of opera. At the same time, many writers became interested in the Northern Opera and wrote large numbers of excellent opera works. Compared with the lyrics of the literati of the Song period, the Northern Opera was simple, direct and sincere, and there was greater freedom in arranging rhythm. The Northern Opera was performed mainly in the form of short lyrics and cycles. As they dealt with various social themes, operas performed in this artistic form were referred to as *zaju* (杂剧 opera of various themes). Writers in the Yuan Dynasty had low social status, so they wrote a large number of Northern Opera works to express their emotions and views. They are represented by Guan Hanqing, Ma Zhiyuan (1251?-1321?), Bai Pu (1226-1306?) and Zheng Guangzu (?-1324?), collectively known as the top four Yuan Opera writers.

引例 Citations：

◎宋世所谓诗余，金元以来所传南北曲者，虽非古之遗音，而犹有此名目也，夫人能为之，而闻之者亦能辨别其是否，诚因今而求之古，循俗而入于雅……因声以考律，正律以定器，三代之乐亦可复矣。(丘濬《大学衍义补》卷四十四)

(宋代所说的词，金元以来所流行的南曲、北曲，虽然不是上古留传下来的音乐，但仍然有宫、商、角、徵、羽这些名目，有人能够制作这些曲子，而听曲子的人也能听得出音律是否正确，其实这是从当代音乐推求古代音乐，由俗乐而进入雅乐……凭所唱的声音来考求音律，再通过标准的音律来确定乐器的声音，如此则夏、商、周三代的音乐都可以复原了。)

Song Dynasty *ci* poetry and the Southern and Northern operas that were popular from the Jin and Yuan dynasties onwards were not music from ancient times, but they were still divided into Do, Re, Mi, Sol and La. Some people could produce these kinds of music, and the audience could also tell if it had the right rhyme. Actually, what was done was to restore ancient music based on current music and make popular music more refined... Rhymes were evaluated through singing, the sound of musical instruments was then determined according to standard rhymes, and this made it possible to restore the music of the Xia, Shang, and Zhou dynasties. (Qiu Jun: *Supplement to the Exposition on The Great Learning*)

◎唱者只二人，末泥主男唱，旦儿主女唱。他若杂色入场，第有白无唱，谓之"宾白"。"宾"与"主"对，以说白在"宾"，而唱者自有"主"也。至元末明初，改北曲为南曲，则杂色人皆唱，不分宾主矣。(毛奇龄《西河词话》卷二)

(演唱的只有两个人，末泥专唱男角，旦儿专唱女角。其他角色入场，只有说白而没有唱腔，称为"宾白"。"宾"和"主"相对，说白属于"宾"的事情，演唱则属于"主"的事情。到了元末明初，北曲受南曲影响而改变，则所有的角色都演唱，不再区分"宾"和"主"了。)

Only two people sang in the performance. One was the male character and the other was the female character. When others joined in, they only talked. As they did not sing, they were known as supporting speakers. Singing was done by leading performers, and speakers only played a supporting role. By the time of the late Yuan and early Ming dynasties, however, this practice changed due to the influence of the Southern Opera, and all performers sang and they were no longer classified as leading or supporting roles. (Mao Qiling: *Mao Qiling's Remarks on Ci Poetry*)

本色 /běnsè/

Bense (Original Character)

原义指本来的颜色，引申指本来的样子、面貌。作为文学批评术语，主要有三种含义：其一，指符合文体规定的艺术特色和风貌；

其二，指符合作家艺术个性的特色和风貌；其三，指作品中真率自然地贴近生活原貌、表达自己真实思想或感情的风格。本色不仅是对作者的要求，也是对作品的要求。宋代文论中，本色多用于评述文体的特性；明清文论中，本色多指诗人作家的个性风格，也用来倡导不加雕饰地贴近生活原貌的创作风格。"本色"常与"当行"连用，相当于"本真"，往往与道家自然之道的思想相联系，用来反对过分雕琢的创作态度与作品风格。

The term originally referred to true colors and has been extended to mean true appearance. As a term of literary critique, *bense* (本色) has three meanings: 1) the artistic style and literary features that are compatible with a given genre; 2) the style and literary features that remain true to the writer's individual character; and 3) the style that makes it possible for the writing to remain true to the author's own experience and that gives truthful expression to his thoughts and feelings. *Bense* is not only a requirement for the writer but also for his works. In the literary criticism of the Song Dynasty, *bense* was often used to describe and evaluate the special qualities of different genres. In the literary criticism of the Ming and Qing dynasties, *bense* usually referred to the individual style of poets and writers and also those styles of writing that remained true to life experience and eschewed literary embellishment. *Bense* is often used together with *danghang* (当行 professionalism) to mean "original and genuine"; it is often associated with the Dao of nature in classical Daoist philosophy, in opposition to the attitude and styles that stress literary embellishment.

引例 Citations：

◎退之以文为诗，子瞻以诗为词，如教坊雷大使之舞，虽极天下之工，要非本色。（陈师道《后山诗话》）

（韩愈以写文章的方法来写诗，苏轼以写诗的方法来写词，就像教坊里的艺人雷大使跳女子舞蹈，虽然技巧高明无比，但并不符合诗词的本色。）

Poems written by Han Yu read like essays and *ci* lyrics by Su Shi read like poems. This is like Master Dancer Lei of the Song Palace Music School performing dances choreographed for women. Although they were good writers, what they wrote was incompatible with the original characters of the genres. (Chen Shidao: *Houshan's Understanding of Poetry*)

◎近来觉得诗文一事只是直写胸臆，如谚语所谓开口见喉咙者。使后人读之，如真见其面目，瑜瑕俱不容掩，所谓本色。此为上乘文字。(唐顺之《与洪方洲书》)

(最近觉得写诗作文只需要直接写出心中所想，就像俗语所说的"开口看见喉咙"。让后人读到这样的作品，就能看到作者的真面目，优点、缺点都不掩饰，这就是本色。能体现本色的作品才是最好的文字。)

Recently I have come to realize that in writing poetry or prose, all that is needed is to write what I have in mind. This is like the Chinese saying, "When you open the mouth, others can see your throat." When readers read such works, they will come to know what the author is actually like. Without hiding either strengths or weaknesses, the author makes his true character fully apparent. The writing that best embodies the author's original character is most desirable. (Tang Shunzhi: Letter to Hong Fangzhou)

◎世事莫不有本色，有相色。本色，犹俗言正身也；相色，替身也。(徐渭《〈西厢〉序》)

(世上之事莫不有本色，有相色。本色，好比说是本来之我；而相色，好比替身。)

Everything in the world has its true appearance and its surrogate. True appearance is what I am, while a surrogate is a substitute. (Xu Wei: Foreword to *Romance of the Western Chamber*)

比德 /bǐdé/

Virtue Comparison

用自然物包括动植物的某些特性比附人的道德品格。引申到文学审美领域，一般是用美好的事物直接比喻高尚的人格精神，将自然现象看作是人的某些精神品质的表现和象征，体现出儒家将审美与文艺道德化的思维模式。人比德于自然，意味着对自然的欣赏其实就是对人自身特别是人所具有的伦理品格的欣赏。后成为修辞与诗歌创作的一种方式。

The term means likening certain characteristics of things in nature, including plants and animals, to human virtues. When extended to the domain of literary appreciation, it generally involves likening desirable objects to a noble personality. To perceive a natural phenomenon as a reflection or symbol of human characteristics is typical of the Confucian school, which takes aesthetic quality as a moral standard for people as well as literature and arts. Likening humans to nature implies that appreciation of nature is actually appreciation of humanity itself, particularly its moral character. It later became a technique employed in rhetoric and poetry.

引例 Citations：

◎昔者君子比德于玉焉，温润而泽，仁也。（《礼记·聘义》）

（从前，君子的道德人格可以和美玉相比，温润而有光泽，体现出的就是仁。）

In the past, the moral integrity of a man of virtue was likened to fine jade, which is smooth, mellow, and lustrous, an exact embodiment of benevolence. (*The Book of Rites*)

◎及三闾《橘颂》，情采芬芳，比类寓意，乃覃及细物矣。（刘勰《文心雕龙·颂赞》）

（到了屈原创作《橘颂》，情感和文采都很出色，用橘来类比并寄托某些寓意，于是延伸到对细小事物的描绘了。）

By the time Qu Yuan wrote "Ode to the Orange," both his sentiment and literary style had become highly refined. He used orange to draw analogy and convey a certain message before preceding to describe details. (Liu Xie: *The Literary Mind and the Carving of Dragons*)

边塞诗 /biānsàishī/
Frontier Poetry

一种以塞外风光、边境战事及戍边生活为主要创作题材的诗歌流派。其作品或描绘奇异鲜明的塞外风光，或反映惨烈的战争场景与艰苦的戍边生活，有些则重点刻画戍边将士们的离别、思乡、报国之情或其配偶之闺怨及对前方亲人的思念等。边塞诗往往反映作者对战争的深切感受和思考，表现出个体生命价值与时代精神之间的一种张力。边塞诗以唐代为主，之后虽也有边塞之作，但规模与气象远不能与唐代相比。

Poems of this kind depicted frontier scenery as well as fighting along the northern border area and the life of soldiers garrisoned there. These poems described the scenic splendor north of the Great Wall, fierce war scenes, or hardships endured by frontier guards. Some of the works were about soldiers' agony caused by long separation from families and about their homesickness, but many such poems also extolled their patriotism. Some of the works voiced the longing for reunion of women left at home when husbands and sons went to the frontier. Frontier poems showed the poets' attitude towards and reflections on war, highlighting the tension between valuing individual lives and the need to respond to call to duty. The most compelling frontier poems were written in the Tang Dynasty. Frontier poems of later generations could not rival the powerful expression of Tang frontier poems.

◎盛唐诸公五言之妙，多本阮籍、郭璞、陶潜……边塞之作则出鲍照、吴筠（yún）也。唐人于六朝，率揽其菁华、汰其芜蔓，可为学古者之法。（王士祯《居易录》卷二十一）

（盛唐诗人们的五言诗，其精妙之处多取法于阮籍、郭璞、陶渊明等人的作品……而边塞诗则是学习鲍照、吴筠的作品。唐代诗人于六朝人的作品中，多能采撷它们的精华而去除它们芜杂枝蔓的毛病，这可以作为向古人学习的典范。）

Five-character-a-line poems written during the prime of the Tang Dynasty emulated the poetic style of Ruan Ji, Guo Pu, and Tao Yuanming, whereas frontier poems in this period were more influenced by Bao Zhao and Wu Yun. Tang poets drew inspiration from the poetry of the Six Dynasties while discarding its defects of random extension and disorderliness. Their poems were therefore representative of classical poetry that we should learn from. (Wang Shizhen: *Records of a Secure and Peaceful Life*)

辨体 /biàntǐ/
Style Differentiation

辨明文学作品的体式与风格。指创作时根据所要表达的思想感情选择合适的文学体式与风格，从而创作出内容与形式高度和谐一致的优秀作品。古代的文学家在从事文学创作时往往首先考虑文章的体式。魏晋南北朝时的文学批评家们详尽探讨了各种文体的艺术特征和艺术规律，强调创作者应根据思想感情表达的需要选择相应的文体进行写作，并应严格遵守所选文体的创作风格、语言形式与表达技巧，这样才能写出优秀的作品。与之相对的是"破体"，指打破各类文章体式与风格的界限，使之相互融合。"辨体"有时也指辨别与追求高尚的文学品格与境界。

The term refers to the differentiation of the form and style of a literary work. It means that before putting words on paper, one needs to decide on the form and style appropriate to the thoughts and feelings to be expressed so as to produce a fine literary work with a high degree of harmony between form and content. In creating literary works, ancient scholars tended to decide on the style before writing. Literary critics in the Wei, Jin, and Southern and Northern dynasties discussed in detail the artistic features and rules of all literary styles and stressed that authors must choose an appropriate form or style to express their thoughts and sentiments and strictly follow the rules of the style, language form, and writing technique required by the chosen form or style. This, they believed, was the only way to create excellent literary works. Contrary to the term "style differentiation," the term *poti* (破体) or "breaking-down styles" refers to the integration of different styles or forms of literary works by breaking down their boundaries. Style differentiation sometimes refers to differentiating the form or style of a literary work in order to attain a lofty character and realm of literature.

引例 Citations：

◎夫情致异区，文变殊术，莫不因情立体，即体成势也。势者，乘利而为制也。（刘勰《文心雕龙·定势》）

（作品所表达的思想情趣既有所区分，文章的创作手法也要因之变化，但都是依照思想感情确定文章的体式，就着体式形成文章的气势。文章的这种气势，是就着文体自身的特点进行创作而形成的。）

Since literary works express different ideas, temperaments, and tastes, the writing skills and techniques used should also differ in order to suit the content. It is the content of a literary work that determines its style, which in turn gives strength to the work. Such strength comes from writing in accordance with the style of the literary work. (Liu Xie: *The Literary Mind and the Carving of Dragons*)

◎夫诗人之思，初发取境偏高，则一首举体便高；取境偏逸，则一首举体便逸。（释皎然《诗式·辨体有一十九字》）

（诗人刚开始构思的时候，如果取境偏于高迈，那么整首诗的意境就高迈；如果取境偏于飘逸，那么整首诗的意境就飘逸。）

When the poet starts to compose a poem, if his conception of the poem tends towards grandeur, then the aesthetic conception of the poem will be grand; if his conception of the poem is free and easy, so will the aesthetic conception of the poem be. (Shi Jiaoran: *Poetic Styles*)

◎先辨体裁，引绳切墨，而后敢放言也。（章太炎《国故论衡·文学总略》）

（先辨明文章体裁，遵循文章体式的要求分出段落，而后才敢放开写作。）

One should first decide on the style or form of an article, decide paragraphs following the rules required by the chosen style or form for the article, and then start writing. (Zhang Taiyan: *Overview of Traditional Chinese Scholarly Learning*)

标举兴会 /biāojǔ-xìnghuì/
Distinctiveness and Spontaneity

亦作"兴会标举"。"标举"有"标明、突出"之义，后来引申出"鲜明、高超、独特"等众多含义。"会"是会聚，"兴会"是创作主体为外物所激发的创作状态及由此产生的丰富的心理感悟，是文学创作时灵感勃发而自然生成的浓厚兴致与意趣。"标举兴会"指文学创作中由"兴"所生发的丰富的心理感悟与情感特征，亦指作品中所呈现的浓厚而强烈的兴致与意趣。"标举兴会"既是一个文学批评术语，也是一种创作理念，它与崇尚自然、反对造作的写作态度相对应，推崇创作者的才华与激情，强调直觉基础上的自由想象和灵感勃发状态下的自由创造。

Also "spontaneity and distinctiveness." *Biaoju* (标举) originally meant "to mark out or stand out." It later extended to mean "superior, unique, distinctive, and outstanding." *Hui* (会) means "to get together." *Xinghui* (兴会) refers to one's passionate creative state and rich perceptions sparked by an object, and keen, naturally-inspired interest and charm in literary creation. The term, as a whole, indicates distinctive, spontaneous perceptions and emotions in literary creation, and intense interest and charm possessed by literary work. It is both a term of literary criticism and a concept of literary creation. Opposing false sentimentality, the term holds in esteem spontaneity, writers' talents and enthusiasm, and emphasizes free imagination based on intuition and free creation in a state of bursting inspirations.

引例 Citations：

◎灵运之兴会标举，延年之体裁明密，并方轨前秀，垂范后昆。
(《宋书·谢灵运传论》)

（谢灵运的诗作意旨鲜明、情致高超，颜延之的诗作结构严谨、语言明晰，他们都取法于前代作家的优秀传统，成为后辈写作的典范。）

The spontaneity and distinctiveness of Xie Lingyun's poems as well as the closely-knitted structure and lucidity of Yan Yanzhi's poems, which both draw inspiration from poets before them, have stimulated poets of later time. (*The History of Song of the Southern Dynasties*)

◎一用兴会标举成诗，自然情景俱到。（王夫之《明诗评选》卷六）

（只要将直觉感受到的鲜明物象与灵感激发的独特感悟写成诗，自然有情有景，情景交融。）

A poem with spontaneity and distinctiveness will automatically blend one's sentiments and the natural setting. (Wang Fuzhi: *A Selection of Ming Poetry with Commentary*)

◎原夫创始作者之人，其兴会所至，每无意而出之，即为可法可

则。……情偶至而感，有所感而鸣，斯以为风人之旨。（叶燮《原诗·内篇下》）

（推究诗歌的创作者，当兴会来临时，往往在无意间写出了至美的作品，这些作品即成为后世学习的典范。……心中的情偶然与外在的物相感，自然要将心中所感说出来，这就是诗人创作的本旨。）

A careful examination shows that a poet, when inspired, creates excellent works without knowing it. Such poems will thus become a model for future generations to emulate... When the poet's inner feelings interact with the external world, he naturally has the urge to express them. That is what poetry writing is all about. (Ye Xie: *Studies on the Purpose of Poetic Writing*)

别材别趣 /biécái-biéqù/
Distinct Subject and Artistic Taste

诗歌应具有的特殊题材和特殊的人生趣味。北宋以来，在黄庭坚（1045—1105）的倡导下，江西诗派追求学问，以议论入诗，忽略诗歌自身的感兴特点。南宋严羽（？—1264）对此深为不满，在《沧浪诗话》中提出这个概念，旨在划清诗与非诗的界限，说明诗歌的本质是吟咏情性，而不是堆砌书本知识、卖弄学问；诗歌重在表现感受、传达意味，而不是单纯阐发义理，诗的义理应融化在审美意象中。"别材别趣"的提出，说明文论家注意到了诗歌自身的审美特性，倡导回归唐诗的创作方式和风格。

Poetry should have its distinct subject and artistic taste. In the Northern Song Dynasty, inspired by Huang Tingjian (1045-1105), poets of the Jiangxi School used poetry as a means to express views on public issues. In doing so, they tended to overlook the use of inspiring and evocative language unique to poetic expression. In *Canglang's Criticism on Poetry*, literary critic Yan Yu

(?- 1264) of the Southern Song Dynasty expressed his dismay at this trend. He argued that poetry should have its distinctive subject and purpose and that poetry should express the poet's sentiment and emotion rather than piling book knowledge or showing off learning or presenting theories. The message of a poem should be expressed through its aesthetic imagery. The advocating of distinct subject and artistic taste by Yan Yu shows that by the time of the Southern Song Dynasty, literary critics had recognized the distinctive features of poetic expression and called for return to the creative style of poetry writing of the Tang Dynasty.

引例 Citations：

◎夫诗有别材，非关书也；诗有别趣，非关理也。(严羽《沧浪诗话·诗辨》)

(诗歌有特殊的题材，跟书本知识没有关系；诗歌有特别的旨趣，跟论理没有关系。)

Poetry has its distinct subject matter and is not about book learning. It also has distinct artistic taste and is not about presenting theories. (Yan Yu: *Canglang's Criticism on Poetry*)

◎三百年间虽人各有集，集各有诗，诗各自为体；或尚理致，或负材力，或逞辩博，少者千篇，多者万首，要皆经义策论之有韵者尔，非诗也。(刘克庄《竹溪诗序》)

(宋朝三百年之间，虽然人人有文集，集中都有诗，诗又各有自己擅长的体式，这些诗或者崇尚义理情致，或者自负才学，或者逞辩夸博，少的上千篇，多的上万首，全都是阐发儒家经义或论述时政对策的文章，只不过押上韵罢了，根本不能算诗。)

During the 300 years of the Song Dynasty, a lot of people published collections of literary works, many of which contained poems dealing with different subject matters. In these poems, some authors showcased their arguments, while others paraded their learning or indulged in scholarly debate. Some published 1,000 poems, and others published even 10,000 poems; but most of them were merely rhymed essays that expounded

Confucian classics or discussed current policies. They were just not poetry.
(Liu Kezhuang: Preface to *A Collection of Lin Xiyi's Poems*)

别集 /biéjí/
Individual Collection

　　汇集某一作家个人诗文作品的集子（与汇集多人诗文作品的"总集"相对）。西汉刘歆（？—23）《七略》有"诗赋略"，录有屈原（前340？—前278？）、唐勒、宋玉等66家的作品，皆以作家为单位，是图书"别集"之始。东汉以后别集渐繁，两汉魏晋南北朝别集见于《隋书·经籍志》的就有886部，历代文人学者几乎人人有集。只收诗作的称为诗集，单收文或诗文并收的称为文集。别集常以作家姓名、字号、谥号、籍贯、居住地等命名。别集保存了某一作家的全部传世作品，是作家心灵世界的真实展示，也是后人认识和研究作家思想与文学成就的主要材料。

The term refers to a collection of works by an individual author, in contrast to an anthology which amalgamates the works of many writers. In the Western Han Dynasty, Liu Xin (?-23) composed *Seven Categories*, one of the categories being "The Catalogue of *Shi* and *Fu*," which collects the literary works of 66 writers including Qu Yuan (340?-278? BC), Tang Le, and Song Yu. Organized by author, "The Catalogue of *Shi* and *Fu*" was regarded as the beginning of individual collections. Many more individual collections were compiled in the Eastern Han Dynasty, as exemplified by the 886 collections of writers from the Han through Wei and Jin to the Southern and Northern Dynasties, recorded in *The History of the Sui Dynasty*. Nearly every author had his own collection. Collections devoted to poetry were usually entitled collection of poems while those concerned with prose or both poetry and prose were entitled collection of writings. An individual collection might be entitled after the author's name, pen name, posthumous title, birth place, or residence. Containing all the major works of an author, an individual collection enables readers to learn about the author's aspirations and therefore provides a valuable source for the study of his ideas and literary achievements for later generations.

引例 Citation：

◎别集之名，盖汉东京之所创也。自灵均已降，属（zhǔ）文之士众矣，然其志尚不同，风流殊别。后之君子，欲观其体势而见其心灵，故别聚焉，名之为集。(《隋书·经籍志》)

（别集的名称，大概是东汉时创立。自屈原以下，写作文章的文士太多了，但他们各自的志向和崇尚不同，风格和遗韵也相差很大。后代的人想通过文章考察作家的风格气势并窥见其内心世界，于是把他们的作品单独汇总在一起，称之为"集"。）

What is known as *bieji* (别集) appeared in the Eastern Han Dynasty. Literary history since Qu Yuan witnessed an increasing number of creative writers with distinctive aspirations, preferences, literary features, and tastes. To examine the style, strength, as well as the spiritual world of a specific author, later generations put together all his works and called it *ji* (集) or collection. (*The History of the Sui Dynasty*)

不黏不脱，不即不离

/bù nián bù tuō, bù jí bù lí/

Neither Obsessed with Nor Detached from the Objects Depicted

指诗歌的咏物不可太执著于物本身，应当既不黏滞又不脱落，既不太过接近又不完全离开。"不黏不脱，不即不离"包含两方面的内容：一指作品所使用的语言、意象等与所咏对象的关系，一指作品的主题与所咏对象的关系。它强调，如果用语太过切近，作品就缺乏味道，粘皮带骨，但如果不切题，又难免捕风捉影，过于浮泛。除了体物的要求，咏物诗还有寓意寄托的要求，寄托之意不能勉强，否则就落入教条。传神写意在微妙的离合之间，才能创作出好的咏物作品。

In writing poetry, poets should neither totally adhere to nor digress too much from the objects depicted. This term includes two aspects: the relationship between words, images and the objects depicted, and the relationship between the poem's theme and the objects depicted. It emphasizes that if the objects depicted resemble the subject too closely, the poem will sound insipid and mundane; but if the objects depicted are too detached from the subject, the poem will sound superficial and farfetched. In addition to the requirement of depicting objects, odes to objects should also convey implied meaning which cannot be forced. Otherwise, they will quite likely fall into a stereotype. Only when a proper balance is achieved between the depiction of objects and its implied sentiment can excellent odes to objects be produced.

引例 Citations：

◎咏物诗难在不脱不粘，自然奇雅。（袁枚《随园诗话补遗》卷六）

（咏物诗创作的难处在于既不脱离又不黏滞，自然奇妙雅致。）

The difficulty of writing odes to objects lies in how to avoid both excessive adherence to and total detachment from the objects depicted. A poem thus created will be marvelous, natural and elegant. (Yuan Mei: *Addendum to Suiyuan Remarks on Poetry*)

◎咏物之作，须如禅家所谓不黏不脱，不即不离，乃为上乘。古今咏梅花者多矣，林和靖"暗香""疏影"之句，独有千古，山谷谓不如"雪后园林才半树，水边篱落忽横枝"；而坡公"竹外一枝斜更好"，识者以为文外独绝，此其故可为解人道耳。（王士禛《跋门人黄从生梅花诗》）

（咏物的作品，应当如禅宗所说既不黏滞又不脱落，既不太过接近又不完全离开，才是最好的。从古至今吟咏梅花的诗太多了，林和靖"暗香""疏影"的句子，独特美好千年流传，黄山谷说不如"雪后园林才半树，水边篱落忽横枝"；而苏东坡"竹外一枝斜更好"，有见识的人认为那是东坡文章之外独特高绝的地方，这其中的缘故只可和懂得诗歌的人讲说。）

The best odes to objects, according to Chan philosophy, should not resemble real-life objects too closely nor be totally detached from them. There have been many poems depicting plum blossoms since ancient times. For example, Lin Hejing's poetic terms like "subtle fragrance" and "scattered shadows" of plum blossoms have been passed on over centuries, but Huang Shangu remarked that they were not so good as Lin's other lines: "A garden of half-blossomed plums after the wintry snow, a slanting twig visible over the fence by the riverside." Insightful people believe that Su Shi's poetic line "Miraculous is the single twig slanting out of the bamboo grove" is unrivalled and that only those who really know how to appreciate poetry understand why this is so. (Wang Shizhen: A Postscript to "The Plum Blossom Ode by Huang Congsheng")

不平则鸣 /bùpíngzémíng/
Cry Out Against Injustice

本义是物体没有放平就容易发出声响，引申为人受到了不公正的对待就要发出不满的声音。唐代著名文学家韩愈（768—824）意在说明文学作品的创作是因为作者受到外界的激发，心中产生"不平之气"，这种不平之气推动作者用文学语言表达出来。这一理论是对孔子（前551—前479）"诗可以怨"和司马迁（前145或前135？—?）"发愤著书"说的继承与发展，北宋欧阳修（1007—1072）进一步提出了"诗穷而后工"的见解，认为诗人在困厄艰险的环境中，幽愤郁积于心，才能写出精美的诗歌作品。

This expression originally denotes an observation that when objects lose their balance, they make sounds. Figuratively, it means that an ill-treated person will make sounds of protest and complaint. Han Yu (768-824), a famous writer in the Tang Dynasty, used the phrase to point out that writers will be driven to write when the outside world invokes in them feelings of injustice. Feelings like this compel writers to expose injustices through literature. This theory is a continuation and development of Confucius' (551-479 BC) idea "Poetry can address grievance" and the Grand Historian Sima Qian's (145 or 135 ?-? BC) concept "Indignation spurs one to write great works." Ouyang Xiu (1007-1072) in the Northern Song Dynasty further proposes "A good poem is the product of pent-up emotions." He believes that only when a poet is trapped in a difficult and even perilous position with pent-up anger and frustration will he be able to compose quality poems.

引例 Citations：

◎大凡物不得其平则鸣。(韩愈《送孟东野序》)

(一般来说，物体因为放置不平就容易发出声响。)

Generally speaking, when things lose their balance, they make sounds. (Han Yu: Farewell to Meng Dongye)

◎太史公曰:《说难》《孤愤》，贤圣发愤之所作也。由此观之，古之贤圣，不愤则不作矣。不愤而作，譬如不寒而颤，不病而呻吟也，虽作，何观乎? (李贽《〈忠义水浒传〉序》)

(司马迁说:《说难》《孤愤》，是圣贤之人为抒发愤懑而写的作品。这样看来，古代的圣贤之人，没有愤懑的情绪是不会写作的。没有愤懑情绪的写作，就如同不寒冷却打寒颤，没生病却痛苦呻吟，即使写出来，又有什么值得看的呢?)

The Grand Historian Sima Qian said: "'On Difficulty' and 'Solitary Anger' are two pieces of writing by sages to give vent to their anger and frustration. Thus, it seems that ancient sages would not write if they were not angry and frustrated. To write without such emotions is to shiver without feeling cold, or to moan without being sick. Who would want to read such things even though they have been written?" (Li Zhi: Preface to *Outlaws of the Marsh*)

不涉理路，不落言筌

/bù shè lǐlù, bù luò yánquán/

Dispense with Theory and Logic; Take Care Not to Fall into Traps of Language

不关涉论理和逻辑，不落入语言的束缚。筌是竹制的一种捕鱼器，比喻束缚、拘碍，"言筌"即指语言文字的束缚。这是宋代严羽（？—1264）在《沧浪诗话》中所提出的有关诗歌学习及创作的要求。这一术语相当于对"妙悟"的解释，诗歌有独特的思维方式和审美要求，它的本质是吟咏情性，注重当下即是的感觉，而不是阐发义理、卖弄学问。学习诗歌，也要避免受到论理和语言文字的束缚。

Poets should not concern themselves with theory, logic or any other convention in the use of language. *Quan* (筌), originally a bamboo fish-catching device, later was used as a metaphor for any form of linguistic constraint on poetic creation. The term "language trap" was first put forward by the Song Dynasty poetry theorist Yan Yu (?-1264) in his *Canglang's Criticism on Poetry*, a work on poetry learning and creation. It can be likened to the idea of "subtle insight." Poetry writing has its distinct ways of thinking and aesthetic requirements. Essentially, it should express the poet's emotions and mood, and emphasize momentary feeling, rather than expound on theories or show off one's learning. Poetry learners should also avoid being shackled by theories or conventions in language use.

◎夫诗有别材，非关书也；诗有别趣，非关理也。然非多读书，多穷理，则不能极其至。所谓不涉理路、不落言筌者，上也。（严羽《沧浪诗话·诗辨》）

（诗歌有特殊的题材，跟书本知识没有关系；诗歌有特别的旨趣，跟论理没有关系。然而不多读书，不多穷究义理，就不能达到极致。只有不关涉论理逻辑、不落入文字束缚的诗，才是上乘的诗。）

Poetry has its distinct subject matter and is not about book learning. It also has its distinct artistic taste and does not bother to dwell on theories. However, if poets do not read widely and pursue reason exhaustively, their poems can never reach perfection. Poetry of the highest class is not restricted by theory, logic or convention. (Yan Yu: *Canglang's Criticism on Poetry*)

◎筌者所以在鱼，得鱼而忘筌。蹄者所以在兔，得兔而忘蹄。言者所以在意，得意而忘言。（《庄子·外物》）

（竹筌是用来捕鱼的，得到鱼就忘记了筌。兔网是用来捉兔子的，得到兔子就忘记了网。语言是用来表达意义的，得到意义就忘记了语言。）

The bamboo fish trap is used to catch fish, but the trap will be forgotten once the fish is caught. The rabbit net is used to catch rabbits, but the net will be forgotten once the rabbit is caught. Words are used to convey meaning, so we should forget the words once we have grasped the meaning. (*Zhuangzi*)

不似之似 /bùsìzhīsì/
Dissimilar in Form but Similar in Spirit

指艺术作品不刻意追求外形与描写对象的酷似，而是在传神达意上达到更高程度的相似。也说"不似而似"。唐宋元绘画理论重视"神似"超过"形似"，到了明代，以石涛（1641—1718?）为代表的画论观点，反对自矜神韵的重意轻形，亦反对刻意求似。他们认为最理想的状态是"不似之似"，"不似"是指笔情恣意，脱离陈旧套路，不过于追求外形的真实；"似"是指以生活真实为基础，而臻于传神写意的真实。不似之似相当于在艺术真实与生活真实中达到巧妙的平衡。

This happens when artists do not aim deliberately for virtual replica in form between works of art and the objects depicted but make every effort to achieve a resemblance in spirit. This is also known as "dissimilar in form but similar in spirit." The Chinese theory of painting in the Tang, Song and Yuan dynasties emphasizes resemblance in spirit over similarity in form. The artistic elite represented by Shi Tao (1641 - 1718 ?) in the Ming Dynasty objected to both the idea that the artist should emphasize a profound artistic ambience at the expense of formal resemblance, and the idea that the artist's sole duty is to blindly imitate the form. They believe that an ideal work of art is both "dissimilar and yet similar at the same time." "Dissimilar" means that an artist should paint with free will, discarding outdated practices, and not excessively pursuing resemblance in form. "Similar" means that painting should be based on true life and artists should strive for similarity in spirit. This principle of allowing for dissimilar form in quest of similar spirit strikes an ingenious balance between artistic reality and the reality of daily life.

引例 Citations：

◎今人或寥寥数笔，自矜高简，或重床叠屋，一味颟顸（mānhān）。动曰不求形似，岂知古人所云不求形似者，不似之似也。彼繁简失宜者，乌可同年语哉！（王绂（fú）《书画传习录》卷四）
（今天的人有的随意画上几笔，就以为自己高远简约了；有的则叠床架屋似的繁杂，一味稀里糊涂。动不动就说不追求形似，不知道古人所说的不追求形似，其实说的是"不似之似"。那些连繁简都处理不当的人，怎么可以和古人相提并论呢！）

中华思想文化术语
文艺卷

Today some painters casually use a few strokes to show their effortless skill and graceful simplicity, while others, muddle-headed as they are, overload their works with complicated structures and details. They always say that they care little about similarity in form, not knowing that artists of ancient times, when saying that they had no appetite for similarity in form, in fact pursued similarity in spirit. How dare those who cannot master either simplicity or complexity compare themselves to great artists! (Wang Fu: *Notes on How to Do Painting and Calligraphy*)

◎ 名山许游不许画，画必似之山必怪。变幻神奇懵懂间，不似似之当下拜。（石涛《大涤子题画诗跋》卷一）

（名山只允许你游玩但不允许你画它，你若画得太相似，那样画出的山一定怪异。只有在你懵懂间无法分辨它的神奇变化，所绘之山不似之似，它才会对你俯伏下拜。）

Famous mountains can be visited but not painted. If a painting is too much like the mountain itself, the mountain in the painting will look unnatural. Only when you depict them as mystically muddled, dissimilar in form but similar in spirit, will they seem subdued under your brush. (Shi Tao: *Dadizi's Comments on His Own Poems Inscribed on Paintings*)

◎ 天地浑溶一气，再分风雨四时。明暗高低远近，不似之似似之。（石涛《大涤子题画诗跋》卷一）

（天地浑然融合一体，再区分为风雨四季。有明有暗，有高有低，有远有近，只有做到了不似之似，才是真正的相似。）

Sky and earth blend into a harmonious whole, distinguished only by the cycle of the four seasons. Artists should use brighter and darker colors to make objects look appropriately high or low, far or near. Genuine similarity is similarity in substance despite dissimilarity in form. (Shi Tao: *Dadizi's Comments on His Own Poems Inscribed on Paintings*)

不学《诗》，无以言 /bù xué《shī》, wú yǐ yán/

You Won't Be Able to Talk Properly with Others Without Studying *The Book of Songs*.

不学习《诗经》，就不能提高与人交流和表达的能力。孔子（前551—前479）时代，《诗经》象征着一个人的社会身份与文化修养。不学习《诗经》，就无法参与君子间的各种交往，就不能提高语言表达能力。孔子对《诗经》与社会交往关系的论述，实际阐明了文学的教育功能或者说文学在教育中的重要地位。

In Confucius' (551-479 BC) time, how well one understood *The Book of Songs* was a sign of his social status and cultural attainment. If one did not study it, one would find it difficult to improve one's ability to express oneself and to converse with people of high social status. Confucius' elaboration on the relationship between studying *The Book of Songs* and social interaction actually expounds on the importance of literature in education.

引例 Citation：

◎尝独立，鲤趋而过庭。曰："学《诗》乎？"对曰："未也。""不学《诗》，无以言。"（《论语·季氏》）

（孔子曾独自站在堂上，儿子伯鱼从堂下庭院经过，孔子问他："学习《诗经》了吗？"伯鱼回答："没有。"孔子说："不学习《诗经》，就不会交流与表达。"）

Confucius was standing alone in the central hall when his son Boyu walked across the front yard. Confucius asked, "Have you studied *The Book of Songs*?" "Not yet," was the reply. Confucius then said, "If you do not study it, you will not be able to express yourself properly." (*The Analects*)

草书 /cǎoshū/

Cursive Script

汉字发展演变中的一种书体。按发展历程可分为草隶、章草、今草、狂草等阶段。它始于汉代，主要是为了书写便捷，提高效率，当时通行的是草隶，后书家损益笔法，逐渐发展为章草。传至汉末，相传张芝（？—192？）摆脱了章草中所保留的隶书形迹，上下字之间的笔势牵连相通，并省减偏旁、相互假借，形成今草（即今天俗称的草书）。发展到唐代，张旭、怀素（725—785，一说737—799）等草书大家相继产生，他们抒发性情、解放怀抱，将草书写得更为自由纵放，笔势绵延环绕，章法跌宕起伏，结字大胆奇诡，形态变化多端，成为"狂草"。后人又称狂草为"大草"，称今草为"小草"。

Cursive script, also known as running hand, is a particular style of Chinese calligraphy. It went through four stages of development: cursive clerical, semi-cursive, regular cursive and wild cursive. It began in the Han Dynasty, aiming to facilitate handwriting and increase efficiency. The first popular form of cursive script was cursive clerical. Later, calligraphers added or subtracted the number of strokes to turn the cursive clerical into semi-cursive. Toward the end of the Han Dynasty, Zhang Zhi (?- 192 ?) allegedly rid semi-cursive script of cursive clerical vestiges, linking the final strokes of the character above with the beginning stroke of the following character, eliminating certain radicals and borrowing strokes from neighboring parts to form regular cursive script (commonly known as "cursive hand" today). During the Tang Dynasty, Zhang Xu and Huaisu (725 - 785, or maybe 737 - 799), regarded as master calligraphers of the cursive style, gave full expression of their feelings and thoughts, and wrote their characters in a freer and more uninhibited manner. Their execution of strokes featured continuous stretches, gracefully circular movement, flowing contours, amazingly bold combinations of characters and a wide variety of patterns, leading to the emergence of "wild" cursive script. People of later generations also called the latter "great cursive" as opposed to "small cursive," which in fact referred to regular cursive.

引例 Citations:

◎往时张旭善草书，不治他技。喜怒窘穷，忧悲、愉佚、怨恨、思慕、酣醉、无聊、不平，有动于心，必于草书焉发之。（韩愈《送高闲上人序》）

（从前张旭善于写草书，无心于其他技艺。遇有欣喜、愤怒、窘迫、困穷，忧伤、悲愤、愉悦、怨恨、思慕、大醉、无聊、不平等，每有心动，都会通过草书发泄出来。）

Zhang Xu is a master of cursive-hand calligraphy with no other interests. Whenever he experienced heart-stirring joy, anger, awkwardness, poverty, sorrow, grief, pleasure, resentment, yearning, drunkenness, boredom, or injustice, he would unleash his feelings through cursive script. (Han Yu: A Few Words in Farewell to Gaoxian, an Eminent Monk)

◎张丞相好草书而不工。当时流辈皆讥笑之，丞相自若也。一日得句，索笔疾书，满纸龙蛇飞动，使侄录之。当波险处，侄罔然而止，执所书问曰："此何字也？"丞相熟视久之，亦自不识，诟其侄曰："胡不早问？致予忘之！"（释惠洪《冷斋夜话》卷九）

（张［商英］丞相喜欢写草书，但是很不精通。当时的人都讥笑他，他却不以为意。一天，他忽然得到佳句，赶忙索要笔墨奋笔疾书，写了满纸，字迹龙飞凤舞。他让侄儿把诗句抄录出来。侄儿抄到笔画怪异的地方，感到疑惑，便停下笔来，拿着丞相所写的字向他询问是什么字。张丞相反复辨认了很久，也没认出来自己写的是什么字，于是就责骂侄儿说："你怎么不早一点问我，以致我也忘了写的是什么！"）

Although Prime Minister Zhang (Shangying) loved writing in cursive style, he was never truly good at it. Many laughed at him, but he didn't mind much. One day, a few poetic lines occurred to his mind, so he asked for his brush and ink and started to write in a lively and vigorous flourish. Then he asked his nephew to copy down those lines for him. Puzzled by some characters with strange-looking strokes, the young man paused and asked what they meant.

The Prime Minister studied them carefully, but they were unintelligible to him as well. So he scolded the boy: "Why hadn't you asked me earlier, before I'd forgotten what those characters were?" (Shi Huihong: *Evening Talks at Lengzhai*)

常州词派 /Chángzhōu cípài/
The Changzhou School of Commentary on *Ci* Poetry

　　清代中期以后影响最大的词学流派，以常州文人张惠言（1761—1802）为首。张惠言编辑《词选》，认为词继承了《诗经》的风雅、比兴传统，强调词"深美闳约""意内言外"等审美特征，推尊词体，大大提升了词的文学地位。其后，周济（1781—1839）继承发扬了张惠言的词论，编辑《宋四家词选》等，提出"夫词，非寄托不入，专寄托不出""浑化"等理论。谭献（1832—1901）、陈廷焯（1853—1892）、况周颐（1859—1926）算是常州词派的第三代，其代表作品《复堂词话》《白雨斋词话》《蕙风词话》等，进一步丰富了品词、作词的方法。常州词派的最大贡献是在理论上阐发了词所具有的载道、言志之价值，使其成为与经典诗文并列的文体。

This term refers to the most influential school of poetic criticism of the mid-Qing Dynasty named after its leader Zhang Huiyan (1761 - 1802), a scholar from Changzhou. He compiled the *Anthology of Ci*, containing 116 *ci* poems by 44 poets from the Tang, the Five Dynasties, and the Song periods. His aesthetic criteria for *ci* poetry included portraying rich emotional content in concise language, and the painting of mood and feeling through subtle associations beyond the words themselves. Thanks to his commentaries, the literary status of the *ci* form was considerably elevated. Zhou Ji (1781 - 1839), who came after Zhang, not only continued in the same practice and theory but also expanded on his ideas and compiled the *Selected Poems of Four Poets of the Song Dynasty*. Zhou proposed a number of theories about writing *ci*: for beginners, to acquire the technique of *ci* writing, it is essential to learn to express their feelings through material references; but to achieve the true depth of the form, material references must not be contrived, and the emotions they represent should both infer yet transcend them. Another theory was "blending." Tan Xian (1832-1901), Chen Tingzhuo (1853-1892), Kuang Zhouyi (1859-1926) were the third generation of this literary school. Their works *Writings on Ci by Futang, Remarks on Ci Poetry from White Rain Studio, Notes and Commentaries on Ci by Huifeng* further enriched and refined the art of writing and critiquing *ci* poetry. The most important contribution of the Changzhou School was to demonstrate from a theoretical angle the value of the *ci* form in expressing philosophical thoughts as well as ambitions and aspirations. This placed it on a par with other classical poetic forms.

引例 Citations：

◎词之为技小矣。然考之于昔，南北分宗，征之于今，江浙别派，是亦有故焉。吾郡自皋文、子居两先生开辟榛莽，以《国风》《离骚》之恉（zhǐ）趣，铸温、韦、周、辛之面目，一时作者竞出，晋卿集其成。（周济《存审轩词·自序》）

（词作为一种技艺，不算重要。然而考察词史，有以北宋词为宗的，有以南宋词为宗的，用今日情形验证，常州（江苏）、浙江发展出两大流派，也是有历史原因的。自从同郡人张惠言、恽敬两位先生开辟词学新路以来，用《诗经·国风》《离骚》的意旨趣味，重现温庭筠、韦庄、周邦彦、辛弃疾等人的艺术风貌，一时之间词人竞相出现，其中董士锡集合了各家优点。）

Ci itself is not a very important poetic technique, however historically it can be traced to both the Northern and Southern Song dynasties, so it is logical that today, there should be two major schools: the Changzhou School (in Jiangsu) and the Zhejiang School. Since Zhang Huiyan and Yun Jing, who came from the same prefecture as me, opened up new paths for *ci* writing by proposing *The Book of Songs* and *Li Sao* as literary references for *ci*, *ci* writing has regained the artistic features of the poetry of Wen Tingyun, Wei Zhuang, Zhou Bangyan, and Xin Qiji. Many other *ci* poets have appeared. The best examples of the various styles have been compiled by Dong Shixi. (Zhou Ji: *Collection of Ci from Cunshen Studio*)

◎金针度，《词辨》止庵精。截断众流穷正变，一灯乐苑此长明，推演四家评。(朱祖谋《望江南》)

(教给别人方法，周济的《词辨》很精当。把众多杂乱的观点一并截断，穷究词体的正源和变化，犹如一盏明灯永久照亮了词苑，这应该归功于周济《宋四家词选》的词评。)

Zhou Ji's *Critique of Ci* is a fine work of instruction. In it he clears up many confused notions, and probes into the origins and evolution of *ci*. Thanks to the commentaries in his *Selected Poems of Four Poets of the Song Dynasty*, he has shed a bright light into the world of *ci* composition. (Zhu Zumou: To the Tune of Wang Jiangnan)

畅神 /chàngshén/
Free Flow of One's Mind

指精神与自然合一时所达到的自由舒畅的一种审美状态。特指欣赏山水画、山水诗时精神融入自然及物象的审美效应。南朝画家宗炳 (375 — 443) 在《画山水序》中指出，欣赏山水画可以领悟古代圣贤寄寓在山水中的哲理与乐趣，可以进入一种摒弃了一切外物和杂念的绝对虚无境界，它是一种全身心的极度愉悦和精神的最高自由。他提出这一术语，不仅揭示了山水画、山水诗及自然美的特殊审美功能，也反映了传统文学艺术对天人和谐、心灵和谐的价值追求。

The term describes a state of mind one achieves when appreciating an artwork, in which process one's inner feelings interact freely and joyfully with nature. In particular, it describes one's aesthetic experience of appreciating landscape paintings and landscape poems, when one feels absorbed with the natural scenes and images depicted. In his "On the Creation of Landscape Paintings," Zong Bing (375-443), painter of the Southern Dynasties, pointed out that by watching landscape paintings, one can appreciate the philosophy and pleasure which sages of past times drew from landscape. When doing so, one becomes oblivious to the external world and is totally free from worldly considerations, thus achieving full satisfaction of both body and mind. This term not only reveals the unique aesthetic function of landscape paintings, landscape poems, and natural beauty, but also demonstrates traditional literature and arts' pursuit of harmony between nature and man and between mind and heart.

引例 Citation：

◎圣贤映于绝代，万趣融其神思，余复何为哉？畅神而已。（宗炳《画山水序》）

（古代的圣贤已经通过想象与思考领略融汇了自然山水中的万般旨趣，我还需要做什么呢？只需体会畅神所带来的快乐就可以了。）

As sages of remote past already discovered the philosophical wisdom inherent in nature through imagination and contemplation, what more do I need to do now? All I have to do is relishing the joy when my mind interacts freely with the depicted landscape. (Zong Bing: On the Creation of Landscape Paintings)

沉郁 /chényù/

Melancholy

指诗歌作品中所表现出的情志含蓄深沉、意蕴丰富深厚的艺术风格。以杜甫（712—770）为代表的古代诗人，关注国家大事，忧心民生艰难，苦思国家兴衰存亡之理而难通，求索安邦济民之策而不得，反映在作品中就表现为情志含蓄深沉、思想丰富深厚。其作品常常一唱三叹，结构、节奏、音调等抑扬起伏，给予读者以特有的"顿挫"美感，读后产生回味无穷的感受。

Melancholy refers to an artistic style in poetic works in which sentiment expressed is subtle and the message is profound. Ancient Chinese poets represented by Du Fu (712-770), keenly concerned about state affairs and people's hardships, tried hard to understand what caused the rise and fall of a nation and sought ways to save the country and the people, but all to no avail. Such frustration and disappointment are thus reflected in their poems. With meticulously crafted structure, rhythm, and tones, their works give readers a special aesthetic appreciation of melody and infinite afterthought.

引例 Citation：

◎所谓沈（chén）郁者，意在笔先，神余言外。（陈廷焯《白雨斋词话》卷一）

（所谓"沉郁"，是指动笔前已有长时间的思想感情积蓄，因而文章有着语言所不能穷尽的精神蕴含。）

Melancholy means that as a writer has given so much thought to the theme before writing, his work, once completed, contains profound sentiments beyond description. (Chen Tingzhuo: *Remarks on Ci Poetry from White Rain Studio*)

陈诗展义 /chénshī-zhǎnyì/
Write Poetry to Express Feeling and Aspiration

诗人创作诗歌是为了展示自己的内心情感和志向。这是南朝诗论家钟嵘（？—518？）在《诗品》中提出的关于诗歌创作动机的重要看法。钟嵘强调四时节物的变化以及社会人事际遇对诗人创作的影响，认为诗人用诗歌来展现内心的情感活动与志向。钟嵘的诗歌美学在注重外部世界激发诗人创作冲动的同时，又强调情感对于诗歌的独立审美价值，这一理论无疑比汉代儒家的"诗教"说要进步许多。

This term, concerning the motivation in poetry writing, was first used by the Southern Dynasty poetry theorist Zhong Rong (?-518?) in his *The Critique of Poetry*. He emphasized the impact upon a poet's creative activities of seasonal changes and encounters between humans, maintaining that the poet uses his work to show his inner feelings and aspirations. Zhong's poetic aesthetics, while recognizing the role of the outer world in inspiring poets, also valued the unique aesthetic value of feelings to poetry. This view was clearly more mature than that of "writing poetry for moral indoctrination only" held by Han Dynasty Confucian scholars.

引例 Citation：

◎若乃春风春鸟，秋月秋蝉，夏云暑雨，冬月祁寒，斯四候之感诸诗者也。嘉会寄诗以亲，离群托诗以怨。至于楚臣去境，汉妾辞宫，或骨横朔野，或魂逐飞蓬……凡斯种种，感荡心灵，非陈诗何以展其义？非长歌何以骋其情？（钟嵘《诗品》卷上）

（至于那春风、春鸟，秋月、秋蝉，夏云、暑雨，冬月、酷寒，这是四季的节令、气候感动诗人从而创作为诗。美好的集会上，诗人写诗来表达亲近和睦之情；离群索居时，诗人用诗歌表达哀怨。至于楚国屈原离开国都，汉朝的王昭君辞别宫廷，或者尸骨横于北方荒野，魂魄追逐着随风飘飞的蓬草……这种种情景，无不感动着人们的心灵，不作诗怎么能够展示诗人的内心情感和志向？不长篇歌咏又怎么能抒发出诗人的情怀？）

Poets are inspired by spring wind and birds, autumnal moon and cicadas, summer clouds and rain, winter moon and desolate cold weather – the cycle of seasons and weather – to create poetry. They write poetry during a beautiful gathering to show affinity among fellow humans, or when they live in solitude to express sorrow. As for Qu Yuan who had to leave the capital of the Kingdom of Chu, Wang Zhaojun who was compelled to bid farewell to the royal court, corpses lying all about in the wilderness in the north, or ghosts chasing artemisia fluttering in mid-air… all this stirs the soul, urging the poet to write and chant poetry as a means of expressing feeling and aspiration. (Zhong Rong: *The Critique of Poetry*)

陈言务去 /chényán-wùqù/
The Necessity of Eliminating Banal Expression

主要有两层含义：其一，指写文章时要去掉那些用腻了的陈旧言辞；其二，指构思文章时要摈除人云亦云的庸俗之见。这是唐代著名文学家韩愈（768 — 824）针对散文写作提出的观点。韩愈强调写文章应该变革创新，努力摒弃一切陈旧的言辞和论点，不可因循守旧。这一见解与韩愈所领导的"古文运动"提出的"文以明道"，提倡古文、反对骈文等观点是一脉相承的。

This term has a two-fold meaning. Firstly, it refers to the need to rid an essay of banal wording. Secondly, it encourages authors to discard mediocre, derivative ideas when writing. It is a term raised by the Tang Dynasty man of letters Han Yu (768-824) about prose writing. Han emphasized that essays should be written in an innovative way. He guarded against stereotyped expression and argument and opposed any rigid convention. This view echoed the idea of "writing to convey Dao" put forward by Han Yu during the Classical Prose Movement he led, a movement which aimed to abandon rhythmical prose characterized by parallelism and ornateness in favor of ancient prose of the Han Dynasty.

◎当其取于心而注于手也，惟陈言之务去，戛戛乎其难哉！（韩愈
《答李翊（yì）书》）

（当把心里所想写出来的时候，一定要把那些陈旧的言辞和论点都
去掉，这是多么费力、困难的事情啊！）

How difficult and exhausting it is to try to eliminate all banal wording
and arguments when a person writes what he feels! (Han Yu: A Letter of
Response to Li Yi)

◎陈言务去，杜诗与韩文同。黄山谷、陈后山诸公学杜在此。（刘
熙载《艺概·诗概》）

（去除陈旧的言词，杜甫的诗歌与韩愈的文章是一致的。黄庭坚、
陈师道诸人学习杜甫的诗歌正在这一点上。）

Du Fu's poetry is no different from Han Yu's prose in that both eliminate
stereotyped wording. Huang Tingjian and Chen Shidao emulated Du Fu
exactly on that point. (Liu Xizai: *Overview of Literary Theories*)

成竹于胸 /chéngzhúyúxiōng/

Have a Complete Image of the Bamboo Before Drawing It / Have a Fully Formed Picture in the Mind's Eye

在文艺创作开始前，艺术形象已在头脑中生成。这一术语揭
示了文艺创作运用形象思维的特点，也是对文艺创作乃至工艺设计
提出的要求。对于文艺创作者来说，思想观念、情感、意志与物象
结合，在心中形成审美意象，艺术构思已经完成，然后才是运用技
巧、借助物质材料外化为具体可感的作品。对于工艺设计者来说，
则有更多的理性思考，允许修改，而成竹在胸则是一种理想状态。

This term means to have an image of the art in one's mind prior to artistic creation. It describes the use of mental imagery in the course of artistic creation, and also sets a requirement for both artistic creation and for design in craftsmanship. For the creator of an artwork, concepts, feelings, intentions and objects should be integrated in the mind to form an aesthetic image. After this artistic conceptualization is completed, technique is used in conjunction with physical materials to form a tangible work. For a craft designer, the emphasis would be more on rational thinking, and revisions would be permissible. Having a fully formed picture in advance is an ideal state.

引例 Citations：

◎故画竹必先得成竹于胸中，执笔熟视，乃见其所欲画者，急起从之，振笔直遂，以追其所见，如兔起鹘落，少纵则逝矣。(苏轼《文与可画筼筜谷偃竹记》)

(所以说画竹一定要先在心中生成竹子的整体形象，拿着画笔仔细观察竹子，然后才可能在心中出现所想要画的竹子，这时要急速起身追赶这一形象，挥笔作画，一气呵成，捕捉住心中所想的竹子，就像兔子跃起、鹰隼俯冲一样迅速，稍一放松，竹子的形象就消失了。)

Thus when drawing bamboo, you must first have a complete image of the bamboo in your mind's eye. First hold the pen while carefully observing the bamboo; only then will the bamboo you wish to draw appear in your mind's eye. Then, as quickly as a leaping hare or a swooping raptor, you must wield your pen and capture this image in one go. The slightest letup and the image of the bamboo will be lost. (Su Shi: An Essay on Wen Yuke's Drawing "The Valley of Bamboos")

◎文与可画竹，胸有成竹；郑板桥画竹，胸无成竹。浓淡疏密，短长肥瘦，随手写去，自尔成局，其神理具足也。(郑板桥《板桥题画·竹》)

(文与可画竹，心里先有竹子的完整形象；郑板桥画竹，心中没有竹子的完整形象。竹子颜色是浓是淡，枝叶是疏是密，竹身是短是长、是肥是瘦，都是随手而画，自成一种形态，也都充分表现出了竹子的纹理神韵。）

When Wen Yuke draws bamboo, he already has a complete image of the bamboo in his mind. When Zheng Banqiao draws bamboo, he does not have a complete image of the bamboo in his mind. The colors of his bamboo might be dark or pale; the leaves might be dense or sparse, the stems might be short or long, thick or slender – they are all drawn spontaneously, assuming a form of their own and fully displaying their own textures and charms. (Zheng Banqiao: *Banqiao's Calligraphies in Paintings*)

程器 /chéngqì/
Assessment of One's Overall Qualities

综合考量文士的器用与文采。由南朝刘勰（465？—520？或532？）在《文心雕龙》中提出。"程"，衡量，考量；"器"，兼指个人品行、治国之能与文才几方面。刘勰认为，汉魏以来有些文人或因品行有失，或因缺乏处理国家军政事务的能力，以致被世人讥诮，作品声誉受到牵累。因此他提出，文士不仅要具备写作才能，还应该具备良好的品行及为国家建功立业的能力。他认为有道德的人必然心怀天下，拥有广博见识，培养多方面才能，在多方面有所作为。他主张将立德、立功、立言统一起来，作为全面评价士人的基本标准。

This term refers to a comprehensive assessment of a scholar's abilities and literary talent. It was first put forward by Liu Xie (465?-520? or 532?) of the Southern Dynasties in his literary critique *The Literary Mind and the Carving of Dragons*. Here *cheng* (程) means to assess; *qi* (器) refers to a person's moral conduct, ability to govern and literary talent. In Liu's view, some scholars since the Han and Wei dynasties had been scorned for their poor moral conduct or their inability to handle political or military affairs. This also harmed their literary reputation. Thus, he advised scholar-officials to not only possess writing skills but also excel morally and perform meritorious deeds for their country. He believed that a virtuous person would embrace noble ideals, be knowledgeable and insightful, be versatile, and fulfill worthy goals. He stressed the need to judge a scholar-official by his statements and moral character and his performance of meritorious service.

引例 Citations：

◎武帝既招英俊，程其器能，用之如不及。(《汉书·东方朔传》)

(汉武帝招揽众多杰出人才之后，马上衡量他们的才能，急于任用他们，好像生怕来不及一样。)

After recruiting talented men, Emperor Wu of the Han Dynasty immediately tested their abilities; he was so eager that he could not wait to assign them to important posts. (*The History of the Han Dynasty*)

◎搞(chī)文必在纬军国，负重必在任栋梁；穷则独善以垂文，达则奉时以骋绩。若此文人，应《梓材》之士矣。(刘勰《文心雕龙·程器》)

(撰写文章一定要像筹划军国大事一样，担负重任一定是要成为国家栋梁；不得志时要独善其身以文传世，仕途通达时要抓住时机建功立业。像这样的文人，应该符合《尚书·梓材》中所说的人才了。)

The act of writing should be performed as if it was a matter of handling major military or state affairs. Those bearing heavy responsibilities should act as pillars of society. When unappreciated, they should preserve their moral integrity and achieve enduring fame through their writings. When serving as officials, they should seize the chance to accomplish great goals. Such scholars fit the description of "outstanding talent" discussed in *The Book of History*. (Liu Xie: *The Literary Mind and the Carving of Dragons*)

澄怀味像 /chénghuái-wèixiàng/

Clear the Mind to Savor the Image

指放空心灵，抛却一切世俗干扰与功利之心，在虚静空明的心境中，观赏、品味由"道"所呈现的物象。"澄怀"是"味像"的前提，唯有不受客观束缚与世俗影响的审美才最接近于"道"。此时，物与我消泯了界限，审美者可由玩味山水而与"道"相通，体会到精神的真正自由与超越。"澄怀味像"是中国古代山水画理论中的重要术语，属于艺术直觉论，它是对老子思想"涤除玄览"的继承与发展，启发了书法、文学等其他领域的创作理论。

This refers to emptying one's mind, casting aside all kinds of worldly interference and eliminating the desire for fame and fortune. In a state of thorough, lucid serenity, one can observe and enjoy physical objects as manifested by Dao. "Clearing the mind" is the precondition for "savoring aesthetic images." People's appreciation of beauty can approach the infinite Dao only by breaking loose from worldly constraints and vulgar influences. At that very moment, the boundary between oneself and external objects disappears. The beholder, feasting eyes on beautiful mountains, rivers and lakes, achieves communion with Dao and thus attains a true mental freedom and transcendence. "Clearing the mind for pure contemplation" is an important term in traditional Chinese landscape painting theory; categorically, it belongs to artistic intuitionism. It carries on and further develops Laozi's notion of cleansing away all distracting thoughts and watching the world with a clear, peaceful mind, which inspires theories of creativity in calligraphy, literature and other artistic fields.

引例 Citations：

◎圣人含道映物，贤者澄怀味像。（宗炳《画山水序》）

（圣人内心涵蕴了"道"因而能映照万事万物，有才德的人放空心灵因而能体味"道"所呈现的物象。）

Sages illuminate objects by embracing Dao, and virtuous people clear the mind to savor the image. (Zong Bing: On the Creation of Landscape Paintings)

◎（宗炳）有疾还江陵。叹曰："老疾俱至，名山恐难遍睹，唯当澄怀观道，卧以游之。"（《宋书·隐逸传·宗炳》）

（[宗炳]生病之后回到江陵。感叹说："我老了，又病了，恐怕难以遍游名山，只有放空心灵而体味"道"所呈现的物象，在屋里躺着观看山水画而权当亲身游历了。"）

Zong Bing returned home to Jiangling after falling ill. He said with a sigh: "I'm old and don't feel well now, so I am no longer able to travel and see famous mountains. All I can do now is to unleash my spiritual self and appreciate objects presented by Dao. I will observe landscapes while lying in bed, which is almost like I was there." (*The History of Song of the Southern Dynasties*)

痴 /chī/

Obsessiveness / Ignorance / Perplexity

痴本义为愚笨、呆傻、疯癫等，引申为痴迷、执著及为人处事上的怪诞、成癖、不通世务等。与世俗的精明算计相比，痴人一往情深，不计代价，形同呆傻，亦往往不追求功名利禄，不慕荣华富贵，与正统教条观念相违背。痴可用于痴情、痴言、痴行等，侧重于一派天真自然，纯任性情，特立独行，不惧世俗眼光。"痴"又为佛教术语，义同"无明"，谓愚昧无知，不明万法事理。佛教将贪、嗔、痴列为"三毒"，认为它们是诸恶产生的根源。

This term originally means stupidity, foolishness or madness, and by extension it becomes closely associated with fascination, persistence, weirdness in dealing with people and things. Compared with shrewd, calculating worldly people, people with obsessions tend to be utterly devoted and passionate to the degree of being like fools. They engage in fond love, fond speech and fond behavior, value innocence, true self and individual character, but they seek no fame, wealth or power, and have no fear of worldly judgment. *Chi* (痴 *moha*) is also a Buddhist term, which means ignorance or perplexity. It is the benighted state of mind, being unaware of the reality of the world. Buddhism lists ignorance as one of the three poisons, the other two being greed and resentment, from which all (other) evils originate.

引例 Citations：

◎诗骨耸东野，诗涛涌退之。有时跟跄行，人惊鹤阿师。可惜李杜死，不见此狂痴。(孟郊《戏赠无本》)

（[贾岛]的诗其内在的骨像孟郊一样高耸，其才思之波涛如韩愈一样翻涌。有时走起路来跟跟跄跄，像是个清瘦如鹤的禅师。可惜李白、杜甫都死了，不能见到贾岛的狂放痴呆。）

Jia Dao's poetic aspiration soars like mine / and his poetic talent matches that of Han Yu. / Sometimes he staggers when he walks / like a thin Chan monk. / What a pity that Li Bai and Du Fu have passed away, / unable to see how other worldly this man appears! (Meng Jiao: *A Poem Playfully Written to Present to Jia Dao*)

◎云何为痴？于诸理事迷暗为性，能障无痴，一切杂染所依为业。(《成唯识论》卷六)

（什么叫"痴"？痴就是迷失心性，不明事理，妨碍正确的认知，因此是一切烦恼存在的依归及根源。）

What is perplexity? It is the loss of one's true nature and the failure to see things in their true light. Perplexity prevents correct understanding, so it is the root cause of all afflictions. (*Collected Commentaries to the Perfection of Consciousness-only*)

赤子之心 /chìzǐzhīxīn/

Utter Innocence

　　本义指婴儿未经世俗染污的纯洁心灵，也指成年人仍然保有的婴儿般的赤诚真心，那种在功利世界里仍能坚守的初心。在政治伦理领域，它指人类善良的真心本性，主要是推己及人的恻隐之心或者是童真一般的尚实求真的品格；在文艺创作与审美领域，它主要指具有丰富情感和美好纯真理想的童心，是超越了一切功利心、尘俗气息以及过于理智、缺乏审美情趣的心理状态。它既是古人推崇的理想人格的一种表征，也是文艺作品中美好人物形象塑造的一种类型。

This term refers to the pure heart and soul of a newborn babe, untainted by worldly affairs. Most often, it refers to adults who retain the utter innocence of an infant, holding themselves aloof from worldly goals. In the field of political ethics, the term highlights humans' natural kindness, calling for empathy with others and child-like wonder for truth. In literary creation and aesthetics, it refers mainly to a pure state of being filled with subtle feelings and noble ideals, transcending all worldly pursuits and sophistication, and rejecting an overly rational mentality lacking aesthetic judgment. The term promotes an ideal personality worshiped by ancient Chinese and represents a laudable type of character often portrayed in literary works.

引例 Citations：

◎含德之厚，比于赤子。蜂虿（chài）虺（huǐ）蛇不螫（shì），猛兽不据，攫鸟不搏。骨弱筋柔而握固，未知牝牡之合而全作，精之至也。终日号而不嗄，和之至也。知和曰常，知常曰明，益生曰祥，心使气曰强。物壮则老，谓之不道，不道早已。(《老子·五十五章》)

（含有深厚德性的人，比得上初生的婴儿。有毒的虫蛇不会叮咬他，猛兽不会伤害他，凶禽不会捕捉他。他筋骨柔弱但拳头握得很紧，不知道男女交合但生殖器却能勃起，这是因为精气充足的缘故。他整天号哭但是嗓子不沙哑，这是因为元气醇和的缘故。理解醇和的道理，就懂得了恒常，懂得了恒常，就可称为明智。纵欲贪生会有不祥，精气任由欲望支配就是逞强。事物过于强盛就会衰老，这叫不合自然常道，不合自然常道就会很早衰亡。）

A man of profound virtue is like a newborn babe. Venomous insects will not sting him, snakes will not bite him, beasts will not harm him, and ferocious birds will not prey on him. He is by no means strong physically, but keeps his fists tightly clenched. Although he knows nothing about intercourse with a woman, his genitals harden because he is full of vital energy. He wails all day without getting hoarse because his energy is mellow. An appreciation of mellow energy promises an understanding of permanence. This, in turn, is akin to wisdom. Indulging in sensual pleasures and unscrupulously craving for life will incur misfortune. If vital energy is dictated by desire, that is an outrageous flaunt. Excessive strength marks the beginning of aging, for it goes against the way of nature. Any violation of this rule will lead to one's fall. (*Laozi*)

◎大人者，不失其赤子之心者也。(《孟子·离娄下》)

（有德行的人，是能保持婴儿般天真纯朴之心的人。）

He who is capable of retaining a childlike heart is a truly virtuous man. (*Mencius*)

冲淡 /chōngdàn/
Quiet Elegance

冲和平淡。用于文艺批评，主要指语言平和质朴、意境闲适恬静的一种诗歌风格。它看似空无所有，实则充盈无限；看似平淡无奇，实则意味悠长。这多与作者冲和平淡的性情相应，反映作者尝遍人生百味之后的心态与境界，是超越一切语言表达与文章法则的真情流露。冲淡作为一种美学理念，不仅影响到文艺创作，也塑造文人学士的心性，影响他们的人生态度。

This term is used in literary criticism to refer to a poetic style marked by the plainness and simplicity of wording and by a leisurely quietude. Despite its seeming sterility, such a style is full of life's potentialities and possesses a profound appeal. This echoes the author's mild and placid temperament, showing his mental attitude and spiritual realm of life after he has gone through life's hardships and struggles – a natural expression of feeling which transcends all forms of verbal articulation and all rules of writing. As an aesthetic notion, quiet elegance has not only influenced artistic creation but also shaped the spiritual being of men of letters, helping to cultivate their outlook on life.

引例 Citations：

◎以虚诞而为高古，以缓慢而为冲淡。(释皎然《诗式·诗有六迷》)

(把虚妄荒诞当作高远古朴，把节奏松缓当作冲和平淡。)

Fabrication and absurdity are mistaken for loftiness and primitive simplicity, and languidness for quiet elegance. (Shi Jiaoran: *Poetic Styles*)

◎唐初王、杨、沈、宋擅名，然不脱齐梁之体。独陈拾遗首倡高雅冲澹之音，一扫六代之纤弱，趋于黄初、建安矣。(刘克庄《后村诗话》卷一)

(唐朝初年，只有王勃、杨炯、沈佺期、宋之问享有盛名，但是尚未摆脱齐梁时期追求形式绮丽的风格。唯独陈子昂最先发出诗歌应当高雅冲淡的声音，一扫六朝以来的纤细柔弱，写作风格自此开始向黄初、建安时期的诗歌靠拢。)

In the early Tang period, Wang Bo, Yang Jiong, Shen Quanqi, and Song Zhiwen were the only ones who enjoyed widespread renown, yet none of them had freed themselves of the obsession with formal beauty pursued by poets of the Qi-Liang era. Chen Zi'ang alone argued for quiet elegance in poetry, making a clean sweep of the cloying sentimentality of the Six Dynasties. After that, the style of poetry shifted toward that of the Huangchu and Jian'an eras of the Wei Kingdom. (Liu Kezhuang: *Houcun's Poetic Remarks*)

◎陶渊明诗所不可及者，冲澹深粹，出于自然。(杨时《龟山集·语录·荆州所闻》)

（陶渊明的诗之所以为后人所不能及，是因为他的诗冲和平淡、深刻纯粹，完全出于自然性情的流露。）

Tao Yuanming's poetry has remained unrivaled because of its quiet elegance, profundity and purity. It fully shows his natural feelings. (Yang Shi: *Collected Works of Yang Shi*)

虫书 /chóngshū/

Insect Script

　　春秋战国时期流行的一种特殊书体。又称"鸟虫书""鸟虫篆"。是篆书的一种变体。因其形态取象于鸟虫之形，故得名。虫书大多铸造或镌刻在兵器、钟鼎上，如湖北宜昌附近出土的越王勾践剑，上面的八字铭文就是鸟虫书。秦朝通行的书体有八种，"虫书"列第四。王莽（前45—公元23）篡位时官方规定的六种书体中亦有"鸟虫书"，用于书写旗帜、符信，或作为印章文字。

Insect script was a special style of calligraphy current in the Spring and Autumn Period and the Warring States Period, also known as "bird-and-insect script" and "bird-and-insect seal script." It was a variation of seal script. Characters written in this style resembled birds and insects in nature, hence the name. Insect script was cast or inscribed on weaponry, bells and cauldrons. For example, the 8-character inscription on the sword of Goujian, the king of the State of Yue, unearthed near Yichang in Hubei Province, adopted this very style. There were eight styles of calligraphy in use during the Qin Dynasty, among which insect script was in the fourth place. After he usurped the throne, Wang Mang (45 BC-AD 23) ordered that insect script be recognized as one of the six official scripts and be used for writing on flags, tallies or seals.

引例 Citations：

◎ 自尔秦书有八体：一曰大篆，二曰小篆，三曰刻符，四曰虫书，

五日摹印，六日署书，七日殳（shū）书，八日隶书。（许慎《说文解字·序》）

（自那时以后，秦朝有八种书体：第一是大篆，第二是小篆，第三是刻符，第四是虫书，第五是摹写刻印，第六是官署之书，第七是殳书，第八是隶书。）

From then on, the Qin Dynasty boasted eight scripts: (1) greater seal script; (2) lesser seal script; (3) engraved script; (4) insect script; (5) ancient imperial seal script; (6) official script; (7) weaponry script; and (8) clerical script. (Xu Shen: *Explanation of Script and Elucidation of Characters*)

◎六体者，古文、奇字、篆书、隶书、缪（móu）篆、虫书，皆所以通知古今文字，摹印章，书幡信也。（《汉书·艺文志》）

（六种字体，分别是古文、奇字、篆书、隶书、缪篆、虫书，书写它们需要通晓古今各种书体，可用来刻写印章、书写符节等。）

Chinese characters may be divided into six forms. They are: archaic style, script adapted from archaic style, seal script, clerical script, deviant seal script, and insect script. One must be well versed in all forms of writing ranging from ancient times up to this day to be able to inscribe seals and write on tallies. (*The History of the Han Dynasty*)

丑 /chǒu/

Ugliness / *Chou* (Role of Clown in a Traditional Chinese Opera)

字本作"醜"，本义指人的样貌难看，引申指丑陋、不好、可恶等义。主要含义有二：其一，作为思想文化术语，它与"美"相对，除了指丑恶、丑陋，还包括芜杂、不修饰、不和谐、不合乎事理等含义。"丑"有时也被看成是有违当下的审美规范、不被大众标准认可的美。对"丑"的认识与接纳，相当于对"美"的范围的突破与延展。其二，传统戏曲中的行当名称，鼻梁上涂抹白粉，饰演相貌丑陋而举止可笑的喜剧人物或反面人物。

The original Chinese character *chou* (醜) literally means "ghastly-looking like a drunkard." It can then be extended to refer to people and things which are ugly, bad or despicable. This term contains two meanings. First, as a concept in Chinese thought and culture, it stands in contrast to "beauty," indicating ugly appearance, as well as the state of being messy, unpolished, unharmonious or unreasonable. "Ugliness" is sometimes used to describe a type of appearance which violates mainstream aesthetic standards and thus is not accepted by the general public. Understanding and accepting the notion of "ugliness" is a breakthrough and extension of the definition of "beauty." Second, the term also refers to clowns who perform funny-looking and amusing characters in a traditional Chinese opera, with a small patch of white chalk painted around the nose.

引例 Citations：

◎桀有得事，尧有遗道；嫫（mó）母有所美，西施有所丑。故亡国之法，有可随者；治国之俗，有可非者。(《淮南子·说山训》)

（桀有做得对的事，尧也有遗漏的事；嫫母有美的地方，西施也有丑的地方。所以亡国的法规，有可以遵循的地方；治理好的国家的习俗，也有可以非议的地方。）

Jie, a tyrannical ruler in ancient China, sometimes also did good things, whereas during the reign of benevolent Yao, certain matters were woefully neglected. The ugly Momu had her attractive aspects, and the beautiful Xishi had her unattractive aspects. Likewise, laws adopted by past countries now perished may have some merits while laws adopted by countries which are still thriving may have demerits. (*Huainanzi*)

◎宁拙毋巧，宁丑毋媚，宁支离毋轻滑，宁真率毋安排，足以回临池既倒之狂澜也。(傅山《作字示儿孙》)

（宁可古朴笨拙而不能精细纤巧，宁可丑陋不工而不能庸俗柔媚，宁可参差不齐而不能轻佻浮滑，宁可自然率意而不能刻意安排，这样足可以扭转学习书法过程中看似将要倾覆的书风。)

Being clumsy and simple is better than being clever and dainty. Being unattractive and crude is better than being vulgar and charming. Being unrefined is better than being frivolous. Being natural and spontaneous is better than being rigidly prearranged. Only by doing so, can a calligraphic style, which seems to face an impending doom, survive and sustain. (Fu Shan: A Work of Calligraphy Written to Advise My Children and Grandchildren)

楚辞 /chǔcí,《Chǔcí》/
Chuci / Odes of Chu

　　楚辞是由屈原（前340？—前278？）创作的一种诗体，后来又成为代表中国古代南方文化的第一部诗歌总集，楚辞运用楚地（今湖南、湖北一带）的文学体式、方言声韵，叙写楚地的山川人物、历史风情，具有浓厚的地域特色，因而得名。"楚辞"之名，西汉初期已有之，后刘向（前77？—前6）辑录成集，收战国时期楚国人屈原、宋玉以及汉代淮南小山、东方朔（前154—前93）、严忌、王褒、刘向等人作品共16篇，后来王逸作《楚辞章句》时增加了自己的一篇，共17篇。楚辞通过独特的文体与文化内涵，反映出南方楚国文化的特点，抒情色彩浓厚，想象丰富，保存了上古许多神话故事，彰显出不同于《诗经》传统的一种全新的文学精神与文学体式，成为与《诗经》并驾齐驱的文学形态，后世称这种文体为"楚辞体"或"骚体"，称研究《楚辞》的学问为"楚辞学"。

Chuci (楚辞 ode of Chu) was a poetic genre first attributed to Qu Yuan (340?-278? BC). It later became the title for the first anthology of poetry depicting the culture in south China. *Chuci* was so named because it made use of Chu (now Hunan and Hubei provinces) dialect, accent, and local special genres to describe the unique landscape, history, and folklore of the State of Chu. The term *chuci* first appeared in the early Western Han Dynasty, and later Liu Xiang (77?-6 BC) compiled a literary collection including 16 pieces written by Qu Yuan, Song Yu, Huainan Xiaoshan (a group of authors of the Western Han Dynasty), Dongfang Shuo (154-93 BC), Yan Ji, Wang Bao, and Liu Xiang. When Wang Yi later compiled *Annotations on Odes of Chu*, he added a work of his own to the collection, making it an anthology of 17 works. Through its distinctive genre and unique cultural elements, *chuci* reflected the special culture of the Chu region in southern China. As a genre, *chuci* is characterized by profound emotions, wild imagination, and rich allusions to the remote historical mythology from the dawn of Chinese history. It demonstrates an innovative and distinctive literary genre and spirit, standing with *The Book of Songs* as twin literary pinnacles. Later generations called this genre *Chuci* Style or *Sao* Style (Flowery Style), and its research *chuci* studies.

引例 Citations：

◎固知《楚辞》者，体宪于三代，而风杂于战国，乃雅颂之博徒，而词赋之英杰也。（刘勰《文心雕龙·辨骚》）

（可以肯定，《楚辞》取法于三代的圣贤之书，但也掺杂有战国的风气，比起《诗经》来，要逊色一些，但却是词赋中的精品。）

It can be ascertained that *Odes of Chu* borrowed literary elements from the classics of the past ages, but also blended some stylistic features from the Warring States Period. Though less outstanding than *The Book of Songs,* they were masterpieces in poetry. (Liu Xie: *The Literary Mind and the Carving of Dragons*)

◎盖屈宋诸骚,皆书楚语,作楚声,纪楚地,名楚物,故可谓之"楚辞"。（黄伯思《新校〈楚辞〉序》）

（大体上说，屈原、宋玉的诸多骚体之作，都是用楚地的方言，用楚地的音乐，描写楚国的地理，称说楚地的风物，因此可称作"楚辞"。）

Generally speaking, the literary works of Qu Yuan and Song Yu used Chu dialect and exploited Chu rhythm and tunes to depict the landscape and scenery in Chu, hence called *chuci*, or odes of Chu. (Huang Bosi: Preface to *Odes of Chu [Revised Edition]*)

传奇 /chuánqí/
Chuanqi (Legendary Story / Legendary Play)

　　作为文艺术语，含义有三：其一，指唐宋时期的一种短篇小说体裁。或认为由六朝时的志怪小说演变而来，内容扩展到对社会生活及各种人情世态的描写。"传"为传说，"奇"为奇异，本义指记述传说或奇异的故事。唐代裴铏的《传奇》一书可能是该术语的最早应用。宋代时以唐代小说《莺莺传》为传奇，元代时称唐人小说为"唐传奇"。与唐传奇相比，宋代传奇更为贴近生活和口语。其二，指宋元时期的诸宫调、戏文、杂剧等戏曲文学类作品。因这一时期的说唱文学、戏曲创作等多取材于唐传奇，故称。其三，指明清时期以唱南曲为主的长编戏曲。由南戏发展而来，也融合了元杂剧的特点，如梁辰鱼（1519 — 1591）的《浣纱记》、孔尚任（1648 — 1718）的《桃花扇》、洪昇（1645 — 1704）的《长生殿》等。各个时期的"传奇"概念，既有题材的沿用与拓展，又有手法的继承与创新，其核心"传奇特之事、演奇特之人"是一以贯之的。

This is a term for a literary form. It refers to three types of artistic works: 1) A type of short story in the Tang and Song dynasties that might be evolved from tales of the supernatural in the Six Dynasties. Later its subjects widened to include social life, and stories about people and events. *Chuan* (传) means "legendary" and *qi* (奇) means "strange and unusual," so the term originally means recounting tales of strange and extraordinary events that have been passed down by word of mouth. The work *Legendary Stories* by Pei Xing in the Tang Dynasty is probably the earliest work that uses the term. In the Song Dynasty, the Tang novel *The Story of Yingying* is considered a *chuanqi*, while the Yuan people called all Tang stories *chuanqi* of Tang. Song Dynasty *chuanqi* were more realistic and vernacular than those of the Tang.

2) Song-speech drama, Southern opera and Yuan *zaju* in the Song and Yuan dynasties, most of which were based on Tang stories.

3) Full-length operas in the Ming and Qing dynasties, which were based on the Southern opera (*Nanxi*), and also included some Yuan *zaju* features. Typical works include *The Story of Washing Gauze* by Liang Chenyu (1519-1591), *Peach Blossom Fan* by Kong Shangren (1648-1718), *The Palace of Eternal Life* by Hong Sheng (1645-1704). The ancient style of *chuanqi* has evolved and been innovated over the centuries, both in story content and performance techniques. However, its main purpose is still to "tell stories of strange happenings and unusual people."

引例 Citations：

◎金元创名"杂剧"，国初演作"传奇"。杂剧北音，传奇南调。杂剧折惟四，唱止一人；传奇折数多，唱必匀派。杂剧但撷一事颠末，其境促；传奇备述一人始终，其味长。（吕天成《曲品》卷上）

（金元时期的"杂剧"名称，到了明朝初年演变为"传奇"。杂剧是北方音乐，传奇是南方曲调。杂剧只有四折，一人主唱；传奇的折数很多，演唱也按角色均匀分派。杂剧只取一件事的首尾，故事情境未免局促；传奇详细演绎主人公的故事原委，自然意味深长。）

The term *zaju* of the Jin and Yuan dynasties became *chuanqi* in the early Ming Dynasty. *Zaju* is northern music, while *chuanqi* is from the south. *Zaju* are composed of only four acts, each with one main performer, while in *chuanqi* there are many acts with several characters of equal importance. In *zaju* the plot is only about one event, which narrows the story, whereas in *chuanqi* the various accounts of the main characters are followed in great detail, which naturally makes it all the more interesting. (Lü Tiancheng: *Comments on Qu Drama: Composers and Their Works*)

◎古人呼剧本为"传奇"者，因其事甚奇特，未经人见而传之，是以得名。可见非奇不传。新，即奇之别名也。若此等情节业已见之戏场，则千人共见，万人共见，绝无奇矣，焉用传之？是以填词之家，务解"传奇"二字。（李渔《闲情偶寄·词曲部·结构》）

（古代人把剧本称为"传奇"，是因为其中所讲述的故事非常奇特，没有人亲眼见过却能在世间流传，所以用这个名称。可见不是奇事就不会流传。"新"就是奇特的另一说法。如果这个情节已经在戏场里演过，则成千上万的人都一同见过，大家绝不会感到新奇了，还用得着特别去"传"吗？因此填写戏曲剧本的人，务必要明白"传奇"二字的含义。）

The ancients called drama scripts *chuanqi* because the extraordinary events, which no one had actually experienced, were passed down the ages. In other words, without the strangeness, no one would bother to pass them on. "Novel" or *xin* is just another term for "strange and unusual." If this particular plot line has been performed before and is familiar to thousands upon thousands of people, then there is nothing novel about it, then what is the need to pass it on? It is thus important for those who write scripts to understand the meaning of *chuanqi*. (Li Yu: *Occasional Notes with Leisure Motions*)

传神写照 /chuánshén-xiězhào/

Convey the Spirit and Capture the Person

指文学艺术作品中所描绘或刻画的人物生动逼真、形神兼备。"传神"是将人物内在的精神世界完全表现出来，使人物栩栩如生；"写照"就是画像，所绘人物形象逼真，如在目前。初为画论术语，后引入文学领域，是画家、文学家在塑造人物形象及一切艺术形象时所追求的艺术境界。

This term refers to literary descriptions of characters which are accurate both in form and in spirit. *Chuanshen* (传神), to "convey the spirit," is to fully express the spiritual world within the character, so that he comes to life; *xiezhao* (写照), to "capture the person," is to create a vivid physical depiction of him. These expressions were originally used in discussions of art but were later introduced into literature. They represent an artistic state which artists and writers try to achieve as they create images of people as well as all artistic images.

引例 Citations：

◎四体妍蚩（chī），本无关于妙处，传神写照，正在阿堵中。（刘义庆《世说新语·巧艺》）

（人物形象的美丑，本来显现不出画作的高妙之处；真正能够让人物形神兼备、生动鲜活起来的地方，就是那个眼睛。）

The heights of artistry do not lie in whether or not someone's physical shape is well portrayed. Rather, it is the eyes which convey the spirit and capture the person. (Liu Yiqing: *A New Account of Tales of the World*)

◎空中荡漾最是词家妙诀。上意本可接入下意，却偏不入。而于其间传神写照，乃愈使下意栩栩欲动。（刘熙载《艺概·词概》）

（在本应接着抒情表意的地方故意转写他事从而留出意义上的空白，是填词高手的妙诀。抒情表意本可前后相接，但作者偏偏没有接写反而转向其他的描写或叙事，通过空白愈发将人物的内心活动鲜活地传达出来，使得接下来的抒情表意更为鲜明灵动、栩栩如生。）

It is a subtle trick of great lyric writers to deliberately change the subject or to leave something unsaid. Where one thought can give rise to another, the author deliberately refrains from doing so, and instead turns to other descriptions or narratives, thus creating a void which conveys the spirit and captures the person. By doing so, lyrical expression becomes even more vivid and lifelike. (Liu Xizai: *Overview of Literary Theories*)

◎描画鲁智深，千古若活，真是传神写照妙手。(李贽《李卓吾先生批评忠义水浒传》)

(作者所刻画的鲁智深，即使千年以后也还活在人们眼前，真是善于传神写照的高手啊！)

The image of Lu Zhishen portrayed by the author remains lifelike even after a thousand years. He is truly a master who can convey the spirit and capture the person! (Li Zhi: *Li Zhi's Annotations on Outlaws of the Marsh*)

纯素 /chúnsù/
Pure and Unadorned

纯粹而素朴。指纯然素朴、不加人工雕饰的本色之美。"纯"即纯然、纯粹，不含任何杂质；"素"本指未经染色的生丝，引申指白色、本色、素朴、不加修饰等义。以老、庄为代表的道家认为"道"是万物之美的总根源，"道"自然无为，最是素朴无华，因此道家美学将自然本色、素朴无华作为审美的最高境界。在古人看来，"纯素"是一种不与物相杂的本真状态，即使混迹于事物之中，它也保持着自然天成的本质，其内在的神气没有一丝亏损。这一思想广泛影响了中国古代文学艺术的创作风格与审美追求。中国古代诗歌崇尚素淡冲远，绘画崇尚平淡天真，都体现了"纯素"的审美追求。

This term refers to natural, unadorned beauty. "Pure" means untainted, unadulterated or containing no impurity. *Su* (素) originally means "undyed raw silk." Later it came to mean "the quality of being white, authentic, unspoiled or undecorated." Daoist thought, represented by Laozi and Zhuangzi (369?-286 BC), held that Dao is the ultimate origin of beauty in everything. Dao is natural, unassertive, simple and unadorned. Thus Daoists consider being natural, unadorned and pure as the highest form of beauty. Ancient thinkers believe that "pure and unadorned" is an authentic state of being, which retains its holistic true status free from external objects. Even if it mixes with the latter, it keeps itself natural and its core essence unimpaired. This idea extensively influenced the writing style and aesthetic pursuit of ancient Chinese literature and art. Plain and quiet poetry and plain and natural painting were upheld in ancient China, which reflect the aesthetic pursuit of the pure and unadorned.

引例 Citation：

◎纯素之道，唯神是守。守而勿失，与神为一。一之精通，合于天伦。……故素也者，谓其无所与杂也；纯也者，谓其不亏其神也。能体纯素，谓之真人。(《庄子·刻意》)

（纯粹素朴的道，就是守持精神。守持而不失，与精神融合为一。"一"的精妙通达，合乎自然天道。……所以"素"，是说没有什么与之混杂；"纯"，是说不亏损本真精神。能够体察"纯"和"素"的，称为真人。）

Within spiritual being lies the value of pure simplicity. If you retain your spirit without fail, you become one with it. In achieving that oneness, you establish contact with the way of heaven... "Simplicity" means "not mixing"; "pure" means "an unimpaired spirit." Only if you embrace pure simplicity can you be called a true man. (*Zhuangzi*)

词 /cí/

Ci (Lyric)

起源于唐五代、发展成熟于宋代的一种新的文学体式，也称"曲子词""乐府""长短句"等。由诗发展演变而来，其主要特点是配乐歌唱。每首词都有一个调名，称"词牌"。不同的词牌在句数及每句的字数、平仄、押韵上都有严格的规定。从篇幅看，词可分为小令、中调、长调；从音乐体制看，词一般分上下两段（古人称为"阕"或"片"），也有分成三四段或仅有一段的，因之音乐也有演奏一遍和多遍的区别；从风格看，词基本分为婉约和豪放两大派：婉约派风格婉转含蓄，多写儿女情长；豪放派则摄取人生情怀及家国大事入词，境界宏大。宋代许多文人学者喜好填词作曲，对推动词的发展起了重要作用。后世的词一般不再配乐歌唱，基本成为按谱填词的一种文学形式。

Ci (词) originated in the Tang and the Five Dynasties, and developed to maturity as a new literary form in the Song Dynasty. Also known as "lyric with a melody," "*yuefu* (乐府) poetry" or "long and short verses," *ci* developed from poetry. Its main feature is that it is set to music and sung. Each piece of *ci* has a name for its tune. There are strict requirements for the number of lines and the number of characters as well as tone pattern and rhyming in different tunes. In terms of length, *ci* is divided into short lyrics, medium lyrics, and long lyrics. In terms of musical system, a piece of *ci* is usually divided into two stanzas of *que* (阕) or *pian* (片), as ancient Chinese called them. Occasionally, it consists of three or four stanzas, or just one. Thus, the music can be played once or many times. In terms of style, *ci* falls into the graceful and restrained school and the bold and unconstrained school. The former is delicate and sentimental, often describing family life and love, while the latter is bold and free, often expressing one's vision about major social issues like the fate of the nation. Many literati and scholars of the Song Dynasty composed *ci* lyrics, which played a significant part in promoting its development. Today, *ci* is generally not set to music and sung. Rather, it is a literary form composed in accordance with the requirements of a music tune.

引例 Citations：

◎古乐府有曰"辞"者，有曰"曲"者，其实"辞"即曲之辞，"曲"即辞之曲也。（刘熙载《艺概·词曲概》）

（在古时的乐府中，有称作"辞"的，有称作"曲"的，其实"辞"就是乐曲的歌词，而"曲"则是与歌词相配的乐曲。）

In the early *yuefu* poems, some are named *ci*, and also some named *qu*. In fact, *ci* means lyrics written for music, whereas *qu* is musical tunes set to accompany lyrics. (Liu Xizai: *Overview of Literary Theories*)

◎宋元之间，词与曲一也。以文写之则为词，以声度之则为曲。（宋翔凤《乐府余论》）

（宋元之时，词和曲是同一个东西，用文句写出来就是词，给它谱上音乐就是曲。）

During the Song and Yuan dynasties, *ci* and *qu* were one and the same thing. When written with words, they were *ci*; when composed with music, they were *qu*. (Song Xiangfeng: *Epilogue to Yuefu Poetry*)

词话 /cíhuà/

Criticism on *Ci* Poetry / *Cihua* (Story-telling with Song and Speech)

主要含义有二：其一，指评论词人、词作、词派，记述词的本事及相关考订的著作，是中国古代诗学文献的一个组成部分。词话借鉴诗话而来，滥觞于北宋，成熟于南宋。著名的词话著作有清代陈廷焯（1853—1892）的《白雨斋词话》、王国维（1877—1927）的《人间词话》等。《人间词话》是王国维在接受了西方美学理论之后，融汇中西美学思想，以崭新的眼光对中国词人与词作做出的评论。表面上看，《人间词话》沿袭了中国传统的诗话、词话一类作品的体例，实际上它已初具理论体系，是晚清以来最有影响的文艺批评著作之一。其二，指盛行于元、明两代的一种说唱艺术形式（其中的"词"主要指词曲），如《大唐秦王词话》，有说有唱，韵文、散文并用。由宋代说话伎艺发展而来，明代中叶以后，逐渐演变为弹词和鼓词两个系统，并且取代了"词话"名称。又，明后期及清前期"词话"还曾用来指称夹杂词曲的章回体通俗小说，如《金瓶梅词话》等。

This term has a two-fold meaning. First, it refers to any work that offers commentaries on *ci* poets, poems, schools of *ci* poetry, the gist of a *ci* poem and textual criticisms. This type of work is a constituent part of scholarly inquiry into classical Chinese poetry. Criticism on *ci* poetry, with relatively long lines interspersed with shorter ones, are derived from criticism on the more usual type of classical Chinese poetry with a fixed number of characters to a line. They proliferated in the Northern Song Dynasty and matured in the Southern Song Dynasty. Famed works of *ci* poetry appreciation include *Remarks on Ci Poetry from White Rain Studio* by Chen Tingzhuo (1853-1892) and *Poetic Remarks in the Human World* by Wang Guowei (1877-1927), both from the Qing Dynasty. The latter work, written after Wang Guowei was influenced by Western aesthetic theories, and fusing Chinese and Western aesthetic thoughts together, was a criticism work on Chinese *ci* poets and *ci* poems made from a brand-new perspective. Although superficially it imitates the traditional way of offering commentaries on *shi* poetry and *ci* poetry, it in fact already attempts to construct a theoretic system. It has remained the most influential work of literary criticism since the late-Qing period.

Second, the term *cihua* also refers to an art of theatrical performance combining narratives and songs popular in the Yuan and Ming dynasties, in which the *ci* part is the singing of rhymed verse. As in *Tales of Prince Qin of the Great Tang Dynasty*, the performance intersperses singing with narrative, and verse with prose. It was developed from the performance of story-telling with speech and song of the Song Dynasty. After the mid-Ming Dynasty, such performances started to adopt two new terms: *tanci* (弹词), or story-telling with the accompaniment of musical instruments such as the Chinese lute, and *guci* (鼓词), or story-telling aided by a drum and clapper. Still later, these two new terms superseded the old. From the last years of the Ming to the first years of the Qing, this term was sometimes also used to refer to a popular novel with each chapter headed by a couplet giving the gist of its content which was interspersed with beautiful verse, for example *Tales of the Golden Lotus*.

引例 Citations:

◎玩月新诗偏有趣，兴唐词话更消闲。(《大唐秦王词话》第四十六回)

(赏月的新诗实在有趣，但讲唱大唐兴起的词话更能使听众消闲。)

The new-style poetry in praise of the moon may be fun, but spoken and sung tales of Li Shimin's rise to the throne are far more intriguing. (*Tales of Prince Qin of the Great Tang Dynasty*)

◎词话者，纪词林之故实，辨词体之流变，道词家之短长也。(谢之勃《论词话》,《国专季刊》第一期)

(词话，用来记录词林的典故，辨析词体的流变，评论词家的优缺点。)

Commentaries on *ci* poetry record the classics of lyrical poetry, analyze the various styles of *ci* poetry, and enumerate the merits and shortcomings of *ci* poets. (Xie Zhibo: On *Ci* Poetry Commentaries)

词曲 /cíqǔ/
Ci (Lyric) and *Qu* (Melody)

词(可以配乐歌唱的长短句诗体)和曲(可以配乐歌唱的韵文体)两种文学体式的并称，在《四库全书》列于集部最末(曲更是有类无目)，这是因为在古人的文学观念中，以诗文为正统，认为诗文可以表现较为正式的内容，而词曲则仅被看作展示个人才情的末技。此外，"词曲"并称有时还用来指戏曲和说唱。

Ci (词 a form of poetry with long or short verses which can be set to music and sung) and *qu* (曲 a form of rhyming compositions which can be set to music and sung) are a combined appellation for two kinds of literary styles. In *Complete Library of the Four Branches of Literature,* they are listed at the very end of the "Collections" section (*Qu* is a sub-genre and is not listed in the table of contents). This is because according to the literary views of ancient scholars, poetry and essays were the only accepted tradition to express important ideas. To write in the form of *ci* (lyric) and *qu* (melody) was only seen as a minor skill showing a person's talent. Sometimes, the combined appellation *ciqu* also refers to traditional opera and genres of performances featuring speaking and singing.

引例 Citation：

◎词曲二体，在文章、技艺之间。厥品颇卑，作者弗贵，特才华之士，以绮语相高耳。(《四库全书总目提要·集部·词曲类》)

（词和曲这两种体式，在文章和才艺之间。它们的地位很低，创作者也不看重它们，只是有才华的人以华丽词句用来相互标榜罢了。）

Ci and *qu* are genres falling between essay and performing skills. They are not highly regarded, and even their authors do not prize them. They are no more than rhetoric with which people show off their literary talent to each other! (*Complete Library of the Four Branches of Literature*)

辞达 /cídá/

Expressiveness

说话、写文章要能简明扼要地表达内心的意思。孔子（前551—前479）反对过度追求辞藻华丽，强调文辞只要能确切而简洁地传达出思想感情即可，并倡导"文质彬彬"的审美观念。

这一术语后来经过刘勰（465？—520？或532？）、韩愈（768—824）、苏轼（1037—1101）等人不断继承与发展，形成了中国文学追求语言自然凝练、反对过分雕琢的美学旨趣与风格。

The term means to put forth one's thoughts in a clear and concise way when speaking and writing. Confucius (551-479 BC) opposed excessive efforts in pursuit of extravagant writing styles. He stressed that writings need only to express one's ideas and feelings clearly and precisely, and he advocated a concept of aesthetics that valued the combination of elegance and simplicity. This concept was successively inherited and developed by Liu Xie (465?-520? or 532?), Han Yu (768-824), Su Shi (1037-1101), and others, resulting in a Chinese literary style that strives for natural and pithy expression as opposed to extravagant embellishment.

引例 Citations：

◎子曰："辞达而已矣。"（《论语·卫灵公》）

（孔子说："言辞能把意思表达清楚就行了。"）

Confucius said, "It's good enough if you express yourself clearly." (*The Analects*)

◎辞至于能达，则文不可胜用矣。（苏轼《答谢民师书》）

（文辞如果能够做到达意，那么文采的运用也就无穷无尽了。）

If one can write expressively, his potential to achieve literary grace is boundless. (Su Shi: A Letter of Reply to Xie Minshi)

辞尚体要 /císhàngtǐyào/

Succinctness Is Valued in Writing.

文辞要切实简要地传达文章想要表达的主要意思或主要内容。"体要"，体现精要。源于《尚书》，原指政令、法规的文辞应体现精要或切实简要，刘勰（465？—520？或532？）将它引入文学批评，强调文辞须切实精当，体现文章的要义。这一术语体现了中国文化推崇的"尚简"传统，即以简练精当的文辞传达出充实、概括性的内容，不能为了追求文辞上的标新立异而忽略文章本来要表达的主要内容。这一要求，后来成为古文写作的基本要求，对文学创作起着重要的指导作用。

Writing should be substantive and succinct in expressing main ideas or key content. "Succinctness" means to capture the essence. The idea comes from *The Book of History*, originally referring to the requirement that government edicts and regulations should be terse and to the point. Liu Xie (465?-520? or 532?) applied this into literary criticism, emphasizing that writing should be both substantive and pithy, striving to capture the essence. This term reflects the traditional pursuit for "succinctness" in Chinese culture, which prefers to convey a rich message in a concise way rather than seek novel expressions that may overshadow the essence of the writing. Later on, this became a fundamental requirement for the classical style of writing and provided important guidance for literary creation.

引例 Citations：

◎政贵有恒,辞尚体要,不惟好异。(《尚书·毕命》)

（国家的大政贵在稳定持久，国家的话语贵在切实简要，不能一味追求标新立异。）

What is most valuable for governance lies in its sustained stability, advocating substantial and straightforward wording, not seeking novelty. (*The Book of History*)

◎盖《周书》论辞, 贵乎体要；尼父陈训, 恶乎异端。(刘勰《文心雕龙·序志》)

(《周书》里讲到文辞，认为重在体现要义；孔子陈述教训，憎恨异端邪说。)

When discussing writing, *The Book of Zhou (of The Book of History)* believes that succinctness matters most. When recounting past lessons, Confucius detested unorthodox beliefs. (Liu Xie: *The Literary Mind and the Carving of Dragons*)

错彩镂金 /cuòcǎi-lòujīn/
Gilded and Colored

涂饰彩色，雕镂金银。形容艺术作品雕饰华美。用于文学作品，主要指诗歌辞藻华丽，讲究技巧。在审美境界上，"错彩镂金"不如"芙蓉出水"高妙："错彩镂金"注重外在形态，处于审美表象阶段；而"芙蓉出水"超越表象，直达本体，是审美意趣的自然呈现。

The term is used to describe an excessively exquisite artistic work as if it were an object painted in bright colors and inlaid with gold and silver. In the literary context, it refers to poems written in a highly rhetorical style. Aesthetically, what is "gilded and colored" is considered undesirable, and the style of "lotus rising out of water" is preferred. The former focuses only on external form and appearance, whereas the latter, as a natural presentation of aesthetic ideas, penetrates appearances and brings out the essence.

引例 Citations：

◎延之尝问鲍照己与灵运优劣,照曰:"谢五言如初发芙蓉,自然可爱；君诗若铺锦列绣,亦雕缋（huì）满眼。"(《南史·颜延之传》)

（颜延之曾经询问鲍照，自己的作品和谢灵运的作品相比哪个更好，鲍照说："谢灵运的五言诗像刚出水的荷花，自然可爱；您的诗像铺开的锦绣，满眼都是雕饰彩绘。"）

Yan Yanzhi asked Bao Zhao, "Whose works are better, mine or Xie

Lingyun's?" Bao said, "Xie's five-word-to-a-line poems are as natural and lovely as lotus having just risen out of water in bloom, while yours are like embroidery embellished with colored decorations." (*The History of the Southern Dynasties*)

◎丹漆不文，白玉不雕，宝珠不饰，何也？质有余者，不受饰也。（刘向《说苑·反质》）

（红色的漆不需要花纹，纯白的玉不需要雕琢，珍贵的明珠不用装饰，为什么呢？本身已非常完美的东西，无需再装饰。）

Red lacquer needs no decorated patterns, white jade needs no carving, and precious pearls need no adornment. Why? Because they are too good to be worked on. (Liu Xiang: *Garden of Stories*)

大巧若拙 /dàqiǎo-ruòzhuō/
Exquisite Skill Looks Simple and Clumsy.

极致的灵巧、技巧看上去就像质朴拙笨一样。最杰出的灵巧一定是浑然天成而非人工刻意雕琢的。出自《老子》。老子提倡纯任自然、无为才能无不为，反对一切形式的卖弄。后用来指文艺创作中的最高技巧与境界。在文艺理论中，大巧若拙并不是"以拙为巧"或完全排斥工巧，而是摒弃过分修饰和刻意追求工巧，提倡朴素自然的浑融之美。它代表了艺术美和艺术技巧的最高境界。大巧若拙是中国古代书法、绘画、园林等艺术形式的共同追求。

The term means that ingenuity and skill at their best look simple and clumsy. The greatest ingenuity should be something completely natural and that it has not been painstakingly worked on. The term comes from the book *Laozi*. Laozi the philosopher believed that everything should be in keeping with nature. He advocated non-action and was against any form of excessive act.

Later, the term came to mean the highest possible level of skill and perfection in artistic and literary creation. In Chinese literary theory, "exquisite skill looks simple and clumsy" does not mean the clumsier the better, nor is it a rejection of skill. Rather, it rejects excessive embellishment and over-pursuit of the exquisite, and encourages well-founded simplicity and naturalness. The phrase represents the highest possible level of perfection in artistic beauty and skill and is also what the people in pre-modern China strove to achieve in calligraphy, painting, gardening, and other forms of art.

引例 Citation：

◎大直若屈，大巧若拙，大辩若讷。(《老子·四十五章》)

（最直的反而像是弯曲一样，最灵巧反而像是笨拙一样，最好的口才反而像不善言辞一样。）

The truly straight will appear crooked; the truly skillful will appear clumsy; the truly eloquent will appear impeded. (*Laozi*)

大收煞 /dàshōushā/
The Grand Finale

指全本戏剧的收场戏。这一术语包含对戏剧全场收束的要求：自然合理而非生硬地交代剧中人物的结局、事件结果，让观众体验到情节有呼有应、有放有收、有始有终、有因有果，心理由紧张到舒释、由期待到满足的审美愉悦，有"团圆之趣"。明末清初曲论家李渔（1611—1680）所言"团圆"不仅是骨肉分离而终聚、有情人终成眷属之类的圆满结局，而是指戏剧结构如同一个完整的环，收场戏就是扣上这个环的最后一步，也是戏剧的高潮。

This term refers to the final part of a drama. It contains a requirement as to how a dramatic or operatic performance should end; i.e., a natural and reasonable rather than stiff outcome of the characters and events in a play, making it possible for the audience to experience the pleasure of a complete plot with both calls and echoes, expansion and withdrawal, a start and an end, a cause and an effect, and a transformation from tension to relief and from expectation to satisfaction. In a word, a good conclusion should feature "a happy outcome for all" as Li Yu (1611-1680), the late Ming to early Qing drama theorist, said. This means not only the reunion of a family after a period of separation or the wedding of a loving couple, but also the completion of a play's circuitous structure. The final part of a play is the last step taken to close that circuit and reach a climax.

引例 Citation：

◎全本收场名为大收煞。此折之难在无包括之痕，而有团圆之趣。（李渔《闲情偶寄·词曲部·格局》）

（全本的最后一折叫做大收煞。这一出戏的难点在于不能有情节拼合的痕迹，又要能够让人感受到自然团圆的乐趣。）

The final scene is the great finale of the entire drama. The challenge here is to avoid just thrusting odd clues together and attain the pleasure of a happy, natural ending. (Li Yu: *Occasional Notes with Leisure Motions*)

大用 /dàyòng/
Maximal Functioning

最大的运用。本义指道在外部世界的各种呈现即是道之最大的显现和运用。道家认为内在的道是主宰外部世界变化的根本，客观世界的各种形态都由作为内在本质的道所造成，是体用统一的结果。唐代司空图（837—908）《二十四诗品》将这一术语引入文学评论，目的是强调诗歌意象丰富多彩的美实际上是作品内在精神与外在形态的统一。人们进行诗歌创作与鉴赏时必须领略现象与本质之美的和谐一致。

Maximal functioning means that all kinds of appearances of Dao in the external world are the greatest manifestation and functioning of Dao. Daoist scholars believe that the internal Dao determines the basis for changes in the external world, and that all kinds of forms in the objective world derive from the active, innate nature of Dao, the result of unity of substance and function. In "Twenty-four Styles of Poetry," Sikong Tu (837-908), a literary critic in the Tang Dynasty, made this notion a term of literary criticism to highlight the view that the rich and colorful imagery in poetry represents unity of the internal spirit of the work and its external shape. In poetry writing and appreciation, one should focus on the harmony between the appearance and the essence.

引例 Citation：

◎ 大用外腓（féi），真体内充。反虚入浑，积健为雄。（司空图《二十四诗品·雄浑》）

（大道呈现于外显得雄浑阔大，真实的本体则充满于内。唯有返回虚静，内心才能到达浑然之境；积蓄精神力量，笔力才能雄放豪健。）

The grand appearance is an external manifestation of Dao, while the true vitality permeates itself internally. Reverting to a tranquil void, one may gain fullness and amass inner strength, and he will produce powerful works. (Sikong Tu: Twenty-four Styles of Poetry)

大篆 /dàzhuàn/

Greater Seal Script / Big Seal Script

汉字发展演变中的一种书体。与"小篆"相对。有广狭两方面含义：狭义专指籀文（先秦刻石书体），以战国时的秦国石鼓文为其典型代表，其特点是笔画凝重，构形多重叠，比金文更为规范、严正；广义指"书同文"之前包括金文、籀文及春秋战国时期各国的刻石文字。秦统一以后为小篆代替。

The greater seal script is a form in the evolution of Chinese characters. Standing in contrast to the lesser seal script, it has two meanings. The narrow meaning specifically refers to the pre-Qin script engraved on stones (*zhouwen* 籀文), modeled after stone-drum script in the Kingdom of Qin during the Warring States Period. It features heavy strokes, duplicated structures and an overall pattern more regular and standard than inscriptions of earlier times on bronze objects. The broader meaning refers to all kinds of stone-engraved characters including inscriptions on bronze ware, greater seal script and the stone script of all kingdoms in the Spring and Autumn Period and the Warring States Period. It was replaced by the lesser seal script after the Kingdom of Qin unified China.

引例 Citations：

◎《史籀》十五篇。[自注]周宣王太史作《大篆》十五篇，建武时亡六篇矣。(《汉书·艺文志》)

(《史籀》一共有十五篇。[班固自注]周宣王时的太史籀创作了《大篆》十五篇，汉光武帝建武年间已经亡佚了六篇。)

Shizhou, the oldest textbook for children in China, has 15 chapters. Ban Gu's own note: During the reign of King Xuan of Zhou, the Grand Historian Zhou wrote 15 chapters for a collection entitled *Greater Seal Script*. By the time of Emperor Guangwu of Eastern Han, six of them had been lost. (*The History of the Han Dynasty*)

◎古籀之亡，不亡于秦，而亡于七国，为其变乱古法，各自立异，使后人不能尽识也。(吴大澂 (chéng)《说文古籀补·叙》)

(大篆的灭亡，不是灭亡在秦朝，而是灭亡在战国七国时期，因为它改乱了古时的书写方法，每个国家都有各自的书写形态，致使后来之人难以全都认识。)

The demise of the ancient script and the greater seal script did not occur during the Qin Dynasty; it had already disappeared in the earlier Warring States Period. The reason is because ancient ways of writing were changed as each kingdom developed its own script, so people in later times had difficulty recognizing all such scripts. (Wu Dacheng: *Ancient Script and Greater Seal Script: A Supplement to Explanation of Script and Elucidation of Characters*)

丹青 /dānqīng/
Painting in Colors

丹和青是中国古代绘画常用的两种颜色，早期中国画常用丹砂、青䃤（huò）一类矿物颜料"勾线填色"，因而用"丹青"代指绘画。代表性的丹青作品有西汉马王堆一号墓帛画，北魏、隋唐时期的敦煌壁画等。后丹青逐渐为水墨所代替。由于丹青颜色鲜艳绚丽，且不易褪色，古代用丹册纪勋、青史纪事。史家多以丹青比喻一个人功勋卓著，永载史册，不会磨灭。

Dan (丹 cinnabar) and *qing* (青 cyan) were two colors frequently applied in traditional Chinese painting. Cinnabar is red and cyan is bluish green. In early times, Chinese paintings often used minerals such as cinnabar and cyan to draw lines or fill in colors. Hence the term *danqing* (丹青) made from the combination of *dan* and *qing* could stand for painting in general. Representative works of this kind included silk paintings unearthed at Tomb No. 1 of Mawangdui of the Han Dynasty as well as the Dunhuang frescoes of the Northern Wei period and the Sui and Tang dynasties. Later, colors made from cinnabar and cyan were gradually replaced by ink and wash. Partly because of their bright, contrastive colors, and partly because mineral colors do not deteriorate appreciably over time, people used red-character books to record merits and bluish-green-character books to record historical events. Historians often use *danqing* to refer to a man's outstanding, indelible work that deserves to be put down in history.

引例 Citations：

◎ [顾恺之] 尤善丹青，图写特妙。谢安深重之，以为有苍生以来未之有也。(《晋书·顾恺之传》)

(顾恺之尤其擅长绘画，画出来的人物奇特精妙。谢安非常器重他，认为他是自有人类以来从未有过的杰出画家。)

Gu Kaizhi was particularly skillful in painting. The figures he portrayed are amazingly vivid and lovely. Xie An held him in high esteem, and regarded him as superior to all other artists, past and present. (*The History of the Jin Dynasty*)

◎ 故丹青画其形容，良史载其功勋。(曹丕《与孟达书》)

(是以画家画下他的相貌，史家记载他的功劳。)

Thus a painter portrays a person's physical features, just as a historian records his accomplishments. (Cao Pi: A Letter to Meng Da)

但见性情，不睹文字
/dàn jiàn xìngqíng, bù dǔ wénzì/

To Impress Readers with True Feelings Oblivious of Its Wording

　　文学作品完美呈现作者的本性真情，让读者全身心感受到性情的真与美，而感觉不到文字的存在。由唐代诗僧皎然（720—796？）提出。此语一是强调性情为本，文字只是工具；二是强调写作者与接受者都要得意忘言；三是突出文学艺术以心会心的特点，只有通过心灵对话才能激活言语之外的多重意蕴。它体现了中国古代文学重视意象、意境构造的特点。

This happens when a literary work reveals to its reader the truth and beauty of its author's innermost feelings, to the point that the reader becomes oblivious to the wording. Such an idea was first raised by the Tang Dynasty poet-monk Jiaoran (720-796?). It emphasizes three points. First, the core value of literature is to express one's true feeling; the wording is only a tool. Second, both the author and reader should focus on the meaning while forgetting the words. Third, tacit understanding is crucial to art and literature. Only through dialogue between souls can a variety of illocutionary implications be activated. The whole term highlights the importance of imagery and artistic ambience in classical Chinese literature.

引例 Citations：

◎两重意已上，皆文外之旨，若遇高手如康乐公，览而察之，但见情性，不睹文字，盖诣道之极也。（释皎然《诗式·重意诗例》）

（诗句具有两重以上的意蕴，都属于言外之旨。如果碰到谢灵运这样的高人，仔细阅读他的作品，你只会感受到诗人的本真性情，不会注意他的文字，这大概是因为他的作品已经臻至诗歌创作的最高境界了。）

Poetic lines carry two or more implications, lying outside of language itself. If you encounter a truly great poet such as Xie Lingyun, you will be struck with his bold and uninhibited expression of feeling and forget his wording. This is probably because his works have reached the highest level of poetic excellence. (Shi Jiaoran: *Poetic Styles*)

◎［杜甫《九日蓝田崔氏庄》］通首八句，一气夷犹，开合顿宕而出。但见情性，不睹文字。（方东树《昭昧詹言·续卷四·杜公》）

（通篇八句诗，好像有一股气从容行于其中，左右开合，跌宕起伏，直至完全抒泄。通篇只感受到诗人的本真情性，不会注意他的文字。）

This eight-line poem is permeated with a calmly executed vital energy. It is sometimes vigorous, sometimes quiet and elegant. It rises and falls rhythmically until it has given full vent to the author's pent-up feelings. So

中华思想文化术语
文艺卷

impressed with the author's true feelings, readers will pay no heed to his actual wording. (Fang Dongshu: *Rambling Words to Expose the Secrets of Poetry Writing*)

淡泊 /dànbó/
Quiet Living with No Worldly Desire

恬淡宁静。最初指清心寡欲、平和恬淡的一种人生态度。道家主张"淡"，认为淡而无味才是至味，这种思想对于"淡泊"审美观念的形成有较大影响。从魏晋时代开始，淡泊被运用于审美领域，指平和清淡的艺术美感与风格，与浓艳富丽相对。淡泊不是淡而无味，是指经过了提纯、熔炼，宁静而空灵，平淡而有深远的韵味。

This term was first used to mean to lead a quiet, peaceful life with few worldly desires. Daoism advocates blandness, believing that lack of flavor is the best possible flavor. It was highly influential in the creation of the aesthetic concept of blandness and quiet living. Beginning in the Wei and Jin dynasties, the term was used in aesthetics, referring to a peaceful and mild artistic beauty and style, as opposed to rich, loud and splendid beauty. The term does not mean insipid with no taste at all; what it refers to is a purified, refined, quiet and ethereal taste, a mild yet profound tone and flavor.

引例 Citations：

◎夫君子之行，静以修身，俭以养德，非淡泊无以明志，非宁静无以致远。（诸葛亮《诫子书》）

（君子的行为，以内心安宁来修养身体，以节俭朴素来培养品德，不恬淡宁静就无法拥有崇高的志向，不安宁平静就无法实现远大的目标。）

In conducting himself, a man of virtue should maintain inner peace to cultivate his moral character and be frugal to cultivate virtue. Unless he is indifferent to fame and fortune, he cannot have aspirations; unless he stays calm and quiet, he cannot reach afar. (Zhuge Liang: Letter of Warning to My Son)

◎独韦应物、柳宗元发纤秾于简古,寄至味于澹泊,非余子所及也。(苏轼《书黄子思诗集后》)

(只有韦应物、柳宗元,在质朴高古中蕴含细腻丰厚,在平静雅淡中蕴含无穷的韵味,是其他人远远不及的。)

Only Wei Yingwu and Liu Zongyuan far exceeded others, because in their poetry, rich delicacy dwells in vintage simplicity and nuanced profundity in serene composure. (Su Shi: Postscript to *Selected Poems of Huang Zisi*)

当行 /dānghǎng/
Professionalism

内行,在行。最初用于诗歌评论,指诗歌创作完全契合诗歌的体制规范。后发展成为中国古典戏曲理论的重要术语。主要含义有二:其一,指戏曲语言质朴自然、浅显通俗,符合人物性格并适合舞台表演;其二,指戏曲中的角色创造及故事情景,真实传神,具有强烈的艺术感染力,能让观众沉浸其中。在明代戏曲理论中,"当行"经常与"本色"连用,能当行、具本色的戏曲作品就是上乘佳作。

The expression was first used in poetry criticism to mean that a poem fully met poetic stylistic standards. It later became an important term in Chinese classical operatic theory. It has two meanings. One is that the language used by a character in a play is simple, natural, easy to understand, and appropriate for the character. The other is that characters and plot of the play are true to life with a strong artistic attraction. In Ming-dynasty operatic theory, "professionalism" and "being true to life" are often used together to describe outstanding opera works.

引例 Citations：

◎ 曲始于胡元，大略贵当行不贵藻丽。(凌濛初《谭曲杂札》)

(戏曲从元代开始，大体上重视通俗浅显，不重视辞藻华丽。)

Beginning in the Yuan Dynasty, professional simplicity, rather than flowery rhetoric, has gained popularity as an operatic style. (Ling Mengchu: Miscellaneous Notes on Opera)

◎ 行家者随所妆演，无不摹拟曲尽，宛若身当其处，而几忘其事之乌有，能使人快者掀髯，愤者扼腕，悲者掩泣，美者色飞。是惟优孟衣冠，然后可与于此。故称曲上乘，首曰当行。(臧懋(mào)循《元曲选·序二》)

(行家根据自己所扮演的角色，无不摹拟相似，曲尽其妙，好像完全置身其中，忘记了所表演的事情并不是真的，能够让人在快乐时胡须张开，在愤怒时握紧手腕，在悲伤时掩面哭泣，在羡慕时神色飞动。只有优孟那样的艺人，才能达到这种效果。因此，说到戏曲上乘，首要的标准就是当行。)

Professional actors can play their roles so vividly as if they were the characters themselves, forgetting that the story is fictional. Their performances can make viewers so happy that their beards will fly up, or make them so angry that they will wring their wrists, or make them so sad that they will sob, or inspire them so much that they will become thrilled. Only artists like Youmeng can create such effect. Therefore, for an opera to be outstanding, it first and foremost must be professional. (Zang Maoxun: *Selected Works of Yuan Opera*)

典雅 /diǎnyǎ/

Classical Elegance

指文章典范雅正。最初指写文章要有经典依据，文章的思想内容应纯正高尚，以经典文献特别是儒家的义理规章作为审美规范，后侧重指文章的文辞和风格高雅优美而不浅俗艳浮。其后，"典雅"这一术语又逐步融入道家自然恬淡、超尘出世的审美意蕴，如司空图（837—908）在《二十四诗品》中用"落花无言，人淡如菊"来描述"典雅"，就很接近道家自然恬淡的风格。

This term refers to a type of writing that is classically elegant. Originally, it meant that a piece of writing should be modeled on ancient classics, express pure and noble ideas, and follow classical literary styles by using Confucian doctrines for aesthetic guidance. Later, the term shifted to emphasize elegant diction and style that were free from vulgarity and frivolity. Later still, it gradually incorporated Daoist aesthetic views, suggesting natural tranquility and spiritual transcendence. For example, in "Twenty-four Styles of Poetry," Sikong Tu (837-908) described classical elegance as being "as quiet as falling flower petals and as modest as unassuming daisies," which is close to the simple, relaxed, and natural style advocated by Daoist scholars.

引例 Citations：

◎ 典雅者，熔式经诰，方轨儒门者也。（刘勰《文心雕龙·体性》）

（所谓典雅，就是取法于儒家经典文献，遵照儒家义理章法。）

Classical elegance is achieved by emulating the Confucian classics and following Confucian doctrines in literary creation. (Liu Xie: *The Literary Mind and the Carving of Dragons*)

◎［徐干］著《中论》二十篇，成一家之言，辞义典雅，足传于后。（曹丕《与吴质书》）

（徐干著《中论》二十篇，成一家之言，文辞有典据而高雅，足以传之于后世。）

Xu Gan wrote his 20-chapter book *Discourses That Hit the Mark*, establishing a distinctive theory of his own. The carefully-researched, well-elaborated and highly elegant writings deserve to be passed on to future generations. (Cao Pi: A Letter to Wu Zhi)

点铁成金 /diǎntiě-chéngjīn/
Turning a Crude Poem or Essay into a Literary Gem

指高明的作者用平常词句或化用前人的词句创造性地表达出神奇精妙的意蕴。亦指高手修改文章，善于从平凡文字中提炼出闪光点。北宋黄庭坚（1045—1105）沿袭刘勰（465？—520？或532？）的"宗经"思想，强调学习、揣摩经典作品的表达技巧，巧妙化用前人的词句，化平常、腐朽为神奇，使自己的文章主旨鲜明而又富有文采。此说推动了宋代及后世关于诗文创作手法的讨论。

The term "turning a crude poem or essay into a literary gem" means creatively expressing novel and exquisite meaning through the use of simple language or by transforming old phrases from past masters. The expression also can be used to describe the way that an accomplished man of letters edits writings. By minor adjustment, he can bring out the splendor in an otherwise ordinary piece. Huang Tingjian (1045-1105), a poet and scholar of the Northern Song Dynasty, valued and promoted literary critic Liu Xie's (465?-520? or 532?) idea that classics offer excellent examples from which to learn, but he stressed the need to study and employ the expressive techniques found in classic masterpieces by cleverly transforming the words found there, altering common and hackneyed forms of "novelty" so as to impart to one's own writing freshness and literary style. In the Song Dynasty and later, this theory gave rise to many debates about methods of creative writing in poetry.

引例 Citations：

◎古之能为文章者，真能陶冶万物，虽取古人之陈言入于翰墨，如灵丹一粒，点铁成金也。（黄庭坚《答洪驹父（fǔ）书》）

（古代那些擅长写作的大家，确实能够将各种文字和物象融为一体，即使是采用前人的陈旧辞句，也像用一颗灵丹就能点铁成金那样［表达出神奇精妙的意蕴］。）

In ancient times the most capable writers could render excellent images of virtually anything mentioned in their writing. Even if old expressions or sentences from former masters entered into their writing, they could transform them like an alchemist who, with a single touch, could turn lead into gold. (Huang Tingjian: *Letter in Reply to Hong Jufu*)

◎"椎床破面枨（chéng）触人，作无义语怒四邻。尊中欢伯见尔笑：我本和气如三春。"前两句本粗恶语，能煅炼成诗，真造化手，所谓点铁成金矣。（吴可《藏海诗话》）

（［有人醉酒后］"捶打坐床撕破脸面触犯他人，满嘴说些无情无义的话激怒四周的人。杯中的酒见到你们的丑态觉得可笑：'我'本是性情温和有如三春的饮品。"前两句本是很粗俗的话，能够锤炼成诗句，真是创意点化的高手，可以说是点铁成金了。）

"When drunk, you strike the bed to offend others, and vex your neighbors with vulgar language. The liquor in the cup laughs at you saying: I am a drink as gentle and warm as the spring weather." The first two sentences were crude, yet for you to transmute such material into a fine poem is true mastery. This is what is called a golden touch! (Wu Ke: *Canghai's Remarks on Poetry*)

独抒性灵，不拘格套

/dú shū xìnglíng, bù jū gétào/

Bold Expression of One's True Self

文学创作抒发自己真实独特的性情，不拘泥于任何格式套路。原为明代文学家袁宏道（1568 — 1610）对其弟弟袁中道（1570 — 1626）文学创作的评语，后来成为公安派的核心理论主张，与当时前、后七子"文必秦汉，诗必盛唐"的复古主义观点形成了鲜明的对抗。公安派强调文艺源于个人性情，讲求独创性，重自由，反拘束，要求诗人不为成法所限。在当时尊古、模拟盛行的风气下，这一命题有个性解放和反传统的意义，对于当时及后代的文艺创作产生了积极影响。

This term indicates that a writer should give expression to his true feelings in literary creation and not be constrained by particular regulations or formulas. It was first used by the Ming Dynasty writer Yuan Hongdao (1568 - 1610) as he commented on the literary work of his younger brother Yuan Zhongdao (1570 - 1626). Later, it became the core idea of the Gong'an School of Literary Writing, firmly opposed to the stubborn emulation of ancient literature as advocated by the Former Seven Masters and the Latter Seven Masters of the time, who highly esteemed prose of the Qin and Han dynasties and poetry of the golden Tang era. The Gong'an School emphasized that literature and art flow forth from the heart, value freedom and originality, and refuse to be bound by any convention. This school urged poets to defy any restriction imposed on them. This view was important to the assertion of individuality and rebellion against tradition, at a time when reverence for and emulation of ancient literature was the trend. It exerted a positive influence on literary creation in that era and later.

引例 Citations：

◎大都独抒性灵，不拘格套，非从自己胸臆流出，不肯下笔。有时情与境会，顷刻千言，如水东注，令人夺魂。（袁宏道《叙小修诗》）

（［他的诗］大都抒发自己真实独特的性情，不拘泥于任何格式套路。只要不是出自本心，绝不肯下笔。有时自己的情感与客观景物融合一片，顷刻成篇，就像大河东流一样，读之夺人心魄。）

Most of his poems express his inner self, without being constrained by any particular regulations or formulas. He would not commit to paper anything not flowing naturally from his inner world. Once his inner feelings and external objects merge into one, words would pour forth to form a magnificent whole, just as a great river flows east undeterred. Readers will be enthralled when reading his works. (Yuan Hongdao: Preface to Xiaoxiu's Poetry)

◎性之所安，殆不可强，率性而行，是谓真人。（袁宏道《识（zhì）张幼于箴铭后》）

（人的性情所形成的习性，大概是不会勉强改变的，只要遵循自己的性情行事做人，就是真性情的人。）

A man's habitual behavior shaped by his own disposition is not quite likely to change. So long as he pursues his true self in his conduct of affairs, he is a true man. (Yuan Hongdao: A Postscript to Zhang Youyu's Admonitory Epigraph)

◎凡诗之传者，都是性灵，不关堆垛。（袁枚《随园诗话》卷五）

（大凡诗歌的流传，都是因为性灵有感染力，与堆砌学识没有关联。）

Poetry spreads far and wide mainly because of its spiritual appeal, not because it is loaded with book knowledge. (Yuan Mei: *Suiyuan Remarks on Poetry*)

读万卷书，行万里路

/dú wàn juàn shū, xíng wàn lǐ lù/

Read Ten Thousand Books and Travel Ten Thousand *Li*

多读书，多走路。比喻要努力读书，尽可能多地丰富书本知识，掌握间接经验；同时要尽可能多地接触实际，丰富自己的亲身体验，开阔眼界，增进见识。理论与实际相结合，间接经验与直接经验相结合，既有真才实学，又能学以致用。

This means one should acquire as much knowledge as possible from books to gain the experience of others. At the same time, one should also have as much direct contact with the world as possible to enrich one's personal experience and broaden one's horizon. When one applies theory in practice and draws on both direct and indirect experience, he will gain true knowledge.

引例 Citation：

◎人生宇宙间，志愿当何如？不行万里路，即读万卷书。（高士奇《扈从杂记》其四）

（人生于天地之间，应当有怎样的志愿？不是走万里长的路，就是读万卷多的书。）

What aspiration should one have? Travel ten thousand *li* to see the world, and read ten thousand books. (Gao Shiqi: Miscellaneous Notes on Escorting Journeys)

夺胎换骨 /duótāi-huàngǔ/

Express the Ideas in Earlier Literary Works in a New Way

原意为脱去凡胎俗骨而换为圣胎仙骨，后比喻在诗文创作中援用前人作品的意思但能用自己的语言另立新意的一种技法。强调师法前人而不露痕迹并能有所创新。在诗歌创作中主要通过换字、换意凸显主旨、生成新意、造就佳句。"夺胎"是发现前人作品中具有某种意味，而予以阐扬、深化、拓展，乃至生成新意。"换骨"是发现前人作品中具有某种高妙的思想、情意但表现不够充分，而用更为恰切的语言予以重新表现，使之更完善、更鲜明。这一技巧体现文艺创作的传承、流变关系，在作品中可以看到很多具体运用的实例。文化学术的继承和发展也可以借鉴这一策略。

This term, which figuratively means to replace the flesh and bones of an ordinary human being with those of an immortal, is used to describe a literary technique in which a writer uses his own words to express new ideas while quoting those from earlier works. The emphasis is on borrowing from the past without showing any traces, yet forming something new in the process. In poetry, this is achieved primarily by substituting words and ideas to highlight a theme, thus creating a beautiful new phrase. *Duotai* (夺胎) is to identify an idea in an existing work and to imbue it with new meaning by expounding, deepening or broadening it. *Huangu* (换骨) is to identify a brilliant idea or feeling in an earlier work which is insufficiently expressed, and to give it greater refinement and clarity by expressing it with a more appropriate choice of words. This technique exemplifies how literature both perpetuates and yet changes tradition. Cultural scholarship can also borrow from this method to build on the past and to further develop.

引例 Citations：

◎然不易其意而造其语，谓之换骨法；窥入其意而形容之，谓之夺胎法。（释惠洪《冷斋夜话》卷一）

中华思想文化术语
文艺卷

（然而不改变前人的意思而换用更恰切的词句，叫做换骨法；从前
人作品中领悟到作者的某个意旨而予以深化和充分发挥，叫做夺胎
法。）

Huangu is to use more appropriate words without changing the meaning
of earlier writers; *Duotai* is to comprehend a certain meaning of an author
and then deepen it and express it more fully. (Shi Huihong: *Evening Talks at
Lengzhai*)

◎文章虽不要蹈袭古人一言一句，然古人自有夺胎换骨等法，所谓
灵丹一粒点铁成金也。(陈善《扪虱新话·文章夺胎换骨》)

（文章虽然不应该袭用前人的一字一句，但前人自有一种夺胎换骨
的方法，就好像用一粒灵丹来点铁成金 [从而创造出更完美的作
品] 一样。）

Though not copying earlier writings word from word, the ancients had a way
of "replacing the flesh and bones" which, like a magic pill turning iron into
gold, brings forward even better works. (Chen Shan: *Daring Remarks on
Literature*)

发愤著书 /fāfèn-zhùshū/
Indignation Spurs One to Write Great Works.

　　因在现实生活中遭遇不平而下决心写出传世著作。源出《史
记·太史公自序》。西汉司马迁（前145或前135？—?）在遭受宫刑
后，强烈的愤懑情绪成为他创作《史记》的驱动力。他借《史记》
表达自己的思想、感情、志向，最终使著作流传于世。"发愤著书"
后多用来解释优秀的文艺作品的创作动机和原因。这一术语揭示了
优秀的文学作品的产生往往与作者个人的不幸遭遇有直接关联。后
世在此基础上又衍生出"不平则鸣""诗穷而后工"等观点。

This term means suffering injustice in life can spur one to create great works. It originated from the "Preface by the Grand Historian to *Records of the Historian*." After Sima Qian (145 or 135 ?-? BC), an official in the Western Han Dynasty, suffered the unjust punishment of castration, his indignation spurred him to write the great work, *Records of the Historian*. In the book he gave expression to his thoughts, feelings, and aspirations, which made the book a classic for later generations. The expression "indignation spurs one to write great works" was used to explain one of the motivations and reasons for creating masterpieces. It points to the fact that injustice suffered by an author often turns out to be the source of inspiration for him to write a literary masterpiece. It later led to similar terms like "cry out against injustice" and "a good poem is the product of pent-up emotions."

引例 Citations：

◎惜诵以致愍兮，发愤以抒情。（屈原《九章·惜诵》）

（痛惜直言进谏却招致谗毁疏远，怀着一腔忧愤抒发衷情。）

I am saddened that my frank remonstration with the king has brought false accusations on me and left me in exile. In anguish and indignation, I am writing these poems to express my strong feelings. (Qu Yuan: Collection of Nine Pieces)

◎《诗》三百篇，大抵贤圣发愤之所为作也。此人皆意有所郁结，不得通其道，故述往事、思来者。（《史记·太史公自序》）

（《诗经》三百篇，大都是圣贤抒发忧愤而创作出来的。这些人都是感情郁结，不能实现志向，所以记述往事，希望将来的人能够了解。）

Most of the 300 poems in *The Book of Songs* were written by sages who were in anguish and indignation. They were depressed over what had prevented them from fulfilling their aspirations, so they composed poems about what had happened in the hope that future generations would understand them. (*Records of the Historian*)

发乎情，止乎礼义 /fā hū qíng, zhǐ hū lǐyì/
Start with Feelings and Control with Propriety

诗歌由情感生发，但是情感的抒发不能超过限度，应该用礼义去节制。其目的是达到委婉讽谏的效果。"发乎情，止乎礼义"由最初批评《诗经》的理论发展成为普遍的文学创作原则，既承认人的本能欲望以及抒发描写本能欲望的需要，同时又强调要用儒家的道德规范来约束指导，不能流于纯自然的宣泄，不能超越社会政治、伦理的规范。因此，诗歌中所表达的情感，既具有个体性，又具有社会性。

Poems and lyrics arise from genuine feelings, which, however, should not be excessive but be controlled by ritual propriety and righteousness, so as to be tactfully persuasive. This term was first used when commenting on *The Book of Songs* and then developed into a guiding principle for literary creation in general. It not only acknowledges people's instinctive desires and the need to express and describe such desires, but also emphasizes that Confucian ethics should be employed to contain and guide feelings, which should neither be improperly vented nor transgress the boundaries of society, politics and ethics. Thus, feelings expressed via poetry are both individual and social.

引例 Citations：

◎国史明乎得失之迹，伤人伦之废，哀刑政之苛，吟咏情性，以风（fěng）其上。达于事变而怀其旧俗者也。故变风发乎情，止乎礼义。发乎情，民之性也；止乎礼义，先王之泽也。(《毛诗序》)

(周代的史官知道政治得失的轨迹，感伤人伦关系的废弛，哀叹刑法施政的严苛，吟唱歌咏自己的情思感受，为的是讽喻人君。这是通晓世事变化而怀念旧时风俗以规谏执政者的缘故。所以"变风"发自内心情感，但不超过礼义规定的限度。发自内心情感，这是出于民众的天性；不超过礼义规定的限度，这是先王教化留下的恩泽。)

Official historians of the Zhou Dynasty were aware of lessons concerning political gain and loss, lamented the abandonment of codes governing human relations, bemoaned the harsh enforcing of laws and government, and sang or chanted to express their feelings and emotions, in order to admonish the monarch. They knew well the vicissitudes of worldly affairs and were nostalgic for bygone customs. "A variation in poetic style" is expressive of poets' inner feelings and, for that matter, an articulation of common folk's natural inclination, but such expression should be kept within the confines of propriety and justice, a good heritage left by the late kings. (Introductions to *Mao's Version of The Book of Songs*)

◎ 不发乎情，即非礼义，故诗要有乐有哀；发乎情，未必即礼义，故诗要哀乐中节。（刘熙载《艺概·诗概》）

（不从情感中生发的，自然不会合乎礼义，所以诗歌中有快乐也有哀伤；从情感中生发的，也不一定就合乎礼义，所以诗歌的哀伤、快乐都要符合礼义规定的限度。）

Not to express feelings and emotions naturally does not conform to propriety and righteousness, so there should be joy and sorrow in poems. Feelings and emotions expressed not necessarily conform to propriety and righteousness, and thus sorrow and joy in poems should be kept within the confines of propriety and righteousness. (Liu Xizai: *Overview of Literary Theories*)

发纤秾于简古，寄至味于淡泊

/fā xiānnóng yú jiǎngǔ, jì zhìwèi yú dànbó/

Intricacy Within Plainness, and Intensity Beneath Quietude

在质朴高古中蕴含细腻丰厚，在平静雅淡中蕴含无穷的韵味。这是北宋文学家苏轼（1037—1101）用来评价唐代诗人韦应物（737？—791）、柳宗元（773—819）诗歌风格的话。这种以质朴、淡泊为至高境界的理念，既代表了苏轼的诗学观，也代表了中国古代的重要美学观念。老子在《道德经》中提出"大音希声，大象无形"，推崇简淡自然之美，是苏轼美学观念的源头。

"Richness dwells in vintage simplicity and nuanced profundity in serene composure." This is how the Northern Song writer Su Shi (1037-1101) praised the poetic style of Wei Yingwu (737?-791) and Liu Zongyuan (773-819). Such insistence on the supremacy of simplicity and composure reflects Su Shi's view about poetry and is an important aesthetic conception of ancient China. "Great music is soundless, and great image is hard to trace," Laozi wrote in his *Dao De Jing*. This shows Laozi's high esteem for simple and natural beauty, which is the source of Su Shi's aesthetic view.

引例 Citation：

◎李、杜之后，诗人继作，虽间有远韵，而才不逮意，独韦应物、柳宗元发纤秾于简古，寄至味于淡泊，非余子所及也。(苏轼《书黄子思诗集后》)

（李白、杜甫之后，诗人相继涌现，虽然中间偶尔也出现具有前人韵味的作品，但是诗人的才华达不到表达相应内容的高度。只有韦应物、柳宗元，在质朴高古中蕴含细腻丰厚，在平静雅淡中蕴含无穷的韵味，是其他人所远远不及的。）

Although there are other poets after Li Bai and Du Fu, they were hardly able to reach a height required to express the content of their poems. Few had the ingenious quality of their poetic predecessors. Only Wei Yingwu and Liu Zongyuan far exceeded others, because in their poetry, rich delicacy dwells in vintage simplicity and nuanced profundity in serene composure. (Su Shi: Postscript to *Selected Poems of Huang Zisi*)

繁缛 /fánrù/

Overly Elaborative

指诗文辞藻华丽、描写详尽（与"简洁"相对）。西晋时期以陆机（261—303）为代表，在文学创作上出现了追求辞藻富丽、文思繁密的倾向。陆机的作品多用典故和对偶句，讲求精雕细琢，文辞繁复华美，同时也有不够清新流畅的弊病。至南朝齐梁时期，刘勰（465？—520？或532？）《文心雕龙》把"繁缛"列为文章八种风格之一。

This term refers to a literary writing style that is ornate and flowery in diction and excessively detailed and exhaustive in description, in contrast to being "simple and concise." The tendency to write elaborately about an idea in ornate language first emerged in the Western Jin Dynasty, represented by the writings of Lu Ji (261-303). His works were rich in allusions and antitheses, meticulous in diction and description, and elaborate and ornate in style. At the same time, these writings suffered from a lack of clarity and novelty. During the Qi and Liang of the Southern Dynasties, this overly elaborative style was listed as one of the eight major literary styles in Liu Xie's (465?-520? or 532?) *The Literary Mind and the Carving of Dragons*.

引例 Citations：

◎繁缛者，博喻酿采，炜烨枝派者也。（刘勰《文心雕龙·体性》）
（所谓繁缛，就是博用比喻，辞藻丰富，文采灿烂，如同树木多枝、河流派分一样。）

An overly elaborative style is known for its profuse use of allusions and ornate language to generate literary effect, like a tree branching out and a river forking into multiple streams. (Liu Xie: *The Literary Mind and the Carving of Dragons*)

◎或藻思绮合，清丽千眠。炳若缛绣，凄若繁弦。（陆机《文赋》）
（写作有时是辞藻华美、文思交会，清新富丽，色彩绚烂。光彩耀目如同装饰繁盛的锦绣，凄切流连如同繁复多变的弦乐。）

Sometimes, one can employ flowery language in writing that makes the idea and language of a work mutually reinforcing, creating a refreshing and appealing effect in a consistently colorful style. It can be dazzling and gorgeous like a piece of exquisitely adorned brocade, or sentimental and lingering like an intricate piece of plaintive string music. (Lu Ji: The Art of Writing)

方圆 /fāngyuán/
Squareness and Roundness

方形和圆形。"方圆"连用，指事物的形状或性状，亦指使事物"方"或"圆"的方法、规则。古人认为天圆地方，天有旋转、圆通、圆融等特性，地有安静、刚直、方正等特性，主张做人行事应当效法天地的特性，外圆内方，既不放弃内心的坚守，又有适度的融通。在文艺创作特别是书法创作中，古人认为楷书要方，草书要圆，但无论哪种书体都应做到方圆之间的相互依存与和谐统一。

"Squareness," used in collocation with "roundness," refers to the shapes and properties of things, or sometimes to the methods and rules of making things square or round. Ancient Chinese believed that heaven is round and earth is square. Heaven revolves, accommodates, and harmonizes. Earth, in contrast, is still, firm, and straightforward. They argued that humans should conduct themselves in imitation of the ways heaven and earth operate, and be "round" on the outside and "square" within, meaning that people should be suitably flexible but firm on issues of principle. In artistic and literary creation, especially in calligraphic creations, ancient Chinese held that regular script should be "square" whereas cursive script should be "round." However, no matter which type of script is adopted, squareness and roundness should be applied in harmony with each other.

引例 Citations：

◎ 离娄之明、公输子之巧，不以规矩，不能成方圆；师旷之聪，不以六律，不能正五音；尧舜之道，不以仁政，不能平治天下。(《孟子·离娄上》)

（即使有离娄的好视力、公输般的高超技巧，如果不用圆规和曲尺，也不能画出方形和圆形；即使有师旷的辨音能力，如果不用六律，也不能校正五音；即使有尧舜的方法，如果不施行仁政，也不能治理好天下。）

Even with Li Lou's keen vision and Gongshu Ban's skillfulness, they cannot draw either a square or a round shape without using compasses or a ruler. Even with Shi Kuang's sharp ear for music, he cannot adjust the five notes without using the six pitch-pipes. Even with Yao and Shun's enlightened methods, they cannot run a country well without practicing benevolent governance. (*Mencius*)

◎ 文有圆有方，韩文多圆，柳文多方，苏文方者亦少，圆者多。(李耆卿《文章精义》)

（文章有的写得圆通，有的写得方正，韩愈的文章大多圆通，柳宗元的文章大多方正，苏轼的文章方正的少而圆通的多。）

The writings of some authors can be round or delicately nuanced, whereas others can be square, or straightforward. Many of Han Yu's essays are round, and many of Liu Zongyuan's are square, while Su Shi's writing is more round than square. (Li Qiqing: *The Essentials of Writings*)

◎ 方圆者，真草之体用。真贵方，草贵圆。方者参之以圆，圆者参之以方，斯为妙矣。(姜夔《续书谱·方圆》)

（对楷书和草书来说，方圆既是书体又是运用上的一种变化。楷书贵在方正，草书贵在圆通。方正的书体要参照圆通的技巧，圆通的书体要参照方正的技巧，如此才能达到绝妙的水平。）

Squareness and roundness are the core essence and useful complement of regular script and cursive script. The merit of regular script is squareness whereas the merit of cursive script is roundness. Only when squareness is complemented by roundness and roundness is complemented by squareness can true calligraphic excellence be achieved. (Jiang Kui: Subsequent Commentaries on Calligraphy)

丰肉微骨 /fēngròu-wēigǔ/
Fleshy Body and Soft Bone Structure

原指女性身材娇小、肌肉丰腴而身段柔软，后用于书画品评，指运笔丰肥、媚浮而骨力纤弱。"骨"即骨法，指笔势或结构上的清劲雄健；"肉"指线条的丰肥、妍媚无力或浓墨重彩。古人强调书画创作应有骨有肉、骨肉匀称，既不失妍美而又雄健有力。因此，"丰肉微骨"是差评，而"丰骨微肉"或"骨丰肉润"则各有千秋。这一术语从人物的鉴赏延伸到艺术作品鉴赏，体现了中国美学概念"近取诸身"的特点。

Originally this term indicated that a woman had a delicate figure, that she was fleshy and limber. Later it was used to judge calligraphy and painting, indicating that the circulation of the writing brush was lavish and vigorous, but that the strength of the bone (structure) was weak. Bone (structure) means skeletal structure, indicating weakness or vigor in the strength of the writing brush and in the structure of the work. "Fleshy" indicates that the lines are sumptuous and charming, but without strength, or that the ink is thick and the colors heavy. In the old days, it was stressed that a work of calligraphy or a painting should have a bone (structure) and be fleshy and that there should be a proper balance between the bone and flesh. There should neither be a lack of elegance nor of vigor and strength. Therefore, "fleshy body and soft bone structure" is regarded as a demerit. But when there is a stout bone structure and soft muscles, or when the bone structure is stout and the muscles are smooth, both are considered desirable. This term shifted from depicting human figures to appreciating art works, giving expression to the Chinese aesthetic concept of "using body parts to describe what is near."

引例 Citations：

◎丰肉微骨，调以娱只。(《楚辞·大招》)

（身材娇小而丰腴柔美的女人哪，舞姿和谐令人欢快轻松。）

With delicate, fleshy and soft figures, the lady dancers delighted the audience with their performance. (*Odes of Chu*)

◎善笔力者多骨，不善笔力者多肉；多骨微肉者谓之筋书，多肉微骨者谓之墨猪；多力丰筋者圣，无力无筋者病。(卫夫人《笔阵图》)

（笔力强的人，其作品的筋骨多清劲雄健；而笔力弱的人，其作品则是多浓墨。骨法鲜明雄健而着墨少的字叫做"筋书"，用墨浓重而不见骨法的字叫做"墨猪"。筋骨饱满有力的作品最高妙，筋骨少而无力属于很差的作品。）

Those who are good at using the writing brush can create fresh and vigorous calligraphic pieces like a body with strong bone structure, whereas those who are not can only produce inky calligraphic pieces. A vigorous calligraphic work done without much ink is called "a sinewy work," while a less vigorous piece done with much ink is called "an inky piglet." A vigorous work is to be highly appreciated, while a less vigorous one is undesirable. (Lady Wei: On Maneuvers of Calligraphy)

丰腴 /fēngyú/
Plump Beauty

中国古代文学艺术的一种风格。"丰腴"一词，本指丰厚、丰富、丰满之意，在书法美学中，主要指笔墨饱满、圆熟润美，引申到诗歌创作中，主要指作品的内容丰富细腻，品味不尽。但仅有丰腴是不够的，只有将"丰腴"和"清癯"结合起来、相反相成，才体现中国古代诗歌及艺术美学的辩证法。宋代著名文学家苏轼（1037—1101）用"质而实绮，癯而实腴"八个字概括陶渊明（365或372或376—427）的诗歌艺术特色，并给予了至高的评价，意思是说，陶渊明的诗歌在质朴中蕴含了华美，看起来清瘦而实际上内容丰富。

Plump beauty is a style prevalent in ancient Chinese literature and art. "Plump" here suggests abundance, richness and fullness. In calligraphic aesthetics, it refers to a state of chubbiness, maturity and lushness. When used in poetic creation, "plump" is associated with a poem's richness in nuance and enduring appeal. However, plump beauty would not work alone; it has to be combined with or complemented by leanness. Only thus can the dual character of ancient Chinese poetry and artistic aesthetics be fully expressed. The Northern Song writer Su Shi (1037-1101) highly lauded the artistic features of Tao Yuanming's (365 or 372 or 376-427) poetry by saying that "it is magnificently beautiful and richly varied under the surface of simplicity."

引例 Citation：

◎吾于诗人，无所甚好，独好渊明之诗。渊明作诗不多，然其诗质而实绮，癯而实腴，自曹、刘、鲍、谢、李、杜诸人皆莫及也。（苏轼语，见苏辙《子瞻和陶渊明诗集引》）

（我对于诗人，没有特别喜欢的，唯独喜欢陶渊明的诗。陶渊明所作的诗数量不多，然而，他的诗在质朴中蕴含了华美，看起来清瘦而实际上内容丰富，从曹操、刘桢、鲍照、谢灵运，到李白、杜甫等诗人都赶不上他。）

I am not particularly fond of any poet except Tao Yuanming. He did not write that many poems, but those he composed are magnificently beautiful. Though seemingly simple, they are richly varied under the surface of insipidity. None of the other poets, including Cao Cao, Liu Zhen, Bao Zhao, Xie Lingyun, Li Bai, and Du Fu, are his equals. (Su Zhe: Preface to *Collection of Su Shi's Poems Following the Rhymes of Tao Yuanming*)

风骨 /fēnggǔ/
Fenggu

指作品中由纯正的思想感情和严密的条理结构所形成的刚健劲拔、具强大艺术表现力与感染力的神韵风貌。其准确含义学界争议较大，但大致可描述为风神清朗，骨力劲拔。"风"侧重指思想情感的表达，要求作品思想纯正，气韵生动，富有情感；"骨"侧重指作品的骨架、结构及词句安排，要求作品刚健遒劲、蕴含丰富但文辞精炼。如果堆砌辞藻，过于雕章琢句，虽然词句丰富繁多但内容很少，则是没有"骨"；如果表达艰涩，缺乏情感和生机，则是没有"风"。风骨并不排斥文采，而是要和文采配合，才能成为好作品。风骨的高下主要取决于创作者的精神风貌、品格气质。南朝刘勰（465？—520？或532？）《文心雕龙》专门列有《风骨》一篇，它是我国古代文学批评史上首篇论述文学风格的文章。

This term refers to powerful expressiveness and artistic impact that come from a literary work's purity of thoughts and emotions, as well as from its meticulously crafted structure. Despite some difference in interpreting the term, people tend to agree that *fenggu* (风骨) can be understood as being lucid and fresh in language while sturdy in structure. *Feng* (风) means "style," which emphasizes that a literary work should be based on pure thoughts, vivid impressions, and rich emotions so as to produce an effect of powerful expressiveness. *Gu* (骨) means "bones" or proper structure, figuratively. It stresses the impact of structure and sentence order, requiring a piece of writing to be robust, vigorous, profound, and yet succinct. If a piece of work is wordy and overly rhetorical but weak in content, then it lacks the impact of a "proper structure," no matter how flowery its expressions are. If such writing is awkward in delivery and has no emotions and vitality, then it lacks expressiveness in "style." *Fenggu* does not preclude, but rather combines with linguistic elegance in order to create a piece of good work. Good command of *fenggu* depends on the personality and dispositions of the author. In *The Literary Mind and the Carving of Dragons*, Liu Xie (465?-520? or 532?) of the Southern Dynasties devoted a chapter to the discussion of *fenggu*, which is the first essay on writing style in the history of classical Chinese literary criticism.

引例 Citations：

◎文章须自出机杼，成一家风骨，何能共人同生活也！(《魏书·祖莹传》)

(文章必须有自己的构思布局，有自己作品的风骨，如何能与他人同一个层次！)

A piece of writing must have its own structure, and its own *fenggu*, that is, expressiveness in style and sturdiness in structure. How can it ever be the same as the writings of other writers! (*The History of Northern Wei*)

◎捶字坚而难移，结响凝而不滞，此风骨之力也。(刘勰《文心雕龙·风骨》)

(字句锤炼确切而难以改动，读起来声音凝重有力而不滞涩，这就是风骨的魅力。)

The charm of *fenggu* in a literary work derives from deliberate and precise diction that is hard to alter, and from powerful and controlled sounds that do not sound awkward when read out. (Liu Xie: *The Literary Mind and the Carving of Dragons*)

◎若能确乎正式，使文明以健，则风清骨峻，篇体光华。(刘勰《文心雕龙·风骨》)

(倘若能够定好正确合适的文体，使文采鲜明而又气势刚健，那么自可达到风神清新明朗，骨力高峻劲拔，通篇文章都会生发光彩。）

Once a good and appropriate style is set to make the writing lucid and vigorous, it will produce the effect of being pure, clear and powerfully impressive, making the writing both remarkable and appealing. (Liu Xie: *The Literary Mind and the Carving of Dragons*)

风教 /fēngjiào/
Moral Cultivation

原义为教育感化，后侧重指风俗教化，即文学艺术作品对改变世情民风所起的教育感化作用。源于《毛诗序》，是儒家关于艺术功能论的重要范畴之一。"风教"强调诗歌、音乐对于人的思想感情的教育引导作用，认为统治者能够用诗歌、音乐为工具，自上而下地传达某种理念、教育感化民众，收到移风易俗的功效。"风教"观念影响深远，从先秦时代的诗歌、音乐到近代的文学艺术作品，大多遵循这一思想，是儒家伦理教育观念的具体体现，也是文学家、艺术家社会责任感的体现。但如果艺术作品过于强调风教，会造成理念先行、理念大过形象，损害艺术作品的审美价值。最好的方式是寓教于乐，让文艺作品在潜移默化中影响人心。

Originally, this term meant to educate and influence people. Later, it came to refer to the function of shaping customary social practices, namely, the educational role of literary and artistic works in changing social behaviors and popular culture. Originating from "Introductions to *Mao's Version of The Book of Songs*," the term is one of the important concepts of the Confucian school on the function of the arts. It believes that poetry and music have a role to play in shaping people's mind, reflecting the notion that rulers can educate and influence the general public by imparting a particular ideology in a top-down fashion, thereby achieving the desired effect of cultivating the general culture. The influence of this concept is far-reaching; it has impacted much of artistic creation in China, all the way from the poetry and music of the pre-Qin period to literary and artistic works in the modern times. It not only reflects the Confucian view on moral education, but also imparts a sense of social responsibility on writers and artists. However, if an artistic work overemphasizes moral cultivation, it runs the risk of placing ideology before artistic form, thus compromising its aesthetic value. The right way is to embed teaching in entertainment and let a literary or artistic work exert its influence on social mentality in a subtle and imperceptible way.

引例 Citations：

◎《关雎》……风之始也，所以风（fèng）天下而正夫妇也。故用之乡人焉，用之邦国焉。风，风（fèng）也，教也，风（fèng）以动之，教以化之。(《毛诗序》)

(《关雎》……是《诗经》十五国风的开始，也是教化的开始，它的功用就是教育感化民众、端正夫妇的行为。风教既可应用于乡间百姓，也可应用于国家层面。风，就是风吹万物，就是教育，像风吹万物一样打动人，以教育感化人。）

"Guan Ju," the first ballad in a collection from the fifteen states in *The Book of Songs,* marks the starting point where moral education was conscientiously pursued. Its purpose was to educate and influence the general public and ensure the proper behavior between spouses. Moral cultivation can be conducted both at the individual and national levels. *Feng* (ballad), with its original meaning of wind, allegorically means to persuade and influence people like the wind touches everything. (Introductions to *Mao's Version of The Book of Songs*)

◎尝谓有能观渊明之文者，驰竞之情遣，鄙吝之意祛，贪夫可以廉，懦夫可以立。岂止仁义可蹈，抑乃爵禄可辞。……此亦有助于风教也。(萧统《〈陶渊明集〉序》)

(我曾经说过，凡是能读懂陶渊明文章的人，就会抛开争名逐利的想法，去除贪鄙吝啬的念头，贪婪的人可以廉洁，懦弱的人可以自立。不只是能够实践仁义，还能辞却一切官爵俸禄。……这就是有助于风俗教化。)

I once said that those who truly understand the writings of Tao Yuanming would be able to resist the temptations of personal fame and gains, and overcome greedy or stingy inclinations. With such understanding, a corrupted person would seek to attain integrity, and a timid one to become self-reliant; people would not only practice benevolence, but also decline offers of any official positions and salaries... This is how moral cultivation can be promoted. (Xiao Tong: Preface to *Collection of Tao Yuanming's Works*)

风神 /fēngshén/
Vim and Vigor

指文学艺术作品的风采神韵。"风神"一词最初见于魏晋时期的人物品评，指风度神采，后引入文艺批评领域。唐代书法理论采用"风神"来形容书法作品的艺术特点，宋代姜夔（1155？—1209）《续书谱》的书论思想更是以"风神"为核心，他认为书法家的品行、师承、技艺、创新、纸笔等共同决定了作品的风采与神韵。文论中对于"风神"的运用，影响较大的是明代茅坤（1512—1601）的文章批评论。他以《史记》为"风神"典范，标举欧阳修（1007—1072）的文章具备"风神"之美，其评价标准注重叙事方面的条畅和情韵方面的感慨。

The term refers to vim and vigor found in a great work of art. It first emerged among comments on famed persons in the Wei and Jin period. Later, it was brought into the field of artistic criticism. The Tang Dynasty's theory on calligraphy adopted the term to describe the artistic features of a calligraphic work. In his essay titled "Subsequent Commentaries on Calligraphy," Jiang Kui (1155?-1209) of the Song Dynasty further argued, on the basis of the concept of "vim and vigor," that the merit of a calligraphic work is jointly determined by the calligrapher's moral character, origin of his style, skill, innovation and the kind of brush and paper he uses. The term gained its popularity when Ming Dynasty's Mao Kun (1512-1601) used it in his critical essays. He praised *Records of the Historian* as its classic example and spoke highly of Ouyang Xiu's (1007-1072) essays for their vim and vigor. His criterion was to see whether a smooth flow of narration was ensured and complicated nuances of feeling admirably expressed in an essay.

引例 Citations:

◎风神者，一须人品高，二须师法古，三须纸笔佳，四须险劲，五须高明，六须润泽，七须向背得宜，八须时出新意。(姜夔《续书谱》)

(书法作品的风神，一要求人品高尚，二要求学习古人，三要求纸笔优良，四要求奇险劲健，五要求高超明智，六要求圆润光泽，七要求笔势的相向与相背适宜，八要求时常写出新意。)

To achieve vim and vigor, a calligrapher should be morally cultivated, emulate master calligraphers of old times, gain access to quality brush and paper, be bold in his execution of strokes, have extra wisdom and skill, be smooth and finely polished, handle his strokes properly whether they proceed toward or away from each other, and often be innovative. (Jiang Kui: Subsequent Commentaries on Calligraphy)

◎西京以来，独称太史公迁，以其驰骤跌宕，悲慨呜咽，而风神所注，往往于点缀指次外，独得妙解，譬之览仙姬于潇湘洞庭之上，可望而不可近者。(茅坤《欧阳文忠公文钞引》)

(西汉以来，我唯独称赞太史公司马迁，因为他的文章纵横跌宕，悲慨呜咽，而文章中所蕴含的风神，往往在字句点缀指示之外，独得精妙的意旨，好比在潇水、湘江、洞庭湖之上看见仙子，可以远望而不可近距离接触。)

Of all the essayists since the Western Han Dynasty, I adore the Grand Historian Sima Qian most. His way of writing is compelling, heroic and deeply sorrowful. The majestic vigor of his essays often lies beyond words and rhetorical devices, holding a truly magical appeal. Like a fairy on the river Xiaohe, Xiangshui or Lake Dongting, it can be viewed from afar but never actually approached. (Mao Kun: A Preface to *Selected Works of Ouyang Xiu*)

风雅颂 /fēng-yǎ-sòng/
Ballad, Court Hymn, and Eulogy

《诗经》中依体裁与音乐对诗歌所分出的类型。"风（国风）"是不同地区的音乐，大部分是民歌；"雅"是宫廷宴享或朝会时的乐歌，分为"大雅"与"小雅"，大部分是贵族文人的作品；"颂"是宗庙祭祀用的舞曲歌辞，内容多是歌颂祖先的功业。"雅""颂"指雅正之音，而"国风"系民间乐歌，因此"风雅颂"既是《诗经》的体裁，同时也有高雅纯正的含义。"风雅"后来一般指典雅与高雅的事物。

In *The Book of Songs,* the content is divided into three categories according to style and tune: *feng* (ballad), *ya* (court hymn), and *song* (eulogy). Ballads are music from different regions, mostly folk songs. Court hymns, divided into *daya* (major hymn) and *xiaoya* (minor hymn), are songs sung at court banquets or grand ceremonies. They are mostly the works by lettered noblemen. Eulogies are ritual or sacrificial dance music and songs, most of which praise the achievements of ancestors. Court hymns and eulogies are highbrow songs while ballads are lowbrow ones. Therefore, ballads, court hymns, and eulogies not only refer to the styles of *The Book of Songs* but also indicate highbrow songs. Later on *fengya* （风雅） generally referred to anything elegant.

引例 Citations：

◎故《诗》有六义焉：一曰风，二曰赋，三曰比，四曰兴，五曰雅，六曰颂。(《毛诗序》)

(所以《诗经》有六项基本内容：即风、赋、比、兴、雅、颂。)

Therefore *The Book of Songs* has six basic elements: ballads, narratives, analogies, associations, court hymns, and eulogies. (Introductions to *Mao's Version of The Book of Songs*)

◎ "三经" 是赋、比、兴，是做诗底骨子，无诗不有，才无则不成诗。盖不是赋便是比，不是比便是兴。如风、雅、颂却是里面横弗 (chǎn) 底，都有赋、比、兴，故谓之 "三纬"。(《朱子语类》卷八十)

(《诗经》中的 "三经" 指赋、比、兴，是作诗的骨架，所有的诗都有，如果没有就不成诗。大概是没有赋就得有比，没有比就得有兴。像风、雅、颂在诗歌里面却起横向的贯穿作用，诗歌中都得有赋、比、兴，所以将风、雅、颂称为 "三纬"。)

The three "longitudes" of *The Book of Songs* refer to narrative, analogy, and association, which serve as the frame of a poem. Without these, they could not be called poems. If narrative is not used in a poem, analogy must be used; if analogy is not used, association must be employed. Ballads from the states, court hymns, and eulogies play a connecting role in the poems. Since the poems have narrative, analogy, and association serving as the "longitudes," ballads from the states, court hymns, and eulogies are therefore called the three "latitudes." (*Categorized Conversations of Master Zhu Xi*)

封禅 /fēngshàn/

Sacrificial Ceremony / An Ode to Sacrificial Ceremony

主要含义有二：其一，指古代帝王登上泰山，祭拜天地以报告成功、感谢天降祥瑞，同时刻石记功、向天下宣示受命于天的一种大典。其中在泰山顶上筑土为坛行祭天礼叫"封"，在梁父（fǔ）或云云等小山上辟除场地行祭地礼叫"禅"。传说中三皇五帝、禹、汤、周武王（？—前1043）等都举行了封禅，秦以后只有秦始皇（前259—前210）、汉武帝（前156—前87）、汉光武帝（前5—公元57）等在泰山举行封禅大典。其二，指封禅文，是古代劝告帝王封禅或记录封禅大典、歌颂功德的一种文体。由西汉司马相如（前179？—前118）创制。南朝刘勰（465？—520？或532？）指出，封禅文作为一个时代的典章，体制庄重宏大、气势壮阔，应当纪事可靠、说理清晰、文辞典雅。为了歌颂帝王的伟大和天地的神奇，封禅文作者要从浩瀚典籍中选用古雅而不晦涩的词语，或者采用新颖而不肤浅的词语，要竭尽想象力和夸饰之能事。封禅文后来演变为庆典致辞以及记录各类庆典活动的文章。遵循刘勰提出的要求写作，庆典文章可以体现一个单位、地区乃至国家的精神与气度，而优秀的庆典致辞或记录庆典的诗文，也有可能成为代表时代水准的大手笔。

This term has two meanings. One is a grand sacrificial ceremony held in ancient times by an emperor after ascending to the top of Mount Taishan to pay tribute to heaven and earth, announce his achievements, thank gods for having brought him and his people good fortune, and inscribe his achievements on a huge stone. He performed this ceremony to declare to the world that his power was bestowed by Heaven. A heaven-worshipping ceremony was held on an earthen terrace on the top of Mount Taishan. An earth-worshipping ceremony was held on a clearing on the Liangfu or the Yunyun Hill near Mount Taishan. According to legend, the Three Sovereigns and the Five Emperors, hero Yu who brought floods under control, King Tang of the Shang Dynasty, King Wu of the Zhou Dynasty (?-1043 BC) all held such ceremonies during their reigns. After the founding of the Qin Dynasty, only the First Emperor of Qin (259-210 BC), Emperor Wu of the Western Han Dynasty (156-87 BC), Emperor Guangwu of the Eastern Han Dynasty (5 BC-AD 57) and several other emperors held such ceremonies on Mount Taishan.

The other meaning of this term is an ode composed to urge the emperor to hold such a sacrificial ceremony or to record its actual process if a sacrificial ceremony was held to extol his achievements. Such an ode was first written by Sima Xiangru (179?-118 BC) of the Western Han Dynasty. Liu Xie (465?-520? or 532?) of the Southern Dynasties held that the ode, as a declaration of royal achievement in its era, should be solemn, grand, factual, eloquent and graceful. To extol an emperor's greatness and the miraculous power of heaven and earth, the author should select old yet lucid words from the classics, or use new words rich in implication. He should give free rein to his imagination. Sacrificial odes later became standard commemorative speeches. Liu Xie's requirements, when observed, may help boost the image or morale of a company, a governmental or cultural institution, a region or even the whole country. Good ceremonial speeches, poems or essays can become representative writings of a particular era.

引例 Citations：

◎伏惟相如《封禅》，靡而不典；扬雄《美新》，典而亡（wú）实，然皆游扬后世，垂为旧式。（班固《典引》）

（我想到司马相如的《封禅》，细密而不够典雅；扬雄的《剧秦美新》，典雅而不够切实。不过它们都传扬于后世，成为典范。）

Sima Xiangru's "The Sacrificial Ceremony" is well-structured yet not sufficiently graceful. Yang Xiong's "The Tyrannical Qin and the Benevolent New Regime" is graceful yet not sufficiently factual. However, both of these writings have been passed down for generations as classics. (Ban Gu: A Commentary on Sacrificial Ceremonies)

◎兹文为用，盖一代之典章也。构位之始，宜明大体：树骨于训

典之区，选言于宏富之路，使意古而不晦于深，文今而不坠于浅，义吐光芒，辞成廉锷，则为伟矣。（刘勰《文心雕龙·封禅》）

（封禅这种文体的意义，堪称一个时代的典章。在构思文章之始，应当先把握它的基本要领：要学习《尚书》中的训典来建立文章的骨干，要从宏伟富丽的作品中选择文辞，使文意古雅而不深奥，用语新颖而不浮浅，内容绽放光彩，文辞展露锋芒，就可称得上杰出作品了。）

An ode to sacrificial ceremony is representative of an era. Before committing one's thought to paper, one should grasp its essence. He should draw upon the tenets of *The Book of History* to develop the basic structure of the writing and the terms from the masterpieces of old times to enrich the expressions, thus making his writing refined yet understandable, novel yet not superficial. If an ode to sacrificial ceremony is appealing in content and grand in style, it will be truly a great work. (Liu Xie: *The Literary Mind and the Carving of Dragons*)

讽咏 /fěngyǒng/
Chanting with Feeling

指的是中国古代阅读、欣赏诗歌的方法。讽，是抑扬顿挫地诵读；咏，指的是吟唱、歌唱。"讽咏"合起来就是指，诗歌要通过反复诵读、吟唱，逐渐感受其节奏、声韵，揣摩其内涵、情感，进而把握作者的作诗用意，甚至产生自己的见解。讽咏的方法，与中国古代诗歌具有较强的音乐性密切相关，不仅可以抑扬顿挫地诵读，而且可以用一定的旋律吟唱出来。

This term refers to the proper way of appreciating classic Chinese poetry in ancient times. Specifically, when reading a poem aloud, it was supposed to intone a poem with cadence; namely, by following a pattern of rising and falling tones with pauses in between. Through repeated chanting and recitals, they captured the rhythm, rhyme, hidden meaning and sentiment of the poem and finally understood the core message conveyed by the author. On that basis, they might even be able to form an interpretation of their own. Chanting played a vital role in poetic appreciation largely due to the musicality of classic Chinese poetry. Readers not only read cadence but sang melodiously as well.

引例 Citations：

◎先须熟读《楚词》，朝夕讽咏，以为之本……以李、杜二集枕藉观之，如今人之治经，然后博取盛唐名家，酝酿胸中，久之自然悟入。(严羽《沧浪诗话·诗辨》)

(先要熟读《楚辞》，每天早晚诵读、吟唱，以此作为基础……将李白、杜甫的诗集放在枕席边随时阅读，就像今人研读经书一样，而后再广泛阅读盛唐时期的名家作品，在心里反复揣摩体会，时间长了自然就会领悟。)

First of all, one should make it a basic practice to learn the *Odes of Chu* by chanting and singing the odes every morning... and place the collected poems of Li Bai and Du Fu beside one's pillow for the convenience of reading at any time, just as scholars of today study non-poetic classics. After that, he should widely read renowned works of the flourishing period of the Tang Dynasty. When he has ruminates on those poems, he will naturally become enlightened. (Yan Yu: *Canglang's Criticism on Poetry*)

◎曰国风，曰雅颂。号四诗, 当讽咏。(《三字经》)

(《诗经》中的《国风》和《大雅》《小雅》及《颂》，加在一起叫做"四诗"，应该经常诵读、吟唱。)

The "Ballads from the States," "Major Court Hymns," "Minor Court Hymns" and "Eulogies" from *The Book of Songs*, the four are collectively known as "the Four Poems." They are meant to be chanted and sung frequently. (*Three-character Classic*)

讽谕 /fěngyù/

Subtle Admonition

指文学作品借用一定事例或思想，含蓄婉转地向统治者传达民情民风、批评时政，从而使统治者能够接受讽谏，革除弊政。"讽"是指讽谏、劝诫，要求诗文中的批评语言含蓄婉转；"谕"是晓谕、表明，文章主旨最终要归结为劝鉴、批评。也就是说，它实际包含密不可分的两方面：一是文学的表达方式（"讽"要婉转含蓄），二是文学的社会功能（"晓谕"统治者）。"讽谕说"由汉代学者解释《诗经》时总结提出，儒家以此倡导文学对朝廷教化和社会民风的干预作用，将其视为文学的特殊使命。唐代诗人白居易（772—846）大量创作讽谕诗，强化诗歌创作的社会功能，推进了这一文学传统，对后世文学创作影响很大。

The term refers to the use of allegories to convey popular mood and public opinion and make critical comments on state affairs to the ruler in a tactful manner in the hope to persuade him to correct wrong policies. *Feng* (讽) represents making critical but persuasive comments subtly through poetry or prose; *yu* (喻) means delivering an explicit message. Such literary writing is intended to be both critical and persuasive; and it has two integral aspects, namely, a subtle literary way of expression as required by *feng*, and its social function of sending explicit messages to the ruler as required. The theory of subtle admonition was advocated by scholars of the Han Dynasty based on their interpretation of *The Book of Songs*. Confucian scholars from then on promoted the use of subtle admonition to influence decision-making of the ruler and social mores in a literary way. Bai Juyi (772 - 846), a poet of the Tang Dynasty, wrote many such poems, further reinforcing the social function of poetry and advancing this literary tradition, which had great impact on literary creation of later generations.

引例 Citations:

◎或以抒下情而通讽谕，或以宣上德而尽忠孝。（班固《两都赋序》）

（有些作品表达臣民的思想感情同时也希望由此将其中的讽喻传达给君王，有些作品则是宣扬君主的恩德同时引导臣民克尽忠孝义务。）

Some literary works use subtle admonition to convey what the subjects think and feel, in the hope that the subtle advice could reach the ruler, whereas other works expound the kindness and benevolence of the ruler so as to guide the populace to fulfilling their duties and obligations. (Ban Gu: Preface to "Essays on Chang'an and Luoyang")

◎古之为文者，上以纫王教，系国风；下以存炯戒，通讽谕。（白居易《策林·六八·议文章》）

（古人写文章，往大了说是为了阐明朝廷教化与社会民风的关联，往小了说是保存谏戒、传达讽喻。）

Writings by ancient scholars could be said that at a higher level they aimed at explaining some kind of link between the ideas of the ruling court and popular sentiment in society. At a more practical level, they sent a clear message of advice to the rulers through allegories. (Bai Juyi: *Collection of Essays in Preparation for the Final Round of the Imperial Examination*)

芙蓉出水 /fúróng-chūshuǐ/
Lotus Rising Out of Water

美丽的荷花从水中生长出来。形容清新、淡雅、自然之美，与"错彩镂金"的修饰之美构成对比。魏晋六朝时崇尚自然，与这种审美理想一致，在艺术创作方面，人们欣赏像"芙蓉出水"一般的天然清新的风格，注重主观意趣的自然呈现，反对过分雕琢修饰。

The term of lotus rising out of water describes a scene of freshness, quiet refinement and natural beauty, in contrast to "gilded and colored" embellishments.

During the Wei and Jin dynasties, people valued nature and favored this aesthetic view. In their artistic creations, they pursued the natural and fresh style like lotus rising out of water. They sought natural presentation of their ideas and were opposed to excessive ornamentation.

引例 Citations：

◎谢诗如芙蓉出水，颜如错彩镂金。（钟嵘《诗品》卷中）

（谢灵运的诗清新自然，像荷花出水；颜延之的诗歌修饰雕琢，像涂绘彩色、雕镂金银。）

Xie Lingyun's poems are natural and refreshing like lotus rising out of water, whereas Yan Yanzhi's poems are elegantly embellished, like gilding an object and adding colors to it. (Zhong Rong: *The Critique of Poetry*)

◎清水出芙蓉，天然去雕饰。（李白《经乱离后天恩流夜郎忆旧游书怀赠江夏韦太守良宰》）

（从清水中生长出的荷花，自然天成没有雕饰。）

It is like a lotus rising out of clear water: natural and without embellishment. (Li Bai: To Wei Liangzai, the Governor of Jiangxia, Written While Thinking of My Friends on My Way into Exile at Yelang Following the War)

赋比兴 /fù-bǐ-xìng/
Narrative, Analogy, and Association

《诗经》创作的三种表现手法。"赋"是铺陈事物直接叙述；"比"是类比；"兴"是先言他物以引出所咏之词，有两层含义，一是即兴感发，二是在感发时借客观景物婉转地表达出某种思想感情。"赋比兴"为汉代儒家所总结和提出，后来演变为中国古代文学创作的基本原则和方法。

These are the three ways of expression employed in *The Book of Songs*: a narrative is a direct reference to an object or an event, an analogy metaphorically likens one thing to another, and an association is an impromptu expression of a feeling, a mood or a thought, or using an objective thing as metaphor for sensibilities. Confucian scholars of the Han Dynasty summarized and formulated this concept of narrative, analogy, and association, which later became the basic principle and method in classical Chinese literary creation.

引例 Citation：

◎赋、比、兴是《诗》之所用，风、雅、颂是《诗》之成形。(《毛诗序》孔颖达正义)

(赋、比、兴是《诗经》创作的三种手法，风、雅、颂是《诗经》体制上的定型。)

In *The Book of Songs,* narrative, analogy, and association are three techniques in its creation, whereas ballad, court hymn, and eulogy represent three established styles of the poems. (Kong Yingda: Correct Meaning of "Introductions to *Mao's Version of The Book of Songs*")

感物 /gǎnwù/
Sensed Externalities

指人为外物所触动产生了创作冲动，经过构思与艺术加工，形成为文艺作品。"物"指直观可感的自然景物、生活场景。古人认为创作缘起于外界事物的感召而激起了创作欲望，文艺作品是外物与主观相结合的产物。这一术语强调了文艺创作源于生活的基本理念。

A person's creative impulse is triggered by one or more externalities, and after conceptualization and artistic treatment, this results in a work of art. Such externalities include both natural sights and scenes from life which can be directly sensed. Ancient Chinese believed that creation resulted from externalities which evoked a desire to create, and that works of art and literature were the result of combining externalities with subjective thinking. This term emphasizes the fundamental idea that artistic creation is rooted in life.

引例 Citations：

◎凡音之起，由人心生也。人心之动，物使之然也。感于物而动，故形于声。(《礼记·乐记》)

(一切音乐都起源于人的内心。人的内心之所以产生活动，是受到外物感发的结果。人受外物的感发而产生内心活动，所以会通过音乐表达出来。)

All music originates in people's hearts. Feelings arise in people's hearts because externalities cause them to do so. Hearts are moved by externalities, hence they express themselves through music. (*The Book of Rites*)

◎人禀七情，应物斯感，感物吟志，莫非自然。(刘勰《文心雕龙·明诗》)

(人具有喜、怒、哀、惧、爱、恶、欲等七种情感，受到外物的刺激而心有所感，心有所感而吟咏情志，所有的诗歌都出于自然情感。)

People have the seven emotions of joy, anger, sadness, fear, love, loathing and desire. He expresses his feelings and aspirations in a poetical way when he is stimulated by the external world and his heart is touched. All poems come from natural emotions. (Liu Xie: *The Literary Mind and the Carving of Dragons*)

高古 /gāogǔ/

Unadorned Antiquity

高远古朴，高雅简古。用于文艺批评，主要指文艺作品中所体现出的意蕴高远古朴、情志高雅，凝重而又深具历史感的艺术风格。"高"体现对空间的超越，不落于现实的具体事物，思想、情感和意愿超然时事和世俗之外；"古"体现对时间的超越，神驰于久远的历史，有拙朴、古雅、凝重的意蕴。"高"和"古"合成一个术语，旨在淡化和超越时代的印记和现实的痕迹，追求一种连接古今、引人追攀又难以企及的意境。它有时也指高人雅士独具的一种人格境界。

This term describes the quality of loftiness or primitive simplicity, and is used primarily in literary criticism to refer to an ancient nobility, an aspiration or sentiment, or an artistic style of historical gravity. "Loftiness" here suggests transcending the limitation of space, not being tied down by concrete objects, and thoughts, moods or wishes staying aloof from current affairs and worldly conventions. "Primitive simplicity" here means breaking loose from the confinement of time and traveling back to the remote past. It also implies an unadorned antiquity or austere dignity. By combining these two concepts, the term aims to weaken the imprint of its time and to transcend the bounds of reality, reaching for a normally unattainable realm linking the present to the past. Sometimes, this term is also used to refer to an elevated state of being attained by noble-minded persons.

引例 Citations：

◎畸（qí）人乘真，手把芙蓉。泛彼浩劫，窅（yǎo）然空纵（踪）。月出东斗，好风相从。太华夜碧，人闻清钟。虚伫神素，脱然畦封。黄唐在独，落落玄宗。（司空图《二十四诗品·高古》）

（不同凡俗的人驾御真气，手持莲花升上天界；渡离人间无边劫难，渺然不见其踪影。月亮从东方升起，伴随着清风飞行。华山的夜色葱茏，人们听闻清越的钟声。心灵清虚纯净，超然尘世之外。独自慕尚纯朴的太古时代，洒脱守持道家玄妙的宗旨。）

A man of noble character, with total control over his vital energies, rises up to the heavenly domain, lotus flower in hand. He thus departs from this bitter world of life, making himself totally invisible. The moon rises from the east, sailing across the sky in a fresh breeze. As night falls, darkness closes in on Mount Hua. Clear sounds of bells can be heard. Tranquility reigns deep within, lifting the soul above mortal chaos. This man, in solitary admiration of the charming rusticity of prehistorical times, obeys the profoundly mystical Daoist principle with perfect ease. (Sikong Tu: Twenty-four Styles of Poetry)

◎惟阮籍《咏怀》之作，极为高古，有建安风骨。（严羽《沧浪诗话·诗评》）

（只有阮籍的《咏怀》诗，极显高远古朴的特色，具有建安诗歌的风采骨力。）

Only Ruan Ji's group of poems "Meditations" display an unadorned antiquity, imbued with the vigorous and forceful features of the poetry of the Jian'an period. (Yan Yu: *Canglang's Criticism on Poetry*)

◎汉人诗文，存于今者，无不高古浑朴。（章学诚《文史通义·内篇五·妇学篇书后》）

（汉代人所作的诗文，凡是流传至今的，无不显得高远古雅、浑厚质朴。）

Prose and poetry by Han Dynasty authors, so long as they have survived to this day, all show a lofty adherence to an unadorned antiquity and a charming rusticity. (Zhang Xuecheng: *General Principles of History*)

歌 /gē/

Song

　　一种篇幅短小、可以吟唱的韵文作品，是集文学、音乐甚至是舞蹈于一体的可以歌唱的文学艺术创作形式。在中国古代，歌与诗的区别是："歌"能入乐歌唱，"诗"通常不入乐歌唱。广义的歌包括了童谣、民谣；狭义的歌与谣有所区别：有固定曲调和音乐伴奏的是歌，没有固定曲调的清唱为谣。歌大多为民间创作的民歌，如汉乐府《长歌行》、北朝民歌《敕勒歌》等；也有小部分是由文士等个人创作的作品，如刘邦（前256或前247—前195）的《大风歌》、李白（701—762）的《子夜吴歌》等。"歌"属于中国古代诗歌艺术的早期形态，古人一般将其归入乐府诗，现在则与诗合称"诗歌"。

Songs are a kind of short, rhyming composition. It is a form of artistic creation combining literature, music, and even dance which can be sung. The difference between songs and poems in ancient China is that the former could be made into music and sung, whereas the latter could not. In a broad sense, the term includes children's ballads and folk ballads. In a narrow sense, songs and ballads are different. Songs have a fixed melody and musical accompaniment, while ballads do not. Songs were created mostly by folk musicians, such as "A Slow Song" of the Han Dynasty and the folk song "Song of the Chile" of the Northern Dynasties. A small number of songs, however, were written by members of the literati, like "Ode to the Great Wind" by Liu Bang (256 or 247 - 195 BC) and "The Midnight Melody of the Land of Wu" by Li Bai (701 - 762). Songs are one of the early forms of ancient Chinese poetic art and were generally classified as *yuefu* (乐府) poetry in ancient China. In modern times, they are called poetic songs as a part of poetry.

引例 Citation：

◎曲合乐曰歌，徒歌曰谣。(《诗经·魏风·园有桃》毛传）

（配上曲调、有音乐伴奏的叫做"歌"，没有固定曲调的清唱叫做"谣"。）

Words sung with the accompaniment of music are called songs, and mere singing and chanting are called ballads. (*Mao's Annotations on The Book of Songs*)

歌行体 /gēxíngtǐ/
Poetic Song

一种由汉魏六朝乐府诗发展而来的诗歌体裁，它的文体特点是篇幅较长，善于抒情写景，句式多变，没有严格的格律要求，形式采用五言、七言、杂言的古体，富于变化。南朝鲍照（414？—466）在学习民歌基础之上，创立了歌行体，唐代李白（701—762）、白居易（772—846）等也常用歌行体创作。

Poetic songs were developed from the officially collected folk ballads and songs of the Han, Wei and the Six Dynasties. They are characterized by great length, bold expression of feeling, diverse sentence patterns and laxity of the requirements of metrical forms. They followed the classic forms of five characters to a line, seven characters to a line and a mixed pattern in a flexible manner. This genre was established by Southern Dynasty poet Bao Zhao (414?-466) who drew inspiration from folk songs. Tang Dynasty poets Li Bai (701-762) and Bai Juyi (772-846) also wrote poems in such style.

引例 Citations：

◎其放情长言、杂而无方者曰歌；步骤驰骋，疏而不滞者曰行；兼之曰歌行。（徐师曾《文体明辨序说·乐府》）

（那些尽情长咏、句式杂而不拘格律叫做"歌"；缓急自由，曲调稍缓但很流畅叫做"行"；二者兼而有之叫做"歌行"。）

Ge (歌 singing) refers to long chanting and offers lines of varying lengths unrestrained by metrical rules; *xing* (行 smooth-flowing) refers to chanting that freely and fluently accelerates or decelerates. If both *ge* and *xing* are involved, it is termed *gexing* (歌行 free and flowing chanting or poetic song). (Xu Shizeng: *A Collection of Introductory Remarks on Various Styles*)

◎歌行则放情长言，古诗则循守法度，故其句语格调亦不能同也。
（吴讷《文章辨体序说·古诗》）

（歌行就是尽情长咏，古体诗则需要遵循一定规则，因此二者的句式、用语、体制、曲调也会有所不同。）

Gexing refers to chanting poetry in a free, flowing and unrestrained manner, as opposed to adhering meticulously to the standard guidelines of classic poetry. Thus, the sentence patterns, phrasing, metrical schemes and tonal effects of these two types of poetry end up being different to some extent. (Wu Ne: *Collected Prefaces for Different Types of Writing*)

格 /gé/

Examine / Study

对人、事、物的考量与推究。是儒家提出的获得正确认识、培养道德良知的途径，具有方法论的意义。"格"亦有规范、准则的意思。用于人物品评，则指人的道德水平和思想境界，即人格。用于文艺批评，主要有三重含义：其一，指诗文写作的基本要求和方法；其二，指作品的品位、品格与境界；其三，指作品的体制、组织结构，是内容特色和形式特征相统一而呈现出的整体格局，仍不离衡量作品水准这一核心意义。

This term means to study or examine things, people or any phenomenon. It is an approach developed by Confucian scholars to help people obtain accurate assessments of things around them and to cultivate morals and ethics, as a kind of methodology. Sometimes the term is used as a noun to refer to a standard or criterion. When the term is used to assess a person's qualifications, it refers to his moral quality which is to say, a person's personality or moral integrity, as well as attainments in learning. In literary criticism, it has three connotations: first of all, it refers to the basic requirements and methods for poem or prose writing; second, it refers to the taste, style, and literary attainment; third, it is about the overall structure of a literary work or how the form and content are integrated. All in all, the term refers to the criteria applied in judging a literary work.

引例 Citations：

◎致知在格物，物格而后知至。(《礼记·大学》)

（获得真知的途径在于推究事实与现象，穷尽事物方方面面的道理，而后才得到真知。）

To study and analyze facts and phenomena is the right approach to obtain knowledge; the truth can only be obtained after facts and phenomena are thoroughly examined and analyzed. (*The Book of Rites*)

◎唐之晚年，诗人无复李、杜豪放之格，然亦务以精意相高。(欧阳修《六一诗话》)

（到了晚唐，诗人们难以再现李杜诗歌那样奔放宏大的境界，但也一定要以构思精巧而一争高下。）

In the late Tang Dynasty, poets no longer possessed the bold, heroic qualities of their predecessors Li Bai and Du Fu. Nonetheless they still competed with each other with regard to the depth of thought and literary refinement. (Ouyang Xiu: *Ouyang Xiu's Criticism of Poetry*)

◎诗之要，有曰格，曰意、曰趣而已。格以辨其体，意以达其情，趣以臻其妙也。(高启《〈独庵集〉序》)

（作诗的关键在于"格"（格局）、"意"（意蕴）和"趣"（趣味）。"格"可以判断其风格体式是否雅正，"意"则是察看其是否表达了真情实感，而"趣"则是衡量其是否达到精妙的境界。）

Structure, content, and appeal are the essentials of poetry. Its structure will reflect the poetic form; its content will convey emotion; and its appeal will determine whether it has achieved a high level of artistry. (Gao Qi: Preface to *Collected Works of Du'an*)

格调 /gédiào/
Form and Melody

指诗歌的体制声调，包括思想旨趣和声律形式两方面，涉及诗歌批评的品味与境界。"格"指诗歌的体制合乎规范，"调"指诗歌的声调韵律。唐宋时期的一些诗论家倡导格调，意在确立诗歌的雅正标准。明清以后的格调说，多强调作品应符合儒家正统思想，这影响了诗人的情感表达与艺术创作。"格调"后来也用到其他文艺领域。

The term refers to the form and metrical patterns, as well as content, of poetry. It relates to artistic taste and appeal in poetry criticism. *Ge* (格) refers to the need to satisfy established metrical rules, while *diao* (调) refers to the need to follow tone and rhyme schemes in poetry. Some poetry critics of the Tang and Song dynasties stressed the importance of form and melody in order to establish a set of elegant and authoritative standards for poetry. Theory on form and melody in the Ming and Qing dynasties often emphasized the importance for poets to abide by Confucian orthodoxy, thus constraining their expression of feelings and artistic creations. The term was later also used in discussions of other forms of art.

引例 Citations：

◎高古者格，宛亮者调。（李梦阳《驳何氏论文书》）

（高雅古朴就是"格"，婉曲清亮就是"调"。）

To be elegant and unaffected is to satisfy the requirements of form; to be tuneful and resonant is to follow the rules of melody. (Li Mengyang: *Arguments Against He Jingming's Views*)

◎白石词以清虚为体，而时有阴冷处，格调最高。（陈廷焯《白雨斋词话》卷二）

（姜夔的词以清新虚空为主要特色，虽然有时有凄清冷寂的地方，但格调最高。）

Jiang Kui's poems are characterized by ethereal purity. Though tinged with loneliness and sadness at times, they are of high standard and taste. (Chen Tingzhuo: *Remarks on Ci Poetry from White Rain Studio*)

隔 / 不隔 /gé / bùgé/
Disharmony / Harmony

　　"隔"指诗文抒情写景不够真切自然，情与景若即若离，让读者产生违和、难以代入的阅读感受；"不隔"指诗文写景抒情真切自然，给读者带来宛如亲见亲历的审美感受。由王国维（1877—1927）在《人间词话》中提出。它传承了古代文艺家以自然为美、注重阅读感受的理念，也受到西方艺术直觉论的影响。直觉关乎艺术经验和心理习惯，有关这对范畴的讨论，表明中西文艺美学思想开始接轨。

"Disharmony" here means an insincere articulation of feeling or an unnatural depiction of scenery. This happens when there is a lack of complete blend of feeling and scenery, causing readers to feel at odds, or unable to identify, with what they are reading. "Harmony," on the other hand, means a true expression of feeling or a natural depiction of scenery, creating an aesthetic feeling of "being right there to witness." This pair of contrasting terms was first used by Wang Guowei (1877-1927) in his critical work *Poetic Remarks in the Human World*, where he combines the appreciation of natural beauty and the emphasis on the reading experience favored by ancient China's literati along with the influence of Western notions of artistic intuition. Intuition relates to artistic experience and psychological habit, and discussion of this pair of opposites shows the convergence of Chinese and Western literary aesthetic thought.

引例 Citations：

◎因采菊而见山，境与意会，此句最有妙处。近岁俗本皆作"望南山"，则此一篇神气都索然矣。（苏轼《东坡题跋·题渊明〈饮酒〉诗后》）

（因采摘菊花而看到南山，随意而见的景与悠然自得的心情相通，"见南山"一句最有妙味。近年通行的刻本都写作"望南山"，那全诗的神韵就都索然了。）

While picking chrysanthemums beneath the eastern fence the poet sees the southern mountains – a harmony between the idyllic scenery his eyes casually fall on and a sense of leisurely contentment. "I see the southern mountains" is a most wonderful phrase. However, in recent block-printed editions this has been changed to "I survey the southern mountains" which takes away the charm of the entire poem. (Su Shi: *A Collection of Su Dongpo's Prefaces and Postscripts*)

◎文以意为主，辞以达意而已。古之文不尚虚饰，因事遣辞，形吾心之所欲言者耳，间（jiàn）有心之所不能言者，而能形之于文，斯亦文之至乎？（赵秉文《〈竹溪先生文集〉引》）

（文章以意蕴为主，言辞能够表达意思就可以了。古人的文章不崇尚无意义的修饰，都是根据内容遣词造句，表达我心中想要表达的，偶尔心中有难以用语言传达的意思，但能用文辞表达出来，这也算是达到写作的最高境界了吧？）

It suffices for an essay to convey its author's meaning with well-chosen words. Ancient men of letters disdained empty rhetoric. They chose their words and constructed sentences on the basis of content, free from unnecessary modifiers. Even though they found it hard, once in a while, to articulate themselves effectively, so long as they could lay bare their hearts in words, it was to be the highest attainment in writing. (Zhao Bingwen: A Preface to *Selected Works of Dang Huaiying*)

公安派 /Gōng'ān pài/
The Gong'an School of Literary Writing

明代后期以湖北公安作家袁宗道（1560—1600）、袁宏道（1568—1610）和袁中道（1570—1626）三兄弟为代表的文学流派。其中以袁宏道声誉最高、成就最大，其次是袁中道，袁宗道又次之。他们提倡"独抒性灵"，反对明代前期一些文士的拟古风气，以"趣"作为文学作品的批评标准，主张文章写作发自内心真情，从胸臆自然流出，不必拘泥于特定的法则。他们的文学成就主要表现在散文、诗歌方面，擅长写闲情逸致。公安派对于民间文学持包容和肯定态度，主张从通俗文学中吸取营养。这一流派的文学主张，在一定程度上反映出明代中期兴起的市民阶层的审美趣味。

This was a literary school represented by three brothers, namely Yuan Zongdao (1560-1600), Yuan Hongdao (1568-1610) and Yuan Zhongdao (1570-1626), who lived in Gong'an, Hubei Province, in late Ming times. Of the trio, Yuan Hongdao was the most accomplished and renowned. Next was Yuan Zhongdao, who in turn outshined his brother Yuan Zongdao. They advocated giving full expression to one's inner self and so opposed some early-Ming men of letters' soulless emulation of ancient literature. They also advocated genuine interest or concern as the criterion for literary criticism, stating that writing should flow forth from one's heart and not be constrained by particular regulations and formulae. Putting their efforts mainly in prose and poetry, they paid particular attention to writing in a leisurely and carefree

中华思想文化术语
文艺卷

mood. The Gong'an School accepted and appreciated folk literature and stressed the need for writers to draw sustenance from vernacular literature. This attitude reflected to some degree the aesthetic tastes of the newly-emerging urban middle class during the mid-Ming period.

引例 Citation：

◎先是，王、李之学盛行，袁氏兄弟独心非之。宗道在馆中，与同馆黄辉力排其说。于唐好白乐天，于宋好苏轼，名其斋曰"白苏"。至宏道，益矫以清新轻俊，学者多舍王、李而从之，目为公安体。(《明史·文苑传·袁宏道》)

（刚开始时，王世贞与李梦阳等人的诗学盛行，唯独袁氏兄弟不以为然，袁宗道在学馆教书时，与同事黄辉竭力反对王、李之学。他们推崇唐代白居易、宋代苏轼的文学创作，袁宗道还以"白苏"来命名自己的书斋。到了袁宏道，越发以清新轻俊的文风来矫正模仿古人的风气，于是学习诗文的人大多舍弃王世贞、李梦阳而追随"三袁"，被称为"公安体"。）

When the theories of poetry advocated by Wang Shizhen and Li Mengyang first flourished throughout the literary community, the Yuan brothers showed reservations about them. Yuan Zongdao, together with his colleague Huang Hui, vehemently opposed Wang and Li's theories. They favored the works of the Tang Dynasty poet Bai Juyi and Song Dynasty writer Su Shi. Yuan Zongdao even applied the name "Bai-Su" for his studio. Yuan Hongdao, in his turn, tried especially hard to rectify the prevalent emulation of old literary styles with his refreshing, innovative way of writing. Thereupon, most literary men abandoned Wang Shizhen and Li Mengyang in favor of the "Three Yuans." Hence comes the term "Gong'an style." (*The History of the Ming Dynasty*)

宫调 /gōngdiào/

Gongdiao (Musical Modes)

中国传统乐学将调式与音高结合，划分、命名音乐类型并描述其特性的基本理论。以宫、商、角、变徵、徵、羽、变宫等七声或其中五声、六声音阶中任何一声为主音，与其他乐音按一定的音程关系（相隔若干音度）组织在一起，均可构成一种调式，其中以宫声为主的调式称"宫"，以其他各声为主者称"调"。七种调式与黄钟、大吕等十二律相配，理论上可配得十二宫七十二调，共为八十四宫调。但在实际音乐中并不全用，如唐宋燕乐只用七宫，每宫四调，共有二十八宫调；南宋词曲音乐用七宫十二调；元代北曲用六宫十一调，南曲用五宫四调；明清以来，最常用者不过五宫四调。有些乐论家对不同宫调所表达的感情特点和适用场合做了规定。宫调理论对于词曲、戏剧、音乐创作具有指导和规范作用，可以运用于古代乐谱翻译，是中国艺术研究的一个重要课题。

Classical Chinese music theory combined tone and pitch to classify and name different types of music, as well as to describe their characteristics. The seven notes are known as *gong* (宫 corresponding to 1 in the numbered musical notation), *shang* (商 corresponding to 2), *jue* (角 corresponding to 3), *bianzhi* (变徵 corresponding to 4), *zhi* (徵 corresponding to 5), *yu* (羽 corresponding to 6) and *biangong* (变宫 corresponding to 7). Any one of them can be used as a major tune along with other notes set in particular intervals to form a mode. The mode with *gong* as the major note is called *gong*, the mode with the rest of the notes as major ones are called *diao*. The seven modes with the accompaniment of 12 temperaments can theoretically have 12 *gongs* and 72 *diaos*, altogether 84 modes of music. However, in practical music, not all the *gongs* and *diaos* were used. Only seven *gongs* with each having four tunes (all together 28 modes of music) were used for imperial court music in the Tang and Song dynasties. Seven *gongs* and 12 *diaos* were used for music to go along with poems in the Southern Song Dynasty. In the Yuan Dynasty, six *gongs* and 11 *diaos* were used for Northern music, and five *gongs* and four *diaos* were used for Southern music. In the Ming and Qing dynasties, only five *gongs* and four *diaos* were often used. Some music critics made rules for different *gongs* and *diaos* to be used for music for different occasions according to their characteristics. The theory of *gongdiao* played a role of direction and regulation in music creation for poems and operas and can be used to translate ancient music. It is an important subject for the study of ancient Chinese art.

引例 Citation：

◎凡《大雅》皆宫调曲，《小雅》皆徵调曲，《周》《鲁》二颂皆羽调曲。十五《国风》皆角调曲。周诗三百篇通不用商调，惟《商颂》五篇则皆商调耳。（朱载堉《乐律全书》卷七下）

（《诗经》中凡是《大雅》用的都是宫调的音乐，《小雅》用的都是徵调的音乐，《周颂》和《鲁颂》用的都是羽调的音乐，而十五《国风》用的都是角调的音乐。周代时《诗经》中有三百篇用的都不是商调，只有《商颂》的五篇用的都是商调。）

In *The Book of Songs*, "Major Court Hymns" are all in the *gong* mode, "Minor Court Hymns" all in the *zhi* mode, "Eulogies of Zhou" and "Eulogies of Lu" in the *yu* mode, and "Ballads" from the fifteen states all in the *jue* mode. Of all the works in *The Book of Songs* in the Zhou Dynasty, only "Eulogies of Shang," altogether five pieces, use the *shang* mode. (Zhu Zaiyu: *A Collection of Writings on Music and Calendar*)

古文运动 /gǔwén yùndòng/
Classical Prose Movement

指唐代中期至北宋时期提倡用古文创作的文学革新运动。其特点是反对六朝以来的骈文创作，兼有思想运动和社会运动的性质。这一运动的代表者，有唐代的韩愈（768 — 824）、柳宗元（773 —

819），以及宋代的欧阳修（1007 — 1072）、苏洵（1009 — 1066）、王安石（1021 — 1086）、曾巩（1019 — 1083）、苏轼（1037 — 1101）、苏辙（1039 — 1112）等人。"古文"相对于"骈文"而言，这一概念由韩愈最先提出，指先秦两汉的散文，其特点是句式长短不限，不追求声律和对偶，在内容上注重表达思想、反映现实生活。"骈文"指六朝以来讲究排偶、辞藻、声律、典故的文体。骈文中虽有优秀作品，但大多形式僵化、内容空虚。韩愈倡导继承两汉的文学传统，文以明道，得到了柳宗元等人的大力支持并形成声势浩大的"古文运动"。韩愈提倡古文的实质是将改革文风与复兴儒学道统结合起来，把文章写作引向为政教服务。但骈文并未就此绝迹，晚唐以后还在流行。北宋欧阳修凭借其政治地位，大力提倡古文，他的同辈苏洵，学生王安石、曾巩、苏轼、苏辙，苏轼门下又有黄庭坚（1045 — 1105）、陈师道（1053 — 1102）、张耒（1054 — 1114）、秦观（1049 — 1100）、晁补之（1053 — 1110）等人，都是古文能手，各树旗帜，最终使宋代古文运动达到波澜壮阔的地步。

It refers to the literary reform movement in the mid-Tang to the Northern Song period. It opposed rigidly rhythmical prose featuring parallelism and excessive elegance that had been popular in the Six Dynasties, and advocated a return to writing in "truly" classical Chinese. This movement was both intellectual and social in nature. Its representative figures included Han Yu (768-824) and Liu Zongyuan (773-819) of the Tang Dynasty and Ouyang Xiu (1007-1072), Su Xun (1009-1066), Wang Anshi (1021-1086), Zeng Gong (1019-1083), Su Shi (1037-1101), and Su Zhe (1039-1112) of the Song Dynasty. In this particular context, the notion of classical prose stood in contrast to rigidly rhythmical prose. Classical prose, first proposed by Han Yu, referred to the prose of the Qin, Western Han, and Eastern Han dynasties. It featured poetic lines of flexible lengths with no particular regard for metric pattern and parallel structure. In terms of content, classical prose aimed to express ideas and reflect real life. Rigidly rhythmical prose, on the other hand, was a style of writing popular in the pre-Tang period which had rigid requirement about the use of parallelism, elegant wording, prosody, melody, and allusions. Although there were good works in this genre, most were rigid in form and hollow in content. In view of this, Han Yu called for a return to the literary tradition of the Western and Eastern Han dynasties to reform literary writing. He gained the strong support of eminent men of letters such as Liu Zongyuan. Together, they launched what was later widely known as the Classical Prose Movement. Han Yu took this initiative to combine the reform of literary writing with the revival of Confucian moralism so as to enable literary writing to promote better governance. But rhythmical prose did not die out altogether; it continued into the late Tang period. Northern Song writer Ouyang Xiu, with strong political influence, championed the revival of classical prose. His contemporary Su Xun, as well as his students Wang Anshi, Zeng Gong, Su Shi, and Su Zhe all wrote classical prose with distinctive styles. Influenced by Su Shi, Huang Tingjian (1045 - 1105), Chen Shidao (1053 - 1102), Zhang Lei (1054 - 1114), Qin Guan (1049 - 1100), and Chao Buzhi (1053 - 1110) also became prominent prose writers. Thanks to the efforts of these literary figures, the Classical Prose Movement flourished in the Song Dynasty.

引例 Citations：

◎时时应事作俗下文字，下笔令人惭。……不知古文，真何用于今世也，然以俟知者知耳。(韩愈《与冯宿论文书》)

(我经常为应付世事而写平庸的应酬文章，下笔时令人惭愧。……不知古文对今世真的有什么用啊，那么还是等待懂的人赏识吧。)

So often, I have to write just for the purpose of socializing. This makes me feel ashamed... What good can classical prose do for today's world? I just hope that there will be people who can truly appreciate our writing. (Han Yu: Letter to Feng Su on Prose Writing)

◎苏子瞻曰："子美之诗，退之之文，鲁公之书，皆集大成者也。"(陈师道《后山诗话》引)

(苏轼说过："杜甫的诗、韩愈的文章、颜真卿的书法，都是集合了各家的优点而达到最高成就的。")

Su Shi said, "Du Fu's poems, Han Yu's prose, and Yan Zhenqing's calligraphy, by drawing on all that is best in great poets, prose writers, and calligraphers, have reached the highest level of artistic attainment." (Chen Shidao: *Houshan's Understanding of Poetry*)

骨 / 肉 /gǔ / ròu/
Bones and Flesh / Literary Framework and Nuanced Expressions

中国古代书画理论或文学批评中用来指称用笔或风格上的遒劲刚健与圆润妍美的一对术语。秦汉时代流行相面术，"骨"指人体骨骼，"肉"指皮肉。汉魏六朝时期，它们被用作文艺批评术语。在书画领域，"骨"指笔力直硬劲拔，"肉"指用墨或着色浓重圆润。在文学创作方面，"骨"侧重指风格上的遒劲刚健，"肉"侧重指辞采上的圆融妍美。这一对术语喻指文艺作品的体格骨力（思想内容、风格特点）与表现之美的关系，也蕴含着文艺作品思想情调与形式妍美的匹配。

These are terms that were traditionally used in painting and calligraphy theory and literary criticism to refer specifically to a vigorous and forceful manner or style of execution in combination with softer, more feminine touches. In physiognomy, which was popular during the Qin and Han period, *gu* (骨) referred to the human frame and *rou* (肉), the skin and flesh. By the late Han, Wei and the Six Dynasties, the term came to be employed in literary criticism as well. In the field of painting and calligraphy, "bones" were virile and energetic strokes whereas "flesh" was the heavy use of ink or color to create an effect of elegant plumpness. In literary writing, "bones" meant a sturdy overall structure, and "flesh," any appropriate rhetorical or formal means employed to fill it out. Bones and flesh, when mentioned together, refer metaphorically to the relation between the framework (i.e., the moral message and structural features) and the nuanced aspects of expression of a literary work. They also imply a union between the essential idea and sentiment of a literary work and its formal beauty.

引例 Citations：

◎骨丰肉润，入妙通灵。（王僧虔《笔意赞》）

（结体要道劲而笔画要圆润，方能抵达精妙境界而与神灵相通。）

Only if one combines robust and powerful strokes with subtler means of expression will he be able to reach a state of supreme sophistication and to communicate with spiritual beings. (Wang Sengqian: In Praise of the Dynamic Beauty of Calligraphy)

◎必以情志为神明，事义为骨髓，辞采为肌肤，宫商为声气。（刘勰《文心雕龙·附会》）

（必须以思想感情作为文章的灵魂，以事实道理作为文章的骨髓，以文采辞藻作为文章的肌肤，以谐合音律增强文章的韵味和气势。）

In writing an essay, content and feeling must be treated as its soul, facts and reasoning as its marrow, and rhetoric and wording as its flesh and skin. Harmony in rhyme must be relied upon to enhance its charm and strength. (Liu Xie: *The Literary Mind and the Carving of Dragons*)

含蓄 /hánxù/
Subtle Suggestion

文艺作品的一种创作技巧与风格，用简约的语言和浅近的艺术形象委婉表达出丰富深远的情感意蕴，使欣赏者能从中获得回味无穷的美感。中国古代的文学艺术作品中既有直率真实的表现方式，亦有含蓄蕴藉的表达手法。含蓄这一术语源于诗歌的讽谏传统及道家思想，主张作品的情感、意蕴应当内敛，外在形象的描写要借助充实的内在意蕴而感染读者，形成言近旨远、意在言外的审美效果。唐代司空图（837—908）将其列为二十四种诗歌风格之一。含蓄是作家修养、创作技巧与文学作品的风格和境界的高度统一。

A technique or style in creating literary works, it refers to the use of concise language in portraying a simple artistic image, whose rich feelings and implications are elicited in a subtle manner, so that readers can intuit multiple hidden meanings. One finds a straightforward and factual manner of expression in early literary and artistic works in China, as well as the subtle mode of expression. Because this technique originally evolved from Daoist thought and, in the early period, was employed as a means of criticizing powerful individuals in poetry, it stresses the expression of emotion in a subtly suggestive manner, such that the depiction of images should be supported by a rich undertone or hidden meaning that can appeal to readers. The language should be simple and plain but still leave sufficient room for readers to seize upon hidden meanings. Sikong Tu (837-908), a literary critic in the Tang Dynasty, listed it as one of the twenty-four styles of poetry writing. Subtle suggestion imparts a high degree of unity to a writer's cultural attainments, creative technique, as well as his literary style and imagery.

引例 Citations：

◎不著一字，尽得风流。语不涉己，若不堪忧。是有真宰，与之沉浮。（司空图《二十四诗品·含蓄》）

（虽然没有写上一字，却尽得其意蕴之美妙。文辞虽没有直接抒写自己的忧伤，读时却使人好像忧伤不已。这是因为事物有着真实自然的情理，在与作品一起或沉或浮。）

Without penning down a word about it, yet it is overfilled with what it intends to express. Without mentioning the writer's own sorrow, yet one can feel it there. It is because the genuine and natural feelings reside there, that one's mood rises and falls with the work that conveys them. (Sikong Tu: Twenty-four Styles of Poetry)

◎语贵含蓄。东坡云："言有尽而意无穷者，天下之至言也。"（姜夔

《白石道人诗说》)

（语言表达以含蓄为贵。苏东坡说："用有限的文辞表达无穷的意义，这是天下公认的至理名言啊。"）

The merit of expressing oneself lies in presenting one's opinions with subtlety. Su Dongpo once said, "There is a limit to the words one can use in writing a poem, but there is no limit to the meaning a poem may deliver. This is universally acknowledged." (Jiang Kui: *The Poetry Theory of Baishi Daoren*)

◎含蓄无穷，词之要诀。含蓄者，意不浅露，语不穷尽，句中有余味，篇中有余意，其妙不外寄言而已。（沈祥龙《论词随笔》)

（有着无限的蕴含是作词的要诀。含蓄就是意蕴不要简单肤浅，用词不要将意蕴全都说完，句子要给人留有回味的余地，整部作品有让人进一步思考的空间，其精妙之处不外就是在有限的词句上寄寓无限的意蕴而已。）

The key to writing great *ci* lyrics is the subtle suggestion of limitless meaning. Subtle suggestion means that the meaning is never simply obvious, yet the words will forever echo in one's mind. A line should leave enough room for further thought, and a poem enough meaning for readers to ponder. The beauty of this method lies in expressing unlimited subtle meaning in simple language. (Shen Xianglong: *Essays on Ci Poetry*)

涵泳 /hányǒng/
Be Totally Absorbed (in Reading and Learning)

原指阅读经典作品时，要像潜泳一样沉浸其中、反复玩味，方能有所收获，激发自己的情志和感悟。作为一种读书做学问的方法，它强调调动自己的经验和学养，努力思考书中的问题、观点、材料及事实，使自己的学问如源头活水而常新。作为一种理解与诠释文艺作品的方法，它强调努力进入作品特定的情境，通过反复体会与咀嚼，最终领略作品的深层意蕴及审美意境。它也表明文艺作品具有兴发志意和感化人心的效力。

This term originally refers to an attitude in reading classics, requiring one to become deeply absorbed in the work as if one were submerged in water, repeatedly ruminating on its meaning until one is able to fully digest its significance so that it informs one's own feelings and insights. In time this becomes a way of learning, impelling one to mobilize one's own experience and accumulated knowledge to think deeply about what he is reading so that knowledge is endlessly renewed and refreshed. As a method of understanding and interpreting literary works, it requires one to place one's own thought in the particular world of the work so that one becomes deeply aware of why the work was so written and can master its subtle meanings and aesthetic conception. This method is premised on the understanding that literary works can be deeply inspiring and enlightening.

引例 Citations：

◎学者读书，须要敛身正坐，缓视微吟，虚心涵泳，切己省察。（《朱子语类》卷十一）

（学者读书，必须收腹端坐，慢慢看，轻声念，放空心灵，沉浸其中，并结合自身经验进行思考和体察。）

When a scholar reads a book, he must sit straight, read attentively, read out softly, focus all his thought on the book, be entirely absorbed in it, and meditate on its significance from his own experience. (*Categorized Conversations of Master Zhu Xi*)

◎此等语言自有个血脉流通处，但涵泳久之，自然见得条畅浃洽，不必多引外来道理、言语，却壅滞却诗人活底意思也。（朱熹《答何叔京》）

（这些语言都有内在的血脉连通之处，只要沉潜其中反复玩味，自然能够理清头绪，融会贯通，不必引用很多外来的道理和言论，这样反而遮蔽诗人真正想要表达的意思。)

Such language has an inner coherence and logical line of thought. When a person has been deeply absorbed in it for long, he naturally understands how to articulate its complexities and unite its core ideas. There is no need to rely on theories and discussions extraneous to the work. To do so would only be to stifle what the poet intended to express. (Zhu Xi: In Response to He Shujing)

◎熟绎上下文，涵泳以求其立言之指，则差别毕见（xiàn）矣。（王夫之《姜斋诗话》卷二）

（细致推究上下文的联系，沉浸其中以求把握文章的主旨，那么不同文章的差别就会完全显现出来了。）

By carefully studying the literary context of a text, and by becoming so absorbed in the text as to master its essence, one will be able to discern the essential differences between different literary works. (Wang Fuzhi: *Desultory Remarks on Poetry from Ginger Studio*)

汉乐府 /hànyuèfǔ/
Yuefu Poetry

指汉代的乐府诗。"乐府"本是秦以后由朝廷设立的用来训练乐工、采集民歌并配器作曲的专门官署，后转指由乐府机关所采集、配乐并由乐工演唱的民歌。乐府诗是继《诗经》之后古代民歌的一次创造，是与"诗经""楚辞"并列的诗歌形态。至今保存的汉乐府民歌有五六十首，大都真实反映了当时社会生活的各个方面，表现出纯真质朴的思想感情，并由此形成反映普通民众声音与情感的文学创作传统。其中最有特色与成就的是描写女性生活的作品。汉代以后将可以入乐的诗歌及仿乐府古题而写的诗歌统称为乐府。

Yuefu (乐府) poems were written in the Han Dynasty. Originally, *yuefu* was a government office set up by the imperial court to train musicians, collect folk songs and ballads, compose music, and match musical instruments to it. It later came to refer to folk songs and ballads collected, matched with music, and played by court musicians. Poems of this style represented a new creation of ancient folk songs and ballads in the years after *The Book of Songs* was compiled, and equaled *The Book of Songs* and *Odes of Chu* in importance. About 50 to 60 *yuefu* poems have been handed down to this day. They truthfully depicted various aspects of society at the time and revealed genuine emotions, thus creating a literary tradition reflecting ordinary people's sentiments. In particular, *yuefu* poems were noted for their vivid depiction of women's life. All poems that could be chanted or were written with *yuefu* themes were collectively called *yuefu* poems in later times.

引例 Citations：

◎自孝武立乐府而采歌谣，于是有代、赵之讴，秦、楚之风。皆感于哀乐，缘事而发……（《汉书·艺文志》）

（自从汉武帝设立乐府并采集歌谣，这之后就有了代、赵之地的吟唱及秦、楚等地的民歌。它们都是受内心悲喜情绪的影响或者受到某件事情的触发而产生的……）

After Emperor Wu of the Han Dynasty set up an office to collect folk songs and ballads, folk songs from the Dai and Zhao regions, and ballads from the Qin and Chu regions could be heard. They were all created to express people's joy and sorrow or were inspired by certain events... (*The History of the Han Dynasty*)

◎乐府者，"声依永，律和声"也。（刘勰《文心雕龙·乐府》）

（乐府诗，就是"随诗的吟唱而有抑扬疾徐的声音变化，再用音律调和声音"。）

Yuefu poems vary in rhythm and tone and are accompanied by music when chanted. (Liu Xie: *The Literary Mind and the Carving of Dragons*)

豪放派 /háofàngpài/

The *Haofang* School / The Bold and Unconstrained School

宋词两大流派之一。内容多写家国大事、人生情怀，其特点是境界壮阔宏大，气象豪迈雄放，常常运用诗文创作手法及典故，而且不拘音律。最先用"豪放"评词的是苏轼（1037 — 1101），南宋人已明确将苏轼、辛弃疾（1140 — 1207）作为豪放词的代表。北宋范仲淹（989 — 1052）《渔家傲》词开豪放之先，经苏轼大力创作"壮词"而成一派词风。中原沦陷后，南宋政权偏安江南，不以收复失地为意，许多词人报国无望，因而逐渐形成慷慨悲壮的词风，产生了豪放派领袖辛弃疾及陈与义（1090 — 1139）、叶梦得（1077 — 1148）、朱敦儒（1081 — 1159）、张元干（1091 — 1170？）、张孝祥（1132 — 1170）、陆游（1125 — 1210）、陈亮（1143 — 1194）、刘过（1154 — 1206）等一大批杰出词人。他们抒发报国情怀，将个体的命运与家国命运紧密联系在一起，进一步拓宽了词的表现领域，丰富了词的表现手法，大大提升了词在文学史上的地位。豪放派词人虽以豪放为主体风格，却也不乏清秀婉约之作，故不可一概而论。有些词作出现议论和用典过多、音律不精或过于散文化，也是毋庸讳言的。

This is one of the two *ci* (词) lyric schools of the Song Dynasty, which mainly dealt with major affairs of the nation and expresses noble aspirations. It featured broad vision and bold expression, often employing the methods of prose poetry and uninhibited by metric stereotypes. The first poet who used the term "bold and unconstrained" was Su Shi (1037-1101) who, together with Xin Qiji (1140-1207), was widely acclaimed by Southern Song critics as the leading poets of this school. The Northern Song writer Fan Zhongyan (989-1052) created this school with his *ci* lyric, A Fisherman's Song, which grew into a major poetic style thanks mainly to Su Shi's contribution. After the Central Plains fell to the Jin forces, the Song court fled south of the

Yangtze River and was too weak to recover the lost territory. Many *ci* poets, led by Xin Qiji and supported by other prominent poets such as Chen Yuyi (1090-1139), Ye Mengde (1077-1148), Zhu Dunru (1081-1159), Zhang Yuangan (1091-1170?), Zhang Xiaoxiang (1132-1170), Lu You (1125-1210), Chen Liang (1143-1194), and Liu Guo (1154-1206), expressed their longing to return to the north in verses of a stirring style. They voiced their patriotic sentiments and identified their own fate with that of the whole nation. They thus enriched *ci* lyrics' ways of expression and greatly lifted its status in the history of literature. Although poets of this school wrote in the bold and unconstrained style, they occasionally wrote graceful and subtle *ci* poems. And some of their works contained too many commentaries and allusions, were careless about the use of metric schemes, and read more like prose than poetry.

引例 Citations：

◎ 词体大略有二：一体婉约，一体豪放。婉约者欲其辞情蕴藉，豪放者欲其气象恢弘。盖亦存乎其人，如秦少游之作多是婉约，苏子瞻之作多是豪放。大约词体以婉约为正。（张綖（yán）《诗余图谱·凡例》）

（词的风格大约有两种，一种是婉约，一种是豪放。婉约风格的词，其词句和情感追求含蓄之美，豪放词则追求气魄宏大。大概是由于作者的气质所致，如秦观的作品多是婉约之作，而苏轼的作品多是豪放之作。大致说来，词的风格以婉约为正宗。）

Ci lyrics can be divided into two types: the graceful and restrained vs. the bold and unconstrained. The first type of poems features subtle expression of one's feelings, whereas the second type is far more explicit and has a broader vision. This distinction is due to different dispositions of poets. Qin Guan's *ci* lyrics are mostly graceful and subtle, whereas Su Shi's tend to be bold and exuberant. Generally, the graceful and restrained style follows more closely the original spirit of *ci* lyrics than the bold and unconstrained style. (Zhang Yan: *The Metric Schemes of Ci Lyrics*)

◎张南湖论词派有二：一曰婉约，一曰豪放。仆谓婉约以易安为宗，豪放惟幼安称首，皆吾济南人，难乎为继矣！（王士禛《花草蒙拾》）

（张綖论词派有二：一是婉约派，一是豪放派。我认为婉约派以李清照为第一，豪放派以辛弃疾为第一，他们都是我们济南人，之后就后继无人了。）

According to Zhang Yan, *ci* lyrics can either be graceful and restrained or bold and unconstrained. I believe that Li Qingzhao is the best of the former and Xin Qiji the best of the latter. They were both natives of Ji'nan. After them, no great *ci* poet has emerged in our province. (Wang Shizhen: *Random Notes on Ci Poetry*)

和 /hé/
Harmony

不同事物之间的和谐共处。古人认为，不同事物的共处及事物间稳定秩序的形成，不能通过消除事物之间的差异来实现，而应在尊重和保全个体差异的基础上，寻求事物之间的和谐共处，这就叫"和"。在"和"的状态下，不同事物可以发挥其各自的特质，相互补充、相互辅助，激发个体乃至整体的活力。

The ancient Chinese believed that coexistence of different things and a stable order among them could not be realized by eliminating their differences; such coexistence could be achieved only by seeking to get along in harmony on the basis of respecting and preserving individual differences. That is what is meant by "harmony." In such a way, different things can develop themselves while complementing each other, stimulating the vitality of both individuals and all.

◎夫和实生物，同则不继。(《国语·郑语》)

（不同的事物相互调和而生成新的事物，只有相同的事物则难以有延续。）

Harmony begets new things; while uniformity does not lead to continuation. (*Discourses on Governance of the States*)

◎君子和而不同，小人同而不和。(《论语·子路》)

（君子与人和谐相处却不会盲目附和，小人盲目附和而不能真正和谐相处。）

A man of virtue pursues harmony but does not seek uniformity; a petty man seeks uniformity but does not pursue harmony. (*The Analects*)

和出于适 /hé chūyú shì/

Harmony Comes from Appropriateness.

音乐的和谐来自音乐的适度及音乐与平和心灵的契合。"和"，和谐，首先指不同声音之间的协调配合；"适"，适度，既指音乐本身高低、清浊的适度，亦指欣赏者对于音乐对象的适度接受。这一术语突出了音乐欣赏过程中作为客观对象的音乐必须与主体心灵的和谐相一致，音乐美感是主客体和谐的产物。

The harmony of music comes from its appropriateness and its concordance with the soul. "Harmony" refers to how different sounds are combined and attuned to each other. "Appropriateness" refers to the pitch and timbre of the music itself, as well as to the degree to which the listener can accept the music. This term highlights the need for harmony and accord between the object – music and the subject – the soul, in order for music to be appreciated. The beauty of music is generated by harmony between the subjective and the objective.

◎声出于和，和出于适。(《吕氏春秋·大乐》)

(音乐产生于不同声音的协调配合，而和谐须与欣赏者的心灵和谐相一致。)

Music comes from harmony, and harmony comes from appropriateness. (*Master Lü's Spring and Autumn Annals*)

和谐 /héxié/
Harmony

相互协调，彼此融洽得当。"和"即协调和睦；"谐"即融洽，适宜得当。"和谐"首先指不同声音之间的配合得当，构成音乐的整体协调；后指良好的社会关系和治理状态，在尊重差异性、多样性的基础上，达成结合共生的关系，从而形成社会的有机整体。在这个整体中，人们各得其所，各安其位，和睦相处，相得益彰，井然有序，生活安康。它是儒家处理人际关系的重要伦理原则和社会政治理想，至今仍被视为核心价值之一。它可泛指人与人之间、团体与团体之间、国家与国家之间和睦、和平、融洽的关系状态。它体现了中华民族反对暴力冲突、崇尚和平秩序的"文"的精神。

This term implies mutual coordination and friendship. The Chinese term *hexie* (和谐) originally referred to the simultaneous combination of different tones that gave rise to a musical work. Later it came to mean a state of governance in which there are good social relations of coexistence based on respect for differences and diversity. In such a society, all people give free rein to their talent and find their proper place to live together in harmony, order and health. *Hexie* is a core Confucian ethical principle for dealing with interpersonal relationship and guiding social and political activities. It now generally refers to the harmonious, peaceful, and amicable relationship between people, between groups, and between countries. Harmony represents the Chinese cultural value of opposing violence and conflicts and cherishing peace and order.

引例 Citations：

◎施之金石，则音韵和谐。(《晋书·挚虞传》)

（将古人的度量标准用于钟磬等乐器，奏出的音乐协调动听。）

When chimes, musical stones and other musical instruments are played according to ancient Chinese metrics, harmonious music pleasing to the ear is created. (*The History of the Jin Dynasty*)

◎和谐则太平之所兴也，违戾则荒乱之所起也。(仲长统《法诫篇》，见《后汉书·仲长统传》)

（相互协调是天下太平的前提，相互抵触是天下大乱的根源。）

Peace will thrive when there is harmony, whereas chaos will prevail when there is mutual opposition. (Zhong Changtong: On Government)

◎君臣相得，政令和谐，治国之道，不过如此。(冯梦龙《东周列国志》第八十六回)

（君臣协调，政令得当，治国的基本原则就是这样。）

Coordination between the emperor and ministers and proper policies are fundamental for ensuring good governance. (Feng Menglong: *Chronicles of the Kingdoms of the Eastern Zhou*)

化工 / 画工 /huàgōng / huàgōng/
Magically Natural, Overly Crafted

品评文学艺术作品风格自然与否的术语。"化工"指作品的工巧自然天成，毫无雕琢痕迹，达到了出神入化的地步；"画工"则是指作品的工巧由刻意雕琢而成，技巧虽高明，但缺乏自然韵味。"化工"是艺术家的作品，"画工"可以说是匠人的作品。这个评价标准，由明代李贽（1527—1602）《杂说》提出，与他所提倡的写文章要有真情、真心是一致的。从文化渊源上来说，"画工"与"化工"的区分，其实来自道家的纯任自然、弃绝机巧的思想。明代文士大都倡导文艺放任天然，否定雕琢模仿的创作立场。

The expressions are about the naturalness of literary and artistic works. The first one, "magically natural," means that a literary or artistic work is completed naturally and achieves the acme of perfection without any sign of craft. The second, "overly crafted," means that a work is meticulously crafted, but it is overly elaborate in style while lacking naturalness and spontaneity. "Magically natural" is used to refer to works accomplished by artists while "overly crafted" is used to describe works done by craftsmen. These two standards were proposed by Ming writer Li Zhi (1527-1602) in his "Random Thoughts," which echoed his idea that writings must reflect the author's true sentiments. Culturally, the distinction between "magically natural" and "overly crafted" is rooted in the Daoist thought of being harmonious with nature while forsaking excessive skills. Most Ming scholars favored literary naturalism and rejected elaboration and imitation.

引例 Citations：

◎吴生虽妙绝，犹以画工论。摩诘得之于象外，有如仙翮谢笼樊。吾观二子皆神俊，又于维也敛衽无间（jiàn）言。（苏轼《王维、吴道子画》）

（吴道子的技巧虽然绝妙，只能说是画工之作。王维的高妙之处则是超越了所描绘的物象，就像仙鸟离飞笼子。我看这两位技法都很高超，对于王维则更钦敬，没有任何可挑剔之处。）

Wu Daozi had superb technical skills, but his paintings were over crafted. What is remarkable about Wang Wei is that he gave free rein to his imagination in his paintings, like a bird that had broken free from its cage. Both of them were highly skilled, but I like Wang Wei better; I can find no fault in his works. (Su Shi: The Paintings of Wang Wei and Wu Daozi)

◎《拜月》《西厢》，化工也；《琵琶》，画工也。夫所谓画工者，以其能夺天地之化工，而其孰知天地之无工乎？（李贽《杂说》）

（《拜月亭》《西厢记》属于"化工"之作，《琵琶记》则是"画工"之作。之所以称"画工"，是人们认为它能够取代天地的造化之功，可是，谁知道天地本就没有这样的造化之工呢？）

The Moonlight Pavilion and *Romance of the Western Chamber* were works of magical naturalness, whereas *A Tale of the Pipa* was an overly crafted work. The latter shows that an attempt made to outdo the magic of nature has proved impossible to achieve. (Li Zhi: Random Thoughts)

化境 /huàjìng/
Sublimity in Art

　　指最佳的艺术境界。"化境"是中国古代文艺批评中的重要命题，与"化""化工"等具有相似内涵。庄子（前369？—前286）《齐物论》"天地与我并生，而万物与我为一"，是化境理论的源头。已臻化境的作品，呈现出物我两忘、人天合一的审美情态，无论诗画，皆浑涵天然，无雕琢斧凿之痕迹。化境生发的机制，是创作者自身的修养积累、心灵体悟与艺术技巧，已到极高境界，然后笔随意动，机缘巧合，方能达成，其效果恍若天工，无法勉强得到。

Sublimity is the highest state of art. It was an important term in literary criticism in ancient China, similar to the ideas of "the oneness of heaven and humans" and "the miraculous work of nature." The assertion that "heaven and earth exist in harmony with me and all things in the universe are inseparable from me," as made in Zhuangzi's (369?-286 BC) "On Seeing Things as Equal," marked the beginning of this theory. A work of art with such excellence shows an aesthetic state wherein one basks in a blissful loss of division between him and his surroundings and heaven and man become completely merged. Whether it is a poem or a painting, it is so naturally created that it bears no mark of men's "carving or chiseling." The sublime in art occurs when the artist has had more than sufficient accomplishment, profound understanding and artistic technique. He will then be able to suit his actual execution of strokes to his fantasy by making everything at his fingertips work. Such an effect is achieved as if only by nature's magical hand, not through human effort at all.

引例 Citations：

◎不知变主格，化主境，格易见，境难窥。变则标奇越险，不主故常；化则神动天随，从心所欲。如五言咏物诸篇，七言拗体诸作，所谓变也。宋以后诸人竞相师袭者是，然化境殊不在此。（胡应麟《诗薮·内编五》）

（人们不知道"变"主要体现为"格"，"化"主要体现为"境"，"格"容易看出来，"境"难以窥见。"变"就是标榜奇特险怪，不主张故旧平常；"化"就是神气自然动而天性随之，可以随心所欲。如杜甫的五言咏物、七言拗体等作品，是"变"的体现。宋代以后的人争着效法学习，然而杜诗的化境根本不在这些方面。）

People do not know that, whereas variation is shown mainly through metrical schemes, sublimity in art is an overall artistic vision. The former is easily discernible but the latter is difficult to get a glance into. Variation entails extra ordinariness and oddity; therefore, it disdains convention or plainness. Sublimity in art, on the other hand, requires the blossoming of one's natural self and that one should always follow the dictates of one's heart. Du Fu's objects-poems with five characters to a line, as well as his metrically deviant poems with seven characters to a line – are good examples of variation. Poets after the Song Dynasty tried especially hard to copy his style, although the sublimity of his poems does not lie there at all. (Hu Yinglin: *An In-depth Exploration of Poetry*)

◎诗家化境，如风雨驰骤，鬼神出没，满眼空幻，满耳飘忽，突然而来，倏然而去，不得以字句诠，不可以迹相求。（贺贻孙《诗筏》）（诗的化境，如同暴风雨忽然来到，鬼神出现又隐没，满眼看到的都是空虚幻影，满耳听到的都是飘忽不定的声音，突然而来，倏然消失，无法解释它的字句，无法探求它的行迹。）

Sublimity in poetry arrives like an unexpected rainstorm. Like when a god or a devil appears and then vanishes, one only sees fleeting fantasies and hears elusive voices – coming and going all of a sudden. Its wording defies any attempt at decipherment and its traces are hard to follow. (He Yisun: *Tools and Methods of Understanding Poetry*)

画道 /huàdào/
Dao of Painting

绘画之道。有广狭二义：狭义指绘画的各种技法；广义则指画作中蕴含的文化理念、人格精神、艺术风格和审美追求，是"道"与"技"的完美融合。"道"决定画所要表现的思想主题、艺术法则和美学风格；画是"道"的具体表象，寄托了画家的文化理念、人格精神、艺术风格和审美追求。故道以画显，画因道而获得提升。杰出的画家追求技进乎道、艺与道合。画道，不仅包含了宇宙自然之道，而且折射了社会人生之道，彰显出中国固有的人文精神。

The term has both broad and narrow meanings. Interpreted narrowly, it means various painting techniques. Interpreted broadly, it means the cultural values, personality, artistic style, and aesthetic aspiration embodied in a painting, suggesting a perfect fusion of Dao and skills. Dao determines the theme a painting conveys as well as the painting's artistic principles and aesthetic style. A painting is a concrete image that illustrates Dao. It reflects the cultural principles followed by the painter as well as his personality, artistic style, and aesthetic aspiration. Therefore, paintings illuminate Dao, which in turn enhances the paintings. Prominent painters seek to access Dao through refining their skills and epitomizing Dao in artwork. The Dao of painting not only encompasses the Dao of nature, but also the Dao of social life, demonstrating the commitment to humanism inherent in the Chinese culture.

引例 Citations：

◎夫圣人以神法道，而贤者通；山水以形媚道，而仁者乐。不亦几乎？（宗炳《画山水序》）

（圣人精神上效法道，而德才杰出的人可以通达于道；山水以其自然形质婉转契合道，使仁者对之喜爱。这难道不是很微妙吗？）

Sages follow Dao with their spirit. Men of virtue and talent may comprehend and practice Dao. Mountains and rivers conform to Dao through their natural shapes. That is why they are loved by benevolent people. Isn't this subtle and profound? (Zong Bing: On the Creation of Landscape Paintings)

◎画之道，所谓宇宙在乎手者，眼前无非生机。（董其昌《画禅室随笔·画源》）

（绘画之道，就是宇宙自然的神奇都能够通过手表现出来，呈现于眼前的全是有生命的景象。）

The Dao of painting enables one to use his hand to depict the wonder of nature and present to viewers a scene full of life. (Dong Qichang: *Essays from Huachan Studio*)

画龙点睛 /huàlóng-diǎnjīng/

Add Pupils to the Eyes of a Painted Dragon / Render the Final Touch

比喻文学艺术创作中在紧要处着墨或写出关键性的词句，以创造出最奇妙的神韵和意境来。孟子（前372？—前289）认为，观察一个人，最好观察他的眼睛，因为眼睛最容易表露一个人内心的善良和丑恶。东晋顾恺之（345？—409）画人物，曾数年不肯轻易下笔点睛。他强调人物传神之关键在于画出眼神。南朝画家张僧繇（yáo）绘画技术高超，传说他曾为画好的龙点上眼珠，龙即刻腾空而去。故后世用"画龙点睛"强调文学艺术创作中应抓住要诀，使形象更加生动传神。

The term is a metaphor about giving the finishing touch, which means providing critical details or key words in an artistic or literary work in order to lend it charm and aesthetic conception. Mencius (372?-289 BC) believed that when observing a person, one should look directly into his eyes because the eyes reveal his nature, be it good or evil. When painting portraits, Gu Kaizhi (345?-409) in the Eastern Jin Dynasty did not add pupils to the eyes in haste. He stressed that the key to painting a vivid portrait lied in painting the eyes. Zhang Sengyao, a painter of the Southern Dynasties, was well known for his excellent painting skills. Legend has it that his painted Chinese dragons flew into the sky as soon as he finished their pupils. The term is thus used by later generations to underline the importance of applying critical touches to add life and charm to a literary or artistic work.

引例 Citation：

◎又金陵安乐寺四白龙，不点眼睛，每云："点睛即飞去。"人以为妄诞，固请点之，须臾雷电破壁，两龙乘云腾去上天，二龙未点眼者见在。（张彦远《历代名画记》卷七）

中华思想文化术语
文艺卷

（[张僧繇]在金陵安乐寺墙壁上画了四条白龙，他没有给龙点上眼睛，常说："点上眼睛，龙立刻就会腾空飞走。"人们都认为他的话荒唐虚妄，一再请他点上眼睛，[张僧繇只好提笔点睛，]即刻天空雷电交加，两条龙乘云腾空而去，而另两条没点眼睛的龙还留在墙壁上。）

Zhang Sengyao painted four white Chinese dragons on the wall of the Anle Temple in Jinling. But he did not paint pupils to their eyes, saying that once he did, the dragons would fly into the sky. People considered his words absurd and repeatedly urged him to add pupils to the dragons' eyes. He eventually did it on two of the four dragons. Suddenly, lightning and thunders struck, and the two dragons with pupils added to their eyes flew into the clouds. The other two remained on the wall. (Zhang Yanyuan: *Famous Paintings Through History*)

幻中有真 /huàn zhōng yǒu zhēn/
Truth in Imagination

指文艺作品的情节与景象虽是通过想象与虚构写成但却具有内在的真实，可以折射社会现实。佛教与道家思想认为，现实社会是变幻不定的，人们不可执迷于这种幻象，而应当超越这种幻象，认识事物的真谛。文艺批评家提出，人们认识文艺作品与生活现实，应当善于透过幻象而把握作品的真实，获取美感。"幻中有真"作为一个文学批评术语，不仅揭示了文艺的审美特征和意义，也揭示了文艺创作的基本规律，即艺术形象的创造须以现实生活为依据，但又不能拘泥于现实生活，而应达到生活真实与艺术真实的高度统一。

The term means that the plot of scenes in a literary work, while imaginary, nonetheless have inner force and reflect reality in society. According to

Buddhist and Daoist thought, society is transitory and shifting and people should not hold on to something unreal; rather, they should transcend delusions and recognise the true essence of things. As pointed out by literary and art critics, to gain keen appreciation of literary works and real life, people should learn to go beyond the imaginary aspect to grasp the truth of a creative work so as to enjoy its beauty. As a term in literary criticism, truth in imagination not only sheds light on the aesthetic function and significance of literature and arts, but also reveals a fundamental principle of literary and artistic creation, that is, art creation should be rooted in real life but not limited by it. Instead, it should aim at blending the truth of life and artistic imagination.

引例 Citations：

◎故不得已描写人生幻境之离合悲欢，以及善善恶恶，令阅者触目知警。（天花藏主人《〈幻中真〉序》）

（因此不得已通过虚构描写人生离合悲欢的情境，以及善得善报、恶得恶报的各种故事，让读者读到这些之后懂得警醒。）

Therefore, [the author] has to describe separation and reunion, happiness and sadness in the illusory world of human life, as well as telling stories of reward for good and punishment for evil deeds, so the reader learns from it and is warned. (Tianhuacangzhuren: Preface to *Truth in Imagination*)

◎即如《西游》一记……师弟四人各一性情，各一动止，试摘取其一言一事，遂使暗中摸索，亦知其出自何人，则正以幻中有真，乃为传神阿堵。（睡乡居士《二刻拍案惊奇》序）

（就拿《西游记》一书来说……师徒四人，各有各的性情，各有各的言行举止，尝试摘出某句话或某一举止，让人不看原书而暗自揣摩，也可以知道出自何人。正因为虚构的人物有现实的影子，才能够产生如见真人的传神效果。）

Take the novel *Journey to the West* as an example… The master and his three disciples each have their distinctive personalities, manners and behavior. If you cite a certain word or action and ask people to guess who did or said it, they will know who it is. Only when there is truth in imagination, can such a life-like effect be achieved. (Shuixiangjushi: Preface to *Amazing Stories, Vol. Two*)

荒寒 /huānghán/
Grim and Desolate

古代诗词绘画作品中所描写的荒僻凄寒的环境及所体现出的孤寂凄冷的心境。唐宋时期一些远戍边关或遭贬谪的诗人，因仕途失意或不为时人理解而倍感环境的荒凉和内心的孤独，在诗歌作品中常常营造一种荒僻凄寒的氛围或意境，以此传达自己百折不回、独善其身的心志，使之成为一种独特的审美追求和超越现实的审美方式。追求荒寒意境的绘画则更充满一种独与天地往来的精神和与自然融为一体的情趣。这类诗画代表着中国文化的一种独特品位与风格。

This term refers to desolate and barren landscapes described or portrayed in classical poems or paintings that convey a feeling of loneliness and desolation. During the Tang and Song dynasties, some poets who were either exiled or sent to work at border garrisons did not only dwell in desolate places but also felt the dire bleakness within as they saw no hope for their future and they were being unappreciated and unrecognized for what they were worth. As a result, in their poetry they would create bleak, desolate scenes with a view to expressing their perseverance and determination to maintain personal integrity. In doing so they created a unique artistic method capable of transcending reality. Paintings depicting grim, desolate scenes suggest the lonely communication of man with nature, expressing as well the integration of man with nature. Such poems and paintings represent a kind of taste and style characteristic of Chinese culture.

引例 Citations：

◎尤工写塞外荒寒之景，殆扈从时所身历，故言这亲切如此。其慢词则凡近拖沓，远不如其小令，岂词才所限欤？（蔡嵩云《柯亭词论》）

（[纳兰性德的词]尤其长于写塞外荒寒的景象，应该是在随皇帝出巡时的亲身经历，因此他的描写才如此亲切。而他较长的词作则近乎拖沓，远远不如他的小令，难道是他作词的才力所限的缘故吗？）

The vivid portrayals of grim and desolate scenes beyond the Great Wall in Nalan Xingde's *ci* poems derive from his personal experience escorting the emperor on inspection tours, so that his portrayals are so close to nature. On the other hand his long *ci* poems are a bit loose, not as good as his short ones. Is it because his talent had its limits? (Cai Songyun: *Keting's Comments on Ci Poetry*)

◎雪图自摩诘以后，惟称营丘、华原、河阳、道宁（nìng）。然古劲有余，而荒寒不逮。（恽格《南田画跋·题石谷雪图》）

（画雪景的作品自王维之后，可以称道的是李成、范宽、李唐、许道宁。然而他们的画作古朴苍劲有余，但荒寒意境上却不及王维的作品。）

As for snowy scenes produced after the time of Wang Wei, those worth notice were by Li Cheng, Fan Kuan, Li Tang, and Xu Daoning. Although their brushwork was amply vigorous, they could not compare with Wang Wei in regards to that sense of grim desolation. (Yun Ge: *Nantian's Comments on Paintings*)

会心 /huìxīn/

Heart-to-heart Communication

不需言说而彼此心领神会。一般是指志趣、性情投合的朋友心意相通，能够互相理解和欣赏。特指自然美欣赏和文艺作品审美中主客体交融的境界。作者创作出美的意境，而欣赏者心领神会，感受到心与物高度融合及心心相印带来的快乐与慰藉。

The term refers to a situation in which people understand each other without the need to utter a single word. It generally means the spontaneous understanding reached by close friends who share common interests, aspirations, and dispositions. In particular, it refers to an aesthetic state in which the subject and the object interact with each other smoothly with no barrier between them, or in which an artist creates a marvelous image and a viewer appreciates it with emotion and understanding. The culmination of such an experience is joy and satisfaction derived from the perfect harmony between the human heart and its surroundings.

引例 Citations：

◎简文入华林园，顾谓左右曰："会心处不必在远，翳然林水，便自有濠濮间想也，觉鸟兽禽鱼自来亲人。"（刘义庆《世说新语·言语》）

（梁简文帝到华林园游玩，转过头对左右随从说："合人心意的地方不一定遥远，这里林木蔽空，其间一湾流水，便自然会产生庄子游于濠水桥上、垂钓于濮水的遐想，觉得鸟兽和鱼儿都主动和人亲近。"）

When Emperor Jianwen of Liang in the Southern Dynasties was touring the Hualin Garden, he turned to his followers and said, "A place which prompts heart-to-heart communication need not be far. This garden is shadowed by trees and has a stream meandering through. Such a place makes one think of Zhuangzi strolling on the bridge of the Haoshui River and angling in the

Pushui River, where birds and fish seemed eager to get close to him." (Liu Yiqing: *A New Account of Tales of the World*)

◎《三百篇》美刺箴怨皆无迹，当以心会心。（姜夔《白石道人诗说》）（《诗经》中的颂美、怨刺与劝谏都没有明显的痕迹，欣赏时应当以心会心。）

The Book of Songs contains odes, satires, and admonitions, but all are veiled. One must engage in a heart-to-heart communication to appreciate them. (Jiang Kui: *The Poetry Theory of Baishi Daoren*)

绘画六法 /huìhuà liù fǎ/
Six Rules of Painting

中国古代关于绘画创作的六种手法与美学原则。南朝齐梁画家谢赫通过品鉴历代名家画作，总结出气韵生动、骨法用笔、应物象形、随类赋彩、经营位置、传移模写等六种基本方法与原则，初步建构起传统绘画理论体系。"气韵生动"是要求画作具有被观者真切感觉到的生气与神韵，是立足审美效果的总体原则。以下五方面是绘画的具体技法要求："骨法用笔"是指运笔能自如呈现人物的各种线条变化，"应物象形"是指造型要顺应对象的外形特征，"随类赋彩"是根据人物对象的特征进行着色，"经营位置"是指构图要合理搭配而呈现整体效果，"传移模写"是通过临摹佳作来掌握绘画技艺。后人据此品评画作，并就五方面技法要求展开论述、总结经验，丰富画论体系。"绘画六法"揭示了中国古代绘画的基本手法与美学原则，也是从事绘画批评的标准，它影响了六朝之后的中国绘画批评与创作实践。

The term refers to six techniques and aesthetic principles for painting formulated by Xie He, a painter between Qi and Liang of the Southern Dynasties. After studying famous painters of the previous age, he summarized his views on painting in six basic rules: dynamic style, forceful brush strokes, life-like image, characteristic coloring, careful arrangement and imitation and copying models. In this way, he established a theoretical framework for traditional painting. "Dynamic style" means that a painting should make the viewers appreciate its vitality and charm. This is a general principle focusing on the aesthetic effect. The other five rules concern specific techniques. "Forceful brush strokes" means being able to wield the brush to portray characters freely with lines of various shapes. "Life-like image" means the image should vividly capture the form of the depicted. "Characteristic coloring" means applying color according to the characteristics of the subject of the painting. "Careful arrangement" means a composition should achieve a good overall effect. "Imitation and copying models" means copying masterpieces to refine one's painting skills. These rules became the basis for later art criticism and discourse on the five aspects of technique, providing a summary of ideal painting techniques and enriching theory on painting. The "six rules of painting" cover the basic techniques and aesthetics of ancient Chinese painting. They also established guidelines for art appreciation and influenced criticism and artistic creation in China from the Six Dynasties on.

引例 Citations：

◎ 六法者何？一气韵生动是也，二骨法用笔是也，三应物象形是也，四随类赋彩是也，五经营位置是也，六传移模写是也。（谢赫《古画品录》）

（绘画的六个法则是什么呢？其一是作品要充满生气，富有神韵；其二是运笔能自如呈现各种线条变化；其三是造型要顺应对象外形特征；其四是要根据对象特征进行着色；其五是构图要合理搭配，呈现整体效果；其六是要临摹佳作以传承前人画技。）

There are six rules for painting. A painting should be full of vitality and artistic appeal; the painting brush should be used in such a way as to make changes in lines natural; image painted should suit the appearance of the painted object; coloring should suit the features of the object portrayed; the painting should be well structured to present an overall visual effect; and masterpieces of past painters should be copied to draw inspiration from them. (Xie He: *An Appraisal of Ancient Paintings*)

◎六法精论，万古不移，然而骨法用笔以下五法可学，如其气韵，必在生知，固不可以巧密得，复不可以岁月到，默契神会，不知然而然也。（郭若虚《画图见闻志·论气韵非师》）

（谢赫提出的绘画六法所论精当，万古不会改变。但是"骨法用笔"以下五方面可以学习，至于"气韵生动"，必定需要与生俱来的天赋，既不能凭借精巧细密而得到，也不能通过长期的积累获得，只能靠心灵去感悟、契合，虽不知怎么做但不知不觉就做到了。）

The six rules of painting are succinct and discerning and will stand the test of time. The latter five rules, starting with "forceful brush strokes," can be learned. But "dynamic style" requires innate aptitude and is not something that can be acquired just through scrupulous efforts or lengthy practice. Only an inspired mind can achieve dynamic style, yet without consciously knowing how. (Guo Ruoxu: *Experiences in Painting*)

绘事后素 /huì shì hòu sù/
The White Silk First, the Painting Afterwards / Beauty from Natural Simplicity

原指绘画须先有白绢作底，引申为美感源于自然质朴。孔子（前551—前479）由此阐发仁义为本、礼教为辅的理念，强调礼的教育起源于人的自然本性。后来这一术语引入文艺创作与批评，它倡导雕饰起源于质素，文质相符，彰显天然之美。

The original meaning of this phrase is that a piece of white silk must be prepared before one can paint. The concept was then extended to mean that beauty comes from natural simplicity. From this, Confucius (551-479 BC) put forward the notion that benevolence and righteousness are fundamental and the code of ethics secondary, emphasizing that the teaching of the rites originates in human nature. This concept was later introduced into literary and artistic creation and criticism, which advocates that elaboration should be based on substance, and that style and substance should be compatible and complement each other to bring out the natural beauty.

引例 Citations：

◎子夏问曰："'巧笑倩兮，美目盼兮，素以为绚兮。'何谓也？"子曰："绘事后素。"(《论语·八佾》)

(子夏问道："'美妙的笑靥那样迷人啊，漂亮的眼睛含羞顾盼啊，就像是白绢上画出了绚丽的画啊！'这几句诗是什么意思？"孔子道："先有白绢才能作画。")

Zixia asked: "A seductive smile with pretty dimples, her lovely eyes sparkling, like a beautiful painting on white silk. What do these lines mean?" Confucius replied: "To paint, one must have a piece of white silk first." (*The Analects*)

◎礼必以忠信为质，犹绘事必以粉素为先。(朱熹《论语集注》卷二)

(礼教必须以忠信为根本，如同绘画必须先要有白绢。)

The ethical code must be based on loyalty and faithfulness, like a painting that must be done on a piece of white silk prepared. (Zhu Xi: *The Analects Variorum*)

活法 /huófǎ/
Literary Flexibility

指诗文创作在遵守规矩法度的同时，又不可死守规矩法度，要有所变化和创新。与拘泥于前人格套、不知变通的"死法"相对立。

使作品具备活法的途径，是善于学习前人，在广泛涉猎、融会贯通的基础上，不拘泥、不胶着，从自己的情感和作品的美感出发，使作品的文法、语言呈现崭新的意义。宋代文论家们受到了圆转灵活的禅风影响，在诗文领域倡导活法，使之成为诗文创作的重要原则。

Literary flexibility means that one should respect the rules for writing poetry or prose but not be bound by them; one should encourage change and innovation. The opposite of literary flexibility is literary rigidity under whose influence the writer mechanically imitates the forms of established writers without innovation. One way to attain literary flexibility in one's works is to draw inspiration from others extensively and absorb their talent while refraining from sticking mechanically to the model. One should base oneself on his own feelings and the aesthetic principles so as to create new styles and new ways of expression. Influenced by the Chan spirit of liberal flexibility, literary critics of the Song Dynasty championed flexibility in literary pursuit and established it as an important principle guiding poetry and prose writing.

引例 Citations：

◎学诗当识活法。所谓活法者，规矩备具而能出于规矩之外，变化不测而亦不背于规矩也。是道也，盖有定法而无定法，无定法而有定法。知是者则可以与语活法矣。（刘克庄《后村集》卷二十四引吕本中《〈夏均父集〉序》）

（学作诗要懂得活法。所谓活法，就是作诗的各种规矩法度全都具备而又能跳出规矩法度的限制，使诗文产生各种不可预测的变化而且还不违背规矩。这个道理就是，说有恒定的规矩法度又没有恒定的规矩法度，说没有恒定的规矩法度却又有恒定的规矩法度。懂得这个道理的人，就可以与他谈论活法了。）

Those who wish to learn to write poetry should master literary flexibility. By this I mean that, while knowing all the rules for poetry, the poet goes beyond them to reflect unpredictable changes in his poetry yet without compromising the rules. The principle underlying this way of writing is that there should be set rules, yet they are not fixed; where there seem to be no rules, rules do exist. You can discuss literary flexibility with others only if they understand this principle. (Lü Benzhong: Foreword to *The Collected Poetry of Xia Junfu*)

◎文章一技，要自有活法。若胶古人之陈迹，而不能点化其句语，此乃谓之死法。死法专祖蹈袭，则不能生于吾言之外；活法夺胎换骨，则不能毙于吾言之内。毙吾言者，[故为死法；]生吾言也，故为活法。(俞成《萤雪丛说·文章活法》)

(写文章这种技艺，必须有自己的活法。如果只是拘泥于古人的陈法，而不能将他们的词句化陈出新，这就叫死法。死法只会因袭模仿，不能让我的文章在语言之外获得新生。活法则能超凡脱俗，不会让我的文章被语言困死。文章被语言困死，[所以称死法；]使文章在语言之外获得新生，所以称活法。)

In writing essays, it is necessary to maintain literary flexibility. If one is bound by the clichés of the classical masters and fails to produce novel ideas, this is what we call literary rigidity. Literary rigidity refers to mechanically copying others without permitting one's own work to acquire new ideas. Literary flexibility, however, allows one's work to free itself from clichés so that the work will not be stifled by stereotyped style of writing. Literary rigidity leads to a literary dead end, while literary flexibility encourages the birth of new ideas by going beyond the limitations of conventional way of writing. (Yu Cheng: *Reflections from Devoted Reading*)

肌理 /jīlǐ/

Reasoning and Structure

本义指肌肉的纹理，引申指事物细密的条理。作为文学术语由清代翁方纲（1733—1818）首先提出，兼指义理与文理两方面：义理是诗歌所阐述的道理或事理，主要指合乎儒家的思想和学问；文理是诗歌的条理或脉理，主要指诗歌的结构、格律和各种创作技法。明清以来，性灵派倡导文学抒发个体性情，摒弃教化；神韵派赞美诗歌意境的空灵玄虚。翁方纲反对这两种诗学主张，推崇宋诗的创作原则与方法，强调诗歌在义理上以经义为准绳，以学问为根底；文理上强调精细缜密，形式雅丽、穷形极变但要内容充实。清代乾嘉时期经学和考据之学盛行，肌理派就是在此背景下形成的诗派。翁方纲宣扬诗歌内容和形式的有机联系，推动了学人诗派的发展，但他一味鼓吹以学问考证作诗，受到同时代及后代文艺批评家的批评。

The term originally refers to the texture of muscle, and later by extension it refers to well-organized principles in things. As a literary term, it was first used by Weng Fanggang (1733-1818), a Qing-dynasty scholar, to refer to two aspects: *yili* (义理 reasoning) and *wenli* (文理 structure). The former is about views or reasoning, primarily concerning Confucian thinking and learning expressed in poetry; whereas the latter represents texture of poetry, especially poetic structures, metrical schemes and rhythms, and other techniques of writing. Scholars of the Xingling School (School of Inner Self) of the Ming and Qing dynasties advocated rejecting dogmatic guidelines and expressing one's emotions and thoughts in literary works, while adherents of the Shenyun School (School of Elegant Subtlety) believed in ethereal beauty and implicitness expressed through poetry. Criticizing both literary trends, Weng promoted the principles and techniques of the Song-dynasty poetry. In terms of *yili*, he emphasized the need to follow classical Confucian tradition and erudition. In terms of *wenli*, he advocated exquisite intricacy, attention to details, and graceful structures with a great many variations, as well as the need to convey a substantive message. During the reign of Emperor Qianlong (1736-1795) and Emperor Jiaqing (1796-1820) of the Qing Dynasty, a boom in the study of Confucian classics and textual research led to the emergence of the Jili School (School of Reasoning and Structure). Weng advocated integration of form and content in poetry, thus promoting the development of poetry based on classic learning. However, his overemphasis on classic scholarliness in poetry was criticized by scholars of both his age and later generations.

引例 Citations:

◎ 同之与异，不屑古今，擘肌分理，唯务折衷。（刘勰《文心雕龙·序志》）

（我不介意自己的见解与前人的见解是否相同，也不介意这些见解来自古人还是今人，只是通过对文章的条理和义理进行细致剖分，力求找到不偏不倚、最为合理的看法。）

I don't care if my views differ from those of others, nor do I care if the differing views are from ancient scholars or my contemporaries. What I do care is analyzing carefully the structure and reasoning of writings in order to arrive at a balanced view. (Liu Xie: *The Literary Mind and the Carving of Dragons*)

◎ 义理之理，即文理之理，即肌理之理也。（翁方纲《〈志言集〉序》）

（诠释儒家经典所追寻的"义理"中的"理"，实质上就是文章的道理和事理，也是文章的脉理和条理。）

Yili in Confucian classics is all about structure and reasoning in writing, i.e., the texture and proper presentation of writings. (Weng Fanggang: Preface to *Collection of Weng's Poems*)

◎ 士生今日，经籍之光盈溢于世宙，为学必以考证为准，为诗必以肌理为准。（翁方纲《〈志言集〉序》）

（士人生于这个年代，正值儒学繁荣昌盛，辉映世间，因此，做学问的人必以查考验证为标准，写诗的人必以遵循肌理为标准。）

Today's men of letters are in an era when Confucian studies are flourishing. It is therefore imperative that scholars base their study on research and verification, and that poets focus on the structure and reasoning of their works. (Weng Fanggang: Preface to *Collection of Weng's Poems*)

寄托 /jìtuō/

Entrust One's Thoughts and Feelings to Imagery

指诗歌作品通过形象化而寄寓作者的主观认识或感受，并能激发读者的联想。"寄"是寄寓一定的思想内容和个人情志，"托"是托物兴咏。是清代常州词派提出的一个文学术语。张惠言（1761—1802）主张词要继承《诗经》的比兴、讽喻传统。周济（1781—1839）进而认为，初学写词应力求有寄托，以提升作品意蕴、激发读者的思考和艺术想象；待入门后，则不能拘于寄托，而要言意浑融，无迹可寻。这一主张实质是反对观念先行，强调文学自身的特性，对于当时的文学创作有积极的导向作用。

The term refers to the entrusting of the poet's subjective understanding or sentiments to imagery in poetic works. It can also stir responsive appreciation of the reader. *Ji* (寄) means having a specific thought or individual feelings, and *tuo* (托) means giving expression to such thought or feelings through the channel of an object. It is a literary term first used by a group of *ci* (词 lyric) poets from Changzhou during the Qing Dynasty. Zhang Huiyan (1761 - 1802) stressed that lyric writing should follow the tradition of analogies, associations and allegories in *The Book of Songs*. Zhou Ji (1781 - 1839) further suggested that an aspiring poet should entrust his thought to imagery in order to raise the artistic appeal of his work and stimulate the imagination of the reader. After having established himself, however, the poet should not be bound by the technique of entrusting to imagery; rather, his words and sentiments should blend seamlessly. This view emphasized the primacy of nature of literature as opposed to the primacy of concept and provided a new guidance for literary creation at the time.

引例 Citation：

◎夫词，非寄托不入，专寄托不出。(周济《宋四家词选目录序论》)（作词，如果没有寄托，就很难深入；如果只专力于寄托，就不能意出词外。)

When writing *ci* poetry, one cannot effectively express one's thoughts and sentiments without entrusting them to imagery. On the other hand, overreliance on imagery will make it hard for one to clearly express his idea. (Zhou Ji: Preface to *Contents of Selected Poems of Four Poets of the Song Dynasty*)

甲骨文 /jiǎgǔwén/

Inscriptions on Bones or Tortoise Shells

商周时期用于占卜记事而刻在龟甲或兽骨上的文字，又称"契文""甲骨卜辞""殷墟文字"，是中国迄今为止发现的最古老文字，距今有三千多年。甲骨文最初出土于河南安阳的小屯村殷墟，一般认为由晚清金石学家王懿荣（1845—1900）于1899年最早发现。商周时期，王室及贵族上自国家大事，下至私人生活，如祭祀、气候、收成、征伐、田猎、病患、生育等等，无不向上天卜问，以占卜结果决定行止。占卜是国家政治生活中的一件大事，有刻辞的甲骨，会被作为国家档案保存起来。目前已出土的甲骨达十万余片，发现的甲骨文单字约4500个，其中能认识的字约1700个。甲骨文已经有较严密的系统，汉字的"六书"造字法在甲骨文中都有所体现，而且有大批形声字产生。甲骨卜辞也是今天研究商周时期历史的第一手资料。

Such inscriptions include oracles and events recorded on bones or tortoise shells of the Shang and Zhou dynasties. They are also known as "script chiseled out with a knife," "oracles on bones or tortoise shells," or "script from Yin ruins." They are the earliest known characters of ancient China dated more than 3,000 years ago. Inscriptions on bones or tortoise shells were first uncovered from among Yin ruins at Xiaotun Village in Anyang in Henan Province, generally believed to have first been discovered in 1899 by Wang Yirong (1845-1900), a late Qing epigrapher. In the Shang and Zhou dynasties, royal families and noblemen would consult heaven about anything ranging from state business to trivial affairs in daily life, such as sacrificial rituals, weather, harvesting, war, hunting, illness, and giving birth. It was the answers they thus elicited that determined what course of action to take. Divination was an important part of a country's governance; the bones and tortoise shells with characters inscribed on them would be stored away as state archives. So far, more than 100,000 bones and tortoise shells have been unearthed, about 4,500 characters have been tallied, and of these, about 1,700 have been understood and interpreted. Characters on bones and tortoise shells have become increasingly systemized, with the six ways of forming Chinese characters (namely, pictographs, self-explanatory characters, associative compounds, pictophonetic characters, mutually explanatory characters, and phonetic loan characters) all reflected in them and a large number of pictophonetic characters (or phonograms) that had merged. Oracles inscribed on bones and tortoise shells are also valuable firsthand material for studying the history of the Shang and Zhou dynasties.

引例 Citations：

◎ 文字之兴，原始于书契。契之正字为"栔（qì）"，许君训为"刻"……"栔"者，其同声段措（jiǎjiè）字也。……毛公诂"契"为"开"。"开""刻"义同，是知栔刻又有施之龟甲者。（孙诒让《契文举例·叙》）

（文字的起源，原本从刻写开始。刻写的本字写作"栔"，许慎训释"栔"为刻……"契"是"栔"的同音假借字。……毛传训"契"为开，"开"与"刻"意思是一样的，由此知道文字又有刻在龟甲兽骨上的。）

Writing began by cutting out or inscribing characters on bones or tortoise shells. The Chinese character 栔, according to Xu Shen, means exactly this... And 契 is a phonetic loan character derived from 栔... According to *Mao's Annotations on The Book of Songs*, 契 means the same as 开, which has the same meaning as 刻 – to carve. Thus we know that some characters are cut out on bones or tortoise shells. (Sun Yirang: *An Interpretation of Some Characters Inscribed on Bones or Tortoise Shells*)

◎卜辞契于龟骨，其契之精而字之美，每令吾辈数千载后人神往。文字作风且因人因世而异，大抵武丁之世，字多雄浑，帝乙之世，文咸秀丽。（郭沫若《殷契粹编·序》）

（占卜之辞刻在龟甲兽骨上，其刻工之精、文字之美，每每令几千年之后的我辈神往。卜辞文字的风格也因人因时而异，大体上说，国王武丁时期，文字大多雄浑，国王帝乙时期，文字都很秀丽。）

Words of divination, cut out on bones or tortoise shells, are truly admirable for their excellent craftsmanship and fine structures. They fascinate me nonetheless today, although they were the work of several thousand years ago. And they also varied in style from time to time and from person to person. Roughly speaking, the characters of King Wuding's time look majestic whereas those of King Diyi's time look elegant. (Guo Moruo: *An Interpretation of Selected Inscriptions on Bones and Tortoise Shells of the Shang Dynasty*)

建安风骨 /Jiàn'ān fēnggǔ/
The Jian'an Literary Style

又称"汉魏风骨"。指汉献帝建安年间（196—220）至魏初这一时期的文学作品中由刚健悲慨的思想感情与清朗遒劲的文辞凝结而成的时代精神和总体风格。汉末政治动荡，战乱频繁，人民流离失所。这一时期的代表作家曹操（155—220）、曹丕（187—226）、曹植（192—232）、孔融（153—208）、陈琳（？—217）、王粲（177—217）、徐干（171—218）、阮瑀（165？—212）、应玚（？—217）、刘桢（？—217）和女诗人蔡琰等人，继承了汉乐府民歌的现实主义传统，在创作中多直面社会动乱，反映民生疾苦及个人怀抱，抒发了建功立业的理想和积极进取的精神，表现出刚健、向上的抱负和豪迈、悲慨的情怀。"建安文学"的总体风格是悲凉慷慨、风骨遒劲、华美壮阔，具有鲜明的时代特征和个性特征，形成了文学史上独特的"建安风骨"，从而被后人尊为典范，其中又以诗歌成就最为突出。

The Jian'an literary style, also known as the Han–Wei literary style, refers to the literary style from the Jian'an era (196 – 220) of the Han Dynasty to the early Wei Kingdom, featuring powerful expression of passion, anxiety, and indignation. The final years of the Han Dynasty saw political turmoil, incessant wars, and displacement of people. Leading literary figures like Cao Cao (155 - 220), Cao Pi (187 - 226), and Cao Zhi (192 - 232), Kong Rong (153 - 208), Chen Lin (?- 217), Wang Can (177 - 217), Xu Gan (171 - 218), Ruan Yu (165 ?- 212), Ying Yang (?- 217), and Liu Zhen (?- 217), as well as female poet Cai Yan, inherited the realistic tradition of the folksongs of the Han Dynasty. In their writings, they dealt with subjects such as social upheaval, the suffering of the people, and the aspiration of individuals, expressing their creative spirit and resolve to pursue a noble cause. Their works demonstrate strength, courage and determination to overcome great odds. With a melancholy and powerful style that was magnificent, unique, and distinctive of its age, Jian'an literature emerged as a unique genre and came to be viewed by later generations as an outstanding literary style, with Jian'an poetry particularly highly regarded.

引例 Citation：

◎ 暨建安之初，五言腾踊，文帝、陈思，纵辔以骋节；王、徐、应、刘，望路而争驱；并怜风月，狎池苑，述恩荣，叙酣宴，慷慨以任气，磊落以使才。（刘勰《文心雕龙·明诗》）

（到了建安初期，五言诗创作空前活跃，魏文帝曹丕和陈思王曹植驰骋文坛；王粲、徐干、应玚、刘桢，随后奋力争先；他们都喜爱风月美景，游玩清池园囿，记述恩宠荣耀，叙写酣饮宴集，慷慨激昂地抒发豪气，洒脱直率地施展才情。）

In the early Jian'an era, the writing of poems in five-word lines gained unprecedented popularity, with Cao Pi (Emperor Wen of Wei) and Cao Zhi (Prince Si of Chen) dominating the literary scene. Other leading poets at the time include Wang Can, Xu Gan, Ying Yang, and Liu Zhen. They enjoyed beautiful scenery, particularly lakes and gardens as well as feasting and drinking; they reflected on the kindnesses they had received and past glories, and wrote about their sentiments and ambition in poems with passion and grace. (Liu Xie: *The Literary Mind and the Carving of Dragons*)

江西诗派 /Jiāngxī shīpài/
The Jiangxi School of Poetry

中国文学史上第一个有正式名称的诗文派别。它以北宋江西籍著名诗人黄庭坚（1045—1105）的"点铁成金""夺胎换骨"说为主要创作理念。该流派写诗以吟咏书斋生活为主，崇尚瘦硬奇拗的风格；强调师承前人，或师承前人之辞，或师承前人之意；重视文字的推敲技巧，追求字字有出处。这一创作理念与唐代诗歌追求兴象风神有着明显的不同，它的影响遍及整个南宋诗坛，甚至影响到近代。

The Jiangxi School of Poetry was the first school of poetry and prose with a formal name in Chinese literary history. It took as its core tenets the notions of "turning a crude poem or essay into a literary gem" and "squeezing new life out of an old sponge," as proposed by Huang Tingjian (1045-1105), a Southern Song Dynasty poet from Jiangxi Province. Members of that school devoted themselves to writing poetry with themes about scholarly life. They championed a vigorously "thin and stiff" style, stressed drawing on the skillful wording or remarkable ideas of their predecessors, and paid close attention to the techniques of writing to ensure that each word used in poetic composition can be traced to its origin. Huang's notions differed from Tang Dynasty poets' pursuit of impromptu inspiration, elegant subtlety of inspiring imagery as well as vim and vigor in poetic creation. The Jiangxi School's influence spread across the poetic community of the Southern Song Dynasty, affecting even early modern-day poetic creation.

引例 Citation：

◎歌诗至于豫章始大出而力振之，后学者同作并和（hè），尽发千古之秘，亡（wú）余蕴矣。录其名字，曰江西宗派，其源流皆出豫章也。（吕本中《江西诗社宗派图》，见《云麓漫抄》卷十四）

（诗歌发展到了黄庭坚时才开始宏大，黄力振诗歌创作，后世学黄的人一并兴起、彼此呼应，诗歌创作的千古秘诀尽被挖掘，再无妙法可言。现在记录下他们的名字，命名为"江西宗派"，因为这一派都起源于江西豫章人黄庭坚。）

It was not until Huang Tingjian's time that poetry started to embrace grandeur. Huang tried hard to boost poetic creation. Poets of later generations, who fashioned themselves after Huang, arose in succession and echoed each other. They solved the millennial mysteries of poetic creation so completely that almost no skill was left unexplored. Hence the term "the Jiangxi School of Poetry" to recognize its founder as a native of Yuzhang, Jiangxi Province. (Lü Benzhong: Branches of the Jiangxi School of Poetry)

结构 /jiégòu/

Structure

　　最初指房屋的构造样式，后指文艺作品的谋篇布局和各部分的组织排列。在书法理论中，"结构"既指单个字的结体，也指整幅作品的章法与分布。其中，笔画的长短粗细俯仰等，决定每个字的形态，故"结体"是书法艺术的根本要求。在诗文理论中，"结构"指诗句起承转合等方面的布置，或用于评价文章的结撰。在戏曲、小说理论中，"结构"用得更加广泛。明末清初曲论家李渔（1611—1680）在《闲情偶寄》中认为"结构"就像造物赋形，先要有轮廓，然后再有血肉，最终五官、躯体具备；又像工匠盖房子，要先胸有成局，不能边建边设计修改。李渔的结构论包括了"立主脑""脱窠臼""密针线""减头绪"等内容，强调戏曲是综合布局的艺术。在说明文艺作品中部分构成整体的组织与安排时，"结构"是最合适的术语。

This term originally referred to the general layout of a building. Later, it came to mean the overall framework and plot development of a piece of work of art and literature. In theories about calligraphy, it refers to both the structure of an individual character and the rules and layout of an entire calligraphic work. Strokes of varying lengths and widths, as well as their upward or downward tilts, determine the shape of a character. Therefore, structure is essential to creating a piece of calligraphic art. In theories about poetry and prose writing, it refers to elements of poetic composition such as introduction, the unfolding of a process, transition to another viewpoint and summing up; it is also used to evaluate the structural merits or demerits of an essay. In theories about fiction and drama, this term is used even more widely. The late Ming to early Qing drama theorist Li Yu (1611-1680) observed in his *Occasional Notes with Leisure Motions* that structure was like forming a concrete creature – one needs to set up a frame and give it flesh and blood until its facial features and body finally take shape. It was also like building a house – a builder should first of all create a general layout in mind; he was not supposed to change the design in the course of house construction. Li Yu's theory about structure included items such as a focus on the main characters and events, abandonment of stereotypes in creating a drama, coherence between parts of a drama and elimination of nonessentials. It emphasized the idea that drama was an art of overall designing. Structure is the most suitable term to explain how parts should be combined into an integral whole.

引例 Citations：

◎凡欲结构字体，未可虚发，皆须象其一物，若鸟之形，若虫食木，若山若树，若云若雾，纵横有托，运用合度，可谓之书。(蔡希综《法书论》)

(但凡要写出每个字的形态结构，不能凭空乱写，都必须要像一个物体，如像鸟的形状，像虫子啃食树木，像山、像树、像云、像雾，笔画纵向、横向都有依托，笔画的运用合于法度，这才可以称为书法。)

In calligraphy, the form or structure of a Chinese word should have a real-life equivalent – it won't do to write just as one pleases. For example, a character can be shaped like a bird or an insect nibbling at a trunk, or like a mountain, a tree, a cloud or a fog. A stroke, whether vertical or horizontal, should be supported by other strokes, and the use of strokes must comply with rules. Such a piece of work deserves to be called calligraphy. (Cai Xizong: *On Exemplary Calligraphy*)

◎至于结构二字，则在引商刻羽之先，拈韵抽毫之始。(李渔《闲情偶寄·词曲部·结构》)

("结构"这两个字，应当放在讲求声律的前面，斟酌用韵、下笔写词的开始。)

The term structure should rank above sound meters in importance. It marks the beginning of good rhyming and a careful choice of words. (Li Yu: *Occasional Notes with Leisure Motions*)

◎[《蟋蟀》]八句中起承转合悉具，可悟诗家结构之法。（牛运震《诗志》）

（《蟋蟀》这首诗一章八句，起头、经过、转折、结尾各个要素都齐备，可以从中领悟作诗的结构方法。）

The poem "Cricket" is complete with an introduction, the unfolding of a process, a transition to another viewpoint and a summing up. One can learn from it about how to arrange the structure of a poem. (Niu Yunzhen: *Commentaries on The Book of Songs*)

解衣盘礴 /jiěyī-pánbó/
Sitting with Clothes Unbuttoned and Legs Stretching Out

原指绘画时全神贯注的样子，引申指艺术家进行艺术创作时排除一切外在干扰而进入一种自由任放的精神状态。《庄子·田子方》讲述了一位画师纯任本性、解衣叉腿恣意作画的情形。"解衣"，敞开胸襟，露出胳膊；"盘（一作'般'）礴"，分开双腿，随意坐着，意谓全神贯注于作画。这一术语揭示了率性不拘、自由无待的精神状态是创作优秀艺术作品的重要条件，对于后世书画理论影响很大。

The term originally referred to the appearance of an artist who is concentrating on painting. It has been extended to mean an unrestrained state of mind free from external interruption when an artist is doing creative work. The book *Zhuangzi* describes a painter drawing freely with his clothes thrown open and legs stretching out. "To unbutton one's clothes" is to expose one's chest and arms; and "to sit with legs stretching out" indicates a casual posture while one is concentrating on painting. This term stresses the importance of a relaxed state and complete freedom of mind to the successful creation of quality artwork. This concept had significant influence on subsequent development of theories on calligraphy and painting in later generations.

引例 Citations：

◎ 宋元君将画图，众史皆至，受揖而立，舐笔和墨，在外者半，有一史后至，儃(tǎn)儃然不趋，受揖不立，因之舍，公使人视之，则解衣般礴，赢。君曰："可矣，是真画者也。"(《庄子·田子方》)

（昔时宋元君准备作画，所有的画师都赶来了，行礼后毕恭毕敬地站着，舐笔调墨，还有一半的人在外面等着。有一个画师来晚了，他悠闲自得，接受了旨意也不恭候站立，随即回到馆舍里去。宋元君派人去看，只见他袒胸露背，叉开腿而坐［正全神贯注作画］。宋元君说："对呀，这才是真正的画家。"）

Once when King Yuan of the State of Song was to do painting, all the painters came. Half of them, after paying him their respects, stood submissively to prepare brush-pen and ink for him. The other half were waiting outside. One painter, however, arrived late and was casual in manner. After receiving the king's instructions, he returned to his hostel instead of standing there respectfully. The king sent somebody to check on him, and he was seen sitting there painting attentively with his chest and shoulders exposed and both legs stretching out. The king exclaimed, "Yes, that is a real painter!" (*Zhuangzi*)

◎ 作画须有解衣盘礴、旁若无人意，然后化机在手，元气狼藉，不为先匠所拘，而游于法度之外矣。(恽格《南田画跋·题石谷为王奉常烟客先生画册》)

（绘画必须解开衣襟、叉腿而坐［排除一切外在干扰］，旁若无人，然后手上仿佛握有造化之精微，天地自然之气纵横散布，不再受先前的画匠束缚，而心神驰骋于各种技法之外。）

When doing painting, one should unbutton one's clothes, sit with legs stretching out, keep himself free from all external interruptions, and ignore spectators. That way, one is able to obtain miraculous creative power, draw inspirations from heaven, earth, and nature, go beyond the rules of previous painting masters, and freely use various painting techniques. (Yun Ge: *Nantian's Comments on Paintings*)

金文 /jīnwén/

Bronze Script

金文是商周时期铸刻在青铜器上的铭文，是在甲骨文基础上发展起来的一种文字。古代青铜器的种类很多，一般分为礼器与乐器两大类，乐器以钟为代表，礼器以鼎为代表，故前人将钟鼎作为古代青铜器的总称，因此金文也称为"钟鼎文"。金文应用的年代起于商代，盛行于周代，下至秦灭六国，计有800多年。据统计，金文有3700多字，其中能认识的字有2420个，较甲骨文略多。金文的内容多是关于当时祀典、赐命、诏书、征战、围猎、盟约等活动或事件的记录，反映了当时的社会生活。

Bronze script refers to writings inscribed on bronze ware in the Shang and Zhou dynasties; it was developed from inscriptions on bones and tortoise shells. There were many sub-types of bronze ware in ancient China, but they were roughly under two main categories: sacrificial vessels and musical instruments. Sacrificial vessels were represented by tripod or quadripod cauldrons, and musical instruments, by chimes. Therefore, ancient bronze ware was formerly known as "chimes and cauldrons," and bronze script used to be called "chime and cauldron inscriptions." The use of bronze script began in the Shang Dynasty, grew very popular in the Zhou Dynasty, and declined in the Qin Dynasty, lasting over 800 years. Bronze script contained over 3,700 characters, of which 2,420 are now intelligible, slightly outnumbering the intelligible characters on bones and tortoise shells. Bronze script was mainly records of sacrificial ceremonies, bestowals, announcements of decrees, declarations of war, hunting expeditions, and pledges of allegiance. It reflected life in those historical periods.

引例 Citations：

◎郡国亦往往于山川得鼎彝，其铭即前代之古文，皆自相似，虽叵复见源流，其详可得略说也。（许慎《说文解字·序》）

（各郡与诸侯国也常常在山间河边挖出钟鼎彝器，上面铸刻的铭文就是前代的古文，它们的字形都很相似，虽然不能看出文字的流变，但是造字的详情也还大致可以说明。）

Various old bronze wares, with epigraphs of old times inscribed on them, were often excavated from the hills and by the riverside in counties and vassal states. The characters looked quite alike. Although nobody can tell exactly how these characters have changed over time, their formative process is more or less traceable. (Xu Shen: *Explanation of Script and Elucidation of Characters*)

◎夫鼎有铭，铭者，自名也。自名，以称扬其先祖之美，而明著之后世者也。（《礼记·祭统》）

（鼎上面多铸刻铭文，"铭"的意思是给自己留名。给自己留名，实际是为了颂扬祖先的美德，让其堂堂正正地传给后世。）

Epigraphs are often inscribed on tripods to leave a name in history and, further, to extol the virtues of one's ancestors so that their reputations will be proudly passed onto posterity. (*The Book of Rites*)

劲健 /jìngjiàn/
Strength and Vigor

强劲刚健。用于文艺批评，主要指作品所显示出的强劲的生命张力、刚劲的语言和矫健的文思，以及所具有的自由奔放的气势和激荡读者心怀的感染力。它要求作者心境澄明、浩气充盈、内在涵养深厚、情志高远深沉，文思纵横无碍，语言丰富多变，强大的精神力量贯穿整个作品。

This term is used mostly in literary criticism to refer to a vigorous life force, the intensity of language, a burst of literary talent, an overwhelming impact, as well as a powerful appeal to readers' hearts. It requires the author to maintain a lucid mind, be filled with positivity, have abundant self-cultivation, embrace noble ideals, be unbridled in literary expression, possess a variety of styles, and infuse spiritual strength into his whole work.

引例 Citations：

◎行神如空，行气如虹。巫峡千寻，走云连风。饮真茹强，蓄素守中。喻彼行健，是谓存雄。（司空图《二十四诗品·劲健》）

（诗人的神思如同翱翔太空，作品的气势好似长虹横贯。仿佛置身于万丈之高的巫峡两岸，伴随疾风的是驰飞而去的云层。涵养真气，培育刚强；蓄积素朴，守持中正。领悟天道永不止息的刚健法则，这就是诗歌需要积存劲力的道理。）

A poet's musings can be likened to a soaring eagle; a literary work should inspire awe like a rainbow across the sky. He feels as if placed on a steep and lofty cliff overlooking the Wuxia Gorge. Clouds swiftly drift away, escorted by a strong wind. Thus, he cultivates vital energies deep inside him, grows in fortitude, and lives out his simple and unadorned life adhering to the principle of propriety. A poet should fully understand the rules governing the robust, ceaseless operation of heavenly forces and needs to accumulate inner strength to produce truly good poetry. (Sikong Tu: Twenty-four Styles of Poetry)

◎延年为人跌宕，任气节，读书通大略，为文劲健，于诗最工而善书。（《宋史·石延年传》）

（石延年为人豪放不羁，崇尚气节，读书粗通其义，但写文章气势强劲刚健，最擅长诗歌，书法也很好。）

Shi Yannian is vigorous and unrestrained. He prizes moral integrity. When reading a book, all he does is to get a basic understanding of its essential meaning. But when he writes, he writes with vim and vigor. He excels at poetry. His calligraphy is also admirable. (*The History of the Song Dynasty*)

竟陵派 /Jìnglíng pài/

The Jingling School of Literary Writing

明代后期的文学流派。因代表人物钟惺（1574—1624）、谭元春（1586—1637）都是竟陵（今湖北天门）人，故称为竟陵派，又称钟谭派。竟陵派重视作家个人的情性流露、反对复古模拟，与公安派主张相同，但他们又认为以袁宏道（1568—1610）等为代表的公安派作品俚俗、浮浅，因而倡导一种幽深孤峭的作品风格，主张文学创作应抒写"性灵"。竟陵派所宣扬的"性灵"，其实是为了追求新奇深奥、与众不同，而刻意雕琢字句，极力造成幽深孤峭、艰涩隐晦的诗歌风格。竟陵派对晚明以后的反拟古文风和小品文的大量产生有促进之功，但他们的创作题材狭窄、语言艰涩，束缚了这一派的发展。

This was a school of literary creation in the late Ming Dynasty represented by Zhong Xing (1574-1624) and Tan Yuanchun (1586-1637), who were both natives of Jingling (today's Tianmen, Hubei Province). It was also known as the Zhong-Tan School. Like members of the Gong'an School of Literary Writing, the Jingling School valued the showing of a writer's true feelings and character and opposed stubborn emulation of ancient literature. However, they regarded works of the Gong'an School represented by Yuan Hongdao (1568-1610) as slangy and shallow. They advocated a serene and solitary style, arguing that literary creation should express the "inner self." But in fact, such an "inner self" pursues only novelty, abstruseness, and aloofness from ordinary mortals. The Jingling School paid excessive attention to wording, trying to create an atmosphere of solitude and profundity. Members of the school contributed to the resistance of stubborn emulation of ancient literature and the emergence of many refined, informal essays. However, the limitation of subject matter and abstruseness of language restrained their further development.

◎惺与同邑谭子元春忧之，内省诸心，不敢先有所谓"学古""不学古"者，而第求古人真诗所在。真诗者，精神所为也。察其幽情单绪，孤行静寄于喧杂之中，而乃以其虚怀定力，独往冥游于寥廓之外。（钟惺《诗归·序》）

（我和同郡人谭元春很担心这种情况，我们在内心反思，不敢先存"学古"或者"不学古"的判断，只是探求古人的诗究竟"真"在哪里。所谓真诗，一定是心神活动的结果。考察这种心神活动，发现它实际是古人幽隐孤寂的情感流露以及在喧杂尘世中所保持的安静独行，它有一种特殊的虚怀和定力，使古人能够独游于苍穹之外。）

My fellow townsman Tan Yuanchun and I share the same worry. Even after much thought, we still hardly dare say whether to emulate ancient literature or not. What we attempt to do is to find out where the "true essence" of old-time poetry lies. True poetry has to be the outcome of spiritual activity. A careful examination of such activity would reveal that it shows the sentiments of ancient people in their reclusion and solitude, as well as the journey they quietly pursued regardless of the noise and bustle of the mortal world. True poetry has a magnanimous mind and quiet confidence; it enabled our ancestors to roam free beyond the horizon. (Zhong Xing: Preface to *The Purport of Poetic Creation*)

境界 /jìngjiè/

Jingjie (Visionary World)

"境界"本指疆域边界、土地边界，后来在佛经翻译中，"境界"一词被用于精神领域，指人破除对于物质世界的沉迷后所达到的精神层次或修为境域。作为文艺术语，主要指文艺作品中所表现出的审美层次和境域，是作者的创造力、理解力和审美能力在精神层面的综合呈现。有境界的作品是作者真实人格的显现，具备超越凡俗的意味，更能引发读者的共鸣，激发读者的想象，甚至提升读者的感受。"意境"形成较早，而"境界"主要受中唐以后佛教思想的影响而形成。近代学者王国维（1877 — 1927）《人间词话》对境界的阐释最多。王国维往往将"意境"与"境界"概念通用。他构建了融合西方美学与中国古典美学为一体的"境界论"。但一般说来，意境侧重作者主观寓意与作品形象的完满融会，通过鉴赏使想象得到发挥，而境界则突出心灵感悟使艺术形象得到升华，强调心灵世界对于作品层次的提升。

Jingjie (境界) originally meant border or boundary. Later, it was used to translate the idea of a mental realm in Buddhist sutras, a state of spiritual cultivation achieved after having overcome bewilderment in the material world. As a literary and artistic term, *jingjie* is mainly used to indicate the aesthetic depth in a literary work so as to give full expression to the author's creativity, comprehension, and aesthetic faculties. A work reaching a high level of *jingjie* manifests the author's true personality, transcends the ordinary, strikes a responsive chord in the heart of the reader, stimulates the reader's imagination, and thus enhances the reader's appreciation of his work. The term *yijing* (意境 aesthetic conception) came into being earlier than *jingjie* which was formed under the influence of Buddhism in the mid-Tang period. In his *Poetic Remarks in the Human World,* modern scholar Wang Guowei (1877 - 1927) wrote extensively about *jingjie.* He often used *yijing* in the same sense as he used *jingjie* or the other way round. He created the theory of *jingjie*, in which he blended classical Western and classical Chinese aesthetics. Generally speaking, *yijing* refers to a perfect combination of the message the author conveys with the images he uses in his works, and it gives full rein to reader's imagination. The concept of *jingjie*, however, foregrounds the sublimation of artistic images through mental insight, and emphasizes the role of the mental world in elevating the work of art to a higher level.

◎山水不出笔墨情景，情景者境界也。（布颜图《画学心法问答》）
（画山水的要素无非就是用笔和墨描绘情与景，情与景融为一体就
是境界。）

Painting landscapes is about depicting with brush and ink the artist's affective response to a natural scene. When the artist's sentiments interact intensely with the natural scene, a realm of what we call the visionary world is reached. (Buyantu: *How to Paint*)

◎言气质，言神韵，不如言境界。有境界，本也；气质、神韵，末
也。有境界而二者随之矣。（王国维《〈人间词话〉删稿》）
（与其用气质、神韵做评价标准，不如用境界来评价。境界是根本，
气质、神韵是末节。有了境界，气质、神韵必然也就随之出现了。）

The visionary world achieved in literary works serves as a better criterion for making critical evaluation than one's personal character or charm. The visionary world is primary, whereas one's personal character and charm are secondary. Once the visionary world is reached, personal character and charm will naturally follow. (Wang Guowei: *Poetic Remarks in the Human World* [*The Deleted Part*])

境生象外 /jìngshēngxiàngwài/

Aesthetic Conception Transcends Concrete Objects Described.

　　诗文中的审美意境往往在物象之外，需要鉴赏者领悟其中的精
神之美。"境"指作品所创造的审美意境，"象"是作品中所呈现出
的具体物象。诗歌由语言文字写成，所描写的都是一个个物象，在
这些具体的物象之外，能够形成整体的审美情境。唐代诗人刘禹锡
（772—842）首次提出这个命题，表达对诗歌意趣的思考，强调文

字与物象是确切的，而审美情境却是微妙而难以言传的。在古典诗论意境说的形成过程中，"境生象外"是一个重要的发展阶段。

The aesthetic conception evoked by a poem or prose transcends what a physical object denotes, and a reader needs to perceive and appreciate the beauty of such aesthetic conception. *Jing* (境) here refers to an aesthetic conception created by a poem or prose, while *xiang* (象) refers to the image of a concrete object portrayed in such writing. Composed of words, a poem describes individual objects through which it evokes a coherent poetic conception beyond the physical appearance of such objects. This proposition was first put forward by poet Liu Yuxi (772-842) of the Tang Dynasty to express his understanding of poetry. He pointed out that words and images were concrete while aesthetic conceptions were abstract and subtle and therefore hard to describe. Liu's proposition, namely, aesthetic conception transcending concrete objects described, marked an important stage in the development of the theory of aesthetic conception in classical Chinese poetry.

引例 Citations：

◎ 夫境象非一，虚实难明，有可睹而不可取，景也；可闻而不可见，风也；虽系乎我形，而妙用无体，心也；义贯众象，而无定质，色也。凡此等，可以偶虚，亦可以偶实。（释皎然《诗议》）

（"境"和"象"不是同一个东西，"虚"和"实"也是难以分清。有的可以看到却不能取用，比如景致；有的可以听到却不能看到，比如风；有的虽然与我的形体有关联，而它神奇的应用却不受形体的局限，比如思想；有的其义理贯穿于万物，本身却无固定的形质，比如色彩。所有这些，可以蕴含于"虚写"，也可以蕴含于"实写"。）

Aesthetic conception and imagery are not the same thing, and it is not always easy to distinguish between what is actual and what is implied. Some things like scenery can be seen but not taken, while others such as wind can be heard but not seen. Still others are like thought: it exists in our body but is not restricted by the body. Some pervades everything but possesses no

中华思想文化术语
文艺卷

particular shape, like color. All these can be expressed concretely or indirectly by implication. (Shi Jiaoran: *Comments on Poetry*)

◎诗者其文章之蕴耶？义得而言丧，故微而难能。境生于象外，故精而寡和。（刘禹锡《董氏武陵集纪》）

（诗歌难道是高度凝练的文章吗？有文章的意蕴却无需那么多语言，所以非常隐微，很难写得非常好。诗的意境往往产生于所描写的物象之外，所以非常精妙，很少有人能臻于完美。）

Is poetry highly condensed prose? A poem can convey the same meaning of a prose without using many words. Therefore, poetry is implicit and subtle, an art that is hard to master. Poetic conception often transcends what is denoted by the objects described, therefore it is subtle and difficult to achieve. (Liu Yuxi: A Preface to *Dong's Notes from Wuling*)

楷书 /kǎishū/

Regular Script

汉字发展演变中的一种书体。亦称"正书""真书""正楷"。为了减少汉隶的波磔流转，端正草书的散漫无则，方便书写和辨识，书家在隶书的基础上更趋简化，横平竖直，逐渐演化出楷书。楷书笔画平整，结体方正，富有法度，可作楷模，故名"楷书"。它始自汉末，经魏晋时期的探索，到唐代成熟定型，通用至今，长盛不衰。按照时期划分，楷书可分为魏碑和唐楷。魏碑是指魏、晋、南北朝时期流行的，由隶书向楷书发展的过渡书体。唐楷是指唐代逐渐成熟的楷书。这个时期名家辈出，唐初的虞世南（558—638）、欧阳询（557—641）、褚遂良（596—658或659），中唐的颜真卿（708—784），晚唐的柳公权（778—865）等，皆是楷书大家，作品为后世所重，奉为习字楷模。

Regular script is one of the scripts of Chinese characters, also known as "proper script," "true script," or "model script." To reduce the curviness and waviness of Han Dynasty clerical script, rectify the undisciplined and unregulated cursive script, facilitate writing and enhance intelligibility, calligraphers shifted toward a simpler style of writing, making both horizontal and vertical lines straighter. Thus, it evolved into the regular script. Characters written in this style looked neat and well laid out, upright and square, showing due reverence for rules governing the writing of calligraphy. This is precisely how it came to be called "model script." It first emerged toward the end of the Eastern Han Dynasty, became better known in the Wei and Jin dynasties, and fully matured and became widely accepted in the Tang Dynasty. It has been flourishing to this day. If divided by historical periods, regular script falls into two styles: Wei stone tablet regular script and Tang regular script. The former represented a transition from clerical script to regular script over the Wei, Jin and the Southern and Northern Dynasties period. The latter was Tang style regular script. Gaining its maturity in the Tang Dynasty, it witnessed many great calligraphers rising to fame, including Yu Shinan (558-638), Ouyang Xun (557-641), and Chu Suiliang (596-658 or 659) in the first years of the Tang Dynasty, Yan Zhenqing (708-784) in the mid-Tang Dynasty and Liu Gongquan (778-865) in the last years of the same dynasty. These calligraphers have since been honored as paragons of Chinese calligraphy. Numerous practitioners have been using their calligraphic works as models of calligraphy through the ages.

引例 Citations：

◎在汉建初有王次仲者，始以隶字作楷法。所谓楷法者，今之正书是也。人既便之，世遂行焉。(《宣和书谱·正书叙论》)

(东汉建初年间有一位叫王次仲的人，开始变化隶书来写作楷书。当时的楷书就是今天所说的正书。人们觉得它书写方便，于是就推行开了。)

During the Jianchu period (76-84) of the Eastern Han, a man named Wang Cizhong gradually changed clerical script to regular script. The regular script of that time was the same as the model script of today. Believing that regular script facilitated writing, calligraphers started to popularize it. (*Collected*

Works of Calligraphy Compiled by the Imperial Court During the Xuanhe Years of Emperor Huizong)

◎［李充］善楷书，妙参钟、索，世咸重之。(《晋书·李充传》)

（李充善于写楷书，他妙悟参透了钟繇（yóu）、索靖的书法真谛，世人都推重李充的书法。）

[Li Chong] excelled at regular script. He had a comprehensive and thorough understanding of the true meaning of the calligraphy of Zhong You and Suo Jing. Both his contemporaries and later generations have respected and admired him for his calligraphic skill. (*The History of the Jin Dynasty*)

空灵 /kōnglíng/
Ethereal Effect

指文学艺术作品中所呈现的飘逸灵动的艺术境界与风格。与"充实"相对。空灵并非空虚无物，它并不脱离具体的物象描写，而是通过有限的艺术形象达到无限的艺术意境，追求一种象外之意、画外之情，给人留下想象发挥的空间，如诗文中不着形迹、不堆砌辞藻和意象，绘画中较少使用浓墨重彩等。空灵用笔洗练，重在传达神韵，具有空灵特点的作品澄澈透明、飘逸灵动，能使人体悟到自由超脱的审美愉悦。

This refers to an open, free, and flexible style of a work of art; it is the opposite of a "densely packed" work of art. Ethereal effect does not mean sheer emptiness; it does not completely avoid imagery, nor does it entirely avoid natural description. Rather its aim is to suggest unlimited possibilities for the viewer's imagination through a highly economical use of brushwork and imagery so as to pursue the "meaning that lies beyond literal form" or "associations beyond the work itself." In this way it leaves room for the viewer's imagination. For example, just as redundant description is deliberately left out of an essay or a poem, along with ponderous wording or unnecessary images, just so thick ink and heavy colors may be avoided in painting. The notion of ethereal effect values simple layout and an economical use of details, seeking to convey character and imagination. Works that make use of ethereal effect convey a wonderful lucidity, and possess openness, freedom, and natural grace. Such works enable viewers to appreciate the aesthetic joy of free imagination.

引例 Citations：

◎古人用笔极塞实处愈见虚灵，今人布置一角已见繁缛。虚处实则通体皆灵，愈多而愈不厌。（恽格《南田画跋·题画》）

（古人绘画，越是在非常具体实在的地方，用笔越有飘逸灵动的感觉。今天的人作画，才画了一角，就已看起来琐碎繁杂。在虚飘的地方用实笔，则整幅作品都显得灵动，所绘物象越多越不会让人生厌。）

When painting, classical artists made use of ethereal effect all the more where a dense collection of objects normally was required. However today's artists no sooner begin to paint than they fill the space with elaborate details. In fact, if a painter applies a few specific details strategically in the empty spaces, then the whole picture will appear more open and alive. Under the circumstances the more images he uses, the less boring the picture. (Yun Ge: *Nantian's Comments on Paintings*)

◎文或结实，或空灵，虽各有所长，皆不免著于一偏。试观韩文，结实处何尝不空灵，空灵处何尝不结实。（刘熙载《艺概·文概》）

（文章或者坚实有力，或者飘逸灵动，虽然各有各的优点，都难免偏于一个方面。试看韩愈的文章，坚实有力的地方未尝不飘逸灵动，飘逸灵动的地方未尝不坚实有力。）

Some essays are written in a substantive style, whereas others feature an ethereal style. Although these two kinds of writing have their respective merits, they are each lopsided in their own way. But if one reads Han Yu's essays, he will find that they are a perfect combination of substantive content and ethereal effect. (Liu Xizai: *Overview of Literary Theories*)

枯淡 /kūdàn/

Dry Plainness

指诗文作品所呈现的质朴干枯、平和清淡的艺术风格。枯淡不是枯涩寡味、平庸浅薄，而是指外表看似干枯平淡、内里丰腴醇厚的一种表现手法，旨在用质朴平淡的语言和描写来表现丰富深刻的思想内容，创造出含蓄深邃、醇厚高远的意境。北宋初期，雕琢华艳的文风盛行，梅尧臣（1002 — 1060）、欧阳修（1007 — 1072）等人倡导诗文革新，标举平淡深邃的风格，认为诗歌的根本在于性情，无需刻意而为。苏轼（1037 — 1101）以陶渊明（365或372或376 — 427）、柳宗元（773 — 819）的诗歌为典范，进一步提出了"枯淡"的概念。"枯淡"与"平淡""淡泊""冲淡"等概念内涵接近，是道家冲和之美与儒家典雅之美的合流。

This refers to a literary style that appears plain and dry, mild and moderate. Here, dry and plain does not mean insipid, dull, common or shallow; rather, it suggests a means of expression that, while appearing prosaic, is rich in substance within. Its aim is to convey, in plain and simple language, a message that is not lacking in breadth or profundity and to create a deep and subtle, rich and far-reaching effect. In the early years of the Northern Song Dynasty, an ornate and sumptuous style prevailed in literature. Men of letters such as Mei Yaochen (1002-1060) and Ouyang Xiu (1007-1072) argued for literary renewal and endorsed a plain and penetrating style. They held that the essence of poetry lies in authenticity and true feeling and that there was no need to be too rhetorical. With the classical examples of Tao Yuanming's (365 or 372 or 376-427) and Liu Zongyuan's (773-819) poetry in mind, Su Shi (1037-1101) went on to put forth the notion of "dry plainness." It comes close in meaning to "calm," "unassuming," or "unpretentious" – a convergence of the peaceful and profound beauty of Daoism and the elegant beauty of Confucianism.

引例 Citations：

◎所贵乎枯淡者，谓其外枯而中膏，似淡而实美，渊明、子厚之流是也。若中边皆枯淡，亦何足道。（苏轼《评韩柳诗》）

（我之所以看重枯淡，是因为它形似干枯而内里丰腴，看似平淡而实际很美，像陶渊明、柳子厚等人的诗歌就是这样。如果中间、边侧都枯淡，那还有什么可称道的呢！）

I value the style of dry plainness because it looks withered and dry outside but is rich inside; it appears plain but is in fact beautiful. Poetry by such writers as Tao Yuanming and Liu Zongyuan is like this. If inner and outer were equally dry, why praise it? (Su Shi: A Critique of Poems by Han Yu and Liu Zongyuan)

◎故观之虽若天下之至质，而实天下之至华；虽若天下之至枯，而实天下之至腴。如彭泽一派，来自天稷者，尚庶几焉，而亦岂能全合哉！（包恢《答傅当可论诗》）

（所以，看起来虽像天下最质朴的，实际上却是天下最华美的；看起来虽像天下最枯槁的，实际上却是天下最丰腴的。像陶渊明等人的诗歌，自然天成，大致达到了这种境界，然而也不能完全符合啊！）

Therefore, what seems most plain in the world is in fact the most resplendent, and what seems most dry and withered is in fact the most fruitful. Poems by people like Tao Yuanming and his followers read naturally; they more or less achieved this artistic effect, though not completely! (Bao Hui: Reply to Fu Dangke's Discussion of Poetry)

苦吟 /kǔyín/

Painstaking Versification

指唐代诗人贾岛（779—843）创作时苦思冥想、反复吟哦的创作方法。苦吟诗人多困顿失意，所以苦吟也被视为诗人借诗解愁的一种方式。有时也指从事文艺创作时精益求精的创作态度。

The Tang-dynasty poet Jia Dao (779-843) found composing his poems quite a painful process, and his creative method was to chant his verses repeatedly to get the right line. Those engaged in "painstaking versification" tended to be exhausted and frustrated, and their poetry is regarded as a way of relief for their sorrows. Sometimes, the term also refers to a perfectionist attitude to literary and artistic creation.

引例 Citations：

◎二句三年得，一吟双泪流。（贾岛《题诗后》）

（两句好诗三年才写出来，一朝吟出不禁泪流满面。）

It took me three years to get two lines right. / So when I chanted them, my tears flowed. (Jia Dao: After Finishing a Poem)

◎吟安一个字，捻断数茎须。（卢延让《苦吟》）

（琢磨出一个恰当的字，捻断了好几根胡须。）

Chanting in search of the right word, / I twisted off several hairs of my beard. (Lu Yanrang: Painstaking Versification)

夸饰 /kuāshì/

Exaggeration and Embellishment

文学作品中所使用的夸张和藻饰的创作手法。目的是增加艺术感染力，吸引读者注意，夸饰运用得好，可以达到写实无法企及的艺术效果，但是过度运用，则会产生华而不实的反面作用，因而古人提出了"夸而有节"的观点，主张夸饰要善于把握尺度。

The term refers to the use of exaggeration and embellishment in a literary work to enhance its artistic appeal. When used as appropriate, exaggeration and embellishment can achieve an artistic effect beyond that of realistic descriptions. However, if overused, it will create the opposite effect, making the writing too flowery to be credible. Therefore, the literary critics of old China believed that excessive use of exaggeration and embellishment should be avoided.

引例 Citations：

◎故自天地以降，豫入声貌，文辞所被，夸饰恒存。（刘勰《文心雕龙·夸饰》）

（因此，自从天地万物生成，就先有了各种声音和形貌，只要用文辞进行描述，夸张和藻饰的手法就会一直存在。）

Therefore, ever since the beginning of heaven and earth, there have been sounds and outward forms. So long as words are used to describe them, exaggeration and embellishment will always be employed. (Liu Xie: *The Literary Mind and the Carving of Dragons*)

◎使夸而有节，饰而不诬，亦可谓之懿也。（刘勰《文心雕龙·夸饰》）

（使得夸张而有节制，藻饰而不虚假，也就可以称为佳作了。）

When exaggeration is used in a restrained way and embellishment is employed without pretensions, a literary work thus created can be considered an excellent one. (Liu Xie: *The Literary Mind and the Carving of Dragons*)

旷达 /kuàngdá/

Broad-mindedness / Unconstrained Style

指诗歌作品中所体现的超然物外、旷放通达的胸襟和艺术风格。是作者通达的人生观及平和心态与作品艺术形象的高度融合。具有旷放性情的作者，多因世事坎坷或社会动乱而落魄或退隐，往往以诗文抒写胸臆，反映在诗歌作品中，既有对世事物情超旷出尘的人生警悟，也有愤世嫉俗、傲岸不羁的真情流露。它的渊源可以追溯到儒家有为和道家顺其自然的思想及魏晋名士超尘脱俗、开朗达观的人生态度。既不逃避世俗，也不贪恋名利，事理通达，心境开阔。唐代司空图（837—908）将其提升为一个诗学、美学术语，强调作品风格与作者心态及人生观的统一，意在倡导一种超脱旷达的人生观与审美心态。

The term means broad-mindedness and a totally unconstrained artistic style in poetic works. It presents a perfect union of the author's outlook on life, his peaceful mind, and the artistic form of his work. A broad-minded writer was often disheartened, who went into seclusion, caused either by frustrations countered in life or social turmoil, and he would naturally seek to express his emotion in literature. As reflected in his writings, such a writer possessed a keen insight into the vicissitudes of worldly affairs. Being cynical and indignant, he also revealed such feelings of disdain for the world and its ways in his writings. The origin of this attitude can be traced back to the Confucian concept of proactivity and the Daoist proposition of following the nature, as well as to the open and cultured way of life characteristic of famous scholars of the Wei and Jin dynasties. Such a writer would not shy away from the worldly, but neither would he cling to fame and wealth. He was completely reasonable in attitude and tolerant in mood. Sikong Tu (837 - 908), a literary critic in the Tang Dynasty, used this term to assess poetic and aesthetic achievement by emphasizing the unity of the style of a work and the mental attitude and the view about human life on the part of the author. The idea is to promote a view about life and an aesthetic attitude that is open-minded and uplifting.

引例 Citation：

◎生者百岁，相去几何。欢乐苦短，忧愁实多。何如尊酒，日往烟萝。花覆茅檐，疏雨相过。倒酒既尽，杖藜行歌。孰不有古，南山峨峨。（司空图《二十四诗品·旷达》）

（人的一生不过百年，寿命长短能差几何。欢乐时光总苦短促，忧愁日子其实更多。哪里比得上手持酒樽，每日在烟绕藤缠的幽静处畅饮。那鲜花覆盖的茅檐下，细雨疏疏飘忽访顾。壶中酒已经喝完，拄着藜杖漫步唱歌。谁没有死的那一天？只有终南山才会巍峨长存。）

There are no more than a hundred years in a man's life, so what difference does it make whether it is long or short! Joys are painfully brief, but sorrows are numerous. There is nothing like holding a goblet of drink, strolling in the mist and the quiet and shady garden, or watching rain drizzling down the thatched eaves covered with flowers! After finishing the drink, I will just take another stroll and sing! Who can escape from one's last day? Only the Zhongnan Mountains will forever stay lofty. (Sikong Tu: Twenty-four Styles of Poetry)

厉与西施，道通为一
/lài yǔ Xīshī, dào tōng wéi yī/

A Scabby Person and the Beautiful Lady Xishi Are the Same in the Eyes of Dao.

身长癞疮的人与美丽的西施，从道的角度看都可相通为一。厉，通"癞"，指长有癞疮的人。这是庄子（前369？—前286）关于审美相对性的著名论述。原意指身长癞疮的人与著名的美女没有区别，因为她们都是"道"的产物及体现。美丑的判断只是人们主观上的感觉而已，而且美丑之间还可相互转化。庄子的这一思想，强调从造物的本原看，美丑都符合道，都具有内在的同一性。这个思想启发后世的文艺评论家从相反相成的维度去看待自然万物与文学创作。

This is a famous statement made by Zhuangzi (369?-286 BC) on how beauty is relative. Originally it meant there was no difference between a beauty and an ugly person, because they both came from and reflected Dao. The character 厉 (*lai*) meant 癞 (*lai*, covered in scabs) in ancient Chinese. Whether a person is beautiful or ugly is but a subjective perspective in the mind of the beholder. Besides, beauty can turn into ugliness, and vice versa. Zhuangzi, from the perspective of the origin of all things, stressed that beauty and ugliness are both in accord with Dao and are inherently the same. This idea has encouraged later literary critics to look at all things, including literary works, from the perspective that opposite things complement each other.

引例 Citations：

◎举莛与楹，厉与西施，恢恑(guǐ)憰(jué)怪，道通为一。(《庄子·齐物论》)

(细小的草茎与高大的庭柱，身长癞疮的人与美丽的西施，还有各种诡变怪异的事物，从道的角度来说都可相通为一。)

In the light of Dao, a small blade of grass or a tall pillar, someone as ugly as a favus patient or someone as beautiful as Lady Xishi, as well as crafty and strange things, are all the same. (*Zhuangzi*)

◎大用外腓(féi)，真体内充。返虚入魂，积健为雄。(司空图《二十四诗品·雄浑》)

(大道呈现于外显得雄浑阔大，真实的本体则充满于内。唯有返回虚静，内心才能到达浑然之境；积蓄精神力量，笔力才能雄放豪健。)

The grand appearance is an external manifestation of Dao, while the true vitality permeates itself internally. Reverting to a tranquil void, one may gain fullness and amass inner strength, and he will produce powerful works. (Sikong Tu: *Twenty-four Styles of Poetry*)

乐而不淫，哀而不伤

/lè ér bù yín, āi ér bù shāng/

Express Enjoyment Without Indulgence and Express Grief Without Excessive Distress

快乐而不放纵，悲哀而不伤身。原是孔子（前551—前479）对于《诗经·周南·关雎》中有关青年男女爱情描写的评语，后世儒家将其作为倡导诗歌及其他文学作品中正平和、情理谐和之美的基本规范与评价标准。这一术语与儒家提倡的中庸思想相一致。近现代以来，其思想内涵也因受到时代潮流冲击而不断更新。

This is what Confucius (551-479 BC) said of the description of love between young men and women in the poem entitled "Guan Ju" in "Ballads of Zhounan," *The Book of Songs*. Later Confucian scholars regarded this as a basic requirement for poems and other literary works to advocate impartiality, peace of mind, and harmony between emotion and reason, making it a criterion for evaluating literary works. Its connotation is in accord with *zhongyong* (the golden mean) of Confucianism. In the more recent history, the connotation of the term has been continuously renewed to keep pace with the times.

引例 Citations：

◎《关雎》乐而不淫，哀而不伤。(《论语·八佾》)

(《关雎》快乐而不放纵，悲哀而不伤身。)

The poem "Guan Ju" expresses enjoyment without indulgence and grief

中华思想文化术语
文艺卷

without excessive distress. (*The Analects*)

◎《国风》好色而不淫,《小雅》怨诽而不乱。(《史记·屈原贾生列传》)
(《国风》虽然描写爱恋情欲，但是并不放纵;《小雅》虽有怨恨与批评，但是并不煽动作乱。)

"Ballads from the States" express passion of love without indulgence. "Minor Court Hymns" make complaints and criticisms without inciting trouble. (*Records of the Historian*)

诔碑 /lěibēi/
Eulogy or Inscription Carved on a Stela

古代文体名称，是为有一定成就或德行的逝者撰写的篇幅短小的誉美性传文。"诔"主要叙述逝者的德行，表达作者的哀伤，通常用韵文写作;"碑"是刻在石碑上的文辞，一般分两部分: 前半简要叙述逝者的生平，后半则用韵文赞美逝者的功业和品德。南朝刘勰（465？—520？或532？）认为，诔碑立传的对象，已经由帝王逐渐延及普通人，立传的目的是让逝者的精神永远不朽。其写作要求是，记载事迹要如实，故应有所选择;评述德行较虚，故可以多加誉美。诔文和碑文是生者缅怀逝者的情感需求，满足每个人追求不朽的心理需求，也有弘扬美德、激励后人的意义，因此要避免轻率为文、简单臧否。

These constitute a genre of short rewriting in ancient times to sing the praise of a meritorious or virtuous deceased person. Such a eulogy, written in rhymed verse, was usually used to recount the deceased person's virtuous deeds and express one's grief over his death. The inscription carved on a stela has two parts, with the first part being a brief account of the life of a deceased person and the second extolling the person's merits and virtues. According to

Liu Xie (465 ?- 520 ? or 532 ?) of the Southern Dynasties, this kind of writing was no longer written for emperors and kings only, but was extended to cover ordinary people. The text was written to see that the deceased person's noble character passes down to posterity. It should highlight the person's deeds truthfully and eulogize his fine deeds and virtue. A eulogy or an inscription carved on a stela was written to cherish the memory of the deceased and satisfy the need of those who were alive to seek eternal solace. It should also promote virtue and inspire later generations to excel. So, it should be discreet and proper in its assessment of the deceased person.

引例 Citations：

◎诔者，累也；累其德行，旌之不朽也。（刘勰《文心雕龙·诔碑》）（"诔"的意思是积累，就是罗列逝者的德行，加以表彰而使之永垂不朽。）

Lei originally meant accumulate, so a eulogy lists a deceased person's meritorious and virtuous deeds and extols him to make him eternal. (Liu Xie: *The Literary Mind and the Carving of Dragons*)

◎夫属（zhǔ）碑之体，资乎史才，其序则传（zhuàn），其文则铭。（刘勰《文心雕龙·诔碑》）

（写作碑文，须有史家的才能。它前面的叙事相当于史传，后面的韵文相当于铭文。）

It requires a historian's talent to write an inscription carved on a stela. Its first half is no different from a biography and its second half, written in rhymed verse, is like an epigraph. (Liu Xie: *The Literary Mind and the Carving of Dragons*)

离形得似 /líxíng-désì/
Transcend the Outer Form to Capture the Essence

文艺创作描绘对象时要善于超越外形而捕捉其精神特征，达到

高度真实。庄子（前369？—前286）认为生命的根本在于精神而
非形体，应该忘记形体存在而让精神自由驰骋。晚唐诗人司空图
（837—908）借鉴这一观点，认为诗歌描绘对象也要追求神似而
超越形似。这一诗歌创作理念和批评术语后来也在书法、绘画领
域得到贯彻。

When describing something, literary writing should be able to go beyond
external appearance to capture the essence so as to reflect a high degree of
reality. Zhuangzi (369?-286 BC) considered that the essence of life lies in the
inner spirit rather than the physical form. One should forget one's physical
existence and give full free rein to the spirit. The late Tang poet Sikong Tu
(837-908) adopted this view and believed that poetic description should
likewise focus on essence rather than form. This concept of poetic creation
and critique was later applied in calligraphy and painting as well.

引例 Citations：

◎有生必先无离形，形不离而生亡者有之矣。（《庄子·达生》）

（生命的存在必定要以形体健全为前提，但是形体没有离开生命而
生命已经死亡的人也是有的啊。）

Life exists in a physical body. However, there are people who are dead due to
lack of spirit although they are alive physically. (*Zhuangzi*)

◎离形得似，庶几斯人。（司空图《二十四诗品·形容》）

（做到离形得似，那才是真正善于描写对象的诗人。）

He who can transcend the outer form aside and capture the essence is truly a
great poet. (Sikong Tu: Twenty-four Styles of Poetry)

◎离形得似，书家上乘，然此中消息甚微，不可死在句下。（姚孟
起《字学臆参》）

（做到离形得似，即是书法作品中的上乘之作，不过这其中的道理
很微妙，不能死抠字面意思。）

The work that transcends the outer form and captures the essence is a masterpiece. However, the theory underpinning this ability is very subtle and is not to be understood mechanically. (Yao Mengqi: *Personal Reflections on the Art of Calligraphy*)

理趣 /lǐqù/
Philosophical Substance Through Artistic Appeal

指文学作品通过艺术形象而展示给人们的某种哲理和审美趣味，亦指读者通过对作品的阅读欣赏而领略到的其中所蕴含的哲理启示与审美趣味。魏晋南北朝出现的玄言诗崇尚玄理，宋人好以议论入诗，皆为后人诟病。因而有些诗歌评论家反对脱离艺术形象而单纯说"理"的创作理念，主张将"理"寄寓在艺术形象中，化为鲜活生动的审美趣味，所以称作理趣。这里的"理"是人生体悟，而非知识和学问，不能用逻辑概念去表达。这里的"趣"是一种审美情趣，是体悟人生哲理后的内心喜悦。"理趣说"将诗歌能否说理的争议转化为哲理与情趣相结合的理论主张，有助于辩证看待一切寄寓思考与体悟的文学作品。

This term refers to the philosophical substance of a work as well as its literary appeal conveyed to readers through its artistic image. In other words, it means the philosophical insights and aesthetic engagement that readers acquire through the process of appreciatively reading classic literary works. For example, poets of the Wei, Jin, or Southern and Northern dynasties were fond of entertaining abstruse schools of philosophy in their poems, while Song-dynasty poets often used poetry to comment on the society of their time. Both practices were treated as faults by some critics of later times. Some later critics even maintained that philosophical content should never figure into a poem apart from artistic images. Instead they insisted that the substantial content of the poem should be conveyed only by means of artistic images so that it could be grasped by readers through their appreciation of the work's artistic features, thus the term "substance through artistic appeal." *Li* (理) in this phrase refers to insights derived from the experience of life rather than bookish knowledge and learning. It is not something that can be acquired or expressed through logical argument. *Qu* (趣) refers to the aesthetic delight readers obtain when they acquire insight into life through reading classic literary works. This concept turns the dispute over whether poems could present logical arguments into a theory of the integration of reason and taste in poetic writing. It helps critics appreciate dialectically those literary works that contain both logic and insight.

引例 Citations：

◎盖古人于诗不苟作、不多作，而或一诗之出，必极天下之至精。状理则理趣浑然，状事则事情昭然，状物则物态宛然。（包恢《答曾子华论诗》）

（大约古人作诗，不轻易作，也不多作，只要创作一首诗，就一定追求天底下最好。说理则哲理与趣味浑然一体，叙事则事情的来龙去脉很明晰，写物则事物的形态让人感觉真切自然。）

Most likely, when writing poems, the classic poets neither wrote carelessly nor wrote many of them. Once they had decided to write a poem, they would strive to create the best work possible. As for philosophical substance, the argument and its aesthetic appeal should be well integrated; when it came to narration, the logic of the story was made perfectly clear, and descriptions were such that the thing described would appear natural and lifelike. (Bao Hui: Letter to Zeng Zihua on Poetry)

◎诗不能离理，然贵有理趣，不贵下理语。（沈德潜《清诗别裁集·凡例》）

（写诗不能背离哲理，但贵在将哲理与审美趣味融为一体，不推崇直接写出哲理。）

A poem cannot avoid philosophical content, yet it is best to integrate the argument with aesthetic appeal. Direct argument is inappropriate for poetry. (Shen Deqian: *Collection of Poems in the Qing Dynasty*)

立主脑 /lì zhǔnǎo/

Focus on What Is Central to a Drama

戏曲创作要围绕主要人物和主要事件展开。由明末清初曲论家李渔（1611 — 1680）提出。李渔认为，古人写文章，必有一篇之"主脑"。所谓主脑，是作者写作的缘由或文章的立意。一部戏曲，也必定围绕一个人、一件事而生发，这一个人、一件事就是戏曲的主脑，它推动戏剧情节和矛盾冲突的发展。这个"人"和"事"可以理解为戏曲的主角和关键事件。所谓关键事件是全剧所有事件中对矛盾冲突起枢纽作用、能够将全部情节串联起来的中心事件。他举例说，《西厢记》的主脑是张君瑞一人、白马将军解围一事，其余皆由此人和此事件引出。立主脑兼指立人、立事而言，很多人创作传奇，知道确立主角，却不知道确立关键事件，导致全本如同断线的珠子、没有栋梁的房屋。"立主脑"对于戏曲的结构非常重要。

The late Ming and early Qing drama theorist Li Yu (1611 - 1680) used this term to suggest that a drama should revolve around main characters and events. He said that when an ancient writer wrote an essay, he would always develop a main theme first. This main theme was what he wanted to write about. A drama, too, should unfold around a key character and a key event, namely, the main theme of the drama, which would spur plot development and interaction between characters. The key event was the one which, of all events in the drama, played a central role in developing the plot and which linked together all plots elements. As an example, Li Yu said the main character in *Romance of the Western Chamber* was Zhang Junrui, whom the White Horse General rescued and around whom all the other characters and events revolved. Main characters and main events were equally important. The authors of many legendary dramas knew how to create a main character but did not know how to set up a main event. As a result, their works looked like broken strings of pearls or houses without pillars. Establishing a main theme was very important to the structure of a drama.

◎古人作文一篇，定有一篇之主脑。主脑非他，即作者立言之本意也。传奇亦然。(李渔《闲情偶寄·词曲部·结构》)

(古人写一篇文章，必然有一篇的主脑。主脑不是别的，就是作者写文章的本来意图和主题。创作传奇也是这样。)

When an ancient writer wrote an essay, he would always develop a main theme first. Such a theme is nothing other than what he intended to convey through the essay. The same is true for dramatic legends. (Li Yu: *Occasional Notes with Leisure Motions*)

◎凡作一篇文，其用意俱要可以一言蔽之。扩之则为千万言，约之则为一言，所谓主脑者是也。(刘熙载《艺概·经义概》)

(凡是写一篇文章，其写作意图都应该可以用一句话概括。扩展开来就是千万句，概括起来就是一句话，所谓主脑就是这个意思。)

When writing an essay, one can sum up its purpose in a single sentence and expand it into thousands of sentences. That is what a "main theme" means – it is roughly a single-sentence summary. (Liu Xizai: *Overview of Literary Theories*)

丽 /lì/

Enthralling Charm

"丽"有成对、美丽、绮丽、附丽等多种含义，彰显华美、绮靡、艳丽等形式美感，是中国古典美学重要范畴之一。从风格而言，它既可表优美，亦可表壮美。就书法而言，它指字的结体之外有余味、余韵，让人兴发美感。就音乐而言，它表现为从清静中发出美妙声音，给人以古淡、素雅之美。

The notion of enthralling charm carries a variety of meanings, such as symmetry, beauty, splendor, and attachment. It highlights the formal aesthetic features of magnificence, intricate beauty, and colorfulness, thus forming a major component of classical Chinese aesthetics. Stylistically, this term indicates elegance and majestic beauty. When referring to calligraphy, it suggests a nuanced taste and a delicate charm beyond the Chinese characters' external structures, arousing one's sense of beauty. When referring to music, enthralling charm appears in a miraculous melody, calling to mind a classical grace and serenity.

引例 Citation：

◎诗人之赋丽以则，辞人之赋丽以淫。(扬雄《法言·吾子》)

(诗人创作的赋华丽而又符合法度，辞人创作的赋华丽却过度修饰。)

The songs by poets are exceptionally beautiful and also comply with rules of musical composition. Those by popular lyricists, on the other hand, are overly flowery. (Yang Xiong: *Exemplary Sayings*)

丽辞 /lìcí/
Ornate Parallel Style

骈文中运用两两相对的方式遣词造句。"丽"即骈俪、对偶。单音独体汉字比较容易形成前后两句对偶的结构，对偶句具有音节配合、意义呼应的整齐美、和谐美。古人借此术语肯定了语言的形式美但又坚持形式与内容相和谐，以最终创作出文质相符、尽善尽美的作品。

The term refers to a classical Chinese literary style generally known as "parallel prose," largely composed of couplets of phrases with similar structure. Monosyllabic Chinese words, each represented with a single written character, are fairly easy to arrange in pairs of expressions with semantic symmetry and prosodic harmony. The ornate parallel style highlights the beauty of the form of the language without neglecting the harmony between form and content; and it is employed to produce fine works of utmost beauty, with form and content reinforcing each other.

引例 Citations：

◎故丽辞之体，凡有四对：言对为易，事对为难，反对为优，正对为劣。（刘勰《文心雕龙·丽辞》）

（丽辞的格式，大凡有四种：文辞的对偶容易，事典的对偶困难，事理不同而旨趣相合的对偶最佳，物类不同而意义相同的对偶最差。）

Thus, the ornate parallel style has four types of couplets: matching words, which is easy; matching facts, which is difficult; matching contrast, which is excellent; and matching sameness, which is poor. (Liu Xie: *The Literary Mind and the Carving of Dragons*)

◎若气无奇类，文乏异采，碌碌丽辞，则昏睡耳目。（刘勰《文心雕龙·丽辞》）

（如果文章在气势上并无奇异的地方，文辞上也缺乏特别精彩之处，有的只是很平常的对偶句，那就让人昏昏欲睡了。）

If a piece of writing has no original appeal, lacks imaginative polish and is full of crude and common parallel phrases, it will bore people to sleep. (Liu Xie: *The Literary Mind and the Carving of Dragons*)

隶书 /lìshū/
Clerical Script / Official Script

汉字发展演变中的一种书体。亦称"隶字""古书"。隶书由篆书简化演变而成，在笔画方面，它改篆书的圆转为方折；在结体方面，其字形多呈宽扁，横画长而竖画短，讲究"蚕头雁尾""一波三折"。隶书相传为秦时小吏程邈所创，实际起源于战国，而程邈为这一书体的整理与定型起了至关重要的作用。与篆书相比，隶书的字形结构趋于简化，书写方式更为便捷。东汉时期普遍使用隶书，使这一书体的发展达到顶峰。魏晋时期也称隶书为"楷书""正书"，实为似隶而体势多波磔的"八分"。

Clerical script is a variety of Chinese calligraphy during its evolution, also known as the "official script" or "ancient style of calligraphy." It evolved from and was a simplification of seal script. In terms of execution of strokes, clerical script changed rounded turns to abrupt turns. Structurally, each character was wider and flatter, with longer horizontal lines and shorter vertical ones, featuring an elegant style like "a silkworm's head and the tail of a wild goose," and "one wave and three bends." Clerical script is said to have been invented by a junior clerk named Cheng Miao who lived in the Qin Dynasty but actually it originated during the earlier Warring States Period. Cheng Miao was the key figure for putting into order and standardizing this calligraphic style. Compared with the seal script, clerical script was simpler in structure and more convenient to write. It became popular in the Eastern Han Period, reaching an unprecedented height of development. In the Wei and Jin period, the clerical script was also referred to as regular script, or proper script, which is similar to clerical style, but with left-falling and right-falling strokes.

引例 Citations：

◎是时秦烧灭经书，涤除旧典，大发吏卒，兴役戍，官狱职务繁，初有隶书，以趣约易。（许慎《说文解字·序》）

（这时秦始皇焚烧经书，废除过去的典籍，大规模征发官吏、士卒去服劳役、守边疆，使得官府、牢狱的事务非常繁多，于是产生了隶书，目的是书写简易便捷。）

The First Emperor of the Qin Dynasty ordered the burning of the classics and sent large numbers of government functionaries and soldiers for forced labor or garrison along the border, leaving a huge amount of routine matters at government offices and prisons unattended. As a result, clerical script was invented to make it easier to deal with the increasing amount of document writing. (Xu Shen: *Explanation of Script and Elucidation of Characters*)

◎秦既用篆，奏事繁多，篆字难成，即令隶人佐书，曰隶字。汉因行之，独符、印玺、幡（fān）信、题署用篆。隶书者，篆之捷也。（《晋书·卫瓘（guàn）传附子恒》）

（秦代使用篆书，由于奏报的事务繁多，篆书非常难写，于是命令隶人帮助抄写文书，故称之为隶书。汉代沿用这一书体，唯独兵符、玺印、作符节的旗帜以及匾额、楹柱等上面所题的字还使用篆书书写。隶书，是篆书的便捷书写。）

The seal script was adopted in the Qin Dynasty. Later, because matters became numerous and it was very difficult to write with the seal script, the Emperor ordered junior clerks to help copy government documents. Hence the name "clerical script." The Han Dynasty continued to use this style of calligraphy, except when carving characters on a commander's tally, an imperial seal, banners used as tallies, horizontal inscribed boards or pillars at the entrance to a hall. The clerical script evolved from the seal script into a more convenient form of writing. (*The History of the Jin Dynasty*)

六观 /liùguān/
Six Criteria

文章鉴赏和批评的六个角度，亦是文章本身所具有的六方面要素，包括"位体"（谋篇布局）、"置辞"（遣词造句）、"通变"（对前人作品风格的继承与创新）、"奇正"（表现手法上的守正与新变）、"事义"（援引事例以证立论）、"宫商"（音律节奏）。"六观"作为批评方法论，是《文心雕龙》整个理论体系的重要一环，它使文章批评自此有章可循，避免了批评的主观性，对后世的诗文评论有着指导与规范的作用，也对现代文学理论建构具有显著影响。

The term refers to the following six criteria on literary appreciation and criticism which are also six key elements in writing: structural layout of writing, choice of words to construct sentences, acceptance and innovation in the style of earlier writers, inheriting and transforming traditional ways of expression, citing examples to support an argument, and musical rhythm. As a school of literary criticism, the six criteria formed a key component in the theoretical system established in *The Literary Mind and the Carving of Dragons*. The six criteria offered rules that could be followed to avoid subjectivity in literary criticism. They also provided a framework of theoretical guidance for later generations of critics and exerted significant influence on the development of literary theory in modern times.

引例 Citation：

◎是以将阅文情，先标六观：一观位体，二观置辞，三观通变，四观奇正，五观事义，六观宫商。（刘勰《文心雕龙·知音》）

（因此阅读和评论文章，先要标明需要考察的六个方面：一是谋篇布局，二是遣词造句，三是对前人作品风格的继承与创新，四是表现手法上的守正与新变，五是援引事例以证立论，六是音律节奏。）

Therefore, we should study and comment a literary work according to the following six criteria: structural layout of writing, choice of words to construct sentences, acceptance and innovation in the style of earlier writers, inheriting and transforming traditional ways of expression, citing examples to support an argument, and musical rhythm. (Liu Xie: *The Literary Mind and the Carving of Dragons*)

六义 /liùyì/

The Six Basic Elements

汉代学者从治理国家与社会教化角度总结《诗经》所具有的六方面意义："风"是用来阐发圣贤思想对民风的教化作用，"赋"是直陈时政善恶，"比"是以类比方式委婉批评时政的不足，"兴"是借助其他美好事物来鼓励善行，"雅"是宣扬正道并作为后世的准则，"颂"是歌颂和推广美德。"六义"原本是儒家用来阐述《诗经》创作手法的术语，后来也用它来说明一切诗歌的创作方式以及文学批评的基本原则。

The six basic elements were drawn from *The Book of Songs* by scholars of the Han Dynasty to promote the state's governance, social enlightenment, and education. The six are: *feng* (ballad), which offers an insight into the influence of a sage's thinking on ordinary folk customs; *fu* (narrative), which directly states the goodness or evilness of court politics; *bi* (analogy), which criticizes mildly the inadequacies of court politics by comparing one thing with another; *xing* (association), which extols a virtue by making an indirect reference to some other laudable thing; *ya* (court hymn), which shows the proper way of doing things as a norm for posterity to follow; and *song* (eulogy), which praises and promotes virtue. All the six elements were originally used by Confucian scholars to expound on the creative techniques in *The Book of Songs*. Later, they were used to emphasize creative styles of all works of poetry. They also served as essential principles of literary criticism.

引例 Citation:

◎风言贤圣治道之遗化也。赋之言铺，直铺陈今之政教善恶。比，见今之失，不敢斥言，取比类以言之。兴，见今之美，嫌于媚谀，取善事以喻劝之。雅，正也，言今之正者，以为后世法。颂之言诵也、容也，诵今之德，广以美之。(《周礼·春官·大师》郑玄注)

(风是从留存的民风习俗了解圣贤的治国之道。赋是铺陈的意思，即直接陈述那些反映时政得失的事情。比是看到时政弊端，但不敢直接指斥，而以类比的方式委婉指出。兴是看到当时政治清明，担心直接赞美好似阿谀谄媚，因此借其他美好事物加以晓谕和勉励。雅是"正"的意思，讲述当今正确的做法，作为后世遵循的准则。颂是"诵"（赞颂）和"容"（仪容）的意思，即通过赞颂仪容来赞美当今君主的品德，并且推广这种美德。）

A ballad tells how to run the country via the customs and folkways that have survived through the ages. A narrative flatly states the positive and negative things in state affairs. An analogy is made when one sees a vice in court politics but dares not directly point it out; it hints at the vice by describing something similar to it. An association, in view of the clean and honest governance of the time, voices its appreciation and support through borrowing from some other commendable thing, in order to avoid arousing suspicions of unscrupulous flattery. A court hymn is related to propriety, describing something rightly done and setting norms for people of later generations to observe. A eulogy praises and promotes a reigning monarch's virtues by admiring his elegant, upright manner. (Zheng Xuan: *Annotations on The Rites of Zhou*)

乱世之音 /luànshìzhīyīn/

Music of an Age of Disorder

指动乱时代的音乐。儒家认为，音乐与社会政治相互联通，音乐能反映出一个国家的政治盛衰得失及社会风俗的变化。如果一个国家政治腐败、社会动荡，其音乐、诗歌等文艺作品一定充满了怨恨愤怒。统治者必须及时检讨并纠正政治弊端，以避免出现败亡的下场。

Confucian scholars believed that music interacts with both society and its political evolution; it also reflects the rise and decline of a state's political strength and changes of social customs. If a state suffers from political corruption and social turmoil, its music and poetry will be full of resentment and anger. Hearing such music and poetry, the ruler must promptly review his governance and correct abuse of power so as to avoid downfall.

引例 Citations：

◎是故治世之音安以乐，其政和；乱世之音怨以怒，其政乖；亡国之音哀以思，其民困。声音之道，与政通矣。(《礼记·乐记》)

（所以，太平时代的音乐祥和欢乐，这是因为政治宽和的缘故；动乱时代的音乐充满了怨恨与愤怒，这是因为政治混乱的缘故；国家将亡时的音乐充满了悲哀忧思，这是因为民众困苦不堪的缘故。音乐所反映出的道理，与一个国家的政治是相通的。）

Hence, the music in time of peace indicates serenity and happiness because of good governance. The music in time of disorder indicates dissatisfaction and anger because of political turmoil. The music of a state on the verge of collapse reveals sorrow and anxiety because its people are in distress. So there is a connection between the music of a state and its governance. (*The Book of Rites*)

◎郑卫之音，乱世之音也，比于慢矣。桑间濮上之音，亡国之音也。其政散，其民流，诬上行私而不可止也。(《礼记·乐记》)

（郑国和卫国的音乐，就是动乱时代的音乐，近乎轻慢无节制了。濮水岸边的桑间所流行的音乐，属于国家将亡时的音乐。它们反映出时政极端混乱，民众流离失所，臣下欺瞒君上、图谋私利而不可制止。）

The music of the states of Zheng and Wei was the music of an age of disorder, bordering on wantonness. The music of Sangjian on the Pushui River was typical of a failing state. The government was dysfunctional, the people were displaced, yet officials cheated on the ruler and pursued selfish gains with no one to stop them. (*The Book of Rites*)

论说 /lùnshuō/

Writings of Argument and Persuasion

泛指古代各种论说文体。"论"是就某一理论问题进行深入研讨的文章，"说"指让人接受某一道理、主张的口头或书面说辞。南朝刘勰（465？—520？或532？）主张，论说文不要依傍前人成说立论，而应有自己的独立见解，须围绕一种理论、一个主题，依据经典和相关材料，综合概括各家见解，周密、深入地思考分析，得出严谨可靠、圆满通达的结论。而对于以说服人为目的的说辞，则要充满诚意，阐明正理和大义，要善于运用典型事例和美好言辞，增强其说服力与感染力，但不能虚假迎合、欺骗诱导。他还指出，论说者要以独立思考去抵达真理，做到师法自心、有创见，笔锋锐利，持论精密。这些见解成为衡量文章优劣的基本标准和文章写作的重要法则。

This term refers to writings of argument and persuasion in ancient times. An essay of argument and persuasion was written to explore a theoretical issue in an in-depth way (*lun*) and make an argument about it to persuade people (*shuo*). According to Liu Xie (465?-520? or 532?) of the Southern Dynasties, in writing an essay of argument and persuasion, one should not blindly copy theories developed by earlier scholars. Instead, one should have his independent views. One should draw his own persuasive conclusion on a theory or a subject by way of reasoning on the basis of numerous facts. He should find support in classics and other relevant sources, draw on previous scholarly reflection and explore an issue comprehensively and elaborately. The wording of such an essay, whose aim is to convince its readers, should be candid and sincere; such an essay should expound truths and uphold the cardinal principle of righteousness. It should increase its persuasive power and emotional appeal by using rhetorical devices and citing concrete examples. But such an essay should not be written to please the readers against one's own will, nor should it be designed to mislead them. One who writes an essay of argument and persuasion should, as Liu Xie pointed out, arrive at a truth through independent thinking, basing his judgment on his own views and conscience. He should be both incisive in wording and elaborate in argument. All these views have become essential criteria for judging the merit of essays and important rules governing their writing.

引例 Citations：

◎圣哲彝训曰经，述经叙理曰论。（刘勰《文心雕龙·论说》）

（圣哲讲述永恒道理的著作叫做"经"，解释经典、说明恒常道理的著作叫做"论"。）

The truths articulated by sages are called classics (*jing*). The interpretations of classics which explain permanent truths are called writings of argument (*lun*). (Liu Xie: *The Literary Mind and the Carving of Dragons*)

◎原夫论之为体，所以辨正然否，穷于有数，追于无形，钻坚求通，钩深取极。（刘勰《文心雕龙·论说》）

（考察"论"这种文体，是为了辨析是非正误，由穷究具体问题，追溯到抽象的道理，突破难题以求贯通，深入钻研直到获取最终道理。）

Writings of argument aim to distinguish right from wrong, explore concrete issues to arrive at an abstract principle, solve a difficult problem in an in-depth way, and make an exhaustive study to attain an ultimate truth. (Liu Xie: *The Literary Mind and the Carving of Dragons*)

◎凡说之枢要，必使时利而义贞，进有契于成务，退无阻于荣身。自非谲敌，则唯忠与信。（刘勰《文心雕龙·论说》）

（对人说理的关键，是一定要抓住有利时机而且道理正当，这样被采纳则有助于成事，不被采纳也无损于自己的声誉。说理不是为了欺骗敌人，因此需要讲求忠实诚信。）

The key to making a convincing argument is to seize an opportune moment and ensure that one's argument is justified. If an argument thus made is accepted, it will enhance one's credibility. If not, it will not harm one's reputation. To reason things out is not to fool one's opponents. Therefore, in making an argument, one should be truthful and credible. (Liu Xie: *The Literary Mind and the Carving of Dragons*)

美刺 /měicì/

Extolment and Satirical Criticism

赞美与讽刺批评。用于文学艺术领域，主要指用诗歌对统治者的品德、政令和作为进行赞美或讽刺批评。孔子（前551—前479）最早指出"诗可以怨"，强调《诗经》具有抒发不满情绪的功用，确定了诗歌创作的基本功能。汉代的诗学则迎合统治者的需要，突出诗歌歌功颂德的功能。汉代诗学作品《毛诗序》和郑玄（127—200）《诗谱序》将"美刺"确立为诗歌批评的基本原则之一，使之成为后世诗人和作家的自觉追求，是他们参与政治、干预社会生活的一种方式，从而构成中国文学的基本功用与重要特色。

This literary term is used in poetry to comment on a ruler's moral character, policies, decrees, and performance, either in praise or criticism. Confucius (551-479 BC) was the first to point out that poetry could be used to vent resentment and thus established a basic function of poetry writing by emphasizing the role *The Book of Songs* played in voicing grievances. In the Han Dynasty, however, poetry tended to be used as a vehicle for extolling the accomplishments and virtues of rulers. In "Introductions to *Mao's Version of The Book of Songs*" and Zheng Xuan's (127-200) "Preface to *On the Categories of The Book of Songs*," two influential writings on theory of poetry published during the Han Dynasty, extolment and satirical criticism was regarded as an underlying principle of poetic criticism. This principle was widely employed by poets and writers of later generations as a way of getting involved in politics and making their impact on the society. This constituted a fundamental function and an essential feature of Chinese literature.

◎［诗］论功颂德，所以将顺其美；刺过讥失，所以匡救其恶。（郑玄《诗谱序》）

（诗歌歌颂朝廷功德，是为了让他们延续光大美好的方面；讽刺批评其过失，是为了让他们匡救改正不好的方面。）

Poems are composed to applaud the rulers to continue to do what is good by extolling their achievements and virtues, and to urge them to change the erroneous course by satirizing and criticizing their wrong doings. (Zheng Xuan: Preface to *On the Categories of The Book of Songs*)

◎汉儒言诗，不过美刺二端。（程廷祚《青溪集·诗论十三·再论刺诗》）

（汉代儒者论说诗歌，不外乎赞美歌颂与讽刺批评两方面。）

To Confucian scholars in the Han Dynasty, poetry has two basic functions: extolment and satirical criticism. (Cheng Tingzuo: *Qingxi Collection*)

妙悟 /miàowù/
Subtle Insight

　　一种特定情境下形成的心理体验状态，在精神自由放松的状态下，直接领会、感知美，然后呈现于诗歌作品中，从而使诗歌整体的美感超越具体的语言文字，达到极高的审美层次。它能够在瞬间的心理体验中，达到物我两忘的境界，领悟诗歌的本质和永恒的精神之美。在佛、道、玄三家的义理中，"妙"指思维方面的精微玄奥，而"悟"则是一种体验式的、不依赖逻辑推理的认识方式。禅宗提倡通过禅修来达到本心清净、空灵清澈的精神境界，这种境界与文艺审美的精神境界有着密切的联系。南宋严羽（？——

1264)《沧浪诗话》借用禅宗的思想，对"妙悟"在诗歌创作中的特征与功用作了充分的阐发，开创以禅喻诗的先河，影响较大。"妙悟"也影响了中国古代的绘画与书法。

This term refers to an inner experience one gains under special circumstances. When the mind is so relaxed and peaceful, it allows one to develop an intimate appreciation and understanding of beauty and then express it in a poem. The beauty of the poem thus inspired transcends words and creates an intense aesthetic experience. Subtle insight enables the reader to appreciate the essence and lasting beauty of a poem by creating a spontaneous experience so engrossing that one becomes oblivious to both himself and the outside world. According to Buddhist, Daoist, and Metaphysical principles, "subtle" refers to the minute and profound nature of thinking, whereas "insight" is an intensely personal experience derived not from logical reasoning. Chan Buddhism promotes meditation as a way to return to the mind's original tranquility and thus achieve a clear and simple state of mind. Such a state of mind comes from literary and artistic experience. In *Canglang's Criticism on Poetry*, literary critic Yan Yu (?-1264) of the Southern Song Dynasty dealt extensively with the function and features of subtle insight in poetry writing by drawing on Chan philosophy. This book is the first one to apply Chan terms to critical writing on poetry and has thus gained great influence. The concept of subtle insight has also influenced traditional painting and calligraphy in China.

引例 Citations：

◎凝神遐想，妙悟自然，物我两忘，离形去智。（张彦远《历代名画记》卷二）

（凝聚心神，自由畅想，对自然之美的体悟达到绝妙境地，忘记了外在世界，也忘记了自身，脱离形体的束缚，抛弃知识的局限。）

By concentrating one's mind and freeing one's thoughts, one can reach such a fascinating state in appreciating the beauty of nature as to become oblivious to the outside world and one's own self, totally free from the constraints of physical forms and limitations of knowledge. (Zhang Yanyuan: *Famous Paintings Through History*)

◎大抵禅道惟在妙悟，诗道亦在妙悟。且孟襄阳学力下韩退之远甚，而其诗独出退之之上者，一味妙悟而已。（严羽《沧浪诗话·诗辨》）

（一般说来禅修最重要的原则是妙悟，作诗最重要的原则也是妙悟。比如孟浩然的学问才力远远比不上韩愈，但是孟浩然的诗却比韩愈水平高，就是因为他一心妙悟。）

Generally speaking, the most important principle of meditation is to achieve subtle insight, and this is the most important principle underlying poetry writing as well. For example, while Meng Haoran is no equal to Han Yu in terms of knowledge and talent, his poems surpass those of Han Yu because he is able to create subtle insight. (Yan Yu: *Canglang's Criticism on Poetry*)

铭箴 /míngzhēn/
Epigraph and Maxim

古代文体名称，是用来针砭过失、褒扬美德并启发哲思的短文。"铭"指铭文，是刻在器物上用以记功颂德的短文，其载体的神圣性及其垂范后世的意图决定了铭文要有宏大格局和雍容气度。"箴"指箴言，是用以规谏劝诫的警语。"箴"的本义是防治疾病的针石，因此有防范过失的含义。"铭"和"箴"都有警示、激励、扬善戒恶的功能，南朝刘勰（465？—520？或532？）认为，这两种文体的共同处在于，所选事例要确切可靠，所说道理要经得起推敲，行文要做到简明而意义深远。

These were two types of writing in ancient times aimed at criticizing errors, upholding virtue, and inspiring philosophical thought. *Ming* (铭), meaning epigraph, is a brief account of merits and virtues inscribed on a vessel. Its sacredness and exemplary nature means such writing should be aspirational and visionary. *Zhen* (箴), meaning maxim, on the other hand, is intended to admonish or warn. In Chinese, it is pronounced as *zhen*, meaning an acupuncture needle, a traditional device for preventing or curing disease. Therefore, a *zhen* should perform the role of preventing an error. Both *ming* or an epigraph and *zhen* or a maxim aim to admonish people against evildoing, promote virtue and punish vice. In the view of Liu Xie (465?-520? or 532?) of the Southern Dynasties, both types of writing should offer true and reliable information and convincing arguments and be succinct in wording and profound in significance.

引例 Citations：

◎故铭者，名也，观器必也正名，审用贵乎盛德。(《文心雕龙·铭箴》)

(所以"铭"就是命名，观察器物必须据其实质确定名称，审视功用重在增进美好的德行。)

Thus, *ming*, meaning "inscription" here is equivalent to appellation. When examining a utensil or an artifact, one should name it on the basis of its nature. The purpose of such scrutiny is to promote moral behavior. (Liu Xie: *The Literary Mind and the Carving of Dragons*)

◎箴者，针也，所以攻疾防患，喻针石也。(刘勰《文心雕龙·铭箴》)

(箴，就是针刺，用来批评过错、防止祸患发生的文辞好比治病的石针。)

Zhen here means to perform acupuncture for a curative effect. To offer a maxim is, like using an acupuncture needle, to criticize wrongdoing to prevent a disaster. (Liu Xie: *The Literary Mind and the Carving of Dragons*)

◎夫箴诵于官，铭题于器，名目虽异，而警戒实同。箴全御过，故文资确切；铭兼褒赞，故体贵弘润。其取事也必核以辨，其摛(chī)文也必简而深，此其大要也。(刘勰《文心雕龙·铭箴》)

(箴言是官员在君王面前讽诵的，铭文则是题刻在器物上的，二者的名称虽然不同，但用于警诫其实是一样的。箴言的作用在于防范过失，所以行文要依靠事实、表达要确切；铭文兼有褒扬赞美的作用，因此贵在格局宏大、文字温润。它们所选取的事例都必须可靠，经得起推敲，行文一定简明而意义深远，这是写作箴言与铭文的基本要求。）

Zhen, or maxim, is cited by an official to advise the emperor face to face, whereas *ming*, or epigraph, is inscribed on a vessel. Although different in name, they both perform a function of admonition. *Zhen* is used mainly to prevent an error, so it should rely on factual presentation and be precise in wording. *Ming*, on the other hand, also commends fine deeds, so it should be profuse and elegant in style. All the instances cited should be perfectly reliable and can stand up to close scrutiny. They should be concise and exert a profound social influence. These are the basic rules for writing *ming* or *zhen*. (Liu Xie: *The Literary Mind and the Carving of Dragons*)

目击道存 /mùjī-dàocún/
See the Way with One's Own Eyes

视野所及而瞬时感悟到"道"的存在。源自《庄子》。庄子（前369？—前286）强调人可以直观感悟到"道"的存在，而无需依赖语言说明和逻辑思辨。后被用于文学创作与鉴赏领域，强调超越耳目感知和逻辑思辨，在涤除一切杂念和外物干扰的心境中领悟并臻于最高的艺术境界。这一术语意在彰显文艺审美中直观感悟与超越功利的特性。

The term, which first appeared in the Chinese classic writing *Zhuangzi* (Zhuangzi 369?- 286 BC), means that one can easily see the existence of Dao with no need to rely on verbal explanation or on logical analysis. Later it was used for literary creations and in the field of connoisseurship. The concept emphasizes the need for one to transcend audio and visual perceptions and logical analysis, and do away with any interfering thoughts or external objects in order to attain true appreciation of art. The concept highlights the importance of seeking intuitive insights unaffected by utilitarian considerations in literature and art.

引例 Citations：

◎子路曰："吾子欲见温伯雪子久矣。见之而不言，何邪？"仲尼曰："若夫人者，目击而道存矣，亦不可以容声矣！"（《庄子·田子方》）

（子路说："先生您想见温伯雪子很久了。见了他却又不说话，为什么呢？"孔子说："像他这种人，只要一见就明白他身上存有的道，无需再用声音表达了。"）

Zilu said: "You, Master, have been wanting to see Wenbo Xuezi for a long time. But you did not say a word when you saw him. Why?" Confucius replied: "As soon as I saw him, I realized that he possesses the Dao! So there was no need for me to say anything." (*Zhuangzi*)

◎夫置意作诗，即须凝心，目击其物，便以心击之，深穿其境。如登高山绝顶，下临万象，如在掌中。（王昌龄《诗格·论文意》）

（当有作诗的打算，就应该凝聚心神，眼睛盯着想要吟咏的物体，用心去接触体会，深深穿透眼前之物而臻于诗的情境。就像登上高山绝顶，向下俯视万物，一切都好像掌握在自己手中。）

If you intend to compose a poem, you should concentrate your mind on it. Fix your eyes on the object which you want to admire in your poem, and appreciate it with your heart. By doing so, you will reach a perfect realm of poetic reflection, as if you have reached the summit of a high mountain, obtained a panoramic view of everything below and gained full command of them. (Wang Changling: *Rules of Poetry*)

南北书派 /nán-běi shūpài/

The Northern and Southern Schools of Calligraphy

中国书法的不同风格流派。宋代欧阳修（1007 — 1072）、赵孟坚（1199 — 1267），清代陈弈禧（1648 — 1709）、何焯（1661 — 1722）等人对南北书风之不同曾有过探讨，清代阮元（1764 — 1849）的《南北书派论》对此问题有更为明确而详备的阐述。他以为南北二派都出于钟繇（yóu，151 — 230）、卫瓘（guàn，220 — 291），索靖（239 — 303）为北派之祖。北派之书以碑为主，上承汉隶，能得古法，书风古朴；南派之书以帖为主，多不习篆、隶，尚真、行、草书，书风妍丽。

The Northern and Southern schools represent two distinctive styles of ancient Chinese calligraphy. Ouyang Xiu (1007 - 1072) and Zhao Mengjian (1199 - 1267) of the Song Dynasty, and Chen Yixi (1648 - 1709) and He Zhuo (1661 - 1722) of the Qing explored the differences of these two styles. Later, Ruan Yuan (1764 - 1849), also of the Qing Period, addressed this issue with clarity and at depth in his "On the Southern and Northern Styles of Calligraphy." In his view, both styles originated with Zhong You (151 - 230, from late Han to the early Three Kingdoms Period) and Wei Guan (220 - 291, the Three Kingdoms Period), while Suo Jing (239 - 303, the Western Jin Dynasty) was the founder of the northern style. The Northern School features calligraphic inscriptions on stones, which displays a primitive simplicity of the official script of the Han Dynasty. The southern style, on the other hand, is mostly found on paper and, rather than following the seal script of the Qin or the clerical script of the Han, adopts the regular script of the late Han, the semi-cursive script of the Western Jin or the cursive script increasingly popular over a much longer period of time. It is charming and beautiful.

引例 Citations：

◎晋宋而下，分而南北……北方多朴，有隶体，无晋逸雅。（赵孟坚《论书法》）

（晋宋时期之后，书法分南北两派……北派书法多质朴，擅长隶书，没有晋朝时的飘逸和雅致。）

In the years after the Jin and Song of the Southern Dynasties, northern and southern styles of calligraphy diverged... In the north simplicity prevailed, and the clerical script was popular, but the formal elegance of the Jin time was lost. (Zhao Mengjian: On Calligraphy)

◎东晋、宋、齐、梁、陈，为南派；赵、燕、魏、齐、周、隋，为北派也。……［南派］长于启牍……［北派］长于碑榜。……至唐初，太宗独善王羲之书，虞世南最为亲近，始令王氏一家兼掩南北矣。（阮元《南北书派论》）

（东晋、宋、齐、梁、陈时期的书法，称之为南派书法；赵、燕、魏、齐、周、隋等时期的书法，可称之为北派书法。……南派书法家擅长于书写奏疏、公文、书信之类……北派书法家擅长于书写碑文、牌匾之类。……唐太宗李世民尤其喜欢王羲之的书法，大臣虞世南效法学习，将王羲之家族的书法发扬光大，兼得南北派书法之长。）

The calligraphy of the Eastern Jin, Song, Qi, Liang and Chen period may be known as the southern style, while that of the Zhao, Yan, Wei, Qi, Zhou, and Sui period, the northern style. The southern style was mostly found in petitions to the throne, documents and letters, whereas the northern style was imprinted on calligraphic inscriptions on stones and plaques... Li Shimin, Emperor Taizong of Tang, was especially fond of Wang Xizhi's calligraphy. One of his ministers Yu Shinan emulated the Wang's style and raised it to a higher level of artistry. His calligraphy had the merits of both the southern and northern styles. (Ruan Yuan: On the Southern and Northern Styles of Calligraphy)

南戏 /nánxì/
Southern Opera

指北宋末年至明末清初流行于南方的汉族戏文。其源头是宋室南渡之时，产生于温州地区的戏种，在当时被称作传奇、戏文等，又被称为温州杂剧、永嘉杂剧、永嘉戏曲等。其特点是将民间唱腔引入杂剧，在村坊小曲的基础上发展起来，起初没有宫调、节奏方面的讲究，只是顺口可歌而已。元代高明（1301？—1370？）创作的《琵琶记》，标志着南戏体制的完备。南戏继承了宋代杂剧，开启明代传奇，篇幅长，角色丰富，而且各种角色都可演唱。《荆钗记》《刘知远白兔记》《拜月亭》《杀狗记》是南戏代表作。我国南方戏曲中有多种声腔都是在南戏基础上发展起来的。

Nanxi（南戏）, the Southern Opera, refers to the Han ethnic opera from the late Northern Song to the late Ming and the early Qing dynasties. The opera was created in the Wenzhou region when the Song court fled south. At the time, it was also known as *chuanqi*（传奇 legendary play）, *xiwen*（戏文 opera）as well as the Wenzhou *Zaju*（温州杂剧 Wenzhou Opera）, the Yongjia *Zaju*（永嘉杂剧 Yongjia Opera）, and the Yongjia *Xiqu*（永嘉戏曲 Yongjia Play）. Drawing on local folk singing styles, the Southern Opera first developed on the basis of village operas without any traces of musical modes and rhymes, and it was noted for being natural and smooth in singing. *A Tale of the Pipa*, a play by Gao Ming（1301 ?- 1370 ?）, marked the maturity of the Southern Opera. The Southern Opera inherited the Song *zaju* and heralded the emergence of the legendary play of the Ming Dynasty. Legendary plays were long enough to accommodate multiple roles and all performers sang. The Southern Opera masterpieces include *The Romance of a Hairpin*, *The Story of the White Rabbit*, *The Moonlight Pavilion*, and *The Killing of a Dog*. Many operas in southern China were created based on the Southern Opera.

引例 Citations：

◎龙楼景、丹墀秀皆金门高之女也，俱有姿色，专工南戏。（夏庭芝《青楼集》）

（龙楼景、丹墀秀都是金门高的女儿，都长得很漂亮，擅长表演南戏。）

Longloujing and Danchixiu were both daughters of Jinmengao. They were beautiful and good at giving South Opera performances. (Xia Tingzhi: *Biographies of Courtesans*)

◎金元人呼北戏为杂剧，南戏为戏文。（何良俊《四友斋丛说·词曲》）

（金、元时代的人把北戏称作杂剧，南戏称作戏文。）

The Northern Opera was known as *zaju* and the Southern Opera as *xiwen* in the Jin and Yuan dynasties. (He Liangjun: *Academic Notes from the Four-scholar Study*)

内美 /nèiměi/

Inner Beauty

内在的美好性情与品德。初见于屈原（前340？—前278？）《离骚》，指先天禀赋的美德，由家族遗传及早期环境造就。与之相随的是"修能"，即初明事理后自觉自主地进行品德修养，并培养更多的才能。后来，用这一术语强调作者应该具有内在的美好性情与品德，高尚伟大的人格决定高尚伟大的文学。

Inner beauty means a fine disposition and moral character. It first appeared in *Li Sao* by Qu Yuan (340 ?-278 ? BC), referring to an inherited innate moral character which was further fostered in one's early living environment. On this basis acquired competence develops, which is achieved when one, after gaining initial understanding of the principles of things, consciously improves his moral character through self-cultivation, and strengthens one's abilities. Later this term is used to emphasize that an author should possess an inner fine disposition and moral character, and that noble and great literature can only derive from a noble and great character.

引例 Citations：

◎纷吾既有此内美兮，又重之以修能。（屈原《离骚》）

（我天生拥有这么多美好的品德，又继续培养自己的卓越才能。）

Armed with such moral qualities given me by birth, I continue to develop competence. (Qu Yuan: *Li Sao*)

◎文学之事，于此二者，不可缺一。然词乃抒情之作，故尤重内美。（王国维《〈人间词话〉删稿》）

（文学创作这件事，要求内在品质和杰出才能两方面，缺一不可。而词是抒发性情的作品，所以尤其注重内美。）

In literary creation, one must have both moral standard and outstanding capabilities. Neither is dispensable. As *ci* lyrics give expression to emotions, one must focus on bringing out the inner beauty. (Wang Guowei: *Poetic Remarks in the Human World [The Deleted Part]*)

拟容取心 /nǐróng-qǔxīn/
Compare Appearances to Grasp the Essence

指诗人在采取比兴手法的时候，通过类比、描摹事物的形象外貌，摄取事物内在的意蕴和义理，从而将原本不同的事物联系、结合在一起。"拟容"说的是重视"比兴"的具体形象；"取心"说的是摄取事物的精神实质，即重视事物形象所包含的内在意蕴和理趣。合起来的意思是，借助能表达一定意义的事物形象，来寄寓、抒写作者的思想感情。见于《文心雕龙·比兴》，由《周易·系辞上》中的"拟物立象"发展而来。刘勰（465？—520？或532？）提出这一术语，主要用以阐释比、兴都是由彼及此，二者又有不同：比为"拟容"，重在贴合事理，忌不伦不类；兴为"取心"，重在感发幽微，以意相联。

This term means a poet uses the techniques of analogy and stimulation to depict the form and the external appearance of things. He takes in internal connotations and the principles of things, thus linking originally different things and combining them. *Nirong* (拟容 comparing appearances) attaches importance to specific forms for *bixing* (比兴 analogy and stimulation). While *quxin* (取心 grasping the essence) aims to get at the spirit and the essence of things, it therefore attaches importance to internal connotations and to the principles contained in the form of things. The combined meaning is that by giving expression to the form of things with a certain meaning, one may imply and express his thoughts and feelings. This notion appeared in *The Literary Mind and the Carving of Dragons*. It developed from *niwu lixiang* (拟物立象 create images through object imitation) in *The Book of Changes*. Liu Xie (465?- 520? or 532?) first used this term, mainly to explain that analogy and stimulation are inter-connected but are different: Analogy here means "comparing appearances." Staying true to the principle of things is most important, and anything far-fetched should be avoided. Stimulation means "grasping the essence," sensing the abstruse and being connected with the meaning.

引例 Citations：

◎诗人比兴，触物圆览。物虽胡越，合则肝胆。拟容取心，断辞必敢。攒杂咏歌，如川之涣。（刘勰《文心雕龙·比兴》）

（诗人在运用比兴手法的时候，能够具体周密地接触、观察事物。即使事物的差异很大，像胡、越一样遥不相及，用比兴合在一起却如同肝胆那样密切。比拟、描摹事物的外在形象，摄取事物的内在意蕴和理趣，判断和措辞一定要果断明白。把繁杂纷纭的事物用比兴纳入诗歌，文思就如同河水一样畅快流淌。）

When a poet uses analogy and stimulation, he comes into close contact with things and observes them thoroughly. Things may be quite disorganized, but when combined they tend to show themselves to be intimately linked. When comparing appearances to grasp the essence of things, one should be concise and resolute in forming judgment. When one incorporates various things in recitations and songs, they will swell and flow like a river. (Liu Xie: *The Literary Mind and the Carving of Dragons*)

◎取象曰比，取义曰兴，义即象下之意。（释皎然《诗式·用事》）
（从事物的外部形象方面着眼是"比"，从事物的内在意蕴方面着眼是"兴"，而意蕴就含在形象之中。）

Analogy means comparing the appearances of things, while association means grasping the essence of things. Meaning is what underlies the appearance. (Shi Jiaoran: *Poetic Styles*)

拟物立象 /nǐwù-lìxiàng/
Create Images Through Object Imitation

通过捕捉自然界和社会生活中具体事物的感性形象，加以模拟与提炼概括，创造出艺术家心目中独有的艺术形象。这一创作理念来源于《周易》。《周易》用设立卦象象征天下的万事万物及其变化规律，启发了文学艺术通过具体的艺术形象对自然界与人类自身进行认识与表达。这种思维方式对中国古代文学、艺术理论产生了深远的影响，孕育了意象理论的产生。

This refers to the process in which an artist creates his unique artistic representations of concrete objects, found in the natural world and social life, by mimicking, refining, and synthesizing their perceptual images. This concept for artistic creation comes from *The Book of Changes*, which uses images of hexagrams to symbolize everything in nature and their rules of change. *The Book of Changes* has inspired literature and art to make use of concrete artistic images to interpret and describe nature and human beings themselves. This mode of thinking has exerted a far-reaching influence on literary and artistic theories in ancient China, nurturing the birth of the theory of imagery.

引例 Citations：

◎圣人有以见天下之赜（zé），而拟诸其形容，象其物宜，是故谓之象。(《周易·系辞上》)

（圣人用《周易》卦爻来察见天下万物的奥妙，从而模拟万物的形态，象征事物之所宜，所以称之为象。）

Sages use the hexagrams and trigrams described in *The Book of Changes* to observe the subtleties of all things under heaven and determine what is fitting through the simulation of shapes in different things. Therefore it is called *xiang* (images). (*The Book of Changes*)

◎子曰："书不尽言，言不尽意。"然则圣人之意其不可见乎？子曰："圣人立象以尽意……"(《周易·系辞上》)

（孔子说："文字不能完全表达言语的意思，言语不能完全表达人的思想。"那么，圣人的思想难道就不可知道了吗？孔子说："圣人设立卦象就是为了全面表达他的思想……"）

Confucius says: "Writing cannot fully express what is spoken, and what is spoken cannot fully express a speaker's thoughts." Then is it ever possible to know the thoughts of a sage? Confucius says: "Sages expressed their thoughts fully through establishing images..." (*The Book of Changes*)

浓淡 /nóngdàn/

Denseness and Lightness

　　浓淡可用于形容颜色、气味、滋味等的深浅、强弱程度。在文艺领域中，浓淡可指绘画色彩的浓淡，文学语言的华美与简淡，艺术风格的浓艳与清淡以及抒情方式的强烈与平淡等含义。"浓"与"淡"是辩证的存在，比如，中国画的笔墨一向有浓有淡，浓不至于浊秽，淡不至于虚缈，尤其水墨画更注重墨色的浓淡，以表现阴阳、向背、虚实、疏密、远近等。理想的艺术境界是浓淡得宜，其他艺术形式对于浓淡的要求与此一致。

This term is used to describe varying degrees of denseness with regard to color, smell or taste. In the fields of art and literature, it refers to the denseness or lightness of a painting's color, ornateness or plainness of literary language, boldness or restraint in artistic style, or to directness or opaqueness of emotional expression. Denseness and lightness are relative to each other. In traditional Chinese painting, for example, the colors chosen can either be dense or light, but they should not be so dense as to be crude or so light as to be insipid. Ink wash painting pays particular attention to the denseness or lightness of color, aiming to achieve a balance between the two. This implies a harmony between the bright and the shady, the front and the rear views, the tangible and the intangible, density and sparsity, and the long- and short-range views. An ideal painting expects denser and lighter hues to set each other off beautifully. This requirement applies also to other genres of art.

引例 Citations：

◎篇章户牖（yǒu），左右相瞰。辞如川流，溢则泛滥。权衡损益，斟酌浓淡。芟（shān）繁剪秽，弛于负担。（刘勰《文心雕龙·熔裁》）

（篇章好像门窗，左右相互配合。文辞好像河流，水满了会泛滥。衡量内容如何减少或增多，斟酌文辞如何加浓或减淡。删去多余剪除杂乱，使文章减少负累。）

A piece of writing is like the shutters on a window, with the left and right sides balanced and well matched. Wording is like a river – if too full, it will flood. We must weigh to see if it needs abridgements or additions, or if it is too ornate or too plain. Any superfluous part should be deleted and any jumbled mass cleaned up so that the composition may not be weighted down. (Liu Xie: *The Literary Mind and the Carving of Dragons*)

◎此卷寂寥简短，不过数笔，而浅深浓淡，姿态横生，使人应接不暇，盖是其得意笔。（尤袤《跋米元晖〈潇湘图卷〉》）

（这幅画意境静谧萧索、尺幅短小，不过寥寥数笔，但是用墨和着色有浅有深、有浓有淡，云雾、山水等各种姿态纷纷呈现，让人目不暇接，应该是他的得意之作。）

The artistic conception of this painting is tranquil and detached. Although small in size and sketchy, it intersperses stronger and milder hues, and heavier and lighter patches. Clouds, mists, mountains, and rivers present themselves in a variety of ways, keeping the eye busy taking it all in at once. It must be the painter's own favorite piece of work. (You Mao: Postscript to Mi Youren's "Landscape Painting of Hills and Rivers in Hunan")

飘逸 /piāoyì/
Natural Grace

指诗歌作品中所表现出的逍遥自适、超凡脱俗、无拘无束的审美情趣和艺术风格。作为一个诗学术语，它也集中体现了诗人思想独立、天性自由的精神气质和审美追求，及"独与天地精神往来"、自由遨游于无限时空的意境，是诗歌意境、诗人与诗中人物融为一体而呈现出的艺术风格。往往与"沉郁"的诗歌风格相对应。

Natural grace, a term for poetic study (often in contrast to the "melancholy" poetic style), refers to free and unconstrained aesthetic style and artistic appeal in poetic works. It gives expression to the imagination of the poet, the natural and free disposition of his spirit, and his pursuit of aesthetic enjoyment. When in such a state of mind, the poet is "totally absorbed in his interaction with heaven and earth," roaming freely in boundless time and space. The concept represents a poetic style in which the poet and what he portrays in his poem merge into a natural whole.

引例 Citation：

◎子美不能为太白之飘逸，太白不能为子美之沉郁。（严羽《沧浪诗话·诗评》）

（杜甫写不出李白那种自由潇洒、超凡脱俗的诗篇，李白也写不出杜甫那种深沉厚重的作品。）

Du Fu could not write as freely and unconstrained as Li Bai, while the latter did not possess the style of melancholy and profoundness typical of Du Fu's poems. (Yan Yu: *Canglang's Criticism on Poetry*)

品题 /pǐntí/
Make Appraisals

对人的品行、才干、风貌等进行品评，判断其高下。盛行于汉末魏晋时期。品题在初兴时具有一定的进步意义，看人不论出身，只论德行才华，是鉴别人才、量才授官的重要手段。魏晋人士清谈的内容之一就是对于人物的识鉴和品藻，当时称为"题目"。但自魏末晋初开始，对人物的品评逐渐倾向于门第权势，九品中正制的形成与此有关。另一方面，品题由对人物的品评转向对于诗文书画的品评，选拔人才的功用削弱，艺术审美的意义凸显，这种风尚影响到南北朝的文学批评，催生了各种诗品、画品、书品等批评著作的出现。

This concept means appraising someone's character, ability, conduct and approach, which was a common practice from the late Han through the Jin and Wei dynasties. The practice was considered a good one when it was first introduced, as people were judged by their moral character and ability, not their family background, making it an important means of selecting officials based on their competence. Appraisal of others was a popular conversational topic among the people in the Wei and Jin dynasties. However, such appraisal gradually shifted towards people's family status, power and influence in the late Wei and early Jin dynasties, which led to the establishment of the nine-rank system for selecting and appointing government officials. There was also a shift in making appraisals away from people towards poetry, paintings and calligraphic works. Thus making appraisals played a less important role in selecting officials while assuming a more significant role in the appreciation of art. This influenced literary criticism in the Southern and Northern Dynasties and led to the creation of works of literary critique on poetry, paintings and calligraphy.

引例 Citations：

◎［许］劭与［许］靖俱有高名，好共覈（hé）论乡党人物，每月辄更其品题，故汝南俗有"月旦评"焉。(《后汉书·许劭传》)

（许劭和许靖都有名望，喜欢聚在一起详细苛刻评论同乡的人物，每个月都要更换品评的对象，所以汝南的人称他们为"月旦（每月初一）评"。）

Xu Shao and Xu Jing were both celebrities in Runan who liked to comment on their fellow townsmen and changed the subjects they commented on every month. What they did was referred to by the locals as "making monthly appraisals." (*The History of the Later Han Dynasty*)

◎诸英志录，并义在文，曾（zēng）无品第。嵘今所录，止乎五言。虽然，网罗今古，词文殆集。轻欲辨彰清浊，掎摭（jǐzhí）病利，

凡百二十人。(钟嵘《诗品》卷中)

(诸位名家编选的总集,意在收罗文章,并没有品评作品的高下。我的《诗品》收录,仅限于五言诗。然而古今的诗人以及他们的代表作品差不多搜罗殆尽了。我就是要辨明诗人的高下,指出作品的优劣,共计品评了一百二十人。)

Compilations of works of famous authors are meant to bring works together on an extensive basis rather than comparing their literary attainment. *The Critique of Poetry* I have compiled, however, is a selection of five-character regulated verses only. As almost all the poets and their masterpieces are already included in other compilations, mine just includes the works of 120 poets, with comments on the merits and demerits of their works. (Zhong Rong: *The Critique of Poetry*)

奇正 /qízhèng/

Qi or *Zheng* (Surprise or Normal)

"奇"是反常的、出其不意的,"正"是正面的、正常的。最早由《老子》提出。主要含义有二:其一,作为军事用语,指两种不同的用兵应敌的方式:"正"指在了解敌方作战意图基础上的正面应敌,"奇"指隐蔽自己的作战意图,灵活地运用偷袭、设伏等手段,以达到出其不意的效果。"奇"与"正"的运用需要相互配合。"奇正"有时也被用来处理、应对日常事务。其二,作为文艺批评术语,用来称说文章思想内容上的纯正与奇诡以及文辞上的典雅与巧丽。南朝刘勰(465?—520?或532?)为了矫正齐梁时期的文坛过于重形式、片面追求新奇的弊病,将"奇正"引入文学批评。他认为,文学创作应当在思想内容上以儒家经典为依归,以文辞上的巧丽奇异为配合,只有执"正"(思想纯正)以驭"奇"

（文辞巧丽），才能使文章的主旨新颖而不邪乱，词采美丽而不浮夸。后世诗歌评论及戏曲批评也用到这一术语。

Qi（奇）means surprise while *zheng*（正）means direct and normal. First advanced by Laozi, the concept has two main meanings. First, it is a military term about two opposing ways of fighting. *Zheng* means meeting the enemy head-on based on an understanding of its intention, while *Qi* means keeping one's intention to oneself and launching surprise attack and laying ambush on the enemy in order to secure surprise victory. *Zheng* and *qi* need to be applied in a coordinated way. While a military term, *qizheng* is also used to deal with daily affairs. Second, as a term of literary and art criticism, it means an article is pure and original in terms of theme and elegant and stylish in terms of diction. Liu Xie (465?–520? or 532?) of the Southern Dynasty first introduced *qizheng* in literary criticism to oppose attaching excessive importance to form and novelty, a trend which was popular in the literary circles in the Qi and Liang dynasties. Liu Xie maintained that literary creation should be based on Confucian classics in terms of theme, to be embellished by stylish rhetoric. He believed that pure thought (*zheng*) must come before rhetoric (*qi*) so that an essay would be original in terms of theme and beautiful but unexaggerated in terms of diction. The term *qizheng* was later also used in literary criticism of poetry and opera.

引例 Citations：

◎ 以正治国，以奇用兵，以无事取天下。(《老子·五十七章》)

（以正规的方式（清静之道）治国，以奇诡的方法用兵，以不搅扰人民来治理天下。）

A state should be ruled by the normal way, fighting should be conducted in a surprised way, while ideal governance should let people handle their own affairs. (*Laozi*)

◎ 凡战者，以正合，以奇胜。故善出奇者，无穷如天地，不竭如江海。(《孙子·兵势》)

（大凡用兵作战，都是以正面应敌，以奇兵取胜。所以善于出奇的人，出奇用兵的手段像天地那样无穷无尽，像江海那样长流不竭。)

In all warfare, the direct way is to meet enemy attack head-on, but surprise attack should be launched in order to secure victory. One who is good at using surprise attack will have at his disposal a rich reservoir of such tactics as inexhaustible as Heaven and Earth and as unending as the flow of rivers and streams. (*The Art of War*)

◎是以将阅文情，先标六观：一观位体，二观置辞，三观通变，四观奇正，五观事义，六观宫商。(刘勰《文心雕龙·知音》)

(因此阅读和评论文章，先要标明需要考察的六个方面：一是谋篇布局，二是遣词造句，三是对前人作品风格的继承与创新，四是表现手法上的守正与新变，五是援引事例以证立论，六是音律节奏。)

Therefore, we should study and comment a literary work according to the following six criteria: structural layout of writing, choice of words to construct sentences, acceptance and innovation in the style of earlier writers, inheriting and transforming traditional ways of expression, citing examples to support an argument, and musical rhythm. (Liu Xie: *The Literary Mind and the Carving of Dragons*)

气骨 /qìgǔ/
Qigu (Emotional Vitality and Forcefulness)

指作品的气势与骨力。多形容文学艺术作品所呈现出的刚健劲拔的精神气度和力度美。"气骨"这一术语出现于南朝，与当时的人物品评风气相呼应，用来形容诗文、书法、绘画等文学艺术作品中劲健的精神气度和内在骨力，与"风骨"含义接近，而与"风姿"（作品外在的风貌姿态）相对。

This term refers to the emotional strength and the vitality of a literary work. It was first used during the Southern Dynasties, resonating with the social practice of making comment on people. The term was used to describe the emotional vigor and forcefulness of artistic works such as poetry, essays, calligraphy, and paintings. It is similar in meaning to *fenggu* (风骨), but contrary to *fengzi* (风姿), a term meaning external elegance of an artistic work.

引例 Citations：

◎言气骨则建安为俦，论宫商则太康不逮。(殷璠(fán)《河岳英灵集·集论》)

(论气势与骨力，能与建安时期的作品相媲美；论音节与韵律，能超过太康时期的作品。)

In terms of its emotional vitality and forcefulness, the poem stands equal to works of the Jian'an Reign period; in terms of its musicality and rhythms, it surpasses the works of the Taikang Reign period. (Yin Fan: *A Collection of Poems by Distinguished Poets*)

◎观鲁公此帖，奇伟秀拔，奄有魏晋隋唐以来风流气骨。(黄庭坚《题颜鲁公帖》)

(观颜真卿这个法帖，奇特雄伟，秀美挺拔，全然具备魏晋隋唐以来的神韵气骨。)

This piece of calligraphy by Lord Lu (Yan Zhenqing) is amazing, vigorous, mellow, and forceful, fully illustrating the admirable emotional vitality and strength that characterized the style since the Wei, Jin, Sui and Tang dynasties. (Huang Tingjian: Inscription on Yan Zhenqing's Calligraphy)

气象 /qìxiàng/

Prevailing Features

原是自然界中景色物候的总称，也指某个时期社会的总体精神风貌。"气象"兼指气概、气势和景色、景物两方面而言。具体到艺术领域，指艺术作品所呈现出的风格与气概，内涵偏重于宏伟壮大，多用"雄浑""浑厚""峥嵘"等来修饰。唐代文论家们开始用"气象"一词来论述诗歌、文章的神采和风貌。从宋代起，"气象"成为文论的重要概念，用以品评诗歌、文章以及书画作品的风格与气概。"气象"往往反映特定文艺时期的精神风貌，例如盛唐气象实即盛唐时代的诗歌风貌，也与创作者个人的襟抱气度相关。

Qixiang (气象), originally a term about the general state of scenery and physical objects in nature, also refers to the prevailing features of a society in a given period of time. This description carries the meaning of great appeal and impact as well as scenery and objects. When applied to art, it refers to the overall style and appeal in a piece of artistic work. It connotes grandeur and magnificence, and is often used in conjunction with such words as "heroic," "immense," and "sublime." Literary critics of the Tang Dynasty began using the term to comment on the style and features of a poem or an essay. Since the Song Dynasty, the term has become an important concept in literary criticism, used to critique the style and artistic flair of poems, essays, calligraphy, and paintings. It is often thought to reflect the prevailing features in literature and art of a particular period. For instance, during the prime of the Tang Dynasty, the term referred to the appeal of both poems and the poets who wrote them.

引例 Citations：

◎盛唐诸公之诗，如颜鲁公书，既笔力雄壮，又气象浑厚。（严羽《答出继叔临安吴景仙书》）

（盛唐诸多诗人的诗作，好比颜真卿的书法作品一样，笔力既雄壮感人，气象又质朴厚重。）

Works of many poets during the prime of the Tang Dynasty struck readers with their powerful expression, just like the calligraphy of Yan Zhenqing. (Yan Yu: *Letter in Reply to Uncle Wu Jingxian in Lin'an*)

◎大凡为文当使气象峥嵘，五色绚烂，渐老渐熟，及造平淡。(周紫芝《竹坡诗话》引苏轼语)

(一般说来，写文章应该做到气象高峻壮美，语言文采绚丽。随着作者年龄增长、阅历丰富及风格逐渐成熟，最终归于平淡自然。)

Generally speaking, one should strive to achieve an elegant style and powerful expression in writing. However, as a writer becomes more experienced with age, his writing will grow simple and natural in style. (Su Shi, as quoted in Zhou Zizhi: *Zhupo's Remarks on Poetry*)

◎五言律体……唯工部诸作气象嵬(wéi)峨，规模宏远。(胡应麟《诗薮·内编四》)

(就五言律诗而言……只有杜甫的作品气象高峻不凡，格局广阔深远。)

Regarding five-character-a-line verses... only Du Fu's poems possess a style that is imposing and original and a quality that is both profound and forceful. (Hu Yinglin: *An In-depth Exploration of Poetry*)

气韵 /qìyùn/
Artistic Appeal

指绘画、书法、文学中所流露出的气势、韵致和生机，是文学艺术作品整体给人的审美感觉。最初仅用于绘画，指用墨、用笔恰当，作品就能表现出自然山水的意态，画幅上就会有流动的生机，令人体味到笔墨之外的精神、韵味。后来逐渐由绘画扩大到诗文、书法等领域。在实际应用中，与"风韵""神韵"等术语近似，是需要借助经验、感悟来获得的审美感觉。气韵虽然通过作品呈现，却与艺术家本人的格调、心胸直接相关，属于自然天成，不能刻意获得。

This refers to the momentum, charm, and vitality in paintings as well as in calligraphic and literary works which together create artistic appeals. The term was first used to refer only to painting, meaning that the proper use of ink and the painting brush could vividly present natural landscape, make the painting flow with vitality, and enable viewers to appreciate its underlying allure. Later, the term was extended to cover poetry, essay, calligraphy and other literary creations. Artistic appeal, which is similar in meaning to such terms as artistic charm and literary charm, is an aesthetic appreciation gained through experiences and feelings. Expressed in a work of art, artistic appeal reflects an author's unique approach to art and inspiration, something that he is born with rather than acquired.

引例 Citations：

◎ 六法者何？一气韵生动是也，二骨法用笔是也，三应物象形是也，四随类赋彩是也，五经营位置是也，六传移模写是也。（谢赫《古画品录》）

（绘画的六个法则是什么呢？其一是作品要充满生气，富有神韵；其二是运笔能自如呈现各种线条变化；其三是造型要顺应对象外形特征；其四是要根据对象特征进行着色；其五是构图要合理搭配，呈现整体效果；其六是要临摹佳作以传承前人画技。）

There are six rules for painting. A painting should be full of vitality and artistic appeal; the painting brush should be used in such a way as to make changes in lines natural; image painted should suit the appearance of the painted object; coloring should suit the features of the object portrayed; the painting should be well structured to present an overall visual effect; and masterpieces of past painters should be copied to draw inspiration from them. (Xie He: *An Appraisal of Ancient Paintings*)

◎气韵有笔墨间两种。墨中气韵，人多会得；笔端气韵，世每鲜（xiǎn）知。（方薰《山静居画论》卷上）

（气韵有两种，分别在笔之间、墨之间。用墨当中的气韵，人们多能领悟；笔端的气韵，世上很少有人知道。）

There are two types of artistic appeal in the use of ink and of the painting brush respectively. The artistic appeal created through the use of ink is readily appreciated; however, such appeal created through the use of the painting brush is not easy to appreciate. (Fang Xun: *On Painting in the Quiet Mountain Studio*)

迁想妙得 /qiānxiǎng-miàodé/
Inspirational Creation Based on Association in Thinking

指画家在艺术构思与创作过程中善于联想，将各种形象、素材通过画家的情感活动重新组织、构图，使画面形神兼备，如同妙手偶得。"迁想"重在想象、选择与构思，所创作的题材、素材来源于现实，却不是现实的完全复制。"迁想"是将画家的思想情感融进、移入作品的形象。"妙得"意思是精妙之得，是"迁想"的最终结果，重在作品的审美效果。它不仅要"得"物之形，还要"得"物之神，如此才称得上"妙"，因此，"妙得"也有妙得灵感的意思。"迁想""妙得"是一个连贯的艺术创作过程，不可分割。这一术语是对艺术构思与审美活动特点的最早概括，后成为中国绘画理论中的一个重要原则。

This concept means a painter should be good at association in thinking in artistic conception and creation. He should give full rein to his imagination and connect and reconstruct a variety of source images and materials so as to create a great painting in both image and spirit. "Association in thinking" stresses imagination, selection, connection and conception. While the subject matter and source materials come from reality, the painting is by no means a replica of it. "Association in thinking" makes it possible for a painter to reconstruct his thoughts and emotions in the image of his work. "Inspirational creation" stresses the aesthetic effects of a good painting that derives from "association in thinking." A good painting should not only create a good image, but also enable the viewer to appreciate the underlying message. Such a painting is one of inspirational creation. "Association in thinking" and "inspirational creation" together constitute an inseparable process of artistic creation. This concept is the earliest definition of artistic conception and aesthetic appreciation in China; it later became an important principle underlying the theory on Chinese painting.

引例 Citations：

◎凡画，人最难，次山水，次狗马，台榭一定器耳，难成而易好，不待迁想妙得也。（顾恺之《论画》，见张彦远《历代名画记》卷五）（凡是画画，画人最难，其次是画山水，再次是画狗马之类的动物，亭台楼榭是固定的器物，难画却容易画好，不需要迁想妙得。）

Painting human figures is most difficult; less difficult is painting the landscape, and then animals such as dogs and horses. Pavilions, which are fixed objects, are also difficult to paint, but it is easy to create accurate image of them because no inspirational creation based on association in thinking is required. (Gu Kaizhi: On Painting, as cited in Zhang Yanyuan: *Famous Paintings Through History*)

◎顾公运思精微，襟灵莫测，虽寄迹翰墨，其神气飘然在烟霄之上，不可以图画间求。（张怀瓘（guàn）《画断》，见张彦远《历代名画记》卷五）（顾恺之运用心思精深微妙，他的襟怀与想法难以预料，虽然依托笔墨来表现，但他的神采气韵却高高飘于云霄之上，不能只在画面中寻求。）

Gu Kaizhi thought deeply before creating a painting, with his vision and thinking hard. His paintings were created through the use of ink and painting brushes, but his artistic appeal and charm have transcended his paintings, reaching high clouds. (Zhang Huaiguan: *An Appraisal of Paintings*, as cited in Zhang Yanyuan: *Famous Paintings Through History*)

巧拙 /qiǎozhuō/
Cleverness and Clumsiness

"巧"是灵巧、聪慧，技艺娴熟精湛；"拙"则是不巧，心思迟钝，技艺笨拙。在艺术领域中，"巧"指文辞、构思、技法等方面的巧妙，其艺术形式修饰性较强。理论家们多重视"拙"，反对刻意工巧。真正的"拙"不是粗劣低级，而是自然天成，是"巧"到极致的浑然状态，看不到斧凿痕迹。但是，"拙"应该是自然而然达成的，如果有意识地追求"拙"，很可能收到相反的效果。"巧"与"拙"相辅相成，尚天然去伪饰，则能达到高妙的艺术境界。

"Cleverness" is a synonym for ingenuity, intelligence or exquisite skills. "Clumsiness," on the other hand, means awkwardness, dullness of the mind or lacking in skill. In the field of art, "cleverness" refers to an ingenious, effortless state of creation whereby general layout, wording, and writing techniques together are at their best. It stresses the ornamental function of artistic form. Many theorists favor the idea of retaining "clumsiness" but oppose deliberate manipulation of skill. "Clumsiness" here isn't the same as shoddy or of a low grade. It means a perfectly natural state of being, or a piece of writing so excellent by its own right as to lose all traces of artificial ingenuity. However, this "clumsiness" should be attained naturally. If a writer deliberately pursues clumsiness, it will only backfire. Cleverness and clumsiness are complementary to each other. Any pretense should be abandoned in favor of what is natural. Only then can artistic excellence be achieved.

引例 Citations：

◎大直若屈，大巧若拙，大辩若讷。(《老子·四十五章》)

(最直的反而像是弯曲一样，最灵巧的反而像笨拙一样，最好的口才反而像不善言辞一样。)

The truly straight will appear crooked; the truly skillful will appear clumsy; the truly eloquent will appear impeded. (*Laozi*)

◎宁拙毋巧，宁朴毋华，宁粗毋弱，宁僻毋俗，诗文皆然。(陈师道《后山诗话》)

(宁可笨拙不要奇巧，宁可朴实不要华丽，宁可粗放不要细弱，宁可生僻不要俗套，写诗作文都是这个道理。)

Better clumsy than deliberately exquisite, better plain than gorgeous, better coarse than dainty, and better rarely seen than conventional – this applies to both poetry and prose. (Chen Shidao: *Houshan's Understanding of Poetry*)

◎文章不难于巧而难于拙，不难于曲而难于直，不难于细而难于粗，不难于华而难于质。可为智者道，难与俗人言也。(李耆卿《文章精义》)

(文章不难写得奇巧而难在重拙，不难写得曲折而难在直接，不难写得繁细而难在粗放，不难写得华丽而难在淳朴。这个道理可以和聪明人讲，难以告诉俗人。)

The difficulty in writing lies not in cleverness, but in clumsiness; not in being meandering, but in being straightforward; not in being meticulous, but in being crude; and not in being gorgeous, but in being plain. This kind of truth can be discussed only with intelligent people, not with the vulgar. (Li Qiqing: *The Essentials of Writings*)

清词丽句 /qīngcí-lìjù/

Refreshing Words and Exquisite Expressions

指立意新颖、情感真挚、物象鲜明而语言清新美妙的诗句。"清"主要针对堆砌辞藻和典故而言，不仅指词句清新自然，还指格调高雅而意境淡远；"丽"指的也不是词语本身的华丽，而是指尽脱俗气，物象鲜明而有真情。作为一个诗学术语，它实际是指包括语言风格在内的诗歌整体风格。

This term refers to verses original in theme, sincere in feeling, distinctive in image, and refreshing in diction. "Refreshing" stands opposed to ornate phrases and excessive literary quotations, and indicates both fresh and natural expressions as well as elegant style and subtle aesthetic conception. What "exquisite" indicates is not that the wording itself is resplendent, but that there is complete freedom from vulgarity, and that the imagery is sharp with real sentiments. As a poetic term, it refers to the general feature of a poem, including its linguistic style.

引例 Citation：

◎不薄今人爱古人，清词丽句必为邻。（杜甫《戏为六绝句》其五）
（学诗既要效法古代名家，也不能轻视当世才俊；一切清新自然、鲜明动人的作品，定要加以亲近揣摩。）

In writing poems, one should emulate past eminent poets. At the same time, he should not ignore contemporary talents either. Every refreshing, natural, distinct, and impressive work should be studied closely. (Du Fu: Six Playful Quatrains)

情发于声 /qíngfāyúshēng/

Feelings Find Expression in Musical Poetry.

当人们受到外界事物的触发，情感在心里激荡，就会用诗歌表现这种情感并用一定的音乐旋律咏唱出来。见于《毛诗序》。这是中国古代关于诗歌起源的一种说法，与《尚书》中的"诗言志"大体接近且一脉相承。在上古时代，诗歌、音乐、舞蹈三位一体，密不可分，"情发于声"体现了上古诗歌的主要特点。到了后来，诗歌逐渐成为单纯的语言艺术，与音乐、舞蹈脱节，"情发于声"的说法也就退出历史舞台了。

When feelings surge up in people's hearts due to inspiration from external objects, they will find expression in poetry and music. This is stated in "Introductions to *Mao's Version of The Book of Songs*," echoing the idea that "poetry expresses aspirations" documented in *The Book of History*. In pre-Qin China, poetry, music and dance were all closely linked together, even merged into one. This idea reflected the special features of that era. Later, poetry became an independent art of language, divorced from music and dance. Thus, the idea took leave from the literary scene.

引例 Citations：

◎诗者，志之所之也，在心为志，发言为诗。情动于中而形于言，言之不足，故嗟叹之，嗟叹之不足，故永歌之，永歌之不足，不知手之舞之足之蹈之也。情发于声，声成文谓之音。(《毛诗序》)

（诗是内心情感意志的表达，藏在心里就是情感意志，用语言把它表达出来就是诗歌。情感在心中激荡而用语言表达出来，用语言还表达不尽，便加上嗟叹的声音，嗟叹还不尽情，就放开喉咙吟唱出来，吟唱仍感不足，于是不知不觉手舞足蹈起来。感情在心里激荡，就会表现为声音，声音按五音的高低组成旋律就成了音乐。)

Poetry is an expression of a person's feelings and aspirations. When hidden in his heart, it is just his feelings and aspirations. When put forth through the medium of words, it becomes what is known as poetry. Feelings are expressed in language. Then if language is insufficient, he will start to hum and sigh. If even that fails to fully express himself, he will burst into song, accompanied sometimes by rhythmical bodily movements. When feelings surge up in his heart, they will naturally find expression via sounds. All five notes of varying heights thus form a harmonious melody. (Introductions to *Mao's Version of The Book of Songs*)

◎大凡人之感于事，则必动于情，然后兴于嗟叹，发于吟咏，而形于歌诗矣。(白居易《策林·六十九·采诗以补察时政》)

(一般来说，人们受外界事物感动，就必然激发内心的情感，随之而发出嗟叹的声音，并用音乐将这种感情吟唱出来，于是就产生了可以歌唱的诗。)

Normally, when a person is moved by external objects or scenery, a feeling will spring up from deep within, thus producing the sound of humming and sighing. Then he will express such a feeling through chanting; hence a poem which can be sung out loud. (Bai Juyi: *Collection of Essays in Preparation for the Final Round of the Imperial Examination*)

情兼雅怨 /qíng jiān yǎyuàn/
A Mixed Quality of Grace and Sorrow

诗歌既表达了诗人的怨苦情感，又不违背雅正的审美标准。这是南朝著名文学理论家钟嵘（？—518？）提出的评判诗歌好坏的标准之一。钟嵘从艺术角度评价曹植（192—232）的诗"情兼雅怨"，其意强调诗歌要抒发诗人内心的怨苦，但这种情感的宣泄一定要适度，符合雅正标准。对于"雅怨"的具体解释，则存在不同看法：一种认为"雅怨"就是"雅正之怨"，重心在"怨"，说曹植的诗虽然抒发了受压抑的怨苦，但诗风温厚平和，符合"雅"的要求；另一种认为"雅""怨"是并立的概念，说曹植的诗同时兼有雅正与怨苦两种艺术特点。不管哪种理解，钟嵘的"情兼怨雅"说，既是对陆机（261—303）"诗缘情"理论的发展，也是对传统诗歌理论"发乎情，止乎礼义"所作的进一步说明。

Poetry should express a poet's grief while not violating the aesthetic rule of proper grace. First raised by the renowned Southern Dynasties literary theorist Zhong Rong (?-518?), this is an important criterion used to judge the merit of poetry. Proceeding from an artistic perspective, Zhong deemed poems by Cao Zhi (192-232) as having "a mixed quality of grace and sorrow." He stressed that a poet should guard against excess emotion and obey the rule of proper grace. As for how to understand the notion of "graceful sorrow," there are two somewhat different interpretations. According to the first, the emphasis of that notion is on sorrow; namely, Cao's poems seek to voice suppressed grief, despite a restrained, proper style of expression. The second interpretation says that "grace" and "sorrow" here are of equal weight, insisting that Cao's poems are both aggrieved and graceful. No matter what, Zhong's theory enhanced Lu Ji's (261-303) idea that "poetry springs from emotions" to a new level and elaborated on the traditional theory that "feelings should be controlled by ritual propriety."

引例 Citations：

◎魏陈思王植，其源出于国风，骨气奇高，词彩华茂，情兼雅怨，体被文质，粲溢今古，卓尔不群。（钟嵘《诗品》卷上）

（魏陈思王曹植的诗可以溯源于《诗经》中的国风，格调气度极高，文采华丽繁茂，情感兼具雅正与怨苦，文采与内容统一，光辉灿烂超越古今，卓然独立而不与众人为伍。）

Poems by Cao Zhi, are profoundly influenced by "Ballads from the States" of *The Book of Songs*. They are majestic and beautiful in style, with a mixed quality of grace and sorrow. Content and form fit together seamlessly. Cao Zhi thus puts all past poetic endeavors to shame and boasts a remarkable edge over his contemporaries. (Zhong Rong: *The Critique of Poetry*)

◎《国风》好色而不淫,《小雅》怨诽而不乱,若《离骚》者,可谓兼之矣。(《史记·屈原贾生列传》)

(《国风》虽然描写爱恋情欲,但是并不放纵;《小雅》虽有怨恨与批评,但并不煽动作乱。至于屈原的《离骚》,可以说兼有《国风》和《小雅》的美。)

"Ballads from the States" express passionate love without indulgence. "Minor Court Hymns" make complaints and criticisms without inciting trouble. As for *Li Sao* by Qu Yuan, it combines the aesthetic merits of both "Ballads from the States" and "Minor Court Hymns." (*Records of the Historian*)

情教 /qíngjiào/
Moral Instruction Carried Out with Emotion

指文学作品所具有的以情动人的教育功能,即文学作品可以通过描写男女爱情及人世间的真情感化读者、净化心灵,并最终影响、改变社会风气。由明末著名通俗文学家冯梦龙(1574 — 1646)提出。冯氏强调"情"是人的一种本能、天性,始于男女,而流注于君臣、父子、兄弟、朋友之间,小说要写真情,有真情才能感动人心,从而起到教化作用。冯梦龙倡立"情教"说,并不是要抛弃道德和说理,只是他认为情比道德和说理更本质、更真切,更贴近人的本性。"情教"说发展了明中叶以来重情尚真的思想,代表了冯梦龙的文学观与世界观。他用毕生精力加工整理并创作了大量通俗文学作品,也是对这一思想的实践。

The educational function of a literary work is best fulfilled through discreet emotional influence, based on the belief that a literary work can affect and purify the reader's soul through descriptions of love between men and women and of true feeling available in the world to finally influence and transform social morality. This term was first used by Feng Menglong (1574-1646), a late-Ming writer of popular fiction. Feng emphasized that "feeling" is an instinct or natural inclination of humans, starting with affection between man and woman and then spreading to relationships between monarch and ministers, father and son, or brothers and friends. Without true feeling, a literary work cannot touch the heart and morally edify people. In imbuing moral instruction with true feeling, Feng did not intend to do away with ethical reasoning. In fact, he held that true feeling is far more fundamental and authentic, adhering more closely to human nature. The theory of imbuing moral education with true feeling arose from a general respect for sincerity and authenticity which burgeoned around the middle period of the Ming Dynasty, reflecting also Feng's literary view and outlook on life. He spent decades compiling and writing popular fictions, thus bringing his ideas to fruition.

引例 Citations：

◎天地若无情，不生一切物。一切物无情，不能环相生。生生而不灭，繇（yóu）情不灭故。……我欲立情教，教诲诸众生。（龙子犹《〈情史〉叙》）

（天地之间若没有真情，就不会生息万物。万物若无情，则不能环环相生。万事万物生生不灭的原因，是由于情始终不绝的缘故……我想要倡立情教，来教诲人世间的芸芸百姓。）

If no true feeling existed between heaven and earth, creatures could not have multiplied. If creatures have no true feeling, the cycle of life will not continue forever. Life goes on solely because true feeling dies hard... I want to advocate the edification of true feeling to guide my fellow humans towards a meaningful life. (Long Ziyou: Preface to *Tales of Romantic Love*)

◎情不知所起，一往而深，生者可以死，死可以生。（汤显祖《〈牡丹亭〉题词》）

（人的情感在不知不觉中被激发起来，而且越来越深，活着时可以因为情而死，死了又可以因为情而生。）

Love can be aroused unconsciously and deepen over time. Because of love, the living can embrace death and the dead be brought back to life. (Tang Xianzu: *A Preamble to The Peony Pavilion*)

情景 /qíngjǐng/
Sentiment and Scenery

指文学作品中摹写景物与抒发情感的相互依存和有机融合。"情"指作者内心的情感，"景"为外界景物。情景理论强调二者的交融，情无景不立，景无情不美。是宋代以后出现的文学术语，相对于早期的情物观念，情景理论更加重视景物摹写与情感抒发、创作与鉴赏过程的互相依赖与融为一体。

This term refers to the mutual dependence and integration of an author's description of scenery and objects, and his expression of feelings in his literary creation. *Qing* (情) is an author's inner feelings, and *jing* (景) refers to external scenery or an object. The theory of sentiment and scenery stresses integration of the two, maintaining that sentiment can hardly be aroused without scenery and that scenery or an object cannot be appreciated without sentiment. This term appeared in the Song Dynasty. Compared with earlier notions about sentiment and scenery, this one is more emphatic about fusing the depiction of scenery with the expression of feelings, and the process of creation with that of appreciation.

引例 Citations：

◎景无情不发，情无景不生。（范晞文《对床夜语》卷二）

（景物若没有情感的注入就不会出现在诗歌中，情感若没有景物的衬托就无从生发。）

Scenery has no place in poetry unless there are feelings for it; feelings cannot be stirred without the inspiration of scenery. (Fan Xiwen: *Midnight Dialogues Across Two Beds*)

◎情景名为二，而实不可离。神于诗者，妙合无垠。巧者则有情中景、景中情。（王夫之《姜斋诗话》卷二）

（情与景虽然名称上为二，但实际上不可分离。善于作诗的人，二者融合巧妙，看不出界限。构思精巧的则会有情中景、景中情。）

Sentiment and scenery seem to be two distinct things, but in fact they cannot be separated. A good poet knows how to integrate them seamlessly. An ingenious combination of sentiment and scenery means scenery embedded in sentiment and vice versa. (Wang Fuzhi: *Desultory Remarks on Poetry from Ginger Studio*)

情以物迁，辞以情发

/qíng yǐ wù qiān, cí yǐ qíng fā/

Feeling Varies with Scenery and Verbal Expression Arises from Feeling.

情志随着自然景物而变化，文辞则由心中的情志而生发。自然物象和社会生活图景激发主体的情志，从而诉诸文字。由南朝刘勰（465？—520？或532？）《文心雕龙·物色》提出。该术语揭示了文学构思时主观情志随自然景物和社会生活图景变化而变化的特征。刘勰关于情、物、辞三者的关系论源自哲学和语言学上的言、意、象关系的命题，但有其特殊的内涵：就学术文章和应用文写作而言，先在心中形成意义，然后用合适的言辞表意，即使涉及到某些物象或场景，亦是用言辞说明，目的在于说明既有主旨，通常不会存在意义随事物或场景变化的情况；而文学创作则是表现主观感受的过程，所以会随时根据依外物而变化的感情来安排文辞。刘勰的这一论述既揭示了文学发生的原理，又解释了文学构思的特征，表明了六朝文学的创作自《文心雕龙》开始上升为理论上的自觉。

Natural or societal phenomena trigger a subjective feeling, which in turn expresses itself in words. This term was first raised by Liu Xie (465?-520? or 532?) of the Southern Dynasties in his critical work on literature and writing, *The Literary Mind and the Carving of Dragons*. It reveals the fact that subjective feeling varies with the changes in natural or societal phenomena. This relation between sentiments, natural or societal phenomena, and verbal expressions originates from the relation between speech, meaning, and phenomena in philosophical and linguistic inquiries, but it has its own peculiar implications. Where academic or practical writing is concerned, meaning takes shape in the mind first, and then it finds expression through words; even when it involves objects or scenery, words are employed to explain and support the existing meaning. In such a process, meaning will not change with external objects or scenery. However, literary creation is a process of expressing subjective feelings; therefore its wording sentimentally varies with external objects or scenery. Liu Xie's observation both reveals the origin of literature and explains the features of literary conception; it made literature conscious of its own subjective status. The Six Dynasties' writings reflect this new trend, as noted by Liu in his *The Literary Mind and the Carving of Dragons*.

引例 Citations：

◎岁有其物，物有其容；情以物迁，辞以情发。（刘勰《文心雕龙·物色》）

（一年四季有不同的景物，每种景物各有不同的形貌；人的感情随着景物变化，文辞则是由心中的感情生发。）

Scenery varies with seasons; each scene features different contours and shapes. Human feeling changes with scenery, with words arising from the bottom of the heart. (Liu Xie: *The Literary Mind and the Carving of Dragons*)

◎人禀七情，应物斯感。感物吟志，莫非自然。（刘勰《文心雕龙·明诗》）

（人具有喜、怒、哀、惧、爱、恶、欲等七种情感，受到外物的刺激而心有所感，心有所感而吟咏情志，所有的诗歌都出于自然情感。）

People have the seven emotions of joy, anger, sadness, fear, love, loathing and desire. He expresses his feelings and aspirations in a poetical way when he is stimulated by the external world and his heart is touched. All poems come from natural emotions. (Liu Xie: *The Literary Mind and the Carving of Dragons*)

屈宋 /Qū-Sòng/

The Qu-Song Duo

战国时期楚国诗人屈原（前340？—前278？）和宋玉。屈原是"楚辞文学"的开创者和伟大的浪漫主义诗人，代表作有《离骚》等。宋玉相传是屈原的学生，是屈原之后楚国著名的辞赋作家，代表作有《九辩》等，后世因以"屈宋"合称，但是宋玉名望和成就远不如屈原。

Qu and Song here refer respectively to Qu Yuan (340?-278? BC) and Song Yu, both being poets of the State of Chu of the Warring States Period. The former was the pioneer of *chuci* poetry and a great romantic poet. His most representative work was titled *Li Sao*. The latter, said to be Qu's student, excelled in the writing of Chu-style *ci* and *fu* poetry after Qu passed away, his representative work being "Jiu Bian" ("The Nine Stanzas" or "The Nine Changes"). Later generations referred to the two as Qu-Song, though Song Yu's literary attainments were far inferior to those of Qu Yuan.

引例 Citations：

◎ 自《九怀》以下，遽蹑其迹；而屈宋逸步，莫之能追。（刘勰《文心雕龙·辨骚》）

(《楚辞》中自王褒《九怀》以下各篇，匆忙地紧追屈原、宋玉的脚步，但屈、宋超逸的境界没有谁能够达到。)

All the verses following Wang Bao's "Jiu Huai" ("Nine Stanzas of Fond Reminiscence") in *Odes of Chu* follow closely in Qu Yuan and Song Yu's footsteps, but no one reached their levels of excellence. (Liu Xie: *The Literary Mind and the Carving of Dragons*)

◎ 相如好书，师范屈宋，洞入夸艳，致名辞宗。(刘勰《文心雕龙·才略》)

(司马相如爱好读书，学习屈原、宋玉的作品，文辞夸张艳丽，赢得了辞赋宗师的称号。)

Sima Xiangru was a book-lover. He took Qu Yuan and Song Yu's works as his models and made his own poetry glowingly beautiful. He thus became honored as a great master of *ci* and *fu* poetry. (Liu Xie: *The Literary Mind and the Carving of Dragons*)

曲 /qǔ/
Qu (Melody)

曲是继诗、词之后兴起的一种文学体式，一般指宋金以来的北曲（音乐多用北方曲调，演唱和念白用北方音）和南曲（音乐多用南方曲调，演唱和念白用南方音）。因鼎盛于元代，故又称为元曲。"曲"与词的体制相近，但句法较词灵活，多用口语，用韵也接近口语。曲大致分为两种类型：一种是进入杂剧、传奇的唱词，属于戏曲（也称剧曲）；另一种是散曲，和诗词一样，可抒情、写景、叙事，能演唱，但没有念白和关于人物动作、表情等的提示语，又称为"清曲"。不过，总体上说，古代戏曲的成就和影响要大大超过散曲，而元代又是中国戏曲史上的黄金时代，当时有姓名记载的戏曲作家就有八十余人。关汉卿、马致远（1251？—1321后）、白朴（1226—1306后）、郑光祖（？—1324前）四位戏曲作家，代表了元代不同时期、不同流派的戏曲创作成就，因此后人称他们为"元曲四大家"。元曲在思想内容和艺术成就两方面都体现了独有的特色，和唐诗、宋词、明清小说一样，成为中国文学史上一座重要的里程碑。

Qu (曲) is a literary form that came into being later than poetry and *ci* (词). It generally refers to the northern- and southern-style melodies created in the Song and Jin dynasties. Northern melodies were composed mostly with tunes in northern China and performed in northern dialect, while southern melodies had southern tunes and southern dialect. Since *qu* reached its peak in the Yuan Dynasty, it is generally known as Yuan *qu* or Yuan opera. *Qu* is similar to *ci* in form but is more flexible in sentence structure, and colloquial language is used. There are two main types of *qu*: one is northern *zaju* (杂剧) opera and southern *chuanqi* (传奇) opera; such *qu* is known as *xiqu* (戏曲) or *juqu* (剧曲). The other type is *sanqu* (散曲) or lyric songs, also known as *qingqu* (清曲). As with other forms of poetry, *sanqu* describes a scene, a sentiment or an event and can be sung, but it has no spoken parts or instructions for performers' movements and expressions. Generally speaking, the old-style opera is much more accomplished and influential than *sanqu*. The Yuan period was a golden age in the development of Chinese opera. There are more than 80 known playwrights from that time. Guan Hanqing, Ma Zhiyuan (1251 ?-1321 ?), Bai Pu (1226 - 1306 ?), and Zheng Guangzu (?-1324 ?) represent different styles from different stages of the Yuan opera, and they are recognized as the four leading Yuan opera writers. Yuan opera has distinctive plots and artistic appeal. Together with Tang and Song poetry and Ming and Qing fiction, it marks an important milestone in the historical development of Chinese literature.

引例 Citation：

◎世称曲手，必曰关、郑、白、马。（王骥德《曲律·杂论》）

（世人称元代戏曲高手，一定推关汉卿、郑光祖、白朴、马致远四人。）

When it comes to leading opera writers of the Yuan Dynasty, Guan Hanqing, Zheng Guangzu, Bai Pu, and Ma Zhiyuan come to mind. (Wang Jide: *On the Melody and Writing of Chinese Operas*)

取境 /qǔjìng/
Qujing (Conceptualize an Aesthetic Feeling)

指诗人在诗歌创作中，选取最能表达内心情感的物象并构思符合诗人自己的审美感受的意境。由唐代诗僧皎然（720 — 796？）在《诗式》中提出。皎然在总结六朝至中唐诗人的创作经验与方式时提出，作诗的时候，要精于构思，立意尽量奇特，不落俗套，在一番苦思冥想之后，灵感迸发、神完气足，才能写出境界上好的诗歌作品。虽然构思险奇，但是最终形成的作品风格要平易自然，不要显露精心思索的痕迹。取境与意境、境界等术语关系密切，属于中国古典诗论中关于"境"的术语系列。

The term means to conceptualize an aesthetic feeling by selecting images that best express a poet's sentiments and appreciation. The term *qujing* (取境) was coined by the Tang monk poet Jiaoran (720-796?) in his *Poetic Styles*. After conducting a review of how poets from the Six Dynasties to the mid-Tang Dynasty wrote poems, he concluded that to write poems, one must structure one's thoughts ingeniously so as to generate a uniquely original conception with no trace of clichés. Then, after some deep thinking, an inspiration will arise and his imagination will run free. In this way, the poet can create a poem with a fine visionary world. Although the conception may be highly original, ultimately the style of the work should be simple and natural without any traces of having been laboriously crafted. This term is closely related to the terms *jingjie* (境界) and *yijing* (意境); together, they are part of a series of terms dealing with *jing* (境) in classical Chinese poetics.

◎夫诗人之思，初发取境偏高，则一首举体便高；取境偏逸，则一首举体便逸。（释皎然《诗式·辨体有一十九字》）

（诗人刚开始构思的时候，如果取境偏于高迈，那么整首诗的意境就高迈；如果取境偏于飘逸，那么整首诗的意境就飘逸。）

When the poet starts to compose a poem, if his conception of the poem tends towards grandeur, then the artistic conception of the poem will be grand; if his conception of the poem is free and easy, so will the aesthetic conception of the poem be. (Shi Jiaoran: *Poetic Styles*)

◎夫不入虎穴，焉得虎子。取境之时，须至难至险，始见奇句。成篇之后，观其气貌，有似等闲不思而得，此高手也。（释皎然《诗式·取境》）

（不进入老虎的洞穴，就抓不住老虎的幼崽。作诗取境的时候，必须从最难最险的地方开始构思，才能创作出奇妙的诗句。全篇完成之后，再看整首诗的气势和面貌，似乎很平常像没经过思索就写成了，这才是作诗的高手。）

Without entering the tiger's den, one cannot catch a cub. When developing one's poetic conception, it is necessary to begin to contemplate what is most difficult and daring before great lines can spring to mind. After one completes a poem, one should review its overall structure and appeal. If it looks so smooth and natural as if written effortlessly, then it will be a great poem. (Shi Jiaoran: *Poetic Styles*)

趣 /qù/

Qu

指文学艺术作品中所表现的作者的志趣、情趣、意趣等。作者的"趣"决定他们对自然、人生的独特体验和理解，以及对作品主题的选择和作品的表现风格。"趣"是作品中无形的精神韵味，通过审美活动而体现出它的价值与品位高下。

Qu is the aspirations, emotions, and interests expressed in the work of a writer or artist. His pursuit of *qu* determines his unique perception and comprehension of nature and life. It also determines what theme he chooses for his work and how he gives expression to it. *Qu* is invisible but manifests its value and appeal through aesthetic appreciation.

引例 Citations：

◎ [嵇] 康善谈理，又能属文，其高情远趣，率然玄远。(《晋书 · 嵇康传》)

（嵇康善谈玄理，又擅长写作，他情趣高雅，率真而旷远。）

Ji Kang was good at explaining profundities and writing. He had a high style and fine taste. A forthright and broad-minded man, indeed! (*The History of the Jin Dynasty*)

◎ 世人所难得者唯趣。趣如山上之色，水中之味，花中之光，女中之态，虽善说者不能下一语，唯会心者知之。……夫趣得之自然者深，得之学问者浅。（袁宏道《叙陈正甫〈会心集〉》）

（世人难以领悟的只有"趣"。"趣"好比山的颜色、水的味道、花的光彩、女人的姿容，即使擅长言辞的人也不能一句话说清楚，只有领会于心的人知道它。……趣，如果从自然之性中得来，那是深层次的"趣"；如果从学问中得来，往往是肤浅的"趣"。）

The only thing really hard to understand in the world is *qu*. *Qu* is like the hues of hills, the taste of water, the splendor of flowers, or the beauty of a woman. Even an eloquent person can hardly find words to put it clearly. Only those with empathy know it well... *Qu* that comes from nature is deep and mellow; if it comes from book learning, it is often shallow. (Yuan Hongdao: Preface to Chen Zhengfu's *Inspirations of the Mind*)

劝百风一 /quànbǎi-fēngyī/

Much Blandishment and Little Criticism

描写奢靡生活占主要篇幅，而用于劝谏的文辞仅占很小比例。形容文章的立意本想使执政者警诫，效果却适得其反。西汉文学家扬雄（前53 — 公元18）认为，司马相如（前179？— 前118）创作的辞赋，虽然文章结尾归于劝谏，但由于他在辞赋中着力描写、渲染汉武帝（前156 — 前87）的奢靡生活，使阅读者的注意力只会为辞赋中描画的帝国宏业所吸引，也由此助长了帝王的奢靡心理，劝谏讽喻的效果并不理想。因此，扬雄对司马相如的辞赋提出了批评。

This term means that an essay dwells too much on the luxurious life of a monarch to the neglect of the author's original intention of admonishing him. In the Western Han Dynasty, writer Yang Xiong (53 BC-AD 18) held that although Sima Xiangru (179?-118 BC) always ended on a note of satirical criticism in his prose-poetry, he devoted too much space to the description and glorification of a monarch's luxurious life, bringing readers' attention to the grand achievements of the empire and feeding the monarch's arrogance, thus impairing the admonitory effect. Therefore, Yang criticized Sima Xiangru for such a style of writing.

引例 Citation：

◎ 相如虽多虚辞滥说，然要其归引之于节俭，此亦《诗》之风（fěng）谏何异？扬雄以为靡丽之赋，劝百而风一，犹骋郑卫之声，曲终而奏雅，不已戏乎？（《汉书·司马相如传》）

（司马相如的辞赋虽然有大量假托的文辞与夸张的说法，但其文章的立意还是归于节俭，这与《诗经》的讽谏有什么不同呢？扬雄认为司马相如华丽的辞赋中，描写奢靡生活的文辞占主要篇幅，用于劝谏节俭的文辞不过百分之一，就好像一支乐队一直尽情演奏淫靡的郑卫之音，只在乐曲终了时才演奏一点儿庄严的雅乐，这不等同于游戏吗？）

Despite much ostentation and exaggeration, Sima Xiangru finally focused on the importance of being frugal. So what difference is there between this and nuanced criticism in *The Book of Songs*? Yang Xiong argued that in Sima Xiangru's beautiful writing, descriptions of luxurious life dominated all space except toward the end of the essay, where admonitory words emerged extolling the merit of frugality. This can be likened to a musical band playing the decadent music of the states of Zheng and Wei up until the end of the performance, when the band finally struck up some majestic, elegant notes. Now isn't it a joke? (*The History of the Han Dynasty*)

人文化成 /rénwén-huàchéng/
Edify the Populace to Achieve a Harmonious Society

根据社会文明的进展程度与实际状况，用合于"人文"的基本精神和原则教化民众，引导民心向善，最终实现有差等又有调和的社会秩序。"人文"指的是诗书、礼乐、法度等精神文明的创造；"化"是教化、教导（民众）并使之改变，"成"指社会文治昌明的实现。"人文化成"的核心在于强调文治，实际上是中华"文明"理想的又一表达形式。

The term is used to describe efforts to teach people essential ideals and principles of *renwen* (人文) and guide them to embrace goodness with the aim of building a harmonious – albeit hierarchical – social order, according to the level of development of a civilization and the specifics of the society. *Renwen* refers to poetry, books, social norms, music, law, and other non-material components of civilization. *Hua* (化) means to edify the populace; *cheng* (成) refers to the establishment or prosperity of rule by civil means (as opposed to force). The concept emphasizes rule by civil means, and is another expression of the Chinese concept of "civilization."

◎观乎天文，以察时变；观乎人文，以化成天下。(《周易·彖上》)

(观察日月星辰的运行状态，可以知道四季的变换；考察诗书礼乐
的发展状况，可以用来教化天下百姓，实现文治昌明。)

By observing the movement of constellations, we can learn about the change
of seasons; by observing development of human culture, we can enlighten the
people and build a civilized society. (*The Book of Changes*)

仁者乐山，智者乐水

/rénzhě-yàoshān, zhìzhě-yàoshuǐ/

The Virtuous Love Mountains and the Wise Love Water.

　　有德行的人喜爱山，有智慧的人喜爱水。山崇高持固，以其
深厚而滋养万物，仁者由此联想到平和安静、心怀仁德而欣喜；水
奔流不息，以其顺势而周流无滞，智者由此联想到顺势而动、随时
应变而快乐。此二句互文见义：仁爱而有智慧的人从自然山水中看
到自己的天性和追求，乃至看到自己精神的映照，所以见山水而欣
悦。这是君子修养的两方面，是君子比德于山水进而移情山水带来
的拟人化的自然之美以及赏会之乐。山水因此联系着人类美好的情
感，成为常见的审美意象，而徜徉于山水也成为文人修养身心的重
要方式。比德是一种富有中国特色的艺术表现方式和思维方式。

According to this term, a mountain is lofty and steadfast, conserving
everything with its infinite forbearance. Thus, a virtuous man feels elated by
associating this with poise, serenity and benevolence. Water, on the other
hand, runs on incessantly, finding its way around without being deterred by
any obstacle. Thus, a wise man feels joyful recalling how water meanders its
course and keeps pace with the seasons. These two statements complement

each other in meaning. Benevolent and wise people note their own nature and aptitude, even their own spiritual state of being, through mountains and water, hence their happiness at the sight of natural scenery. This represents two aspects of a noble-minded person's self-cultivation. It is a personification of natural beauty and an experience of aesthetic appreciation brought about by comparing virtue to, and empathizing with, mountains and water. Thus, mountains and water are often associated with beautiful feelings and have become a common aesthetic image. Wandering among mountains and streams is also seen as an important way for a man of letters to cultivate himself. This comparison made between virtue and natural scenery is typical in Chinese artistic expression and thought.

引例 Citations：

◎岁寒，然后知松柏之后凋也。(《论语·子罕》)

(每年到了天气最寒冷的时节，才知道松树和柏树是最后凋谢的。)

Only when the year turns deadly cold do we see that pines and cypresses are the last to wither. (*The Analects*)

◎知 (zhì) 者乐水，仁者乐山。知者动，仁者静。知者乐，仁者寿。(《论语·雍也》)

(有智慧的人喜爱水，有德行的人喜爱山；有智慧的人好动，有德行的人好静；有智慧的人快乐，有德行的人长寿。)

A wise man loves water; a virtuous man loves mountains. A wise man is active; a virtuous man stays peaceful in mind. A wise man is happy; a virtuous man enjoys a long life. (*The Analects*)

镕裁 /róngcái/
Refining and Deleting

对文学作品的基本内容与词句进行提炼与剪裁，使之达到更高的水准与境界。属于文学写作的基本范畴。最早由南朝刘勰（465？—520？或532？）《文心雕龙》提出。主要指作者在写作过程中，根据所要表达的内容以及文体特点，对于创作构思中的众多素材加以提炼，同时对文辞去粗存精、删繁就简，以求得最佳表现效果。这一术语既强调文学写作的精益求精，同时也彰显了文学创作是内容与形式不断完善的过程。明清时期的戏剧创作理论也颇受其影响。

This term refers to improving a literary work by refining its basic content and making the presentation concise. Refining and deleting is a basic process in literary writing. The term was first mentioned by Liu Xie (465?-520? or 532?) of the Southern Dynasties in his *The Literary Mind and the Carving of Dragons*. It means that in producing a literary work, the author should select the right elements from all the material he has, delete unnecessary parts and keep the essence, and write in a concise way to best present what he has in mind and to best suit the styles of writing. It shows that literary creation is a process of constantly striving for perfection in terms of both content and form. This idea had a great impact on the theory of theatrical writing in the Ming and Qing dynasties.

引例 Citations：

◎规范本体谓之镕，剪截浮词谓之裁。裁则芜秽不生，镕则纲领昭畅。（刘勰《文心雕龙·镕裁》）

（"镕"是规范文章的基本内容和结构，"裁"是删去多余的词句。经过剪裁，文章就没有多余杂乱的词句；经过提炼，文章就会纲目清楚、层次分明。）

Refining means to shape the basic content and structure of a literary work, while deleting means to cut off redundant words or sentences. Once done, the essay will be well structured, with a clear-cut theme. (Liu Xie: *The Literary Mind and the Carving of Dragons*)

◎［谢］艾繁而不可删，［王］济略而不可益。若二子者，可谓练镕裁而晓繁略矣。（刘勰《文心雕龙·镕裁》）

（谢艾的文章用词虽然堆砌，但都是必不可少的，不能删减；王济的语言虽然简略，但能够充分表达意思，不能增加。像这两位，可以说是精通镕裁的方法，明了繁简得当的道理了。）

Xie Ai's essays are ornate in expression yet free of unnecessary sentences or words, with nothing to be deleted. Wang Ji's writing is concise in style; it sufficiently expresses an idea without the need for using more words. Men of letters like them surely command the art of refining and deleting by using a proper amount of words and expressions. (Liu Xie: *The Literary Mind and the Carving of Dragons*)

山水诗 /shānshuǐshī/
Landscape Poetry

一种以描写山水名胜为主要题材的诗歌流派。主要摹写自然山川的秀美壮丽并借以抒发闲情逸致，特点是写景状物逼真细致，语言表达富丽清新。东晋时期，南渡的士大夫在自然山水中寻求精神抚慰和解脱，激发了山水诗创作的灵感。其开创者是晋末宋初的大诗人谢灵运（385—433），他把自然美景引入诗歌创作，将诗歌从枯燥乏味的玄理中解放出来，后经谢朓（tiǎo，464—499）、何逊（？—518？）、阴铿等人的创作实践而逐步成为诗歌史上的一个重要诗派。到唐代特别是盛唐时期，山水诗的创作更是蔚为大观，涌现出王维（701？—761）、孟浩然（689—740）等著名山水诗人，中唐时期的刘长卿（？—789？）、韦应物（737？—791）、柳宗元（773—819）等人的创作也有特色。山水诗开启了新的诗歌风貌，标志着一种新的审美观念的产生。

Landscape poetry, as the name suggests, describes the beauty and charm of natural scenery, and landscape poets express their emotions through extolling the enchanting scenery. Landscape poetry is characterized by vivid description of sights with rich and refreshing language. During the Eastern Jin Dynasty, scholars who had fled war-torn homes in the north sought solace and escape in nature in the south, and this found expression in poetic description of mountain and river scenes. Xie Lingyun (385-433), a great poet of the late Eastern Jin and early Song Dynasty of the Southern Dynasties, created this poetic style. He introduced the depiction of natural beauty into poetry writing, freeing poetry from bland and insipid moral preaching. Further developed by Xie Tiao (464-499), He Xun (?-518?), Yin Keng, and others, landscape poetry became an important literary school. It gained prominence in the Tang Dynasty, especially in the prime of Tang, during which such landscape poets like Wang Wei (701?-761) and Meng Haoran (689-740) distinguished themselves. Mid-Tang poets including Liu Changqing (?-789?), Wei Yingwu (737?-791), and Liu Zongyuan (773-819) also became famous for writing landscape poems. This gave rise to a new form of expression in poetry and a new trend of aesthetic appreciation.

引例 Citation：

◎宋初文咏，体有因革。庄老告退，而山水方滋；俪采百字之偶，争价一句之奇，情必极貌以写物，辞必穷力而追新，此近世之所竞也。（刘勰《文心雕龙·明诗》）

（[南朝]宋初期的诗文，风格上有继承有变革，表现老庄思想的玄言诗退出诗坛，而山水诗正在崛起；文人用数百字的骈偶堆砌辞藻，为了某一句的新奇而攀比争胜，描绘外物务求穷形极胜，遣词造句必定竭力追求新异，这就是近代人们所竞相追逐的目标。）

The literature and poetry of the early Song Dynasty of the Southern Dynasties saw some changing trend: metaphysical poetry implicating Laozi and Zhuangzi's thoughts declined and landscape poetry gained in popularity. Poets sometimes used a few hundred words of parallel prose just to describe a scene, or competed with each other in writing an unusual line. In describing scenes, they tried to depict every detail; in composing a literary work, they racked their brains to achieve what is unusual. This has become the current trend in literary writing. (Liu Xie: *The Literary Mind and the Carving of Dragons*)

神思 /shénsī/
Imaginative Contemplation

文艺创作过程中的一种精神状态，指的是作者在饱满的情感驱动下，超越时间与空间的限制，进入到自由想象或特殊的灵感状态，最后通过特定的文学艺术形象和语言而传达出来，创作出自然而美好的文艺作品。这一术语，在魏晋南北朝的文艺理论中得到广泛运用，南朝刘勰（465？—520？或532？）《文心雕龙》对此有专门论述。"神思"是文艺创作中一种独特的心理活动，不同于其他认识活动。

The term refers to a state of mind in the process of literary and artistic creation. It suggests that the author, fully inspired by emotions, transcends the constraint of time and space, and enters into a state of free imagination or a special mood for literary and artistic creation, before producing a natural and beautiful work of literature or art, either in language or in imagery. This term was popularly used in literary and artistic theories of the Wei, Jin, and Southern and Northern dynasties. Liu Xie (465 ?- 520 ? or 532 ?) of the Southern Dynasties devoted one chapter especially to this term in *The Literary Mind and the Carving of Dragons*. Imaginative contemplation is the unique mental activity in literary and artistic creation, different from other cognitive activities.

引例 Citations：

◎古人云："形在江海之上，心存魏阙之下。"神思之谓也。文之思也，其神远矣。（刘勰《文心雕龙·神思》）

（古人说："身在民间，心却想着朝廷。"这说的就是神思。文章写作时的想象和思绪，其神奇是可以超越时空的呀！）

An ancient saying goes, "Though he lives among the common folks, deep in his heart he concerns himself with affairs of the imperial court." This is called imaginative contemplation. When one writes, his imaginations and thoughts may transcend time and space. (Liu Xie: *The Literary Mind and the Carving of Dragons*)

◎ 属（zhǔ）文之道，事出神思，感召无象，变化不穷。（《南齐书·文学传论》）

（写文章的规律，来自于神思，人对万物的感触没有形迹，变化无穷。）

The guiding principles for literary creation come from imaginative contemplation. Man's feelings and thoughts about the external world are formless and highly changeable. (*The History of Qi of the Southern Dynasties*)

神与物游 /shényǔwùyóu/
Interaction Between the Mind and the Subject Matter

文艺创作中人的精神与外物交融、自由驰骋的构思活动。在这一构思活动中，一方面人的精神感觉和想象投射到客观事物上，使客观事物具有了审美色彩；另一方面，虚无缥缈的精神感觉和想象也借助客观事物得以表达和呈现。"神"与"物"的自由融合，超越了时间与空间的限制，形成艺术形象，然后经过语言的表现，产生了美妙的文艺作品。这一术语源自《庄子》的"乘物以游心"，后经南朝刘勰（465？—520？或532？）《文心雕龙》的系统阐发，成为对"神思"这一术语的概括性论述，突出艺术构思过程中心灵与物象交融、自由想象的特点，既说明了艺术创作中的构思活动，也高度概括了文艺创作中的审美心理与创作自由的特点。

This term refers to the creative process through which a writer interacts with subject matter and gives free rein to his imagination. During the process, he projects onto real objects his mental sensations and imaginings, and endows them with an aesthetic tone. Conversely, his imaginary sensations and imaginings are given concrete expression by real objects. The free interaction between mind and subject matter, transcending the limitations of space and time, creates a superb artistic work depicted in language. The term originated in the words of "taking advantage of the circumstances to let your mind wander freely" in *Zhuangzi*. Later, this idea was systematically developed by Liu Xie (465 ?- 520 ? or 532 ?) in *The Literary Mind and the Carving of Dragons* during the Southern Dynasties to describe imaginative contemplation. The term stresses the importance of interaction between the mind and the poetic subject matter as well as free imagination in the process of artistic creation. It demonstrates the process of thinking in artistic creation and succinctly summarizes the underlying features of aesthetic appreciation and freedom in artistic creation.

引例 Citations：

◎ 其始也，皆收视反听，耽思傍讯。精骛八极，心游万仞。其致也，情瞳眬（tónglóng）而弥鲜，物昭晰而互进。（陆机《文赋》）

（在开始写文章时，必须停止一切视听活动，凝聚心神，广为求索，精神奔驰于八方极远之地，心灵飞翔至万仞极高之境。到极致时，情感由朦胧而渐趋明朗，物象也随之清晰而在眼前交替呈现。）

When starting to write an essay, one should keep away sounds and sights and keep his mind focused so as to allow the imagination to search freely in the universe. When his mind reaches the farthest end, all confusion will dissipate, and images will clearly emerge in his mind one after another. (Lu Ji: The Art of Writing)

◎ 故思理为妙，神与物游。神居胸臆，而志气统其关键；物沿耳目，而辞令管其枢机。（刘勰《文心雕龙·神思》）

（所以写作构思的奇妙之处，可以使思绪和想象与外在事物自由地连接交融。思绪和想象蕴藏于内心，由人的情志、气质主宰；外物通过听觉、视觉来认识，而将其表达出来却是由言辞负责的。）

What is marvelous about composing a poem is that it makes it possible for the mind and the imagination to interact freely with external objects. The feelings and imaginings that well up from within are determined by a writer's aspirations and temperament. We recognize external objects through hearing and vision, but these objects are expressed through the use of language. (Liu Xie: *The Literary Mind and the Carving of Dragons*)

神韵 /shényùn/
Elegant Subtlety

指文学艺术作品中清远淡雅的意蕴和韵味。原本是对人物的风度神情的评价，魏晋时人认为人格之美在于内在精神气韵，不同于汉代人推重外形。后来这一概念进入书画理论，指作品内在的精神韵味。明代人从书画理论引入诗歌理论，使神韵成为对诗歌风格的要求，清代王士禛（1634—1711）是"神韵说"的发扬光大者，他特意编选了《唐诗神韵集》，借编选理想的诗歌阐发自己的审美趣味，又在诗歌理论著作中大力倡导，构建起独具特色的诗歌艺术审美体系，从而使"神韵说"得以完善定型，最终成为清代诗学的一大流派。

This term refers to the subtle elegance of literary and artistic works. It was originally used to depict a person's mien and manner. During the Wei and Jin dynasties, the propriety inherent in a person was valued, whereas during the previous Han Dynasty, a person's external appearance was stressed. Later on, this concept was incorporated into the theory of calligraphy and painting to refer to the elegant subtlety of a work. In the Ming Dynasty, the concept was extended to the theory of poetry, and elegant subtlety became a requirement for composing poetry. Later, Wang Shizhen (1634-1711) of the Qing Dynasty further developed the theory of elegant subtlety. In compiling *The Elegant Subtlety of the Tang Poetry*, he elaborated on his aesthetic views. In his writings on poetry theory, Wang Shizhen championed these views and created his own unique poetical aesthetics, enriching the theory of elegant subtlety, and making it a major school of the Qing-dynasty poetics.

◎诗之佳，拂拂如风，洋洋如水，一往神韵，行乎其间。（陆时雍《诗镜·总论》）

（好诗如同拂面的清风，如同流过的浩大河水，仿佛有种神韵行进在诗的字里行间。）

Just as gentle breeze touching one's face and the river flowing past, a good poem has elegant subtlety permeating its lines. (Lu Shiyong: *A Comprehensive Digest of Good Ancient Poems*)

◎予尝观唐末五代诗人之作，卑下嵬（wéi）琐，不复自振，非惟无开元、元和作者豪放之格，至神韵兴象之妙以视陈隋之季，盖百不及一焉。（王士禛《〈梅氏诗略〉序》）

（我曾经读唐末五代时的诗人作品，格调卑下猥琐，气势不振，非但没有开元、元和年间诗作的豪放风格，在神韵、兴象的绝妙方面，甚至连陈、隋衰微时期的诗作的百分之一都比不上。）

I have read the works by poets of the late Tang Dynasty and the Five Dynasties and found their poetry mean-spirited, trivial, and depressed. They were far less bold and daring than those poems written between the Kaiyuan and Yuanhe periods of the Tang Dynasty. Worse still, they did not have the slightest traces of the elegant subtlety and inspiring imagery that were evident in the poetry written in the State of Chen during the Northern Dynasties and in the Sui Dynasty when poetry was already in decline. (Wang Shizhen: Foreword to *Poetry by the Mei Family*)

审虚实 /shěn xūshí/

Balance Fiction and Reality

戏曲创作必须把握好人物、故事情节的虚构与真实的关系。由明末清初曲论家李渔（1611—1680）在《闲情偶寄》中提出。李渔认为，戏曲所用素材，有古代的，有当今的，有据耳目传闻虚构，有据真人真事改编，大多跟寓言故事一样，能承载一定的教化功能即可，不必实有其人其事。尽管如此，作者在创作传奇戏剧的时候，仍然要把握好虚实的度，使传奇中的人物和情节发展合乎人情事理。"审虚实"认可艺术虚构的合理性与必要性，以合乎人情事理为艺术真实的判断标准，强调艺术真实不同于现实真实，这是对于文学创作规律的合理认识。

This term was first used by the late Ming and early Qing drama theorist Li Yu (1611-1680) in his *Occasional Notes with Leisure Motions*. It means that in dramatic creation, one should maintain a good balance between fiction and non-fiction in characterization and plot development. According to Li, material for dramatic creation could be ancient or current, could be based on what one heard from others or what actually happened. A piece of dramatic creation was just like a fable. As long as it had a good message to convey, whether its plot was real or not did not matter much. Nonetheless, a writer of legendary drama should strike a balance between reality and fiction, suiting characterization and plot development to people's natural way of thinking. The effort to balance fiction and reality acknowledges the need of artistic creation, taking reason and human feelings as the criterion judging artistic reality; and it highlights the difference between artistic reality and mundane reality. This view represents a proper understanding of laws governing literary creation.

引例 Citations：

◎传奇所用之事，或古或今，有虚有实，随人拈取。……传奇无实，大半皆寓言耳。欲劝人为孝，则举一孝子出名，但有一行可纪，则不必尽有其事。（李渔《闲情偶寄·词曲部·结构》）

（创作传奇所用的题材，有些是古代的，有些是当今的，有些是虚构的，有些是真实的，是否取用取决于创作者的需要。……传奇一般都不是实有其事，大多数像寓言。如果要勉励世人孝敬父母，就找一个孝子作为传奇的名字，只要有一项德行值得记述，就不必要求真有这样的事情。)

Material used for writing a legendary drama may be either old or new and can be both fictitious and based on reality. The writer selects whatever material that meets his need... A legendary drama tends to be fictitious, just like fables. If you want to urge people to be filial to their parents, you can then use the name of a filial son for the play. If a virtuous deed deserves to be told, there is no need for it to have actually happened. (Li Yu: *Occasional Notes with Leisure Motions*)

◎ 凡为小说及杂剧戏文，须是虚实相半，方为游戏三昧之笔，亦要情景造极而止，不必问其有无也。（谢肇淛（zhè）《五杂组》卷十五）

（凡是写小说和杂剧戏文的，应该是虚实各半，才是得写作真谛的笔法，情与景的描写也要达到极致才停笔，而不必问这情景实际上有没有。）

A writer of fiction or drama needs to strike a balance between reality and imagination. Then his writing will be engaging and unrestrained. He should give full rein to emotions and plot development in his descriptions; whether they are true or not is not really important. (Xie Zhaozhe: *An Orderly Narration on Five Assorted Offerings*)

审音知政 /shěnyīn-zhīzhèng/

Assess Governance by Listening to Music

通过审察音乐了解一个国家的政治教化情况。是儒家文艺观的具体体现。儒家认为，乐为心声，能传达人的情感和感受，因此，国家政治是否清明、百姓生活是否富足、社会风气是否淳厚，往往会通过音乐表现出来。《左传》记载，春秋时期吴国公子季札出使鲁国，观赏鲁国人演奏的周代不同诸侯国或地区的音乐，并据此评析音乐中所反映出的各国治政状况。这应该是审音知政的源头。这一思想方式产生于秦汉时期，它打通了艺术和政治的界限，将艺术审美活动导向社会现实生活，体现出儒家文艺观以政教为本的特点，使中国古代文艺理论染上了浓郁的政治伦理色彩。

This term is an example of Confucian literary thinking. Confucian scholars believed that music gave expression to people's thinking and emotions, so a country's music reflected whether government integrity was upheld, whether people enjoyed prosperity, and whether the social atmosphere was amiable and sincere. According to *Zuo's Commentary on The Spring and Autumn Annals*, during his diplomatic mission to the State of Lu in the Spring and Autumn Period, Prince Jizha of the State of Wu learned about the governance of various vassal states and regions at the time by listening to their music performed by the people of Lu. This should be the origin of the term "assessing governance by listening to music." This concept first emerged in the Qin and Han dynasties, which removed the boundary between art and government and made artistic aesthetics a part of public life. It gave expression to Confucian literary thinking which was based on governance and ethics and added a political and ethical dimension to the ancient Chinese literary and art theory.

引例 Citations：

◎是故治世之音安以乐，其政和；乱世之音怨以怒，其政乖；亡国之音哀以思，其民困。声音之道，与政通矣。(《礼记·乐记》)

(所以，太平时代的音乐祥和欢乐，这是因为政治宽和的缘故；动乱时代的音乐充满了怨恨与愤怒，这是因为政治混乱的缘故；国家将亡时的音乐充满了悲哀忧思，这是因为民众困苦不堪的缘故。音乐所反映出的道理，与一个国家的政治是相通的。)

Hence, the music in time of peace indicates serenity and happiness because of good governance. The music in time of disorder indicates dissatisfaction and anger because of political turmoil. The music of a state on the verge of collapse reveals sorrow and anxiety because its people are in distress. So there is a connection between the music of a state and its governance. (*The Book of Rites*)

◎凡音者，生于人心者也。乐者，通伦理者也。是故知声而不知音者，禽兽是也。知音而不知乐者，众庶是也。唯君子为能知乐。是故审声以知音，审音以知乐，审乐以知政，而治道备矣。（《礼记·乐记》）

（凡是乐音，都是从人的内心产生。音乐则和社会的伦理相通。因此，知道声响但不懂得更高级乐音的，是禽兽。知道乐音但不懂得更高级音乐的，是众人。只有君子才能懂得音乐。因此，审察声响可以知晓乐音，审察乐音可以知晓音乐，审察音乐可以知晓一个国家的治政情况，如此则治理国家的方法就齐备了。）

All musical sounds come from human mind. Music is connected with social ethics. Therefore, those who know sounds but do not know the modulations are animals; those who know the modulations but do not know music are the common folk. Only men of virtue can really appreciate music. Therefore, one must examine sounds in order to know its modulations, and examine the modulations in order to know music. One must examine the music in order to assess governance. And so the way of governance is complete! (*The Book of Rites*)

声律 /shēnglǜ/

Tonal and Rhythmical Patterns

指诗文中将汉语的声、韵、调互相配合以形成音韵美的一般法则。南朝齐梁时的文士周颙（yóng）将汉语的自然发音区分为平声、上声、去声、入声，沈约（441—513）在此基础上提出声调高低互相调节、平声和仄声前后配合的诗歌创作规则，以及在声调、声母、韵母搭配上存在的八种弊病。刘勰（465？—520？或532？）《文心雕龙》指出，诗歌上下文以声调的飞扬与沉降（相当于平声和仄声）相配产生节奏美，以韵母相同的字收尾押韵产生呼应美。刘勰将音韵和谐协调的要求推及一切文章，既是为了利于传播和接受，也表明对诵读美本身的重视，反映了南朝文人对形式美的追求，启示唐人写出工整优美的律诗。早期的声律理论多借助于音乐概念，后来发展为专门的汉语音韵学。

This term refers to rules and practices which create tonal and rhythmical beauty in prose and verse by blending sounds, rhythms and tones together. Zhou Yong, a scholar of the Qi and Liang periods of the Southern Dynasties, divided the intonation of the Chinese language into four tones: the level tone, the rising tone, the entering tone and the falling tone. On that basis, Shen Yue (441-513), another scholar, proposed his rules for poetry writing, whereby high pitches are countered by low ones and level and rising tones are countered by entering and falling tones. He also analyzed the eight types of poor matches between tones, initial consonants and ensuing vowels. In his representative work *The Literary Mind and the Carving of Dragons*, Liu Xie (465?-520? or 532?) pointed out that rhythmical beauty in poetry can be created by using various tones alternately (i.e., countering even and rising tones with entering and falling tones). Likewise, beauty of echoing can be produced by adopting the same vowel at the end of each poetic line. Liu Xie extended this rule of tonal and rhythmical harmony to other genres of writing to both ensure readability and express his love for the beauty of chanting. His effort shows Southern Dynasties scholars' pursuit of the beauty of formalism, which later inspired Tang Dynasty literary figures to create neat and beautiful metrical poetry. The early theories of metrical beauty, drawing heavily from traditional musical terminology, later developed into the phonology of the Chinese language.

引例 Citations：

◎夫五色相宣，八音协畅，由乎玄黄律吕，各适物宜。欲使宫羽相变，低昂互节，若前有浮声，则后须切响。(《宋书·谢灵运传论》)
（五种颜色互相映衬，八类材质的乐器发出的声音和谐流畅，让色彩和乐音各自有合适的调配。诗歌也要做到平声与仄声有相应的变化，低沉和高昂的声音相互调节，如果前面声调轻扬，后面的声调就要短促响亮。）

The five colors set each other off beautifully, and musical instruments made of eight materials produce harmonious and smooth sounds. One should make all colors and musical notes fit together nicely. Poetry, too, should vary in intonation, alternating between the even and rising tones and the entering and falling tones, and also between low and high sounds. If a tone rises gently, the tone that follows it should be loud and short. (*The History of Song of the Southern Dynasties*)

◎夫音律所始，本于人声者也。声含宫商，肇自血气，先王因之，以制乐歌。故知器写人声，声非学器者也。故言语者，文章神明枢机，吐纳律吕，唇吻而已。（刘勰《文心雕龙·声律》）

（音律是根据人的声音创制的。人声包含有五音变化，这是先天禀赋，古代帝王根据人的声音制作乐歌。可见乐器是模仿人的声音，而不是人的声音模仿乐器。因此，语言是文章表达思想的关键，至于语言符合韵律，只是调节人的唇吻而已。）

Metrical rules are derived from human sounds. Human sounds have naturally developed pentatonic scale. Ancient kings and emperors produced melodies and songs in imitation of human sounds. Apparently, it is musical instruments that mimic human sounds, not vice versa. Therefore, language is crucial to the expression of thought. As to suiting language to metrical rules, it is only to make verbal utterance easier. (Liu Xie: *The Literary Mind and the Carving of Dragons*)

声无哀乐 /shēngwú'āilè/

There Is No Such Thing as Joyful or Sad Music.

音乐本身没有哀乐之情，只是可以寄寓和激发情感。由三国时期的嵇康（223—262，或224—263）提出。嵇康将心情、意志与音乐区分开，认为情志由心灵主宰，可以表现为多种音乐形式，作者用音乐所表现的情志不等于听者由音乐所激发的情志，以乐观政的实质是执政者先了解社会状况和民众情志，然后借助音乐进行教化：乐师将正确的道理、健康的情志、美好的理想表现为和谐优美的音乐，使音乐与某种特定的意蕴结合，成为广大受众共同的认定，由此影响人心、改变社会风俗，并进而强化音乐的特定意蕴。"声无哀乐"说启示后世文艺批评家将历史变迁、社会风俗、作者的精神世界与受众的心理接受等多种要素结合起来进行考察，更为合理地认识文艺的本质与功能。

Music itself should not be divided into joyful music and sad music – it can only accommodate or inspire feelings. This idea was first raised by Ji Kang (223-262 or 224-263) of the Three Kingdoms period. Ji held that music should be separated from emotion and aspiration. Emotion and aspiration, he said, are controlled by the soul and show themselves in many musical forms. The feelings or aspirations expressed by a musician are different from those evoked in the listener's heart. The relation of music to the governance of a country is that rulers should first know more about the livelihood and aspirations of ordinary people and then moralize them accordingly. Musicians can incorporate truths, wholesome aspirations, and noble ideals into harmonious and beautiful music, linking music to certain implications cementing among the audience a broad consensus so as to exert positive impact on the popular belief, improve social customs, and in the process further strengthen messages implied in the music. This theory of non-differentiation between joyful music and sad music urges literary critics of later generations to examine a combination of factors such as historical changes, social customs, the inner worlds of authors, and the psychological reception of audiences, and to understand the essence and functions of art and literature more rationally.

引例 Citations：

◎声音自当以善恶为主，则无关于哀乐；哀乐自当以情感，则无系于声音。(嵇康《声无哀乐论》)

（声音原本以好听与不好听为标准，跟人的悲哀与快乐没有关系；人的悲哀与快乐原本是感情受到激发以后产生的，与声音没有直接联系。）

Music should be judged on the basis of whether it sounds pleasant or not. It has nothing to do with men's joy or sorrow. Men's joy or sorrow is evoked by actual events; it should not be directly linked to sounds. (Ji Kang: On Non-differentiation Between Joyful Music and Sad Music)

◎夫哀心藏于苦心内，遇和声而后发；和声无象，而哀心有主。（嵇康《声无哀乐论》）

（悲哀的情感蕴藏在悲苦的心中，遇到音乐旋律便借助它表现出来；音乐的旋律没有固定的形象，但悲哀的情感则是由内心支配的。）

Sad feeling, buried in a grief-stricken heart, will burst forth through musical melodies. Musical melodies have no fixed form, whereas sad feeling is controlled by the heart. (Ji Kang: On Non-differentiation Between Joyful Music and Sad Music)

声一无听，物一无文
/shēng yī wú tīng, wù yī wú wén/

A Single Note Does Not Compose a Melodious Tune, Nor Does a Single Color Make a Beautiful Pattern.

单一声响不构成动听的旋律，单一颜色不构成美丽的花纹。其本质强调文学艺术的美在于多样性的统一与和谐，只有在多样性的统一与和谐中才能创造美。这一命题后来构成中国古代文艺理论的重要原则，推动文艺的繁荣与发展。

This statement suggests that the beauty of literature and art lies in the unity and harmony of diverse elements. It became an important principle in ancient

Chinese theories on literature and art, and facilitated the development of literature and art.

引例 **Citations：**

◎声一无听，物一无文，味一无果，物一不讲。(《国语·郑语》)
(单一声响不能构成动听的旋律，单一颜色不能构成美丽的花纹，单一味道不能成为美食，单一事物无法进行比较。)

A single note does not compose a melodious tune; a single color does not form a beautiful pattern; a single flavor does not make a delicious meal; and a single thing has nothing to compare with. (*Discourses on Governance of the States*)

◎五色杂而成黼黻 (fǔfú)，五音比而成韶夏，五情发而为辞章，神理之数也。(刘勰《文心雕龙·情采》)
(五色交错而成灿烂的锦绣，五音排列而组织成悦耳的乐章，五情抒发而成动人的辞章，这是自然的道理。)

When silk threads of various colors are woven together, a beautiful piece of embroidery is created. When the five musical notes are properly arranged, a beautiful melody is composed. When the five emotions are forcefully expressed, a beautiful piece of writing is created. This is all too natural and obvious. (Liu Xie: *The Literary Mind and the Carving of Dragons*)

盛唐之音 /shèngtángzhīyīn/
Poetry of the Prime Tang Dynasty

指唐玄宗开元 (713 — 741)、天宝 (742 — 756) 年间的诗歌创作与艺术成就。与初唐、中唐、晚唐时期的诗歌相对应。这一时期是"安史之乱"前唐帝国的黄金时代，当时，社会稳定、政治清明、经济繁荣，南北文化融合，中外交通发达，这一切为"盛唐之音"营造了很好的社会氛围和文化基础。在唐诗初、盛、中、晚四个阶段中，盛唐最短，但艺术成就最为辉煌，被后人誉为"盛唐气象"。这一时期，不但出现了诗仙李白（701—762）、诗圣杜甫（712—770），而且还出现了张说（yuè，667—731）、张若虚、张九龄（673或678—740）、孟浩然（689—740）、王维（701？—761）、高适（700？—765）、岑参（shēn，715—770）、王昌龄（？—756？）、王之涣（688—742）、崔颢（？—754）、李颀（？—753？）、王翰等一大批卓有成就的诗人。他们赞美山川，向往功业，抒发个人情志，记述社会现实，诗风豪迈浑厚，意境宏阔高远，语言清新天然，富有生命活力与进取精神，创造了中国古典诗歌的最高成就。就诗派而论，这一时期则有山水田园诗派、边塞诗派等。

This term refers to the poetic creation and achievements during the Kaiyuan (713–742) and Tianbao (742–756) reign periods of Emperor Xuanzong of the Tang Dynasty, as compared with poetic writing in the early Tang, mid-Tang, and late Tang periods. This period, marked by good governance, prosperity, and stability, was a golden era for the great Tang empire before it was disrupted by the An Lushan and Shi Siming Rebellion. There was cultural infusion between the north and south, and travels to and from the outside world were frequent. All this made it possible for artistic creation to blossom. Of all the four periods of poetic creation, i.e., the early Tang, the prime Tang, the mid-Tang, and the late Tang, the prime Tang was the shortest, but its artistic attainment was most remarkable. This period produced legendary poet Li Bai (701-762) and poetic genius Du Fu (712-770) as well as a galaxy of outstanding poets such as Zhang Yue (667-731), Zhang Ruoxu, Zhang Jiuling (673 or 678-740), Meng Haoran (689-740), Wang Wei (701?-761), Gao Shi (700?-765), Cen Shen (715-770), Wang Changling (?-756?), Wang Zhihuan (688-742), Cui Hao (?-754), Li Qi (?-753?), and Wang Han. These poets extolled natural scenery, expressed noble aspirations, and depicted real life. Their writing style was both vigorous and unrestrained. They were broad in vision and were adept at using fresh, natural language, and their poems were full of power, vigor and an enterprising spirit. Their poems represented the highest attainment in classical Chinese poetry. This period also saw the thriving of the natural landscape school and the frontier school in poetry writing.

引例 Citations：

◎盛唐诸公之诗，如颜鲁公书，既笔力雄壮，又气象浑厚。（严羽《答出继叔临安吴景仙书》）

（盛唐诸多诗人的诗作，好比颜真卿的书法作品一样，笔力既雄壮感人，气象又质朴厚重。）

Works of many poets during the prime of the Tang Dynasty struck readers with their touching, powerful expression and simple yet dignified style, just like the calligraphy of Yan Zhenqing. (Yan Yu: *Letter in Reply to Uncle Wu Jingxian in Lin'an*)

◎盛唐气象浑成，神韵轩举。（胡应麟《诗薮·内编五》）

（盛唐时期的诗歌气象浑然一体、天然生成，其精神气韵也就自然昂扬飞举。）

Poetry in the prime of the Tang Dynasty is noted for being expressive, smooth and natural, creating a soaring and uplifting spirit. (Hu Yinglin: *An In-depth Exploration of Poetry*)

诗 /shī/

Shi (Poetry)

中国古代文学的主要体式，也是中国古代最早产生的文学体式。它按照一定的节奏、韵律、字数和句式要求，用凝练的语言、丰富的想象反映社会生活、表达思想情感。"诗"与"文"是中国古代文学的主要形态，古人所说的"诗"主要分古体诗和近体诗，一般不包括唐以后出现的词曲。古体诗也叫古风，是近体诗产生前除楚辞体之外的各种诗体的通称，其格律比较自由，不拘对仗、平仄，押韵较宽，篇幅长短不限，句子有四言、五言、六言、七言、杂言；近体诗也叫格律诗，它的字数、押韵、平仄、对仗都有严格的规定，有五绝、七绝、五律、七律、排律等。诗与词曲的区别是：诗不配乐，词曲可配乐歌唱。在中国，诗已有两千多年的历史，古人认为诗能够连通人与自然、表达志向、抒发情性，集中体现了中国文学艺术的精神特质与审美追求，这与西方将诗看作文学的门类很不相同。在中国古代，儒家思想对诗的创作有重要指导作用，而道家与佛教思想对于诗的意境理论影响深远。因中国最早的诗集是《诗经》，所以后世也用"诗"专指《诗经》。

Shi (诗) is a major genre of ancient Chinese literature, the earliest literary form that emerged in China. Observing the requirements of a certain rhythm, rules of rhyming, number of characters, and type of verses, and using concise language and rich imagination, it reflects social life and conveys thoughts and emotions. *Shi* and *wen* (文 essay) are two principal forms of ancient Chinese literature. *Shi*, as referred to by the ancient Chinese, consists of the older type of poetry and the latter type of poetry. It generally does not include *ci* (词 lyric) and *qu* (曲 melody), which appeared as literary genres after the Tang Dynasty. The older type of *shi* is also called *gufeng* (古风), meaning ancient style, which is a general appellation for all kinds of poetic forms produced prior to the latter type of *shi*, except the style employed in *Odes of Chu*. With relatively few restrictions in rules and forms, *shi* is not constrained by any antithetical arrangement or a fixed tone pattern, and its rhyme is fairly free. In addition, the length of a piece is not limited. A verse may have four, six, seven, or a mixed number of Chinese characters. The latter type of *shi* is also called *gelüshi* (格律诗), meaning poetry with fixed patterns. Its number of characters, rhyming, tone pattern, and antithetical arrangement are all strictly fixed. A poem of this type may contain four lines (known as *jue* 绝), each with five or seven characters, or eight lines (known as *lü* 律), each with five or seven characters. Occasionally, it is much longer than normal, expanding to one and a half dozen lines, which is referred to as *pailü* (排律). The difference between *shi*, and *ci* and *qu* is that the former is not set to music, while the latter may be set to music and sung. *Shi* has existed as a literary form for more than 2,000 years in China. Ancient Chinese used *shi* to connect humans with nature, voice aspirations, and give expression to emotions. It embodied the spirit and aesthetic pursuits of literature and art in ancient China, which is very different from the West, which only sees poetry as a category of literature. In ancient China, Confucian thought played an important guiding role in poetic creation, while Daoist and Buddhist thoughts had a profound influence on the theory of poetry's artistic conception. Since *The Book of Songs* was China's earliest collection of poems, later generations also used *shi* to refer to *The Book of Songs* in particular.

引例 Citations：

◎诗言志，歌永言，声依永，律和声。(《尚书·舜典》)

（诗是表达内心志向的，歌是用语言来吟唱的。五音（宫、商、角、徵、羽）的高低变化要随吟唱而定，音律则要与五音谐和。）

Poems express aspirations deep in one's heart, whereas songs are verses for chanting. Undulation of tunes of five notes depends on chanting, and meter and melody must be in harmony with the five notes. (*The Book of History*)

◎诗，言其志也；歌，咏其声也；舞，动其容也。三者本于心，然后乐器从之。(《礼记·乐记》)

（诗，用语言表达人的志向；歌，用吟唱表达内心的想法；舞，是将内心的想法呈现于形体的各种舞姿。这三者都发自内心，之后才以乐器演奏加以配合。）

Shi expresses aspirations through written words, whereas songs do so via chanting. Dancing is a sequence of body movements to project one's emotions. All these three forms of art come forth from the heart, accompanied by musical performance. (*The Book of Rites*)

◎气之动物，物之感人，故摇荡性情，形诸舞咏。照烛三才，晖丽万有，灵祇（qí）待之以致飨，幽微藉之以昭告。动天地，感鬼神，莫近于诗。(钟嵘《诗品》卷上)

（四季的气候引起景物变化，景物变化感发人的内心，引起人的性情起伏跌宕，并通过舞蹈、吟咏表现出来。它辉映着天、地、人，让万物亮丽生辉，天上的神祇依赖它接受享祀，幽冥的神灵也通过它明告世人。而感动天地、鬼神的，没有比诗更接近的了。）

The four seasons bring changes in scenery, which in turn stir one's emotions. One gives expression to such emotions through dancing and chanting. Poetry thus illuminates heaven, earth and humans, making everything clear and bright. The gods in heaven rely on it to receive sacrificial rituals and the spirits in the nether world use it to communicate with the world. Among those which move heaven, earth and the spirits, nothing comes near poetry! (Zhong Rong: *The Critique of Poetry*)

诗话 /shīhuà/

Criticism on Poetry / *Shihua* (Story-telling with Song and Speech)

主要含义有二：其一，指评论诗人、诗作、诗派及记载诗人逸事及相关考订的著作，是中国古代诗学文献的一个组成部分。诗话肇始于南朝梁代钟嵘（？—518？）的《诗品》，第一部完整意义上的诗话是北宋欧阳修（1007—1072）的《六一诗话》，南宋严羽（？—1264）的《沧浪诗话》是宋代最负盛名、对后世影响最大的诗话。此后，诗话成为评论诗作、发表诗歌创作理论的主要著作形式，明、清两代诗话作品数量巨大，其中以清代王夫之（1619—1692）的《姜斋诗话》和袁枚（1716—1798）的《随园诗话》成就最大。明清时期还刊行了《历代诗话》《历代诗话续编》《清诗话》等，辑集了历代重要的诗话著作。诗话的一般特点是，不追求系统严密的理论体系，主要以评论者的细腻感悟为特色，以若干短句为一则，对诗歌创作中的具体问题或某些艺术规律提出自己的感受和意见。诗话具有较强的文学性和文学欣赏价值。中国诗话以其鲜明的文化特色，有别于西方思辨式的文学理论体系建构和科学严密的语言表述。其二，指中国古代的一种说唱艺术。有说有唱，韵文、散文并用，韵文多为七言诗赞，用于唱；散文即"话"，用于说。现存最早的作品是宋元时期刊印的《大唐三藏取经诗话》。

This term has a two-fold meaning. First, it refers to any work that contains critiques or commentaries on poets, poems, schools of poetry, anecdotes about poets, and textual research. This type of work is a constituent part of scholarly inquiry into classical Chinese poetry. The tradition of offering commentaries on poetry had its origin in *The Critique of Poetry* by Zhong Rong (?- 518?) of the Liang Period of the Southern Dynasties. The first somewhat complete commentary on poetry and poets was *Ouyang Xiu's Criticism of Poetry*, by Ouyang Xiu (1007-1072) of the Northern Song Dynasty. The Song Dynasty's most renowned work of poetry commentary, which also had the greatest influence on scholars of later generations, was *Canglang's Criticism on Poetry* by Yan Yu (?-1264) of the Southern Song Dynasty. After that, notes of this kind became a principal medium through which to offer commentaries on poetry and propose theories of poetry composition. The Ming and Qing dynasties boasted the largest number of works of poetry commentary. The best of such works were *Desultory Remarks on Poetry from Ginger Studio* by Wang Fuzhi (1619-1692) and *Suiyuan Remarks on Poetry* by Yuan Mei (1716-1798), both from the Qing Dynasty. During the Ming and Qing periods, *Commentaries on Poetry from Past Dynasties*, *A Sequel to Commentaries on Poetry from Past Dynasties* and *Qing Dynasty Commentaries on Poetry* were also published, all of which contain important works of poetry critiquing of all dynasties. Commentaries/critiques on poetry essentially shun a comprehensive and elaborate theoretical system and focus instead on articulating the critic's personal, nuanced appreciation and evaluation of poetry. Each of them contains only a few terse remarks, airing views on finer points in poetic composition and revealing personal feelings and thoughts on rules governing artistic creation. Commentaries on poetry are themselves highly literary and deserve to be appreciated from that perspective. Such commentaries on poetry, with their distinctly Chinese cultural features, distinguish themselves from Western scholars' obsession with systematic construction of literary theories and strictly scientific modes of expression.

Second, the term *shihua* may also refer to a kind of age-old art of theatrical performance that intersperse singing with narrative, and verse with prose. Rhymed verse, which normally consists of seven characters to a line, is employed for singing. Prose, on the other hand, is used as in vernacular speech. The earliest extant work of this kind is *Tales of Xuanzang's Journey to the West* compiled and published during the Song and Yuan periods.

引例 Citations：

◎诗话者，辨句法，备古今，纪盛德，录异事，正讹误也。(许颛 (yǐ)《彦周诗话》，见何文焕辑《历代诗话》)

(诗话的作用是为了辨析诗歌文法，细述古今流变，记载朝廷盛德，实录奇闻逸事，辨正创作讹误。)

Commentaries on poetry serve to expound rules guiding the composition of poetry, detail the evolution of poetry from past to present, note the imperial court's meritorious deeds, record anecdotes and hearsay, as well as to rectify malpractices in poetic composition. (Xu Yi: *Yanzhou's Commentaries on Poetry*)

◎诗话之源，本于钟嵘《诗品》。(章学诚《文史通义·诗话》)

(诗话的源头，来自于钟嵘的《诗品》。)

The tradition of offering commentaries on poetry is traced back to Zhong Rong's *The Critique of Poetry*. (Zhang Xuecheng: *General Principles of History*)

诗家三昧 /shījiā sānmèi/

The Key to Poetic Creation

指诗歌创作的秘诀。"三昧"一词，源于梵文samādhi音译，意思是止息杂念、使心神平静，是佛教的重要修行方法，后借指事物的要领、真谛，被诗歌、绘画、书法等各领域借用，成为各领域要领、技巧、秘诀的代名词。"诗家三昧"由南宋著名诗人陆游（1125 — 1210）在《九月一日夜读诗稿有感走笔作歌》中使用，后用以指代诗歌创作过程中出现的一种灵感突发、文思泉涌的生命状态。陆游在这首诗中讲述年轻时学诗未有心得，后从军，驻守南郑，火热、紧张、刺激的军营生活，使其诗风发生巨变，灵感纷至沓来。从陆游的创作历程可以看出，诗歌来源于生活，"诗家三昧"只有在表现生活、反映现实的创作活动中才能获得。

Sanmei（三昧）originates from the Sanskrit word *samādhi*, meaning "the mental state of being firmly fixed on a single object" or "meditative absorption." Samadhi used to be Buddhism's important way to engage in self-cultivation. Later, it took on the meaning of "the gist or true essence of things." This Sinicized phrase thus made its way into the fields of poetry, painting, and calligraphy and began to be used in the sense of a "knack," a "trick" or a "secret." The whole term, "the key to poetic creation," was first put forward by the Southern Song poet Lu You (1125 - 1210) in his poem "Poetic Lines Scribbled Down on the Night of the First Day of the Ninth Lunar Month." Over time, it became used to refer to a burst of inspiration, with words pouring forth like the flow of a spring, in poetic creation. In that poem, Lu You describes how his initial effort to learn to write poetry failed in his youth and how life in the army at Nanzheng, hectic, vibrant, and exciting as it was, thoroughly changed his poetic style and brought forth great ideas. The way Lu You wrote poetry shows that poetry has its origins in life. The inspiration of poetic creation can be drawn solely from the creative activity of reflecting and portraying life through poetry.

引例 Citations：

◎长沙僧怀素，好草书，自言得草圣三昧。（李肇《唐国史补》卷中）

（长沙僧人怀素喜爱草书，说自己悟到了草圣张旭书法的诀窍。）

Huaisu, a Buddhist monk in Changsha, loved the cursive style of calligraphy. He said that he had fortunately captured the key to the calligraphic work of cursive-style master Zhang Xu. (Li Zhao: *A Supplement to Liu Su's Dynastic History*)

◎诗家三昧忽见前，屈贾在眼元历历。天机云锦用在我，剪裁妙处非刀尺。（陆游《九月一日夜读诗稿有感走笔作歌》）

（我突然领悟了作诗的诀窍，屈原、贾谊文章的奥秘在眼前清晰呈现。天赋灵机与云锦般文章全在自己灵活运用，素材选取与文章构思绝非随意尺量刀剪。）

I suddenly captured the key to poetry writing. The secret of success of the poems of Qu Yuan and Jia Yi clearly presents itself before my eyes. Swift inspiration endowed by heaven and truly beautiful writing depend on an author's flexible use of such a knack. The choice of material and structuring of an article should not subject themselves to arbitrary measurement with a ruler or cutting with a pair of scissors. (Lu You: Poetic Lines Scribbled Down on the Night of the First Day of the Ninth Lunar Month)

◎余尝观荆浩论山水而悟诗家三昧，曰：远人无目，远水无波，远山无皴（cūn）。（王士禛《香祖笔记》卷六）

（我曾经从荆浩的山水画论中悟到了写诗的诀窍，他说：画远处的人不可画眼睛，画远处的河不可画水波，画远处的山不可画褶皱。）

I came to see the key to poetic creation through Jing Hao's commentaries on landscape painting. He said: "He who depicts a distant human figure should not try to draw his eyes; he who depicts a distant river should not draw its ripples; he who depicts distant hills, not their folds." (Wang Shizhen: *Notes Written in the Orchid Studio*)

诗界革命 /shījiè gémìng/

The Revolution in the Circle of Poets

　　中国近代发生的一场以诗歌革新为内容的文化运动，是"文界革命"的一部分。梁启超（1873—1929）首倡"诗界革命"，他在《夏威夷游记》中提出，写诗要汲取古人的风格体式，但必须有新的意境和语句。他反对旧体诗的语言晦涩与格律束缚，认为若不进行诗界革命，诗运就会断绝，主张新诗的语言应该通俗，应该承载新的思想、传播先进观念，以引导、教化国民。梁启超、黄遵宪（1848—1905）、严复（1854—1921）、夏曾佑（1863—1924）、谭嗣同（1865—1898）、邱炜萲（xuān，1874—1941）等人均写作新体诗，并在报刊上登载。"诗界革命"中产生的诗作总体上艺术成就不高，往往是旧体诗堆砌新名词，表达生硬，不伦不类，但其创新精神直接启迪了白话新诗。

The Revolution in the Circle of Poets was a cultural movement in early modern China. A part of the Revolution in the Literati Circle, it aimed to reform poetic expression. Liang Qichao (1873-1929) was the first one to champion this movement. In his work "My Days in Hawaii," he argued that modern poetry should draw on the style and format of classical poetry, but it must also develop new artistic conception and expressions to depict contemporary life. He opposed the obscurity and formal restraints of classical Chinese poetry, arguing that without a revolution among poets, poetry in China would wither. He said that new poetry should be simple in language, convey new ideas, and disseminate modern values to enlighten people in China. Liang Qichao, Huang Zunxian (1848-1905), Yan Fu (1854-1921), Xia Zengyou (1863-1924), Tan Sitong (1865-1898), and Qiu Weixuan (1874-1941) all wrote poetry in modern Chinese and published their writings in newspapers and magazines. Generally speaking, verses written under the influence of the Revolution in the Circle of Poets did not have high artistic value. Rather, they were old in style but new in content, yet they did not make smooth reading. However, their creative spirit later gave rise to truly vernacular new poetry.

引例 Citations：

◎过渡时代，必有革命。然革命者，当革其精神，非革其形式。吾党近好言诗界革命。虽然，若以堆积满纸新名词为革命，是又满洲政府变法维新之类也。能以旧风格含新意境，斯可以举革命之实矣。苟能尔尔，则虽间杂一二新名词，亦不为病。不尔，则徒示人以俭而已。（梁启超《饮冰室诗话》）

（过渡时期，必须要有革命。然而革命，应当是革除其精神，而不是革除其形式。我们这些人最近喜好谈诗界革命。虽然这是对的，但是如果以为满篇堆积新名词就是革命，这又是清政府变法维新一类的做法了。能够用旧风格蕴含新意境，这才是倡举革命的实质。如果能做到这样，虽然夹杂一两个新名词，也不算弊病。做不到这样，不过是将内容的贫乏展示给别人看罢了。）

There bound to be a revolution during the transitional period, but the revolution is designed to eradicate the substance of old-style poetry, not its form. Nowadays, many of us like to talk about the need for a revolution among poets. That's exactly right, but if we think the revolution means using a pile of newly-coined phrases, we will just turn ourselves into quasi-reformists like those in the Qing court. The goal of the revolution is to introduce a new vision in the old style. If this can be done, one modern phrase or two here and there in a poem will be no big problem. If not, the poet is only showing the poverty of content to his readers. (Liang Qichao: *Notes on Poets and Poetry from the Ice-drinker's Studio*)

◎近世诗人能镕铸新理想以入旧风格者，当推黄公度。（梁启超《饮冰室诗话》）

（近一个时期的诗人，能够在旧的风格中融入新的思想观念的，应当推举黄遵宪。）

Among all poets today, Huang Zunxian figures prominently, because he incorporates new ideas into the old form. (Liang Qichao: *Notes on Poets and Poetry from the Ice-drinker's Studio*)

诗穷而后工 /shī qióng ér hòu gōng/

A Good Poem Is the Product of Pent-up Emotions.

诗人只有在遭受困厄艰险的环境中，幽愤郁积于心，方能写出上乘的诗歌作品。这里的"穷"，并非指物质生活上的"穷困"，而是指广义的人生逆境。"工"，工致精美。这一命题由北宋著名文坛领袖欧阳修（1007—1072）提出。欧阳修认为，诗人因人生逆境而能对现实利益有所超脱，这有助于诗人抒写出曲折入微而又带有普遍性的世况人情。欧阳修的"诗穷而后工"继承发展了司马迁（前145或前135？—？）的"发愤著书"说与韩愈（768—824）的"不平则鸣"说，但它不再强调诗人自身愤懑的宣泄，而是揭示了优秀诗歌作品之所以产生的规律。欧阳修之后，此说成为文学批评理论中关于优秀文学作品产生规律的带有普遍意义的说法。

A poet will be able to produce a quality poem only when he is in a difficult and perilous environment, feeling suffocated with pent-up anger and frustration. The word *qiong* (穷 difficulty) does not mean the physical deprivation of material means but refers more broadly to adverse situations in life. *Gong* (工 quality) means artistically refined and beautiful. This idea was put forward by Ouyang Xiu (1007-1072), a renowned leader in the literary world of the Northern Song Dynasty. He believes that adverse situations will enable poets to transcend the desire for worldly gains and assist them to depict with sophistication and insight scenes and people in the real world that have a universal significance. Ouyang Xiu's theory not only continues but also develops Sima Qian's (145 or 135 ?-? BC) "indignation spurs one to write great works" and Han Yu's (768-824) "cry out against injustice." This concept no longer focuses on expressing the poet's own indignation or frustration but seeks instead to shed light on the way a great poem comes into being. Later on, the proposition became a mainstream theory in literary criticism regarding the origins of literary masterpieces.

◎予闻世谓诗人少达而多穷，夫岂然哉！盖世所传诗者，多出于古穷人之辞也。……盖愈穷则愈工。然则非诗之能穷人，殆穷者而后工也。（欧阳修《梅圣俞诗集序》）

（我听到世人说，诗人很少有仕途通达的，大多人生不顺。果真是这样吗？大概是世间流传的那些诗，多是出于古代不得志的诗人们的创作吧。……大概诗人越是命运不顺，他们的诗就写得越是精美。这样看来，并不是写诗让人命运不顺，恐怕是诗人命运不顺，然后做的诗才精美吧。）

I hear that poets seldom fare well in their pursuit of official positions. Many suffer ups and downs. Is that really true? Maybe it is because poems circulated among people are mostly written by those frustrated in their ambitions. Perhaps they are more likely to produce quality poems when they suffer ill fortune. It seems it is not writing that brings people ill fortune, but, rather, poets are better able to produce exquisite poems when they suffer ill fortune. (Ouyang Xiu: Preface to *The Collection of Poems by Mei Yaochen*)

诗史 /shīshǐ/
Historical Poetry

指诗歌的内容能够真实反映某一历史时期广阔的社会现实和重大的历史事件而具有"史"的价值。《诗经》有些诗篇反映当时历史，孔子（前551—前479）据此提出《诗经》"可以观"，即包含了对《诗经》以诗征史的肯定，汉代学者很看重诗歌承载历史的功能。后来的诗论家大都强调优秀诗歌须将审美与反映现实结合起来，从而彰显诗歌的审美与认识、教育功能的统一。唐代诗人杜甫（712—770）的诗歌被称作"诗史"，就是因为他的诗能够反映

"安史之乱"时的真实社会，体现出深刻的忧国忧民之情。

This term refers to poetry that reflects social realities and major events of a historical period, thus possessing historical value. Some of the poems in *The Book of Songs* were about the realities of its time, which prompted Confucius (551-479 BC) to exclaim that "*The Book of Songs* enables one to understand society." This means that he viewed *The Book of Songs* as using poetry to reflect history. Han-dynasty scholars stressed the importance of poetry as a means of recording history. Subsequently, Chinese scholars of poetry believed that poetry should reflect reality through aesthetic means so as to provide aesthetic enjoyment, understanding as well as education. The poems of Tang poet Du Fu (712-770) are called "historical poetry" because they reflected what the country went through during the An Lushan-Shi Siming Rebellion and the author's acute sense of sadness about the misery the country and its people suffered in times of national crisis.

引例 Citations：

◎杜逢禄山之难，流离陇蜀，毕陈于诗，推见至隐，殆无遗事，故当时号为"诗史"。(孟棨（qǐ）《本事诗·高逸》)

（杜甫遭逢安禄山叛乱引发的灾难，先后漂泊甘肃、四川一带，所经历的一切，全都写在诗中，后人由此推知当时的很多隐约细节，几乎没有什么遗漏，所以当时人称他的诗为"诗史"。）

Du Fu fled to the provinces of Gansu and Sichuan to escape turbulences caused by the An Lushan-Shi Siming Rebellion and wrote about his experiences in poems. As his poems gave vivid and detailed accounts about events of the time, they became known as "historical poetry." (Meng Qi: *The Story of Poetry*)

◎昔人评杜诗为"诗史"，盖其以咏歌之辞，寓纪载之实，而抑扬褒贬之意，粲然于其中，虽谓之"史"可也。(文天祥《集杜诗自序》)

（过去的人评价杜甫诗为"诗史"，大概是因为他能够以诗歌形式记载真实的事件，同时批评讥刺与表扬赞美的意旨显然蕴含其中，所以称他的诗为"史"完全合适。）

People regarded the poems of Du Fu as historical poetry mostly because they described what really happened in his age, and they contained criticisms or praises of historical events. So his poems were aptly called "historical poetry." (Wen Tianxiang: Preface to *Poems Composed by Rearranging Du Fu's Verses*)

诗无达诂 /shīwúdágǔ/
Poetry Defies Fixed Interpretation.

原指《诗经》没有恒定不变的训诂或解释，后用为文学鉴赏与批评术语，泛指由于时代变化与鉴赏者的思想、阅历、修养等个性差异，对同一作品往往有不同的解释或解读。由汉代大儒董仲舒（前179—前104）提出。"诗无达诂"源于春秋时代的"赋诗言志"，当时的为政者从实际的政治和外交需要出发常常引用《诗经》诗句，不一定符合诗句本意，甚至有时断章取义；汉儒诠释《诗经》，也因不同学术取向而分为数家。董仲舒提出这一命题，其意在为汉儒的不同解释提供依据。作为一种文学理论，"诗无达诂"属于鉴赏论，侧重于读者感受，体现出不同读者在文本解读与艺术审美上的差异性；同时，诗歌语言具有暗示、含蓄、曲折的特点，言不尽意，所以不能仅照字面意思直解，读者须按照自己的理解、想象与学识，以心会心，体悟诗中的寄托和寓意。"诗无达诂"的价值在于揭示了作品自身语义的模糊性与解释者个人的差异性，但不等于可以随意解释作品的意义。

This term originally referred to the absence of a universally accepted interpretation or explanation of *The Book of Songs*. It was first put forward by the great Han Dynasty Confucian scholar Dong Zhongshu (179-104 BC). Later, it came to be used as a general term in literary criticism, which suggests that as the result of the changing historical conditions and different life experiences of readers there bound to be varied interpretations or explanations of the same literary work. The idea that poetry defies any attempt at fixed interpretation derived from the traditions of the Spring and Autumn Period, when poetic lines were recited to express one's view, stance, or emotion. To justify themselves politically or diplomatically, politicians at the time would quote from *The Book of Songs*, yet without bothering to find out the exact meaning of the quotes, sometimes even distorting their meaning. Confucian scholars of the Han Dynasty interpreted *The Book of Songs* in several different ways due to different academic orientations. Dong Zhongshu raised this idea to provide theoretical support for such divergence. As a view of literary theory, it is concerned with different readers' divergent interpretations of a text and its aesthetic values. This view argues that as poetic terms are suggestive, ambiguous, and intricate, readers should not settle for a superficial understanding of a poem. Instead, they should delve into the poet's heart and develop their own understanding, interpretation, and insight of his poem. The argument that there is no fixed interpretation of poems is valid, because it shows that poetic language can be ambiguous in meaning and that interpretations can therefore vary. However, this does not mean that one should interpret a poem too freely.

引例 Citations：

◎ 所闻《诗》无达诂，《易》无达占，《春秋》无达辞。从变从义，而一以奉人［天］。（董仲舒《春秋繁露·精华》）

（我听说《诗经》没有恒定不变的解释，《周易》没有恒定不变的占卜，《春秋》没有恒定不变的词句。遵从变通的原则，遵从经典的本来意义，将两者合一即可不违背圣人的思想［天道］。）

I hear that there is no fixed interpretation of *The Book of Songs*, no fixed divination in *The Book of Changes*, and no unchangeable wording in *The Spring and Autumn Annals*. We should obey principles flexibly and capture the underlying messages of classics. Then, we should merge these two aspects into one without violating sages' moral instructions or the way of heaven. (Dong Zhongshu: *Luxuriant Gems of The Spring and Autumn Annals*)

◎ 余尝谓《诗经》与诸经不同。故读《诗》者亦当与读诸经不同。

盖诗人托物引喻，其辞微，其旨远。故有言在于此而意属于彼者，不可以文句泥（nì）也。（何良俊《四友斋丛说·经一》）

（我曾经说《诗经》与别的儒家经典不一样。所以读《诗经》也应当与读其他经典不同。大概是诗人借某些事物引申比喻，其用词精微，其意旨深远。所以有字面意思说的是这个而实际意旨说的是那个，不可以拘泥于《诗经》的文句。）

I once said that *The Book of Songs* was different from other Confucian classics. So it should be read in a different way. Poets in the book probably used certain things in life to make allusions about things. Their wording was nuanced and their message was profound. Yet, they often said something but meant quite another. Therefore, we should not be too strict in interpreting the lines of the book. (He Liangjun: *Academic Notes from the Four-scholar Study*)

诗言志 /shī yán zhì/

Poetry Expresses Aspirations.

诗歌表达作者内心的志向。"志"指诗歌作品中所表达的作者的内心志向、思想，兼及情感因素。"诗言志"最先见于儒家经典《尚书·舜典》，是中国诗论的"开山纲领"（朱自清语），经过历代诗论家的演绎，其蕴涵不断得以丰富，并由此确立了中国文论关于文学特征的基本观念。

A poem expresses aspirations in one's heart. *Zhi* (志) here means the author's aspirations, emotions, and thoughts. The concept of "poetry expressing aspirations," first seen in the Confucian classic *The Book of History,* was hailed by Zhu Ziqing as the "manifesto" of Chinese poetry. Enriched by poetry critics through the generations, it was later established as a basic concept in Chinese literary criticism.

◎诗言志，歌永言。(《尚书·舜典》)

(诗是表达内心志向的，歌是用语言来吟唱的。)

Poems express aspirations deep in one's heart, whereas songs are verses for chanting. (*The Book of History*)

◎诗者，志之所之也，在心为志，发言为诗。(《毛诗序》)

(诗是内心情感意志的表达，藏在心里就是情感意志，用语言把它表达出来就是诗歌。)

Poetry is an expression of a person's feelings and aspirations. When hidden in his heart, it is just his feelings and aspirations. When put forth through the medium of words, it becomes what is known as poetry. (Introductions to *Mao's Version of The Book of Songs*)

诗缘情 /shī yuán qíng/
Poetry Springs from Emotions.

诗歌缘于诗人内心的情感。西晋陆机(261 — 303)《文赋》提出，诗人情动于心，而后才有诗歌创作。"诗缘情"说与"诗言志"说互为补充，强调文学的抒情性与审美特征，表现出魏晋时代文学观念的变迁。因此，"诗缘情"也成为中国古代关于诗歌与文学本质看法的另一代表观点。

Poems originate from the poet's heart-felt feelings. Lu Ji (261-303) of the Western Jin Dynasty said in "The Art of Writing" that a poet must have a surge of feeling deep in his heart before he could create a poem. This view, complementing the concept of "poetry expressing aspirations," stresses the lyrical and aesthetic nature of literary works and echoes the evolution of literary tastes during the Wei and Jin dynasties. "Poetry springing from emotions" represents another viewpoint on the nature of poetry and literature in ancient China.

引例 Citations：

◎诗缘情而绮靡。（陆机《文赋》）

（诗歌源于情感因而形式华丽好看。）

Poetry, springing from emotions, reads beautifully in its form of expression. (Lu Ji: The Art of Writing)

◎人禀七情，应物斯感，感物吟志，莫非自然。（刘勰《文心雕龙·明诗》）

（人具有喜、怒、哀、惧、爱、恶、欲等七种情感，受到外物的刺激而心有所感，心有所感而吟咏情志，所有的诗歌都出于自然情感。）

People have the seven emotions of joy, anger, sadness, fear, love, loathing and desire. He expresses his feelings and aspirations in a poetical way when he is stimulated by the external world and his heart is touched. All poems come from natural emotions. (Liu Xie: *The Literary Mind and the Carving of Dragons*)

诗中有画，画中有诗
/shī zhōng yǒu huà, huà zhōng yǒu shī/

Painting in Poetry, Poetry in Painting

诗中有画意，画中有诗情。指诗歌与绘画作品所呈现出的审美意境融合相通的美学效果。语出苏轼（1037—1101）《书摩诘〈蓝田烟雨图〉》。绘画是造型艺术，通过众多物象构成画面给人以审美感受；诗歌是语言艺术，通过文字营造意境给人以审美感受。前者是"无声有形"的艺术，后者是"有声无形"的艺术。这一术语旨在提倡"诗歌"与"绘画"的相互渗透与融合，进而创造出天然清新、具有"诗情画意"的审美境界。苏轼这一思想对后世文学与绘画艺术的发展有着深远的影响。

This expression highlights the connection between poetry and painting in their ability to create aesthetic imagery. This idea was first put forward by Su Shi (1037-1101) in his "Notes to Wang Wei's Painting 'Mist and Rain over Lantian.'" Painting creates an aesthetic effect through images presented. Poetry, on the other hand, is a language art, which creates an aesthetic effect through the use of words. The former is an art that has shape but no sound, while the latter is an art that has sound but no shape. The term means that good poetry and painting should be fused so that a spontaneous and novel aesthetic realm can be created by a "picturesque poem" or a "poetic picture." This idea of Su Shi's had a far-reaching influence on the subsequent development of literature and painting in China.

引例 Citations：

◎味摩诘之诗，诗中有画；观摩诘之画，画中有诗。（苏轼《东坡题跋·书摩诘〈蓝田烟雨图〉》）

（品味王维的诗，诗中有画的意境；观看王维的画，画中有诗的情感。）

When reading Wang Wei's poems, one can conjure up a picturesque image. When viewing Wang Wei's paintings, one can experience a poetic sentiment. (Su Shi: *A Collection of Su Dongpo's Prefaces and Postscripts*)

◎诗中画，性情中来者也，则画不是可拟张拟李而后作诗；画中诗，乃境趣时生者也，则诗不是便生吞生剥而后成画。真识相触，如镜写影，初何容心？今人不免唐突诗画矣。（石涛《大涤子题画诗跋》卷一）

（所谓诗中有画，源自诗人的本真性情，故而诗中的画不是随便描摹哪个姓张姓李的人的画便能写出诗来；所谓画中有诗，乃是由当时特定的意境、情趣生发出来的，故而画中的诗不是生搬硬套某一首诗便能画成画。内心的识见与自然碰撞相融，如同镜子显现物象那么逼真，起初哪里是有意于此，今天的人［不懂得这一点］所以免不了要胡乱冒犯诗画了。）

Painting in poetry is a natural creation deriving from a poet's true aspiration; such poems cannot be composed by imitating others' paintings. Poetry in painting is inspired by a specific scene or sentiment at a given time, so it is not possible to artificially insert a poem into a painting. The way that a mind interacts with nature is as direct and unaffected as a life-like image reflected in a mirror. The effect is not deliberately intended at first. Nowadays, people do not understand this point. No wonder poetry and painting have become abused. (Shi Tao: *Dadizi's Comments on His Own Poems Inscribed on Paintings*)

时序 /shíxù/
Change Along with Times

即时世和时代变化。这一术语旨在揭示文学创作与时代变化的关系。南朝刘勰（465？—520？或532？）指出文学发展不是孤立的现象，而是受到时代多重因素的影响，包括当时的社会政治状况、统治者的个人爱好、学术思潮等。

The term suggests that literary creation is affected by changes of the times. Author and literary scholar Liu Xie (465?-520? or 532?) of the Southern Dynasties who used this term pointed out that literary creation is not an isolated phenomenon. Rather, it is affected by numerous historical factors, such as the prevailing social and political conditions, the personal preferences of rulers, as well as intellectual trends.

引例 Citations：

◎ 故知歌谣文理，与世推移，风动于上，而波震于下者。（刘勰《文心雕龙·时序》）

（因此知道诗歌的文采情理随时代变化而变化，时政教化对诗歌的影响如同风在水面上吹，而水波就在下面震荡一样。）

Thus we know that songs and literary style change with the times, just like when the wind blows, waves are stirred up in the water. (Liu Xie: *The Literary Mind and the Carving of Dragons*)

◎ 文变染乎世情，兴废系乎时序。（刘勰《文心雕龙·时序》）

（文章的变化受到当世各种情况的影响，它的兴衰取决于时代的变化。）

Literary changes are affected by the ways of the world. A literary style's rise and decline in popularity is caused by changes of the time. (Liu Xie: *The Literary Mind and the Carving of Dragons*)

识书之道 /shíshūzhīdào/
The Way to Recognize Good Calligraphy

指辨识书法艺术的要诀。南朝王僧虔（426—485）、唐代张怀瓘（guàn）等人主张，鉴赏书法时以精神气韵为首要标准，其次才是书法的笔墨形式。他们将富有风神骨气的书法看作上品，将崇尚美丽形体和功用目的的书法看作下品。这一观念，代表中国古代书法的主流欣赏标准。

This refers to the way to judge the artistic quality of calligraphy. Wang Sengqian (426-485) of the Southern Dynasty and Zhang Huaiguan (dates unknown) of the Tang Dynasty held that the primary criterion for appreciating calligraphy is whether it features a spiritual liveliness; the concern about the way of how to use the brush and ink is secondary. Both of them valued a calligraphic work's spiritual verve and structural integrity and despised an excessive obsession with superficial decorum and practical usefulness. This preference represents a major criterion for appreciating ancient Chinese calligraphy.

引例 Citations：

◎深识书者，惟观神彩，不见字形。若精意玄鉴，则物无遗照，何有不通？（张怀瓘《文字论》，见张彦远《法书要录》卷四）

（深通书法的人，主要是观摩作品内在的神采，而不是外在的字形。如果洞察书法的神韵意趣，那么作品中的所有方面都能清晰照见，还有什么不能通达的呢？）

A truly good calligrapher cares mainly about a calligraphic work's innate charm, not about characters' external appearances. Provided that a deep insight is gained into the spiritual profundity and liveliness of calligraphic script as a whole, all minor aspects of it will become recognizable as well. (Zhang Huaiguan: On Characters with and without Analyzable Components)

◎智则无涯，法固不定，且以风神骨气者居上，妍美功用者居下。（张怀瓘《书议》，见张彦远《法书要录》卷四）

（智慧没有边际，法度本不固定，书法作品中以富有风韵、神采、筋骨、气势等品格的列为上品，而追求外形华丽和功用目的的则列为下品。）

Wisdom has no boundary; rules are by no means fixed. All calligraphic works with an innate appeal, liveliness, structural integrity, and overall impact are excellent, whereas those whose sole aim is to pursue superficial pomp and functional relevance are shoddy works. (Zhang Huaiguan: Comments on Calligraphy)

势 /shì/

Situation / Trend

事物存在与发展的态势、趋势。"势"的形成、存在与变化，取决于事物之间的格局、力度及相互关系。"势"可指自然的形势，如空间位置上以高临下之势，也可指人类社会中因身份地位或行为举动所造成的态势、趋势。在文艺创作领域，"势"也表现为由作品结构或风格所造就的作品内在的流动之势。"势"对于人和事物的影响，体现着自然与社会运行的法则。人可以通过顺应、把握外在的"势"而有所作为，在一定条件下甚至可以通过造"势"改变事物发展的趋向。

This refers to the situation or trend in the development of things. The formation, existence and change of a situation hinges on how things are organized, their relative strength, and how they interact with each other. It also refers to topography, such as occupying a commanding position at a high location. It may also refer to how people behave as influenced by their social positions. In terms of literary work, a trend refers to a particular force running through a literary work arising from its structure and style. The impact of a tendency upon people and social affairs gives rise to laws governing nature and social development. One can accomplish great things by following and gaining a good command of social trends. Under certain conditions, one changes the developmental course of things by creating trends.

引例 Citations：

◎水因地而制流，兵因敌而制胜。故兵无常势，水无常形，能因敌变化而取胜者，谓之神。(《孙子·虚实》)

（水根据地形而决定水流的形态和方向，用兵根据敌人的情况而制定取胜之道。因此用兵没有不变的形式，水流没有固定的形态，能够根据敌人的变化而取胜的人，可以称得上神妙。）

Topography decides where and how water flows. Similarly, the strategy to win a war should be made based on an understanding of the situation in the enemy's camp. So, just as there is no fixed form of flowing water, there is no fixed strategy in commanding an army. Those who win the war by changing their strategy in response to changes in the enemy's situation are truly master of warfare. (*The Art of War*)

◎君执柄以处势，故令行禁止。柄者，杀生之制也；势者，胜众之资也。(《韩非子·八经》)

(君主执掌权柄、占据权势，因此有令则行，有禁则止。权柄，是对生杀权力的控制；权势，是任使民众的凭借。)

With power to dictate the trend, a sovereign can ensure that his orders and prohibitions are enforced. Power means control over the life and death of others, while the ability to dictate a trend is the means to govern the general public. (*Hanfeizi*)

◎夫情致异区，文变殊术，莫不因情立体，即体成势也。(刘勰《文心雕龙·定势》)

(作者的情趣各不相同，因而文章的手法也多种多样，但都会根据所要表达的具体内容来确定体裁，就着体裁形成具有特定风格的文章气势。)

With different temperaments and tastes, different writers have different approaches to writing, and they will use different literary styles according to what they want to write about. In doing so, they create a particular literary force. (Liu Xie: *The Literary Mind and the Carving of Dragons*)

瘦硬 /shòuyìng/
Thin and Strong

细瘦而劲硬。"瘦"义为细瘦、不丰满，与"硬"连用，侧重指作品的骨力。用于诗歌创作，主要指少铺陈，不堆砌华美的辞藻，不做细腻柔媚的描写，而通过峭拔新奇的声律、刚劲简洁的词句，达成瘦硬的艺术风格；用于书法绘画，主要指笔触细瘦遒劲，具有刚劲挺拔的气质，但又不同于雄浑风格为主的刚健气质。

As employed in traditional Chinese art and literature, "thin" here means bony or not plump; it is used in collocation with "strong," emphasizing a work's strong structural force. Used in poetic composition, the term refers to a layout devoid of elaborate writing, flowery wording or excessively subtle description. Instead, amazingly new metrical patterns and bold, concise phrases and sentences are preferred to achieve a "thin and strong" style. When used in painting and calligraphy, it refers to thin but vigorous strokes executed to highlight a quality of unbending rigidity, unlike other more robust styles.

引例 Citations：

◎书贵瘦硬方通神。（杜甫《李潮八分小篆歌》）

（书法注重细瘦劲硬，方能达到非凡的境地。）

Calligraphy, only when performed with thin and strong strokes, will be truly remarkable. (Du Fu: *Ode to Li Chao's Modified Lesser Seal Script*)

◎宋子京词是宋初体，张子野始创瘦硬之体，虽以佳句互相称美，其实趣尚不同。（刘熙载《艺概·词曲概》）

（宋祁的词作反映宋朝初年的样貌，张先始创细瘦劲硬的词风，虽然他们相互称赞对方的佳句，其实各自的趣味和追求并不相同。）

Song Qi's *ci* poetry reflects the style of the early years of the Song Dynasty, whereas Zhang Xian was the first to create the "thin and strong" *ci* style. Although the two poets praised each other, they differed in artistic taste and pursuit. (Liu Xizai: *Overview of Literary Theories*)

书道 /shūdào/
The Way of Calligraphy

指通过书法创作追求身心合一进而体悟宇宙与生命真谛的艺术境界。受孔子（前551—前479）"志于道，据于德，依于仁，游于艺"的思想影响，尤其是庄子（前369？—前286）"技进乎道"的美学精神导引，书家对书法有更高的艺术追求，希望超越书法的形式与技艺，达到"道"的境界。因唐代书家重视书写的笔法、技法，故改称"书法"。"书法"是"书道"的初级阶段，属于技法的、有形的、形而下的范畴；"书道"是"书法"的最高阶段，属于普遍的、抽象的、形而上的范畴。"书道"这一术语后来传至日本，被赋予了更多修身、养性、悟道等方面的内容，这些又影响了中国近现代书法艺术的发展。

This term refers to an artistic state wherein a calligraphic artist pursues a unity between body and soul through calligraphic creation, so that he may embrace the truths about the universe and life. It was influenced by Confucius (551-479 BC) who said: "[Cultivated people] should follow Dao, adhere to virtues, embrace benevolence, and are well versed in various arts and skills." It was influenced even more by Zhuangzi's (369? - 286 BC) aesthetic view, "If we can achieve perfection in a particular area of skill, we come close to the great Way itself." The calligrapher aims higher than the mere art of calligraphy, aspiring to attain the great Way by transcending calligraphy as a mere skill or form of art. By the Tang Dynasty, because calligraphers put more emphasis on the different forms and skills of calligraphy, they started to use a new term "calligraphic technique." Calligraphic technique represented an initial stage of calligraphy – a tangible, superficial and somewhat "lower" level. The calligraphic Way, on the other hand, was an advanced stage of calligraphic technique, paying attention to universal, abstract and therefore much "higher" aspects of calligraphy. This latter concept spread to Japan and took on the broader implications of self-cultivation and enlightenment later on. It, in turn, influenced the development of modern Chinese calligraphic art.

引例 Citations：

◎ 唐中叶以后，书道下衰之际，故弗多得云。(黄伯思《东观余论·跋叚(xiá)柯古靖居寺碑后》)

(唐代中期之后，书道开始走向衰落，故而上乘书作不可多得。)

After the mid-Tang Dynasty, the way of calligraphy started to decline, and excellent works of calligraphy became scarcely available. (Huang Bosi: *A Chief of Imperial Archives' Other Works Appended to a Collection of Essays*)

◎ 隶书生于篆书，而实是篆之不肖子，何也？篆书一画、一直、一钩、一点，皆有义理，所谓指事、象形、谐声、会意、转注、假借是也，故谓之"六书"。隶既变圆为方，改弦易辙，全违父法，是六书之道由隶而绝。(钱泳《履园丛话·书学》)

(隶书由篆书生发出来，实际上是篆书的不肖之子，为什么这么说呢？篆书的一画、一直、一钩、一点，都蕴藏着义理规律，即通常所说的指事、象形、谐声、会意、转注、假借，故而称之为"六书"。隶书将篆书圆润的书写形态变为方正，全然改变篆书的结构规律，违背了篆书的造字方法，所以六书所蕴含的造字规律由隶书而开始断绝了。)

Clerical script was derived from seal script. It was an "unfilial son" of seal script. Why? In seal script, the execution of each horizontal or vertical line, hook or dot is governed by certain reasons and laws. They are ideographic, pictographic, ideophonetic, associative compound, or with transferred meaning and borrowed meaning, hence the term "six ways of constituting characters." The clerical script, by changing seal script from smooth roundness to angular abruptness, transforms the structural pattern altogether and violates the methodology of forming seal script. Thus, the reasons and laws implicit in the six ways of forming characters became lost as clerical script came to prevail. (Qian Yong: *Collected Writings on the Study of Calligraphy at Lüyuan*)

书契 /shūqì/

Documents on Bamboo or Wooden Slips

主要有两种含义：一指书写于简牍上的文字；二指纸张发明以前用竹木制作的券契或文书凭证，竹木正面用文字记录事项，竹木的一侧刻有一定数量的齿，通常会有两份，由当事双方各执其一，便于将来复验。两汉以后，简牍书写逐渐退出历史舞台，但作为券契或文书凭证用的竹木书契仍有使用。

This term has two meanings. One refers to script in general inscribed on bamboo or wooden slips. The other refers to documentary proofs, particularly proof of property ownership inscribed on bamboo or wooden slips before paper was invented. Various activities and matters were recorded on the front side. A number of tooth-like marks were carved on one side. There are usually two copies of the document, each held by one of the two parties concerned for future re-verification. After the Western and Eastern Han dynasties, script inscribed on bamboo or wooden slips gradually fell into disuse, whereas documents of proof carved on the same medium continued to be used.

引例 Citations：

◎上古结绳而治，后世圣人易之以书契。(《周易·系辞下》)

(上古时期的人通过结绳的方法来记录事情，后世的圣人用文字记录取代了这一做法。)

In Chinese high antiquity people tied knots to keep records. The sages of later generations, on the other hand, used writing for the same purpose. (*The Book of Changes*)

◎书者文字，契者刻木而书其侧，故曰"书契"也。一云：以书契约其事也。(陆德明《经典释文·尚书音义上》)

("书"指的是文字，"契"是在竹木的一侧刻上与事项有关的标识，所以称之为"书契"。另一种说法是："书契"是就有关事项进行约定的文书凭证。)

The character *shu* refers to written characters, whereas *qi* means the marks made on one side of bamboo or wooden slips to record matters and activities. Another interpretation is that *shuqi* refers to documents that guarantee the validity of a pledge or proof. (Lu Deming: *An Interpretation of Confucian and Other Classics*)

书圣 /shūshèng/
The Sage of Calligraphy

东晋时期著名书法家王羲之（303 — 361，一作307 — 365，又作321 — 379）的"别称"。"圣"指神圣，中国古代往往将精通某门技艺或在某一方面造诣达到极深之人尊称为"圣"，以此肯定和称赞一个人的卓越成就、杰出地位和深远影响。"书圣"一词，既强调了王羲之书法艺术的高超，也称赞了王羲之道德人格的高尚。王羲之精研体势，心摹手追，广采众长，兼善隶、草、楷、行各体，摆脱了汉魏书风，自成一家。其代表作《兰亭集序》，被誉为"天下第一行书"。因梁武帝萧衍（464 — 549）、唐太宗李世民（599 — 649）、宋太宗赵光义（939 — 997）等帝王的大力推崇，历史上曾出现过三次大规模学习王羲之书法的高潮，由此树立了王羲之千古"书圣"的美名。

This title was given to the renowned calligrapher Wang Xizhi, who lived from 303 to 361 (or possibly 307 - 365 or 321 - 379) of the Eastern Jin Period. The word "sage" here refers to a person of supreme attainment. People in ancient China tended to honor a person with an exceptional talent or skill as a "sage" in recognition of his outstanding accomplishments, prominent achievements, and profound influence. The term "Sage of Calligraphy" not only highlights Wang Xizhi's superb mastery of calligraphic art but also commended his moral integrity. By carefully studying the features of calligraphy, and by imitating and practicing, Wang learned widely from the strong points of others. He was extraordinarily good at all four major forms of calligraphy – clerical script, cursive script, regular script, and running script. His calligraphy abandoned the special traits popular in the Han and Wei dynasties and formed a style of his own. His most noted and famous work, "Preface to the Collection of Poems Composed at the Orchid Pavilion" has been honored through the ages as the best running script ever written. Promoted by Xiao Yan (464-549), Emperor Wu of the Liang Dynasty, Li Shimin (599-649), Emperor Taizong of the Tang, and Zhao Guangyi (939-997), Emperor Taizong of the Song, there appeared three upsurges of emulating Wang's calligraphy on a massive scale. Hence his prestige as the greatest calligrapher of all times.

引例 Citations：

◎王羲之书字势雄逸，如龙跳天门，虎卧凤阁，故历代宝之，永以为训。(《梁武帝评书》，见陈思《书苑菁华》卷五）

(王羲之的书法，体势雄浑飘逸，好像是蛟龙跃进天宫大门，猛虎卧在皇宫楼阁，[可谓达到极致,]所以历朝历代都将其视为珍品，作为永远的典范。)

Wang Xizhi's calligraphy, both vigorous and graceful, calls to mind a great Chinese dragon leaping through the gate of the Heavenly Gate or a fierce tiger crouching in the Royal Palace. It has reached a supreme level! Therefore, people through the ages have viewed it as a treasure and eternal classic model. (Emperor Wu of Liang's Comments on Calligraphers from the Han Dynasty to the Liang of the Southern Dynasties)

◎详察古今，研精篆素，尽善尽美，其惟王逸少乎！(《晋书·王羲之传论》)

(仔细考察古今书法，对前人的作品透彻精研，所写书法全都尽善尽美，古今只有王羲之一个人啊！)

Wang Xizhi is the only one to have studied both ancient and contemporary calligraphy carefully and elevated it to a level of perfection! (*The History of the Jin Dynasty*)

书者，散也 /shū zhě, sǎn yě/
Calligraphy Expresses Inner Conditions.

写好书法，先要抒放情性、摒除一切杂念。是东汉著名书法家蔡邕（133—192）在《笔论》中提出的书法观念。它论述了书法艺术抒发主体情怀的创作心态，强调书家在创作时应先抒放情性、排除一切牵累与功利之心，并将其视为决定书法作品成功与否的关键要素。

To become a good calligrapher, one must first set one's mind at ease and dismiss all distracting thoughts. This is an argument raised by Cai Yong (133-192), a famous Eastern Han calligrapher, in his treatise "On Calligraphic Script." He says that the art of calligraphy discloses the calligrapher's personal feeling, stressing the need to unleash one's true self and to eliminate all of life's burdens and practical considerations. This view takes such actions as being crucial to the success of a calligraphic work.

引例 Citations：

◎ 书者，散也。欲书先散怀抱，任情恣性，然后书之，若迫于事，虽中山兔豪不能佳也。（蔡邕《笔论》，见陈思《书苑菁华》卷一）

（从事书法活动，先要抒放情性、排除一切杂念。动笔之前，必须舒展心胸，任凭性情恣意挥洒，然后再展毫书写，如果是被迫应事，即使是用中山产的兔毫佳笔，也写不出优美的书法作品来。）

To engage in the practice of calligraphy, one should first unleash his pent-up feelings and eliminate all distracting thoughts. Before setting brush to paper, he is advised to open his heart and give free rein to his fantasy. Only then can he expect to carry out his actual task. If he is reluctant to do it, even if he uses a rabbit-hair brush from Zhongshan, he will still fail to produce a fine work of calligraphy. (Cai Yong: On Calligraphic Script)

◎ 夫欲攻书之时，当收视反听，绝虑凝神，心正气和，则契于玄妙。心神不正，字则欹（qī）斜；志气不和，书必颠覆。（李世民

《笔法诀》，见陈思《书苑菁华》卷十九）

（想要书写之时，首先应当对外界之事不看不听，杜绝思虑，凝聚心神，心思纯正，气息平和，才能写出玄妙的作品。如果心神不端正，那么所写的字就会歪斜；气息不平和，所写作品就会失败。）

When doing calligraphy, he should stay totally free from what is going on outside, let go of all worries and anxiety, concentrate his energy, purify his mind, and breathe with perfect ease. Only thus would he be able to produce a real piece of work of art. If his mind is in a jumble, his written characters will be crooked; if his breath is uneven, his work will turn out a failure. (Li Shimin: The Craft of Calligraphy)

疏密 /shūmì/

Sparsity and Density

由"疏""密"两个意义相反的词构成，有稀疏与稠密、简略与详细、粗疏与精密、宽松与严密、疏远与亲密等含义。在书法绘画等艺术批评中，疏密主要指结构或布局方面的安排以及笔墨运用的浓淡粗细等。在文学批评中，"疏"与"密"经常联用，"疏"义为疏荡、疏阔、粗略等，多指诗文创作中的随意、粗疏、不严密；"密"义为精密、严密、紧凑等，多指诗文创作中在构思、逻辑、用语等方面严谨周密，有时亦指密集堆砌的毛病。中国古人认为，"疏"与"密"对立统一，好的作品在结构、布局上应当疏密相间。

This concept consists of several pairs of opposites: sparsity and density, brevity and thoroughness, roughness and precision, flexibility and rigor, and estrangement and intimacy. In the artistic criticism of painting and calligraphy, the term is used to mainly describe the structural arrangement, general layout, as well as dark or light, thick or thin execution of strokes in these two art forms. In literary criticism, "sparsity" and "density" often occur together. "Sparsity" means carefree, rough or sketchy. It refers especially to thoughtlessness, carefreeness or looseness in the creation of prose and poetry. "Density" means meticulous, tight or compact. It often refers to rigor and thoroughness in theme development, logic, and wording in the creation of prose and poetry, and occasionally to the demerit of piling too many words up for no good reason. Ancient Chinese believed that sparsity and density represent a unity of opposites. A good work of art should balance density with sparsity in both structure and layout.

引例 Citations：

◎试笔成文，临池染墨，疏密俱巧，真草皆得，似望城扉，如瞻星石。（萧纲《答湘东王上王羲之书》）

（[王羲之]下笔成文，在砚池边蘸墨挥毫，无论是疏朗还是精密都很巧妙，真书、草书都精心写就，其静处如同远观城门，其动处好似瞻望天上的陨星。）

Wang Xizhi wrote swiftly and skillfully, dipping his brush in the concave inkstone from time to time. His calligraphic writing, whether sparingly or densely spaced, looks truly beautiful. Both his regular script and cursive script were written with immense care. In repose, his flow of words can be likened to watching a city gate from far away. In motion, it can be likened to watching a meteorite in the sky. (Xiao Gang: In Answer to Prince Xiangdong for Kindly Presenting Me with a Calligraphic Work by Wang Xizhi)

◎古无真正楷书…… 至国朝，文征仲先生始极意结构，疏密匀称，位置适宜。（谢肇淛（zhè）《五杂组》卷七）

（古代没有真正的楷书…… 到我们明朝，文征明先生才开始致力于书体结构，他的作品无论疏朗、严密都非常匀称，位置适当。）

There was no real regular script in ancient times... It was not until the Ming Dynasty that Wen Zhengming started to explore rules governing the structure of characters in calligraphy. His works feature a perfect balance between sparsity and density. Each stroke is in its proper place. (Xie Zhaozhe: *An Orderly Narration on Five Assorted Offerings*)

◎词贵疏密相间。(陈廷焯《词坛丛话》)

(词的写作贵在疏朗与严密相互交错。)

The merit of *ci* poetry composition rests on the balance of sparsity and density. (Chen Tingzhuo: *Random Remarks on Ci Poetry Creation*)

水墨画 /shuǐmòhuà/
Ink Wash Painting

指中国画中纯用水墨、不用色彩的一种绘画形式。也称国画、中国画。以水、墨、毛笔和宣纸作为主要材料，通过调配清水的多少，引为浓墨、淡墨、干墨、湿墨、焦墨等，画出浓淡层次不同的作品。一般的水墨画，只有水与墨，黑色与白色。进阶的水墨画，也有工笔花鸟画，色彩艳丽，又称彩墨画。中国水墨画讲究远处抽象、近处写实，渲染色彩、营构意境，崇尚"气韵生动"。

This refers to a style of painting in which ink shades are manipulated through dilution, and color use is minimal. It is also known as traditional Chinese or typically Chinese painting. The materials used include ink and water, a painting brush, and rice paper. Through adjusting the proportion of water to ink, the final image varies between light and dark, wet and dry, and thick and thin ink, thus producing varying degrees of color intensity. An ink wash painting normally consists of only ink and water, or of black and white. A more refined ink wash painting, on the other hand, may also feature an elaborate style of painting with flowers and birds in splendid hues, also known as "colored ink wash painting." On the whole, Chinese ink wash painting is impressionistic when depicting distant objects, but realistic about nearby ones. Through the skillful manipulation of color contrasts and the production of artistic ambience, the painter brings forth the value of a painting's "spiritual liveliness."

◎夫画道之中，水墨最为上。肇自然之性，成造化之功。或咫尺之图，写千里之景。东西南北，宛尔目前；春夏秋冬，生于笔下。（旧题王维《画学秘诀》）

（在绘画技法之中，水墨画法是最上层的一种。它发端于水墨的自然质性，却成就了天地造化的神奇。数尺长的画幅，能绘制出长达几千里的景色。它将天下四方的景色，都呈现在观者眼前；四季的物象，都通过画笔表现出来。）

Ink wash is the cream of all painting techniques. Making use of the natural properties of ink and water, it creates a miraculous view of heaven and earth. About several *chi* (3 *chi* ≈ 1 meter) of a painting would suffice to demonstrate a several-thousand-*li*-long landscape. It captures the scenic beauty of all quarters of the world, showing seasonal changes through the execution of a painting brush. (Wang Wei: Key to Good Paintings)

◎余曾见破墨山水，笔迹劲爽。（张彦远《历代名画记》卷十）

（我曾见〔王维〕用破墨之法创作的山水画，它的线条很是劲健、爽朗。）

I saw some landscape paintings produced by Wang Wei rendered with the use of an "alternating technique," namely alternating light ink with thick ink or vice versa, or alternating wet ink with dry ink. They struck me as vigorous and bold. (Zhang Yanyuan: *Famous Paintings Through History*)

说话 /shuōhuà/
Tale Telling

　　古代一种用说唱方式讲说故事的伎艺。"话"即故事。"说话"渊源于先秦时代，优人以俳谐方式讲故事。汉末魏晋时期，佛教、道教人士以通俗的语言、生动的故事讲述宗教经义，后发展为唐代的"俗讲"。在前代基础上，宋代说话伎艺进入兴盛时期，从寺院的俗讲变为勾栏瓦舍的大众娱乐，其内容非常广泛，包括讲史、小说、说诨话、说三分、五代史等。南宋时说话大体可以分为四类：小说（银字儿）、铁骑儿、讲史、说经说参请。说话艺人能讲能唱，擅长打趣调笑，表演时有锣、鼓等乐器伴奏，开场先念诵几首诗词，讲一个小故事，俗称"得胜头回"，相当于拖延一下时间，等观众差不多到齐后，再"言归正传"，末了常以诗词收尾。说话堪称宋代最受欢迎的市井伎艺，由此衍生发展出的话本小说，是中国古代通俗白话小说的重要组成部分。

Tale telling was an artistic form of telling stories through talking and singing that originated in the pre-Qin times. By the late years of the Han Dynasty to the Wei and Jin period, Buddhists and Daoists started to interpret religious scripts with vernacular language and vivid stories. In the Tang Dynasty, monks used talking and singing to interpret religious doctrines. On the basis of these early attempts, tale telling prospered in the Song Dynasty. It was no longer confined to temples, but became a form of popular entertainment on stages and at marketplaces. It included many subgenres such as histories based on works of authors of the Han to the Tang dynasties, skits with talking and singing, farces, stories of the Three Kingdoms and stories of the Five Dynasties and Ten Kingdoms. In the Southern Song Dynasty, tale telling covered four subjects: stories told to the accompaniment of a wind instrument, war stories, histories of past dynasties as well as Buddhist allegories and tales about wise thoughts inspired by worshipping at shrines. Tale telling entertainers were good at talking, singing and telling jokes; and drums, gongs and other musical instruments were used to enhance the appeal. Poetic lines were read and an anecdote was told at the beginning of the show, a trick used by performers that drew cheers and applause from early comers and ensured that late arrivals would not miss the main show. Performances would often end with a recitation of other poetic lines. Tale telling was very popular among common folks throughout the Song Dynasty. The scripts thus developed became an important part of old-time vernacular Chinese fiction.

引例 Citations：

◎说话有四家。一者小说，谓之银字儿，如烟粉、灵怪、传奇。说公案皆是搏刀赶棒及发迹变泰之事，说铁骑儿谓士马金鼓之事。说经谓演说佛书，说参请谓宾主参禅悟道等事。讲史书讲说前代书史文传兴废争战之事。(灌圃耐得翁《都城纪胜·瓦舍众伎》)

(说话分为四家。一是小说，又称"银字儿"，如讲说烟花女子的爱情故事、讲说神灵鬼怪的故事、讲说男女爱情的传奇之类。说公案讲说的都是使刀弄棒的江湖游侠或某人发迹发达的故事，说铁骑儿就是战斗打仗的故事。说经就是讲说佛经故事，说参请就是讲说宾主间参禅悟道的故事。讲史书就是讲说前代史书、文章、传记所记载的王朝兴废及争战的故事。)

Tale telling covers four subjects: first, prostitutes' yearning for love, spirits good and evil, and romance between men and women; second, legendary fiction involving weapon-wielding knights-errant or men who leap from rags to riches; third, war heroes; fourth, Buddhist stories or discussion between host and guest when the latter visits a temple. Besides, tale telling also deals with history and the wars as well as rise and fall of dynasties as recorded in articles and biographies. (Naideweng, the Gardener: *Wonders of the City of Lin'an*)

◎说话者谓之"舌辨"。(吴自牧《梦粱录》卷二十)

(说话可以说是凭口舌伶俐辩给争胜。)

A tale teller strives to achieve success with smooth tongue. (Wu Zimu: *Notes of Past Dreams*)

思无邪 /sīwúxié/
No Depraved Thoughts

思想纯正而无邪念。这是孔子(前551 — 前479)评价诗歌总集《诗经》时提出的著名观点。孔子认为,《诗经》三百多篇的宗旨可以用一句话概括,即作品的思想纯正而没有邪念,符合中和之美。由于孔子和《诗经》在中国历史上的重要地位,历代学者对这一理念都非常重视,常用这一标准来要求和批评作家和作品。但是《诗经》中的一些作品往往在思想情感上富有激情与真率,并不都符合"思无邪"的标准。

This refers to a state of mind that is pure and proper with no depraved or evil thoughts. This is a well-known critique made by Confucius (551 - 479 BC) on *The Book of Songs*, a collection of more than 300 poems. In his opinion, these poems may be summarized as pure and proper in thoughts with no depravity, keeping with the beauty of balanced harmony. This concept has always been held in high respect among scholars over the years because of the important position in history enjoyed by both Confucius and *The Book of Songs*. It is often used to judge and critique writers and writings, although some of the poems in *The Book of Songs* are not fully up to the standard of "no depraved thoughts" due to their unbridled feelings and candidness.

引例 Citation:

◎子曰:"《诗》三百,一言以蔽之,曰'思无邪'。"(《论语·为政》)
(孔子说:"《诗经》中三百多首诗,用一句话来概括,就是思想纯正而没有邪念。")

Confucius said: "One phrase can sum up the more than 300 poems in *The Book of Songs*, namely, no depraved thoughts." (*The Analects*)

中华思想文化术语
文艺卷

思与境偕 /sīyǔjìngxié/

Blend Sentiment with Scenery

指诗人的主观情思与作品所描绘的客观景物浑融一体。为唐司空图（837—908）评论同时期诗人王驾五言诗作的用语。"思"指诗人的思想、思绪、情感等；"境"指与审美主体相对的客观景物，也指作品所创造的审美意境；"偕"是齐等合一。心中的"思"，与外在的"境"观照合一，从而泯灭了主客体之间的界限，呈现为诗中浑融一体的意境。"思与境偕"被后世批评家看作意境理论的核心。

This term refers to blending a poet's own sentiments with the scenery depicted in his poem. It was first used by Tang Dynasty poetry critic Sikong Tu (837 - 908) when he commented on the five-character-per-line poems by Wang Jia of the same period. *Si* (思 sentiments) here means the poet's thoughts, emotion, and moods, whereas *jing* (境 scenery) is external scenery as well as the artistic ambience created by the poem. *Xie* (偕 blending) means the oneness of external things and the poet's inner world. When the poet's sentiments and the scenery come together, the boundary between subjectivity and objectivity disappears, and a perfect unity in the art of poetry is achieved. Later critics regarded this idea as the core conception of artistic theory.

引例 Citations：

◎然河汾蟠郁之气，宜继有人。今王生者，寓居其间，浸渍益久，五言所得，长于思与境偕，乃诗家之所尚者。（司空图《与王驾评诗书》）

（然而黄河、汾河的山川秀气长年在该地区盘绕积蓄，理应还会有杰出的诗人出现。现在的王驾，居住在此，濡染浸淫在其中很久了，他写的五言诗有所成就，长于思与境偕，这是诗人所推崇的。）

The captivating landscape of the Yellow River and Fenhe River region should produce outstanding poets. Our contemporary Wang Jia lives here. He has long been immersed in this atmosphere. This has given his five-character poems a chance to excel. He is good at blending sentiment with scenery, thus winning recognition from many other poets. (Sikong Tu: Letter to Wang Jia with Comments on Poetry Writing)

◎文学之事，其内足以摅（shū）己，而外足以感人者，意与境二者而已。上焉者意与境浑，其次或以境胜，或以意胜。（樊志厚《〈人间词〉序二》）

（文学创作之事，向内足以抒发自己的思想情感，向外足以感动别人，是因为有"意"与"境"二者罢了。上等的作品是"意"与"境"浑然一体，次一等的作品或是在"境"上胜出，或是在"意"上胜出。）

A piece of literary creation voices one's emotions and thoughts; but it moves others because it blends sentiment with scenery. A good poem features a perfect union between these two factors, whereas other poems excel either in sentiment or scenery. (Fan Zhihou: Preface II to Wang Guowei's *Poetic Remarks in the Human World*)

宋杂剧 /Sòng zájù/
Poetic Drama of the Song Dynasty

宋代产生的由滑稽表演、歌舞、杂戏组合而成的综合性戏曲形式，是以唐代参军戏为基础并吸收当时的歌舞、曲艺等发展起来的早期戏剧形式。内容上以滑稽讽刺为主，演出形式多采用"一场两段"，有时候会增加"杂扮"。宋杂剧角色有四到五人，一人主唱，主要通过演唱大曲叙事，其他角色则承担宾白、插科打诨、歌舞表演等。北宋时期的戏剧演出非常普遍，开封、洛阳两地尤其兴盛。整个两宋期间，杂剧也在不断演变中，角色分工更细，造型手法更多样，戏剧情节更复杂。宋杂剧是元代北杂剧的前身，其艺术形态、艺术手法等也直接影响了后世的其他戏剧形式。

Poetic drama of the Song Dynasty refers to a combination of comic shows, song and dance, and variety shows. It is an early form of traditional Chinese drama based on *Canjunxi* (comic dialogical plays of the Tang Dynasty) and drawing elements from song and dance plus other forms of folk art. It is mainly jocular and satirical. Its performance is divided into two sections. The first is a warming-up show whereas the second section is the "real thing." Sometimes, skits will be added to a regular show to enhance the fun. Each poetic drama has four or five characters, with one of them being the main singer who narrates events by singing major arias while the others do the spoken parts, throw in impromptu remarks for comic relief, or simply sing and dance. Dramatic performances were very popular in the Northern Song Period, especially in Kaifeng and Luoyang. Throughout the Northern and Southern Song dynasties, poetic drama kept on growing and reached a new height, further dividing roles, varying postures and making plots more intricate. Poetic drama of the Song Dynasty predated that of the Yuan Dynasty. Its artistic forms and techniques directly influenced later forms of drama.

引例 Citations：

◎杂剧中，末泥为长，每四人或五人为一场，先做寻常熟事一段，名曰艳段，次做正杂剧，通名为两段。末泥色主张，引戏色分付，副净色发乔，副末色打诨，又或添一人装孤。（灌圃耐得翁《都城纪胜·瓦舍众伎》）

（杂剧中，末泥是主要角色，每四人或者五人表演一场戏。先演出日常生活中大家熟悉的题材，称为"艳段"，然后演出正式的杂剧，这通常称为"两段"。末泥主导表演，引戏负责引导吩咐，副净负责装憨弄傻，副末负责插科打诨，又或者添一个角色装孤。）

In the poetic drama of the Song Dynasty, *moni* is the main male role while four or five characters perform the whole play together. They begin by acting out a familiar situation adapted from daily life (*yanduan*), a warming-up section of the performance. Then they put on the poetic drama itself. Of the entire cast of characters, *moni* is always in the limelight. *Yinxi*, for his part, guides the show by giving directions or dropping a hint where necessary. *Fujing* is supposed to act like a clown, whereas *fumo* makes comical remarks. Sometimes, there may appear a government official to suit the need of plot development. (Naideweng, the Gardener: *Wonders of the City of Lin'an*)

◎ 山谷云："作诗正如作杂剧，初时布置，临了须打诨，方是出场。"盖是读秦少游诗，恶其终篇无所归也。(王直方《王直方诗话》，见曾慥（zào）编《类说》)

（黄庭坚说："写诗就像写杂剧，开始的时候经营布置，临到最后要打诨，方才结局完整。"大概是他读秦观的作品，不喜欢秦观的作品写到最后都无所归附。)

As Huang Tingjian puts it, "Writing poetry is like writing drama. You start out by making overall arrangement, while toward the end, you have to sound conclusive by making some offbeat remarks for fun." This is perhaps because he didn't like Qin Guan's works for their lack of purpose after he read them. (Wang Zhifang: *My Commentaries on Poetic Creation*)

颂赞 /sòngzàn/
Extolment and Commendation

歌颂、赞扬美好的人物、事物、功德、品行等，并弘扬其积极意义和正面价值的文体。"颂"本指仪容，作为文体名称，有"描摹仪容""颂扬"双重含义，意思是通过描写仪容状貌颂扬人的德行；"赞"是赞美，用于对人的功德或美好事物的赞美与评价。二者的共同点都是以歌颂赞美为宗旨，篇幅简短，句式整齐，多用韵文。南朝刘勰（465？—520？或532？）高度推崇颂赞文学的思想性和教化功能，认为"颂"的对象已由神明、帝王扩展到普通人，"颂"的范围已由国家大事扩展到一切美好事物；"赞"同时有评价的功用，通过积极、肯定的评价可以提升赞美的意义。在中国文学中，"颂""赞"不仅可以独立成文，而且常常附着于各类文艺、新闻作品，这些作品以歌颂或正面评价的方式，在中华思想文化中有承载传播正能量的功能。

Essays of extolment and commendation were written to pay tribute to laudable persons, things, merits and virtues, thus promoting their positive influence. The purpose of both an extolment and a commendation is to exalt good persons and things. Such essays are short, neatly patterned and rhymed. Liu Xie (465?-520? or 532?) of the Southern Dynasties valued the intellectual and educational value of extolment and commendation essays. He found that the objects of extolment had extended from gods, emperors and kings to ordinary people and the scope of extolment was no longer limited to state affairs; it had been extended to cover all beautiful things. To him, an essay of commendation also functions as an evaluation and a positive evaluation enhances the significance of commendation. In Chinese literature, writings of extolment or commendation are not only essays in their own right; they are sometimes attached to various literary works or even news reports. These works, through extolment and positive evaluation, convey the traditional Chinese thought and culture.

引例 Citations：

◎四始之至，颂居其极。颂者，容也，所以美盛德而述形容也。（刘勰《文心雕龙·颂赞》）

（《风》《小雅》《大雅》《颂》表现王道兴衰的起始，代表着诗歌的最高意义，而《颂》在其中更具有终极的意义。"颂"是形容状貌的意思，指通过描述形容状貌来赞美伟大的德行。）

The "Ballads from the States," "Minor Court Hymns," "Major Court Hymns," and "Eulogies" trace the rise and decline of the kingly way, and they represent the loftiest realm of poetry. Of all these, the "Eulogies" are of the greatest poetic significance. *Song* (颂) originally means demeanor; it then goes on to mean "extolment of great virtues through a depiction of demeanor." (Liu Xie: *The Literary Mind and the Carving of Dragons*)

◎原夫颂惟典雅，辞必清铄。敷写似赋，而不入华侈之区；敬慎如铭，而异乎规戒之域。揄扬以发藻，汪洋以树义。（刘勰《文心雕龙·颂赞》）

（推求颂文的写作，要求内容典美雅正，文辞清新明丽。铺叙描写接近赋，但不会到过分华丽浮夸的地步；庄重谨慎如铭文，但又不同于后者的规劝警诫。它是本着颂扬的宗旨来展开文辞，着眼宏大的内容来确立意义。）

By definition, an essay of extolment should be refined and proper in content and refreshing and elegant in style. Its narration should resemble rhapsodic prose but should not indulge in verbosity. Its solemn and prudent style should resemble that of an epigraph but should not contain admonition. An essay of extolment is written to pay homage to the goodness of a person or a thing, focusing on major accomplishments to highlight its significance. (Liu Xie: *The Literary Mind and the Carving of Dragons*)

◎然本其为义，事生奖叹，所以古来篇体，促而不广，必结言于四字之句，盘桓乎数韵之辞；约举以尽情，昭灼以送文，此其体也。（刘勰《文心雕龙·颂赞》）

（由"赞"的本义来看，它产生于对人或事物的赞美与感叹，所以自古以来，赞的篇幅都很短小，一定是用四言诗句，长短在几个韵之间。简明扼要地讲清情由，明白鲜亮地结束文辞，这就是它的写作要点。）

By definition, commendation means praise or admiration. Since ancient times, essays of commendation have been brief, with poetic lines of only four characters each, and the whole essay contains no more than a few rhymed stanzas. It sets out the facts succinctly and ends on a clear-cut and forceful note. These are the essential rules for writing an essay of commendation. (Liu Xie: *The Literary Mind and the Carving of Dragons*)

随物赋形 /suíwù-fùxíng/
Writing That Flows like Water

原意指水流无常形，随地理形貌或自然物而呈现千变万化的形态。宋代文学家苏轼（1037—1101）用它来形容文艺创作应像水流一样流畅自然而又灵活多变，既遵循客观事物的规律，又体现作家自由创作意志，从而达到立意与表现技巧自在圆融，情、景、事、理妙合无间的审美境界。这一术语可能受了道家"上善若水"、水"几于道"与佛教"随缘自适"思想的影响，也是艺术家人格、学养、技艺的综合体现。

This term originally referred to water, which, without a fixed shape, flows along the contours of objects or land. Song Dynasty writer Su Shi (1037 - 1101) used it to describe literary writing that was smooth and free like water, showing both the writer's creative power and his adherence to the laws of nature and human society. This style of writing endeavors to achieve harmony between a motif and expressive techniques and to merge emotion, landscapes, events and moral lessons into an aesthetic whole. This term may have been influenced by the Daoist beliefs that "great virtue is like water" and that "water is the most exact equivalent of the Way" as well as the Buddhist faith in following karma. It also gives expression to an artist's personality, artistic attainment and capability.

引例 Citations：

◎天下之至信者，唯水而已。江河之大与海之深，而可以意揣。唯其不自为形，而因物以赋形，是故千变万化而有必然之理。（苏轼

《滟滪（yànyù）堆赋》）

（天下最有诚信的，只有水罢了。江河之大与海洋之深，都可以凭想象揣测。只因为水没有自己固定的形态，只是凭借自然物而获得形态，所以水虽然千变万化但有其必然如此的道理。）

The most honorable thing in the world is definitely water. The mightiness of a river and the depth of a sea can be envisaged through imagination. As water has no fixed shape of its own, it assumes different shapes when passing over various landforms. So, though the flow of water varies miraculously, it follows an inherent law of nature. (Su Shi: Ode to the Yanyu Rock at the Qutang Gorge of the Yangtze River)

◎吾文如万斛（hú）泉源，不择地皆可出，在平地滔滔汩（gǔ）汩，虽一日千里无难。及其与山石曲折、随物赋形而不可知也。所可知者，常行于所当行，常止于不可不止，如是而已矣。（苏轼《自评文》）

（我写文章就像上万斛泉水，不用选择地势，随处都可以涌出，在平地上流淌起来滔滔不绝，即使一天流淌千里也无难处。而到了顺随山石而曲折变化，依据地理形貌而获得各种形态，这种情况不可预知。所能知道的是，经常行进在应当行进的地方，经常停止于不得不停止的地方，就这样罢了。）

When I write, words keep pouring forth like springs come from numerous sources. They will flow in from everywhere in the mountains without having to choose a commanding height to do so – words that, like water, flow so profusely over flat ground that they travel a long distance a day with perfect ease. Then rocks of all kinds appear, but words flow around them, taking on shapes as determined by various terrain. It is hard to predict what will emerge eventually, but I do know that I will pause or move on whenever necessary. (Su Shi: A Commentary on My Own Writing)

太康体 /Tàikāng tǐ/
The Taikang Literary Style

西晋初年和中期大约三十多年时间里的诗歌风格，指晋武帝（236 - 290）太康（280 — 289）年间以左思（250？— 305？）、潘岳（247 — 300）、陆机（261 — 303）等人为代表的诗体。与建安（196 — 220）时代积极进取、昂扬向上的诗风不同，太康诗人讲究辞藻华丽和对偶工整，诗歌技巧更臻精美。其中，左思的作品语言质朴，但内容充实，气势雄浑，在太康诗风中独树一帜。

This term refers to a poetic style popular for about 30 years from the early to mid-Western Jin Dynasty, particularly in the Taikang era (280 – 289) during the reign of Emperor Wu (236 - 290). Among the poets of this tradition were Zuo Si (250 ?- 305 ?), Pan Yue (247 - 300), and Lu Ji (261 - 303). Taikang poets focused excessively on the use of rhetorical description, verbal parallelism, and refined poetic techniques, representing an abrupt departure from the Jian'an (196 - 220) poetry with its passion, boldness, and vitality. Standing out among the Taikang poets was Zuo Si, who used plain language, but whose works had substance and were imbued with passion and strength.

引例 Citation：

◎太康中，三张、二陆、两潘、一左，勃尔复兴，踵武前王，风流未沫，亦文章之中兴也。（钟嵘《诗品》卷上）

（西晋太康时期，张载、张协、张亢，陆机、陆云，潘岳、潘尼和左思，突然复兴建安时期的兴盛局面，追寻前代杰出者的足迹，这是建安文学的风流未尽，也是诗文的中兴啊！）

In the Taikang era of the Western Jin Dynasty, scholars including Zhang Zai, Zhang Xie, Zhang Kang, Lu Ji, Lu Yun, Pan Yue, Pan Ni, and Zuo Si revived the literary legacy of the Jian'an period by following the footsteps of the masters of that period. It signalled the continuation and beauty of the Jian'an style and a resurgence of poetry writing. (Zhong Rong: *The Critique of Poetry*)

体 /tǐ/

Ti

"体"作为文艺学、美学范畴，主要含义有三：其一，指文学艺术的某一门类、流派、体式、作品区别于其他文学艺术门类、流派、体式、作品的整体特征。它是包含了文学艺术的体式、内容、语言、风格等诸要素在内所呈现出的总体形态与艺术特征。其二，指文学艺术作品的风格，不包括体式、形式等方面的内容。其三，指文学作品的基本样式，即文体或文学体制。历代文论家对文体的分类不尽相同，比如南朝梁昭明太子萧统（501—531）《文选》将文体分为38种。中国古代文学的文体丰富多样，各有自己的基本样式与写作要求，而风格即是作者的艺术个性在作品中的显现，有时也表现为一个时代、一个流派的文学特征。这一术语经常与人名、朝代名等结合，如骚体、陶体、建安体等，用来指称与作品风格相关的艺术特征并广泛运用于文艺批评与鉴赏中。

Ti (体) has three different meanings in the study of literature, art, and aesthetics. First, it refers to features that distinguish one particular category, form, or literary school from others. These features represent the overall form and artistic characteristics, including the structure, content, language, style, and other essential elements. Second, it refers only to literary and artistic style, not their form or shape. Third, it refers to the basic literary and artistic form, i.e., the writing style and literary genre. Scholars of literary theory in different historical periods did not use the same standards to classify literary styles. For example, Xiao Tong (501-531, Crown Prince Zhaoming of the Liang Dynasty during the Southern Dynasties) classified literary and artistic works into 38 styles or categories in his *Selections of Refined Literature*. There is a wide range of writing styles and literary genres in classical Chinese literature, each with its own style and writing requirements. The style of a literary work reflects the author's individual artistic temperament, and, sometimes, also the literary and artistic trend in a particular era. This term is often used together with the name of a person or a dynasty to describe literary and artistic features peculiar to a school of literature. Examples are the Sao Style (represented by the famous poem, *Li Sao*, written by renowned poet Qu Yuan), Tao Style (represented by poet Tao Yuanming), and Jian'an Style (named after the period of Jian'an during the Han Dynasty). The term is widely used in literary criticism and appreciation.

引例 Citations：

◎夫人善于自见，而文非一体，鲜能备善，是以各以所长，相轻所短。(曹丕《典论·论文》)

(人总是善于看到自己的优点，然而文章不止一种文体，很少有人擅长所有文体，因此各人总是以自己所擅长的文体写作而轻视别人所不擅长的文体。)

People are always quick to see their own strengths. However, given the rich variety of literary styles, few people are accomplished in all of them. Therefore, people always write in the styles they are good at while taking lightly other people's works written in styles they happen to be weak in. (Cao Pi: On Literary Classics)

◎自汉至魏，四百余年，辞人才子，文体三变。(《宋书·谢灵运传论》)

(自汉至魏，四百多年，写诗文的才子[众多]，而诗文的体制风格，也经历了三次大的变化。)

For more than 400 years from the Han Dynasty to the Wei Dynasty, numerous talented poets came to the fore, and the styles of poetry and essay writing went through three major transformations. (*The History of Song of the Southern Dynasties*)

体性 /tǐxìng/

Style and Temperament

作品风格与作者个性的统一与结合。是关于文学风格的重要术语。"体"在这里主要指文章风格,"性"指作者个性因素。源出于南朝刘勰(465？—520？或532？)《文心雕龙·体性》。该文提出作者的个性特点与文章风格有着内在的关联,文如其人。这启发了后人从作者个性着眼去分析文学作品不同的风格类型,奠定了中国古代文学风格论的基本思想。

This is an important term about literary style that stresses the unity and integration of the styles of writings with the temperaments of their authors. The term originated by Liu Xie (465?-520? or 532?) of the Southern Dynasties in his *The Literary Mind and the Carving of Dragons*. One chapter of the book discusses how the styles of writings are related to the temperaments of the writers, and argues that the writings truly reflect the temperaments of their authors. This has encouraged later generations to analyze different styles of literary works based on the authors' temperaments and became a basic line of thought on ancient Chinese literary style.

引例 Citations:

◎夫情动而言形,理发而文见(xiàn)。盖沿隐以至显,因内而符外者也。然才有庸俊,气有刚柔,学有浅深,习有雅郑;并情性所铄(shuò),陶染所凝,是以笔区云谲(jué),文苑波诡者矣。(刘勰《文心雕龙·体性》)

(情感激发而形成语言,道理表达便体现为文章。也就是将隐藏在内心的情和理逐渐彰显、由内至外的过程。不过人的才华有平凡和杰出之分,气禀有阳刚与阴柔之别,学识有浅深之异,习性有雅正和鄙俗之差。这些都是由人的先天情性所造就,并由后天的熏陶积聚而成,所以他们的创作奇谲如风云变幻,文章诡秘似海涛翻转。)

When emotions stir, they take the form of language. When ideas emerge, they are expressed in writings. Thus the obscure becomes manifest and the internal feelings pour into the open. However, talent may be mediocre or outstanding, temperament masculine or feminine, learning deep or shallow, upbringing refined or vulgar. All this results from differences in nature and nurture. Hence the unusual cloud-like variations in the realm of writing and the mysterious wave-like undulations in the garden of literature. (Liu Xie: *The Literary Mind and the Carving of Dragons*)

◎故性格清彻者音调自然宣畅，性格舒徐者音调自然疏缓，旷达者自然浩荡，雄迈者自然壮烈，沉郁者自然悲酸，古怪者自然奇绝。有是格，便有是调，皆情性自然之谓也。莫不有情，莫不有性，而可以一律求之哉？（李贽《读律肤说》）

（所以那些性情开朗透明的人所作诗的音律自然直接流畅，性情迟缓的人所作诗的音律自然疏朗宽缓，性情旷达的人所作诗的音律自然磊落浩荡，性情雄奇豪迈的人所作诗的音律自然强劲壮烈，性情沉郁的人所作诗的音律自然悲凉酸楚，性情古怪的人所作诗的音律自然不同寻常。有什么性情，便有什么音律，这都是个性气质所自然决定的。人莫不有情感，莫不有个性，怎么可以用一个音律标准去要求所有的诗歌呢？）

So it is natural that those with an open and easy-going temperament create poems with tonal rhythms that are direct, smooth, and easy to understand; those with a slow temperament write in relaxed tonal rhythms; those with a broad mind, magnificent and uninhibited; those with a heroic character, powerful and gallant; those with a depressed personality, sad and miserable; those with a weird temperament, out of the ordinary. Temperament decides the tonal rhythms of an author's writings. People have their own emotions and personalities. How can all the poems be judged by the same standard for tonal rhythms? (Li Zhi: *My Understanding of Poetic Genre*)

田园诗 /tiányuánshī/
Idyllic Poetry

　　一种以描写田园景色和田园生活为主要题材的诗歌流派。由东晋诗人陶渊明（365或372或376—427）开创。陶渊明的诗大部分取材于田园生活，语言质朴，画面平淡，但清新自然，意境深远，韵味醇厚。田园诗为中国古典诗歌开辟了一个新的境界，影响了六朝之后的诗歌发展。

A genre created by Tao Yuanming (365 or 372 or 376 - 427) of the Eastern Jin Dynasty, idyllic poetry depicts rural life and scenery. Taking country life as his favored theme, Tao Yuanming used plain language to portray rural scenes. His poems were unpretentious, refreshing, and natural, thus creating a far-reaching aesthetic conception and a lasting charm. Idyllic poetry represented a new stage in classical Chinese poetry and shaped poetic development in the Six Dynasties period and beyond.

引例 Citation：

◎以康乐之奥博，多溺于山水；以渊明之高古，偏放于田园。（白居易《与元九书》）

（谢灵运的诗深奥博大，但是多耽溺于山水；陶渊明的诗超拔古朴，却又多放情于田园。）

Xie Lingyun's poems are profound in implication, but focused excessively on mountain and water scenes, while Tao Yuanming's poems are graceful and simple, depicting mainly rural scenes. (Bai Juyi: Letter to Yuan Zhen)

同光体 /Tóng-Guāng tǐ/
The Tong-Guang School of Poetry

形成于清末同治（1862—1874）、光绪（1875—1908）年间，延续于民国初年的诗歌流派，因同治、光绪年号而得名。主要诗人有陈三立（1852—1937）、沈曾（zēng）植（1850—1922）、陈衍（1856—1937）、郑孝胥（1860—1938）等。他们推崇宋人诗歌，主张"学人之诗"与"诗人之诗"合一，将言志、缘情、学问、修养相结合，多以议论入诗，重锤炼之功，风格雄健瘦硬，标举所谓"荒寒之路"。因地域和风格的不同，同光体又有闽派、浙派、江西派之分。

The Tong-Guang School of poetry, which first emerged during the reigns of Tongzhi (1862-1874) and Guangxu (1875-1908) of late Qing, continued to flourish in the early years of the Republic of China early in the 20th century. It was thus named by combining the initial characters of the two emperors' reign titles. Chen Sanli (1852-1937), Shen Zengzhi (1850-1922), Chen Yan (1856-1937) and Zheng Xiaoxu (1860-1938) were representative figures of this school. They valued Song *ci* poetry, a kind of lyric classical Chinese poetry using a poetic meter based upon certain patterns of fixed-rhythm formal types. Their aim was to blend "the poetry of a poet" with "the poetry of a scholar," merging a poet's aspirations, feelings, academic learning and moral accomplishment into an integral whole. They incorporated commentaries into their poems and carefully weighed their words. Stylistically, they pursued a vigorous brevity and straightforwardness, trying to blaze "a way through desolate wilderness." Due to regional and stylistic differences, this school of poetic creation is further divided into the Fujian, Zhejiang and Jiangxi branches.

引例 Citations：

◎同光体者，苏堪与余戏称同光以来诗人不墨守盛唐者。（陈衍《沈乙盦（ān）诗叙》）

（所谓同光体，是郑孝胥和我用来戏称同治、光绪以来写诗不遵守盛唐风格的诗人的用语。）

"The Tong-Guang School of poetry" is a jocular term Zheng Xiaoxu and I invented for those since the Tongzhi and Guangxu times who, when writing poems, did not comply with the rules of poetry prevalent in the most prosperous period of the Tang Dynasty. (Chen Yan: A Preface to *Collected Poems of Shen Zengzhi*)

◎往余在京华，郑君过我邸。告言子沈子，诗亦同光体。杂然见赠答，色味若粢醍（jītǐ）。（陈衍《冬述四首视子培》其三）

（过去我在京城的时候，郑孝胥来到我的住处。他告诉我沈子写的诗，与我同为同光体。我们互相赠答的多篇作品，色泽味道至今仍似浅红色的清酒。）

When I was in the capital, Zheng Xiaoxu once came to see me. He told me that Shen Zengzhi's poems, like mine, belonged to the Tong-Guang School of poetry. The many works we wrote in salute to each other were like mellow wine, whose color and flavor would never diminish over time. (Chen Yan: Four Pieces Written During Winter for Presentation to Shen Zengzhi)

桐城派 /Tóngchéng pài/

The Tongcheng School of Writing

清代影响最大的古文流派，因代表人物都是安徽桐城人，故名。形成于康熙（1662—1722）年间，鼎盛期在乾隆（1736—1795）、嘉庆（1796—1820）年间，文脉绵延近二百年。创始人方苞（1668—1749）提出"学行继程朱之后，文章在韩欧之间"，该观点奠定了学派的风格基调。主要人物先后有戴名世（1653—1713）、刘大櫆（kuí，1698—1779）、姚鼐（nài，1732—1815）、

梅 曾（zēng）亮（1786—1856）、方 东 树（1772—1853）、吴 汝 纶
（1840—1903）等。桐城派普遍重视文与道的关系，要求在内容上
"文以载道"，形式上"雅洁"，其重要理论有方苞提出的"义法"
说，姚鼐提出的"义理、考据、辞章"说，以及刘大櫆提出的"神
气"说。桐城派继承了中国古文写作的优良传统，对散文创作做了
系统的理论总结，长期享有盛誉，直至近代梁启超（1873—1929）
等人倡导"文界革命"，桐城派才被认为是保守的象征而受到诟病。

This school of writing represented the Qing Dynasty's most influential style
of classical Chinese writing. Its representative figures were all natives of
Tongcheng, Anhui Province, hence the name. It was formed during the reign
of Emperor Kangxi (1662-1722) and reached its height during the reigns
of Emperor Qianlong (1736-1795) and Emperor Jiaqing (1796-1820). Its
founder, Fang Bao (1668-1749), believed that men of letters should follow
the style of writing of the Neo-Confucian moralists Cheng Hao (1032-1085),
Cheng Yi (1033-1107), and Zhu Xi (1130-1200), and that of great men
of letters like Han Yu (768-824) and Ouyang Xiu (1007-1072). This set
the tone for this school of writing. Among its prominent figures were Dai
Mingshi (1653-1713), Liu Dakui (1698-1779), Yao Nai (1732-1815), Mei
Zengliang (1786-1856), Fang Dongshu (1772-1853), and Wu Rulun (1840-
1903). Writers of this school emphasized that writings should convey moral
ideals and be refined and well-laid out in form. Such a style of writing was based
on Fang Bao's "guidelines for writing good prose," Yao Nai's stress on "conveying
righteous messages, facts and evidence, and rhetoric and technique," and Liu
Dakui's theory about "a piece of writing and its author's charm." The Tongcheng
School of Writing inherited Chinese scholars' tradition of writing in classical
Chinese and offered a theoretical summary about prose writing. It enjoyed high
prestige until the Revolution in the Literati Circle led by Liang Qichao (1873-
1929), when it came under attack as a symbol of conservatism.

引例 Citations：

◎神者，文家之宝。文章最要气盛，然无神以主之，则气无所附，
荡乎不知其所归也。神者气之主，气者神之用。神只是气之精处。

古人文章可告人者惟法耳，然不得其神而徒守其法，则死法而已。
（刘大櫆《论文偶记》）

（"神"是写文章的人最要看重的东西。写文章最是要"气"盛，但如果没有"神"统帅"气"，那么"气"就会没有东西可以依附，就像在空中飘荡而无所归依。"神"是"气"的灵魂，而"气"是"神"的具体应用。"神"是"气"的凝聚与精华。古人能告诉别人的只是文章的技法，但如果得不到文章的"神"而只是遵守技法，那这些技法不过是死的东西而已。）

"Inner strength" is what prose writers endeavor to express. An essay does need to sound vigorous, but it should convey the author's inner strength. Without it, the so-called vigor of an essay will have no foundation, drifting aimlessly in the air. The author's inner strength is the soul of the essay's vigor; the latter is the concrete manifestation of the former. The author's inner strength is the condensed form and essence of the essay's vigor. Our ancestors can only pass skills of writing onto us. If a writer fails to capture the essence of writing and obeys only superficial rules, he will only be hindered by them. (Liu Dakui: *Occasional Thoughts About Writing*)

◎ 为文章者，有所法而后能，有所变而后大。维盛清治迈逾前古千百，独士能为古文者未广。昔有方侍郎，今有刘先生，天下文章，其出于桐城乎？（姚鼐《刘海峰先生八十寿序》）

（写文章的人，有所取法然后能写好，有所变化然后能光大。如今大清太平盛世，超越前代千百倍，唯独能写古文的文士不多。[写文章最好的，]过去有侍郎方苞，现在有刘大櫆先生，天下的好文章，大概都出自桐城吧？）

Good writing involves not only complying with rules but also bold departure from them. Ours is a time of prosperity infinitely greater than any previous era, but there are few men of letters who are good at writing classical Chinese. The two best writers are Vice Minister Fang Bao of the past and our great Lord Liu of today! The best literary prose of the country has probably been written by scholars of Tongcheng origin! (Yao Nai: A Congratulatory Message on Liu Haifeng's Eightieth Birthday)

脱窠臼 /tuō kējiù/

Avoid Stereotypes

指戏曲创作应摆脱陈旧的创作模式。所谓窠臼，不仅指以往作品的窠臼，还包括创作者个人的窠臼。由明末清初曲论家李渔（1611－1680）在《闲情偶寄》中提出。李渔认为，戏曲创作的取意、填词应力求新颖，不能蹈袭前人，才可称得上"传奇"。这一术语的提出既是为了满足观众的审美心理，也体现了文艺创作必须创新求变的宗旨。

This term means that a writer should not fall into old patterns when writing a drama. He should not only avoid stereotypes of previous works but also resist attempts to do so in his own creations. The term was proposed by the late Ming to early Qing drama theorist Li Yu (1611 - 1680) in his *Occasional Notes with Leisure Motions*. In his view, dramatic creations should be original in both content and wording, and previous works should not be blindly followed. Only such works deserve to be called legendary stories. This call to avoid stereotypes was made to encourage creativity and variety in artistic pursuit to delight the audience.

引例 Citations：

◎吾谓填词之难，莫难于洗涤窠臼，而填词之陋，亦莫陋于盗袭窠臼。（李渔《闲情偶寄·词曲部·结构》）

（我认为填写曲词的困难之处，莫过于洗净一切陈旧的套路，而填写曲词的鄙陋之处，也莫过于盗取袭用已有的套路。）

The greatest difficulty in writing lyrics, I believe, lies in ridding them of stereotypes, and the thing not to do when writing such lyrics is to copy old stereotypes. (Li Yu: *Occasional Notes with Leisure Motions*)

◎非特前人所作，于今为旧，即出我一人之手，今之视昨，亦有间（jiàn）焉。昨已见而今未见也，知未见之为新，即知已见之为旧矣。（李渔《闲情偶记·词曲部·结构》）

（不仅前人的作品，到现在已经陈旧了，即使出自我个人之手的作品，今天看昨天写的，也是有毛病的。昨天见过而今天没有见过，才知没见过的是新的，已见过的是旧的。）

Not that only the works by our predecessors have become largely obsolete; even those I myself wrote yesterday need to be improved when examined today. Only when I no longer see today what I saw yesterday do I realize that what I haven't seen is new and what I have seen is old. (Li Yu: *Occasional Notes with Leisure Motions*)

外师造化，中得心源
/wài shī zàohuà, zhōng dé xīnyuán/

Draw Artistic Inspiration from Both Within and Without

艺术创作向外得自师法自然万物，向内得自心中的悟性。"造化"即大自然；"心源"为佛教语，意指内心的妙悟为一切法的根源。是唐张彦远在《历代名画记》中所记载的唐代画家张璪（zǎo）的话。原意指创作山水松石类画作，应当以大自然为师，观察山水景物真实的纹理、形状、色彩等，用心领悟山水景物之美，进而在画作中提炼呈现，使画作既逼真又超脱，以达到传神境界。"造化"与"心源"是相通融合而非彼此对立的关系。唐代诗论中对"心"与"心源"也有应用，文论家们对于写诗过程的描述，与张璪所言绘画过程并无区别。中国古典诗文创作提炼物象、熔铸意象，重视作品的韵致之美，与画论具有共通性。

According to this precept, in pursuing artistic creation, one needs to draw inspiration from all things in nature and his innermost thoughts. *Zaohua* (造化) means nature. *Xinyuan* (心源) is a Buddhist term, meaning that the true awakening of one's mind is the root of all Buddhist teaching. This view, originally described by the Tang Dynasty painter Zhang Zao, was quoted later by the Tang Dynasty author Zhang Yanyuan in his *Famous Paintings Through History*. It originally was a principle governing the painting of landscapes. It aimed to achieve both verisimilitude and ephemeralness and convey the subtle nuances of mountains, rivers, lakes, trees, and rocks in real life by carefully observing their true grains, shapes, and colors. The painter was encouraged to experience their beauty with his heart and capture it in a painting. "Nature" and "inspiration from within" are complementary rather than confrontational – they have a relationship of unity rather than opposition. Tang Dynasty essays about poetry, too, referred to the "soul" and "inspiration from within." Descriptions of poetry writing were not very different from Zhang Zao's interpretation of the process of painting. Classical Chinese prose and poetry are similar to painting in that they stress the importance of molding different physical images into an aesthetic whole. They value the charm of a literary work, fusing outer nature and inner thought.

引例 Citations：

◎初，毕庶子宏擅名于代，一见惊叹之，异其唯用秃毫，或以手摸绢素，因问璪所受。璪曰："外师造化，中得心源。"（张彦远《历代名画记》卷十）

（起初，左庶子毕宏在当时很有名气，见到张璪忍不住惊叹，奇怪于他仅仅用秃毫笔作画，有时还用手摸作画用的绢素，因此询问张璪从哪里学习的。张璪说："向外得自师法自然万物，向内得自心中的悟性。"）

Bi Hong, an official who oversaw the management of the crown prince's residence, was well-known. He marveled at Zhang Zao's ability to paint with an almost worn-out brush. When he saw Zhang Zao touched from time to time the undyed silk Zhang was painting on, he asked Zhang how he had learned this skill. Zhang said, "I have learned it all from both nature and within." (Zhang Yanyuan: *Famous Paintings Through History*)

◎心源为炉，笔端为炭。锻炼元本，雕砻（lóng）群形。纠纷舛错，逐意奔走。（刘禹锡《董氏武陵集纪》）

（内心的悟性就像是熔炉，笔端就像是炭火。用熔炉提炼出万物的根本，用笔端雕琢刻画出具体的物象。错杂纷乱的词句和描写，随着作者的思绪恣意奔驰。）

Inspiration from within is like a furnace, and the tip of a writing brush is like a burning charcoal fire. An artist extracts the essence of all things from the furnace and carves out concrete objects with his brush. His thoughts and feelings pour out a free flow of multitude of vivid expressions. (Liu Yuxi: A Preface to *Dong's Notes from Wuling*)

婉约派 /wǎnyuēpài/

The *Wanyue* School / The Graceful and Restrained School

宋词两大流派之一。内容多写儿女之情、离别之绪，其特点是"专主情致"，表情达意讲究含蓄柔婉、隐约细腻，音律婉转谐和，语言圆润清丽。婉约词出现较早，名家辈出，唐五代有温庭筠（？—866）、李煜（937—978），宋初有柳永（987?—1053?）、晏殊（991—1055）、欧阳修（1007—1072）、晏几道（1038—1110），之后又有秦观（1049—1100）、贺铸（1052—1125）、周邦彦（1056—1121）、李清照（1084—1151？），南宋则有姜夔（1155？—1209）、吴文英（1212？—1272？）、张炎（1248—1314后）等一大批词人。在一千多年的词学发展中，婉约词风支配词坛，无论是数量还是质量，婉约派都占据主流和正统地位。需要说明的是，婉约派词人也抒写感时伤世之情，只是多将家国之恨、身世之感寓于抒情咏物，别有寄托，故不能一概以柔媚视之。

As one of the two *ci* (词) lyric schools of the Song Dynasty, the graceful and restrained school mainly dealt with romantic love or parting sorrow. It featured sentimental and nuanced expression of one's feelings, graceful and melodious metric patterning, and mellow and subtle use of language. *Ci* lyrics of this school emerged early, and many poets were famed for writing this style of *ci*, especially Wen Tingyun (?- 866) and Li Yu (937 - 978) of the Five Dynasties period, Liu Yong (987 ?- 1053 ?), Yan Shu (991 - 1055), Ouyang Xiu (1007 - 1072), Yan Jidao (1038 - 1110), Qin Guan (1049 - 1100), He Zhu (1052 - 1125), Zhou Bangyan (1056 - 1121), and Li Qingzhao (1084 - 1151 ?) of the Northern Song Dynasty, as well as Jiang Kui (1155 ?- 1209), Wu Wenying (1212 ?- 1272 ?), and Zhang Yan (1248 - 1314 ?) of the Southern Song Dynasty. The graceful and restrained school occupied a dominant position in terms of both quantity and quality in over one thousand years of poetry's development. It should be mentioned that poets of this school also cared deeply about the fate of the nation, but they tended to express their concerns in a personal and sentimental way, often through depicting scenery. Therefore, their poems should not be regarded as lacking of vigor and energy.

引例 Citations：

◎ 至论其词，则有婉约者，有豪放者。婉约者欲其辞情蕴藉（jiè），豪放者欲其气象恢弘，盖虽各因其质，而词贵感人，要当以婉约为正。（徐师曾《文体明辨序说·诗余》）

（至于说到词，则有婉约风格的，有豪放风格的。婉约词其词句和情感追求含蓄而有意蕴，豪放词则追求气魄和境界宏大壮阔。这虽然是词作者的气质不同所致，但是词讲究以情动人，大体还是应该以婉约为正宗。）

Some *ci* lyrics are graceful and restrained, and some are bold and exuberant. The former are written in a nuanced way, whereas the latter are powerful and unrestrained. This difference is due to different temperament of poets. But *ci* lyrics are about expressing one's nuanced feelings, so the graceful and restrained school is representative of *ci* lyrics. (Xu Shizeng: *A Collection of Introductory Remarks on Various Styles*)

◎ 易安为婉约主，幼安为豪放主，此论非明代诸公所及。（沈曾（zēng）植《菌阁琐谈》）

(李清照是婉约词第一人，辛弃疾是豪放词第一人，这一见解明代诸位评论家并未提及。)

Li Qingzhao was the best *ci* poetess of the graceful and restrained school, whereas Xin Qiji was the best of the bold and unrestrained school. This view, important as it is, was not mentioned by literary critics of the Ming Dynasty. (Shen Zengzhi: *Random Notes on Ci Lyrics from Junge Studio*)

亡国之音 /wángguózhīyīn/
Music of a Failing State

　　国家将亡时的音乐，后多指颓靡荒淫的音乐。儒家认为，一个国家即将灭亡时，音乐多颓靡荒淫；而生活于社会底层的民众却困苦不堪，其音乐、诗歌等文艺作品一定充满了悲哀忧思。统治者若还不警醒，亡国也就为期不远了。

This term refers to the music of a state that is about to disintegrate. Later, it also refers to decadent and immoral music. The Confucian view was that music of a state on the verge of collapse tended to be dejected and demoralizing. As the downtrodden people endured immense suffering, their music and poetry were invariably full of sorrow and bitterness. If the ruler failed to wake up to the reality, the fall of his state was imminent.

引例 Citations：

◎亡国之音哀以思，其民困。(《礼记·乐记》)

(国家将亡时的音乐充满了悲哀忧思，这是因为民众困苦不堪的缘故。)

The music of a state on the verge of collapse reveals sorrow and anxiety because its people are in distress. (*The Book of Rites*)

◎郑卫之音，乱世之音也，比于慢矣。桑间濮上之音，亡国之音也。其政散，其民流，诬上行私而不可止也。(《礼记·乐记》)

(郑国和卫国的音乐，就是动乱时代的音乐，近乎轻慢无节制了。濮水岸边的桑间所流行的音乐，属于国家将亡时的音乐。它们反映出时政极端混乱，民众流离失所，臣下欺瞒君上、图谋私利而不可制止。)

The music of the states of Zheng and Wei was the music of an age of disorder, bordering on wantonness. The music of Sangjian on the Pushui River was typical of a failing state. The government was dysfunctional, the people were displaced, yet officials cheated on the ruler and pursued selfish gains with no one to stop them. (*The Book of Rites*)

温柔敦厚 /wēnróu-dūnhòu/
Mild, Gentle, Sincere, and Broad-minded

指儒家经典《诗经》所具有的温和宽厚的精神及教化作用。秦汉时期的儒学认为，《诗经》虽然有讽刺、劝谏的内容，但是重在疏导，不直言斥责，大多数诗篇情理中和，在潜移默化中使读者受到感化，养成敦实忠厚的德性，从而达到以诗教化的目的。温柔敦厚的诗教观是儒家中庸之道的体现，以中正、平和为审美标准，这也成为对于文艺创作风格的要求，体现为以含蓄为美、以教化为重。

This term refers to the mild and broad-minded manner with which the Confucian classic, *The Book of Songs*, edifies people. Confucian scholars during the Qin and Han dynasties believed that although some poems of *The Book of Songs* were satirical and remonstrative in tone, it still focused on persuading people instead of just reproving them. Most of the poems in the book were moderate in tone and meant to encourage the reader to learn to be moderate and honest. Encouraging people to be mild and gentle, sincere and broad-minded is a manifestation of Confucian doctrine of the mean, and being fair and gentle is an aesthetic value, which is also a standard for literary and artistic style that stresses the need for being gentle in persuasion and for edification.

引例 Citations：

◎入其国，其教可知也。其为人也，温柔敦厚，《诗》教也。(《礼记·经解》)

(进入一个国家，能看出国民的教养。民众的为人如果温柔敦厚，那就是《诗经》的教化之功。)

When you enter a state, you can find out whether its people are proper in behavior. If they show themselves to be mild and gentle, sincere and broad-minded, they must have learned it from *The Book of Songs*. (*The Book of Rites*)

◎温柔敦厚，诗教之本也。有温柔敦厚之性情，乃能有温柔敦厚之诗。(朱庭珍《筱 (xiǎo) 园诗话》卷三)

(温柔敦厚，是诗歌教化的根本。只有具备温柔敦厚的性情，才能写出温柔敦厚的诗歌。)

Teaching people to be mild and gentle, sincere and broad-minded is the basic purpose of poetry education. One can write poetry with such characteristics only if one is endowed with such good qualities. (Zhu Tingzhen: *Xiaoyuan's Comments on Poetry*)

文笔 /wénbǐ/
Writing and Writing Technique

泛指各类文章。经历了不同时期的概念变化，两汉时泛指文章的技法、风格及各类文章。魏晋南北朝时期，文论家们认识到不同文体的特性，首先将文笔与经典解释类著作相区分，用"文""笔"分别指纯文学写作和应用文写作；继之又以外部形式作为区分标准，将诗赋颂赞等文学类作品与奏章书策等"杂笔"进行区分，提出有韵为文、无韵为笔的观点。梁元帝萧绎(508—554)以内容为尺度，进一步提出"文"（诗赋等）不仅有韵，还应该表达内心的情感并有华丽的辞藻；而"笔"（应用文）只需要一般写作能力即可。今"文笔"主要指文章的技法与语言风格。

The term generally refers to different types of writings. Its meanings have evolved over time. During the Western and Eastern Han dynasties, it generally referred to writing techniques, writing styles, and various types of articles. During the Wei, Jin, and the Southern and Northern dynasties, literary scholars began to identify different features in different types of writings. They distinguished, for the first time, literary writings from those interpreting classical works, and identified pure literature as literary writings and practical writings as technical writings. They subsequently distinguished, on the basis of form, literary works such as poems, *fu* (赋 descriptive prose interspersed with verse), *song* (颂 essays of extolment), and *zan* (赞 essay of commendation) from essays such as memorials, documents, and policy proposals submitted to the emperor by officials. They concluded that all writings with rhyme were literary writings and those without were technical writings. Xiao Yi (508-554), Emperor Yuan of the Liang Dynasty, argued further that literary writings should not only have rhyme, but also express the author's inner feelings and use elaborate rhetoric, while technical writings required only general writing skills. Today, this term mainly refers to writing techniques and language styles.

引例 Citations：

◎无韵者笔也，有韵者文也。（刘勰《文心雕龙·总术》）

（没有固定节奏和韵律的作品称为"笔"，有固定节奏和韵律的作品称为"文"。）

Writings without rhyme or rhythm are technical writings while those with rhyme and rhythm are literary ones. (Liu Xie: *The Literary Mind and the Carving of Dragons*)

◎少有志气，博学洽闻，以文笔著称。(《晋书·习凿齿传》)

([习凿齿]少年时有志气，博学多闻，以写文章著称。)

Ambitious and studious from a young age, Xi Zaochi was an erudite scholar known for his writings and writing techniques. (*The History of the Jin Dynasty*)

文界革命 /wénjiè gémìng/
The Revolution in the Literati Circle

中国近代发生的一场以语言文学革新为内容的文化活动。1899年，梁启超（1873 — 1929）有感于戊戌变法失败、国民精神亟须提升，转而寻求以变革文章的方式输入欧美新思想，启蒙、教化国民，以达到革新思想的目的。"文界革命"所针对的主要是桐城派古文及骈文，变言文分离为言文合一，采用新文体、新词句，传达先进的西方思想观念。梁启超自创新文体，大量使用俗语、外国文法，笔锋充满感情，对于"文界革命"起到了引领作用。"文界革命"与"诗界革命""小说界革命"是相同主题的文风改革诉求，促进了白话文的广泛应用，直接启发了"五四"时期的文学革命，为白话诗文成为文坛主导开辟了道路。

The Revolution in the Literati Circle, which took place in early modern China, was a cultural movement aimed at transforming classical Chinese language and literature. In 1899, Liang Qichao (1873 - 1929), frustrated by the failure of the Reform Movement of 1898, saw an urgent need to reform and uplift the national character of the Chinese people. He used writing to introduce new ideas from the West, hoping that this would help enlighten and educate his fellow countrymen and change their ways of thinking. One target of this revolution was the prose of the Tongcheng School, which was founded by some natives of Tongcheng County, Anhui Province in the early years of the Qing Dynasty. Another target was *Pianwen*, rhythmical prose characterized by parallelism and ornateness. This revolution aimed to merge classical oral Chinese and classical written Chinese into one form and use a new style and wording to convey modern Western concepts and ideas. Liang Qichao created a new style by employing many colloquial expressions and the grammar of foreign languages. His writings were full of emotion. The Revolution in the Literati Circle shared goals of the Revolution in the Circle of Poets and the Revolution in the Circle of Fiction Writers: to promote a reform in the style of writing. It enhanced the popularity of vernacular Chinese, inspired the literary revolution of the May 4th period (1919), and paved the way for vernacular poetry and prose to gain dominance in the Chinese literary writing.

引例 Citations:

◎德富氏为日本三大新闻主笔之一，其文雄放隽快，善以欧西文思入日本文，实为文界别开一生面者，余甚爱之。中国若有文界革命，当亦不可不起点于是也。（梁启超《夏威夷游记》）

（德富苏峰是日本三大新闻主笔之一，他的文章雄奇奔放、隽永轻快，善于把西方欧洲的作文方法引入日本文章中，确实为文学界另外开辟了新局面，我特别喜欢他的文章。中国如果有文界革命，应当也是不可不以此作为起点的。）

Tokutomi Sohō is one of Japan's three great journalists. His writing is free, unrestrained, profound and graceful in style, incorporating the Western way of writing into Japanese literature. He created a new horizon for the literati circle. I love his writing. If a literary revolution is ever to happen in China, this should be the way it starts. (Liang Qichao: My Days in Hawaii)

◎启超夙不喜桐城派古文，幼年为文，学晚汉魏晋，颇尚矜炼，至是自解放，务为平易畅达，时杂以俚语韵语及外国语法，纵笔所至不检束，学者竞效之，号新文体。老辈则痛恨，诋为野狐。然其文条理明晰，笔锋常带情感，对于读者，别有一种魔力焉。（梁启超《清代学术概论》二十五）

（我从来不喜欢桐城派的古文，小时候写文章，学习汉末魏晋时人所写的文章，很崇尚严谨而精练的风格，到现在自我解放了，务必做到平易流畅，有时夹杂一些俚俗语、押韵词句及外国语法，信笔所至不加约束，学者竞相仿效，称为新文体。老一辈的人则痛恨这种文风，诋毁为"野狐禅"。然而我写的文章条理明晰，笔端常常带有感情，对于读者来说，别有一种吸引人的魔力。）

I never liked the Tongcheng style of prose. When writing while I was a boy, I imitated the style of Wei and Jin literati and adored their meticulous and concise way of writing. Now that we have liberated ourselves, we can pursue ease and facility by using some slang, rhyming expressions, and foreign grammar. I am uninhibited in my writing. Many scholars take pride in imitating me, calling my writing a "fresh and new style." People of the older generation, however, hate it, deriding it as being "shamelessly deviant." But what I write is logical, well laid-out and full of passion. It has a magical appeal to my readers. (Liang Qichao: *An Outline of Qing Dynasty Academic History*)

文气 /wénqì/
Wenqi

作品中所表现出的作者的精神气质与个性特点。是作家的内在精神气质与作品外在的行文气势相融合的产物。"气"原指构成天地万物始初的基本元素，用在文论中，既指作家的精神气质，也指这种精神气质在作品中的具体表现。人禀天地之气而形成不同的个性气质，表现在文学创作中，便形成不同的文气，呈现出独特的风格特点及气势强弱、节奏顿挫等。

Wenqi (文气) is the personality an author demonstrates in his works, and is a fusion of his innate temperament and the vitality seen in his works. Originally, *qi* (气) referred to the basic element in the initial birth and formation of all things, as well as heaven and earth. In literary criticism, it refers to an author's distinctive individuality and its manifestation in his writings. Humans are believed to develop different characters and traits endowed by the *qi* of heaven and earth. Reflected in literary creation, such different characters and traits naturally find expression in distinctive styles and varying degrees of vigor as well as rhythm and cadence.

引例 **Citations:**

◎文以气为主，气之清浊有体，不可力强而致。（曹丕《典论·论文》）
（文章由作家的"气"为主导，气有清气、浊气两种形态［决定人的气质优劣与材质高下］，不是强行可以获得的。）

Literary writing is governed by *qi*. Either clear or murky, *qi* determines the temperament of a writer, refined or vulgar, and his talent, high or low. *Qi* cannot be acquired. (Cao Pi: On Literary Classics)

◎气盛则言之短长与声之高下者皆宜。（韩愈《答李翊（yì）书》）
（文章的气势很强，那么句子长短搭配和音调的抑扬顿挫自然都会恰当。）

If a piece of writing has a vigorous style, the length of the sentences will be well-balanced and the choice of tone and cadence will be appropriate. (Han Yu: A Letter of Response to Li Yi)

文人画 /wénrénhuà/
Literati Painting

泛指中国古代文人士大夫的绘画，区别于民间的或宫廷画院的绘画，是中国画的一种。又称"士夫画""南画""南宗画"。宋代苏轼（1037—1101）首提"士人画"，明代董其昌（1555—1636）视唐代王维（701？—761）为"文人画"的创始人。文人画作者多取材于山水、花鸟、竹木等，侧重于抒发主体性灵，表达人的内心世界，间或寄托、书写对社会现实的不满与愤慨之情。文人画讲究笔墨情趣，超越形式技法，强调神韵意境。

This refers to paintings produced by ancient Chinese scholars and writers, as distinguished from those by craftsmen or court-hired artists. It is a sub-category of traditional Chinese painting, also known as "scholarly painting," "southern school painting," or simply "southern painting." Although Su Shi (1037-1101), a renowned Song Dynasty poet, first advanced this idea, Ming Dynasty painter and calligrapher Dong Qichang (1555-1636) regarded the Tang Dynasty poet Wang Wei (701?-761) as the true pioneer of literati painting. Its authors typically drew inspiration from scenery and image of mountains, rivers, trees, flowers, and birds, focusing on expressing their subjective perceptions and inner selves. Their works sometimes showed resentment and discontent with certain social phenomena. Stressing skillful use of brush and ink, literati painting transcended the restraints of form and technique, imbuing itself with real taste and verve.

引例 Citation：

◎观士人画，如阅天下马，取其意气所到。乃若画工，往往只取鞭策皮毛槽枥刍秣，无一点俊发，看数尺许便倦。汉杰真士人画也！
（苏轼《东坡题跋·又跋汉杰画山二则》）

（观赏士大夫绘画，如品阅天下的骏马图，当择取其中构意和气势俱佳的作品。如果是普通画匠，往往在皮毛、马鞭、马槽、饲料上用心，不能让人产生一点儿才情勃发的感觉，看几平尺就让人困倦。宋汉杰的绘画，才是真正的士大夫绘画。）

Examining scholarly paintings is like looking at galloping steeds of the world: one must choose only those works good in both structure and vision. A mediocre painter pays too much attention to trifles such as the fir and hair, horse whip, manger, and fodder, which are not quite able to enhance our aspirations. We would start to feel tired after we have looked at the first ten inches or so of such a painting. Song Hanjie's works alone show the intrinsic quality of a true scholar. (Su Shi: *A Collection of Su Dongpo's Prefaces and Postscripts*)

文学 /wénxué/

Literature / Scholars / Education Officials

原义为博通前代文献，"文"指文献，"学"是关于文献的学问。后泛指文章、文献以及关于文章、文献的各种知识与学问。主要含义有三：其一，先秦两汉时期，指关于古代文献特别是诗书礼乐、典章制度等人文方面的知识与学问。魏晋南北朝以后，"文学"一词大体与今天的文学概念接近，但包含人文学术的内容。近代以来，西方的文学观念传入中国，"文学"一词逐步演变指用语言创造审美形象的一门艺术，但传统意义上的"文学"范畴仍为章太炎（1869—1936）等少数学者沿用。这一术语的最初含义决定中国现当代主流的文学观念仍坚持从大文化的意义上看待文学现象，强调文学的审美价值与人文学术的内在联系，而与西方的"文学"术语强调文学之独立审美价值有所区别。其二，泛指古代各类文章及文献。其三，指以著书立说、教学等方式传播学问的文人与掌管文教的官员。

Originally, the term meant to command a good knowledge of documents from pervious dynasties. *Wen* (文) referred to documents, and *xue* (学) referred to the study of these documents. Later, the term referred to articles and documents in general as well as the knowledge about those documentations. The term had three main meanings. Firstly, from the pre-Qin period to the end of the Eastern Han Dynasty, it meant knowledge of ancient literature, especially that of humanities including poetry, history, rites and music, as well as works of laws and regulations. Starting from the Wei and Jin dynasties, the term basically became equivalent to today's concept of literature, but it also referred to academic writings on humanities. With the introduction of the Western concept of literature in recent history, the term gradually evolved to mean a pursuit that uses language to create aesthetic images. However, a few scholars, such as Zhang Taiyan (1869-1936), stuck to its traditional definition. The original meaning of the term determined the mainstream view on literature in contemporary China, which focuses on examining a literary phenomenon in the broader cultural context and emphasizing the intrinsic relationship between the aesthetic values of literature and liberal arts. This is somewhat different from the Western notion of literature which highlights the independent nature of literary appreciation. Secondly, the term refers broadly to various kinds of articles and documents in ancient times. Thirdly, it refers to scholars who promote learning through writing and teaching, as well as officials in charge of culture and education.

引例 Citations：

◎文学：子游、子夏。(《论语·先进》)

([弟子中]博学与熟悉古代文献的，是子游和子夏。)

Among the disciples of Confucius, Ziyou and Zixia have a good knowledge of ancient literature. (*The Analects*)

◎于是汉兴，萧何次律令，韩信申军法，张苍为章程，叔孙通定礼仪，则文学彬彬稍进，《诗》《书》往往间(jiàn)出矣。(《史记·太史公自序》)

(这时汉朝兴起，萧何编订法令，韩信申明军法，张苍订立历数和度量衡标准，叔孙通确定礼仪，而后文章与学问出众的人才逐渐进入朝廷，失传的《诗经》《尚书》等典籍也不断被发现。)

At that time, the Han Dynasty was on the rise, with Xiao He codifying laws, Han Xin promulgating military rules, Zhang Cang formulating the calendar and measurements, and Shusun Tong establishing ceremonial rites. Soon, literary talent who excelled in writing and learning took up positions in the imperial court. Lost classics such as *The Book of Songs* and *The Book of History* were rediscovered one after another. (*Records of the Historian*)

◎ 大抵儒学本《礼》，荀子是也；史学本《书》与《春秋》，马迁是也；玄学本《易》，庄子是也；文学本《诗》，屈原是也。（刘熙载《艺概·文概》）

（大致来说，儒学以《礼》为依据，荀子即是这样；史学以《尚书》和《春秋》为典范，司马迁即是这样；玄学以《周易》为根基，庄子即是这样；文学以《诗经》为本源，屈原即是这样。）

Generally speaking, Confucian studies are based on *The Book of Rites*, as exemplified by Xunzi. Historiography is modeled on *The Book of History* and *The Spring and Autumn Annals*, as exemplified by Sima Qian. Metaphysical studies are based on *The Book of Changes*, as exemplified by Zhuangzi. Literature has its root in *The Book of Songs*, as exemplified by Qu Yuan. (Liu Xizai: *Overview of Literary Theories*)

文以意为主 /wén yǐ yì wéi zhǔ/
The Message Matters More than the Rhetoric.

写文章要以立意为主导。"意"就是文章的思想内容。这是中国古代重要的文学理论命题，在宋、金、元、明文论中，多次被强调，并为后世学者所接受。这一理论认为，在立意与辞章文采两者中要把立意放在首要地位。这一观点与唐宋时人提出的"文以明道"说和"文以载道"说有密切的关联，是中国古代文学理论优良传统的一脉传承，但这里的"意"，远比"道"的内涵要宽泛。

Writing is done mainly to convey a meaning. Here, "meaning" refers to what an article is essentially about. This is an important theoretic notion in ancient

Chinese literary theory. It was often emphasized in essays of the Song, Jin, Yuan and Ming dynasties and accepted by scholars of later generations. According to this theory, the meaning is weightier than the rhetoric; it should always be put first. The theory is closely associated with the ideas of writing to illuminate Dao and writing to convey ideas first raised by Tang and Song scholars. It continues the fine literary theoretical tradition of ancient China. However, the word "meaning" covers far wider implications than Dao or truth.

引例 Citations：

◎常谓情志所托，故当以意为主，以文传意。以意为主，则其旨必见（xiàn）；以文传意，则其词不流。（范晔《狱中与诸甥侄书》，见《宋书·范晔传》）

（我常常说文章寄寓着人的情感与志向，本应以思想内容为主，以文辞来传达思想内容。以思想内容为主，则文章的立意会得到很好的展现；以文辞来传达思想内容，则文辞就不会散乱无章法。）

I often say that a person's feelings and aspiration dwell in his writing. Essays should focus much more on content and use rhetoric to better serve content. As long as an essay's focus is on content, its message will be clearly conveyed. When rhetoric is used to convey the message, it will not fall into disarray. (Fan Ye: A Letter Written In Prison to My Nephews)

◎无论诗歌与长行文字，俱以意为主。意犹帅也，无帅之兵谓之乌合。（王夫之《姜斋诗话》卷二）

（无论是诗歌还是长篇幅的文字，都是以立意为主。立意就如同军队的主帅，没有主帅的士兵只能是乌合之众。）

Whether it is poetry or a longer piece of writing, the author's main concern should be with its core message. A core message is like the commander-in-chief of an army. Without a commander-in-chief, soldiers will be reduced to a badly-organized crowd. (Wang Fuzhi: *Desultory Remarks on Poetry from Ginger Studio*)

文以载道 /wényǐzàidào/

Literature Is the Vehicle of Ideas.

儒家关于文学与道关系的论述。"文"指的是文学创作及作品；"道"指的是作品中的思想内容，但古代文学家与理学家将"道"主要理解为儒家所倡导的思想和道德。中唐时期古文运动的领袖韩愈（768—824）等人提出"文以明道"的观点，认为文章主旨应合乎并发挥圣人的经典。宋代理学家周敦颐（1017—1073）进一步发展为"文以载道"，提出文学像"车"，"道"即是车上运载的货物，文学不过是用以传播儒家之"道"的手段和工具。这一命题的价值在于强调文学的社会功用，强调文学作品应该言之有物、有正确的思想内容。但它轻视文学自身的审美特性，故后来受到重视文学自身价值的思想家与文学家的反对。

This term is a Confucian statement about the relationship between literature and ideas. *Wen* (文) refers to literary creations and works, while *dao* (道) refers to the ideas conveyed by literary works. Writers and philosophers in ancient China explicated these ideas as Confucian thought and ethics. Han Yu (768-824), leader of the mid-Tang-dynasty Classical Prose Movement advocating the prose style of the Qin and Han dynasties, and some others proposed that the purpose of writings should be in line with the classics of the ancient sages as well as promote them. Zhou Dunyi (1017-1073), a Neo-Confucian philosopher of the Song Dynasty, expounded the principle of literature serving as a vehicle of ideas. He concluded that literature was like a vehicle while ideas were like goods loaded on it, and that literature was nothing but a means and a vehicle to convey Confucian ideas. This theory was valuable because it stressed the social role of literature and emphasized that writers should know what they were writing about to ensure that their works conveyed correct ideas. However, it underestimated the aesthetic value of literature and later met opposition from thinkers and writers who emphasized the value of literature per se.

引例 Citation：

◎ 文所以载道也。轮辕饰而人弗庸，徒饰也，况虚车乎？文辞，艺也；道德，实也。（周敦颐《通书·文辞》）

（文章是用来承载思想和道德的。车轮与车辕过度装饰而没人使用，白白装饰了，更何况那些派不上用场的车呢？文辞，只是一种技艺，而道德才是文章的实质。）

Writings are meant to convey ideas and ethics. When vehicles are not used, even if the wheels and shafts are excessively decorated, it is simply a waste. Fine language is only a means for writing, whereas ethics are the essence of writings. (Zhou Dunyi: *The Gist of Confucian Thought*)

文章 /wénzhāng/
Literary Writing

泛指一切著述，包括今天意义上的文章和著作。先秦时这一术语包含在文学之内，两汉时"文章"一词与"文学"对举，指一切用文字写下来的文辞、篇章、史书、论著，六朝时"文章"与"文学"并列，开始指后世所说的审美范畴的"文学"，但仍作为统括一切文体的范畴使用。"章"意为一曲音乐演奏完毕，或一首完整的音乐，故此术语强调作品意义和结构的完整，注重文章写作手法与技巧；"文"和"章"都有花纹、色彩错杂的意思，"文章"相当于美的形式，故此术语隐含了审美观念。早期"文章"的概念与"文学"概念有一定联系又有所区别。"文章"偏重于辞章美文，说明了人们对于文章审美价值的逐渐重视。

The term refers to all kinds of writings, including what we call essays and books today. In the Pre-Qin period, this term was subsumed under literature.

During the Han Dynasty, the term referred to writings other than *wenxue* (文学documents of previous dynasties) to specifically mean essays, articles, history books, and treatises. In the Six Dynasties, the term, together with *wenxue*, began to assume the meaning of what later generations meant by literature, that is, writings for aesthetic appreciation which encompass every type of literary works. *Zhang* (章) also implies a movement of music played to its finish, or a single piece of music. Therefore, the term focuses on both meaning and structure as well as writing skills and techniques. Both Chinese characters in the term have the meaning of interwoven patterns and colors. Together, they signify a beautiful form, giving the term an aesthetic connotation. The earlier concept of the term is related to but different from that of *wenxue*, with the former focusing more on elegant diction and style, indicating increasing attention to the aesthetic value of literary works.

引例 Citations：

◎文章者，盖情性之风标，神明之律吕也。蕴思含毫，游心内运，放言落纸，气韵天成。(《南齐书·文学传论》)

(所谓文章，乃是人的感情性格变化的风向标、内在精神的一种量器。下笔之前蓄积文思，内心思绪自由驰骋，等到形诸纸墨时，文章的气韵自然天成。)

Literary writings reflect one's moods and disposition, or give expression to one's inner world. Before writing, one should gather his thoughts and free his mind so as to transcend the limitations of time and space. Thus, once he starts writing, his work will achieve its flavor naturally. (*The History of Qi of the Southern Dynasties*)

◎圣贤书辞，总称"文章"，非采而何？(刘勰《文心雕龙·情采》)

(古代圣贤的著作文辞，都叫做"文章"，这不是因为它们都具有文采吗？)

Writings by sages in ancient times are all called "literary writings." Isn't this because they all have literary elegance? (Liu Xie: *The Literary Mind and the Carving of Dragons*)

卧游 /wòyóu/

Enjoy Sceneries Without Physically Travelling

以观赏山水画代替游历山水，借以体味山水之乐。南朝画家宗炳（375 — 443）晚年因病无法游历名山大川，于是将游玩过的山水绘成画作挂在墙上，以卧游的方式权当山水之游。这一术语体现了古代文人乐（yào）山乐水的传统，还肯定了艺术对于人生的特殊意义，推动了绘画艺术的发展。

Artists often admire natural scenery beholding landscape paintings rather than traveling to actual spots. When the Southern Dynasty painter Zong Bing (375-443), due to illness in old age, could no longer tour great mountains and rivers, he painted the landscapes he had once seen and then hung the works on the wall, thus fulfilling his dream of seeing those beautiful sights again. This term illustrates the tradition of loving mountains and rivers among ancient literati, affirms the significance of art to life, and promotes the art of painting.

引例 Citations：

◎（宗炳）有疾还江陵。叹曰："老疾俱至，名山恐难遍睹，唯当澄怀观道，卧以游之。"凡所游履，皆图之于室。(《宋书·宗炳传》)

（[宗炳]生病之后回到江陵。感叹说："我老了，又病了，恐怕难以遍游名山，只有放空心灵，向内省察而领悟真谛，在屋里躺着观看山水画而权当亲身游历。"于是将自己游玩过的地方都画出来挂在室内墙上。)

Zong Bing returned to Jiangling to convalesce. With a sigh he said, "I'm old and sick, so touring famous mountains and rivers is now quite beyond me. What I should do is to unleash my soul and look inwardly to seek truth. I can look at landscape paintings even when lying in bed, as if I were actually there." Thus he hung on the wall all the paintings he had done of the places he had been to. (*The History of Song of the Southern Dynasties*)

◎一畦杞菊为供具，满壁江山入卧游。（倪瓒《顾仲赟过访闻徐生病差（chài）》）

（以一畦枸杞和菊花为酒食，满壁的山水画都可躺着观赏。）

With a plot of wolfberries and chrysanthemums to go with my wine, I rove the landscapes covering the walls while reclining in my bed. (Ni Zan: Gu Zhongzhi Visits to Find Mr. Xu Fully Recovered)

吴带当风 /Wú dài dāng fēng/
The Sashes in Wu's Painting Flutter as if in the Wind.

唐代吴道子绘画笔势圆转飘逸，画中人物的衣带宛如随风飘扬。较之顾恺之（345？—409）的画作笔法细密而宛若真人实景，吴道子作画运笔自如，线条流畅，动感强而传神，呈现全新风格和特殊审美效果，体现了绘画艺术的发展。

Wu Daozi of the Tang Dynasty executed his brushstrokes in a curvy and graceful manner, so that sashes on the people in his paintings seem flutter in the wind. Compared with Gu Kaizhi (345?-409), Wu's painting is more nuanced and lifelike. He used his brush with perfect ease and fluency. His works are dynamic and vivid, presenting a distinctly new style and aesthetic effect, reflecting the development of the art of painting.

引例 Citations：

◎吴带当风，曹衣出水。（郭若虚《图画见闻志·论曹吴体法》）

（吴道子所画人物的衣带如同随风飞扬；曹仲达所画人物衣衫紧贴身上，犹如刚从水中出来一般。）

The sashes worn by the figures in Wu Daozi's paintings flutter gracefully like in the wind, while the clothing in Cao Zhongda's paintings cling fast to bodies as if just emerged from water. (Guo Ruoxu: *Phenomena and Anecdotes in the History of Painting*)

◎其傅彩于焦墨痕中，略施微染，自然超出缣（jiān）素，世谓之"吴装"。（汤垕（hòu）《画鉴·唐画》）

（吴道子在焦墨痕中加上色彩，略加点染，人物逼真自然，似乎要溢出画布。后人称之为吴道子笔下的衣装。）

Wu Daozi used to add hues to traces of thick ink. With a gentle touch here and there, the figures in his painting all look natural and lifelike, as if about to come forth from the painting. People of later times called this style "Wu's unique skill of painting." (Tang Hou: *Appreciating Paintings*)

五音 /wǔyīn/
The Five Notes

五声音阶，即宫、商、角、徵、羽等五个音高递增的音符，大致对应于今天简谱中的1、2、3、5、6。在角后、徵前加变徵，在羽后加变宫，即为七声音阶。音阶细分意味着旋律多变，不过基于五声音阶的古典音乐尽管变化相对较少，亦自有一种单纯、质朴、静穆、悠扬的美。因为古代雅乐、民歌多用五声音阶，所以常用"五音"泛指音乐。

The term refers to the five musical notes that rise in pitch, from *gong* (宫), *shang* (商), *jue* (角), *zhi* (徵), to *yu* (羽), which correspond roughly to the notes of 1, 2, 3, 5, and 6 in today's numbered musical notation. When a *zhi* minus is placed before *zhi* and a *gong* plus after *yu*, this pentatonic scale becomes heptatonic. Such division of the musical notes gives rise to a variety of tunes. Although Chinese classical music based on a five-note scale does not vary that much, it retains the beauty of a simple, quiet, and lyrical style. As ancient refined music and folksongs were mostly based on a five-note scale, this term often referred to music in general.

中华思想文化术语
文艺卷

◎高渐（jiān）离击筑，荆轲和（hè）而歌，为变徵之声，士皆垂泪涕泣。（《战国策·燕策三》）

（高渐离敲着筑，荆轲和着节拍唱歌，发出变徵的音调，送行的人都流着眼泪低声哭泣。）

Gao Jianli struck the *zhu* instrument. Jing Ke sang to the beat, uttering a *zhi*-minus note. Those who saw him off broke out in tears. (*Strategies of the Warring States*)

◎五色令人目盲；五音令人耳聋；五味令人口爽；驰骋畋（tián）猎，令人心发狂；难得之货，令人行妨。是以圣人为腹不为目，故去彼取此。（《老子·十二章》）

（缤纷的色彩，使人眼花缭乱；嘈杂的音调，使人听觉失灵；丰盛的食物，使人舌不知味；纵情狩猎，使人心情放荡发狂；稀有的物品，使人行为不轨。因此，圣人但求吃饱肚子而不追逐声色之娱，所以摒弃物欲的诱惑而保持安定知足的生活方式。）

A riot of color makes one dizzy; discordant melody damages one's hearing; plenty of food numbs one's taste bud; hunting to excess causes one to lose control over oneself; and a valuable object tempts one into stealing it. Therefore, a sage, once having eaten enough, will not seek sensual pleasures. Rather, he will abandon the desire for material comfort and be content with living a simple life. (*Laozi*)

◎五色杂而成黼黻（fǔfú），五音比而成韶夏，五情发而为辞章，神理之数也。（刘勰《文心雕龙·情采》）

（五色交错而成灿烂的锦绣，五音排列而组织成悦耳的乐章，五情抒发而成动人的辞章，这是自然的道理。）

When silk threads of various colors are woven together, a beautiful piece of embroidery is created. When the five musical notes are properly arranged, a beautiful melody is composed. When the five emotions are forcefully expressed, a beautiful piece of writing is created. This is all too natural and obvious. (Liu Xie: *The Literary Mind and the Carving of Dragons*)

物色 /wùsè/

Physical Features

泛指各种自然事物的形貌。"物色"本义为牲畜的毛色，引申指物体的颜色，进而指景物、景色。南朝刘勰（465？—520？或532？）在《文心雕龙·物色》中专门对自然景物与文学创作的关系进行了讨论。他认为"情以物迁，辞以情发"，自然景物作为审美对象能够引发人们的创作冲动，从而发为文章。优秀的文学作品，既要做到"写气图貌，既随物以宛转"，细腻描摹景物；也要"属采附声，亦与心而徘徊"，情景交融。《昭明文选》中赋类有"物色"一目，专门收录写景出众的作品。

This term refers broadly to the appearances and patterns of everything in nature. It was originally used to describe the colors of animal furs; later it became associated with the colors of all physical objects, such as the splendor of scenery and landscape. Liu Xie (465?-520? or 532?) of the Southern Dynasties discussed at some length the relationship between natural features and literary creation in his book *The Literary Mind and the Carving of Dragons*. In his view, "Literary writing is created only when the writer's innermost emotion is stirred up by external things." That is, as objects of aesthetic appreciation, natural features can inspire one to turn his emotions into words. A fine piece of literary work should "depict the external traits of an object and capture its hidden momentum or spirit by varying the style in accordance with circumstances." At the same time, such work should "carefully choose words and poetic rhythm in response to a call from deep within the author." It should fuse emotions and scenery into one. This type of writing can be found in the "Rhapsodic Prose" section of *Selections of Refined Literature Compiled by Prince Zhaoming*, which has vivid accounts of scenery and landscape.

引例 Citations：

◎春秋代序，阴阳惨舒；物色之动，心亦摇焉。（刘勰《文心雕龙·物色》）

(四季不断交替，阴冷天气使人沉郁而温暖阳光使人舒畅；自然景物不断变化，也使得人的心情随之波动。)

Seasons change. Cold weather makes people feel depressed, whereas warm sunshine makes them happy and relaxed. Natural scenery and objects change with time, causing change in one's mood. (Liu Xie: *The Literary Mind and the Carving of Dragons*)

◎物色延暮思，霜露逼朝荣。(鲍照《秋日示休上人》)

(黄昏的景色使人愁思绵长，秋天的霜露让清晨的花草感到寒意逼近。)

The scenery at dusk makes one feel downhearted. The frost and dew of early autumn morning chill flowers and grass, signaling the advent of winter. (Bao Zhao: An Ode to Autumn Written in Tribute to My Revered Buddhist Friend Huixiu)

西昆体 /xīkūn tǐ/
The Xikun Poetic Style

北宋初年出现的以追求辞藻华美、对仗工整为主要特征的诗歌流派。宋初，杨亿（974—1020）、刘筠（970—1030）、钱惟演（977—1034）等人聚集在皇帝藏书的秘阁（"西昆"代指皇帝藏书的地方），编纂历代君臣事迹，诏题《册府元龟》。他们在编书之余，写诗相互唱和，并结集为《西昆酬唱集》，时人因称之为"西昆体"。"西昆体"诗人提倡学习李商隐（813？—858？），讲求用典精巧、意旨幽深，重视音律与借代，其作品词采精丽、音节铿锵、属（zhǔ）对工整，一扫晚唐五代以后平直浅俗的诗风，在诗歌发展史上有一定影响。由于是酬唱之作，大都雕琢太过，缺乏真情实感，常流于艳浮，为后人诟病。

This poetic style pursued rhetorical beauty and symmetrical structure. In the early years of the Northern Song Dynasty, poets such as Yang Yi (974-1020), Liu Yun (970-1030), and Qian Weiyan (977-1034) gathered in the emperor's private library to compile *Important Mirrors for Governance*, a book that records the activities of monarchs and their ministers in all previous dynasties. During spare time, they wrote poems to each other. Later, they put these poems into a collection titled *A Collection of Xikun Poems*. (Xikun, in an ancient Chinese legend, was a place where books of emperors were supposedly housed, thus the title for their collected poems.) Xikun style poets drew inspiration from Li Shangyin (813?-858?), who was meticulous about the use of allusions and whose poems had subtle appeal. These poets prized metrical rigor and metonymy. Their works were exquisite in diction, highly rhythmical, and strictly parallel, doing away with the insipid and shallow features of poetic style in the late Tang as well as the following Five Dynasties and Ten States period. Xikun style poetry exerted a considerable influence on poetry writing in the later periods. However, being written impromptu just to echo each other, such poems tend to be overly polished and lacking in true sentiments, and their vanity was frowned upon by later critics.

引例 Citation：

◎盖自杨、刘唱和，《西昆集》行，后进学者争效之，风雅一变，谓之"昆体"。由是唐贤诸诗集几废而不行。（欧阳修《六一诗话》）

（大约自从杨亿、刘筠开始唱和，《西昆酬唱集》风行，后辈学人争相效仿，诗风为之改变，因而称之为"昆体"。从这以后，唐代诗人的诗集几乎被人遗忘而不流传了。）

After Yang Yi and Liu Yun wrote poems to each other, *A Collection of Xikun Poems* became popular, and its style was emulated by poets of the later periods, thus transforming the poetic style. A new way to write poetry, known as the Xikun style, emerged. From then on, collections of Tang poems were all but forgotten. (Ouyang Xiu: *Ouyang Xiu's Criticism of Poetry*)

檄移 /xíyí/

Condemnation and Admonition

古代文体名称。"檄"即檄文，是战前誓师讨伐敌人的宣言；"移"即移文，多用于劝诚百姓移易不良风俗或不当言行的公告。南朝刘勰（465？—520？或532？）在《文心雕龙·檄移》中认为，檄文的作用是声讨敌人的罪过，鼓舞士气，赢得人民支持，打击敌人斗志，因此，在行文时一定要气势刚强，有理有据，表述清晰，可以运用夸饰、渲染甚至是诡诈的手法。而移文的作用是揭示内部存在的问题及危害，公开颁布命令要求改正，因为针对的是自己人，应该多一些宽容和理解，要就事论事，不要夸饰渲染；要直陈其事，不要拐弯抹角，更不要欺瞒。檄文和移文的共同点是在抨击罪恶现象和不良风气时均义正辞严，所持立场和态度是一致的。

This term means two types of imperial decrees in ancient times. *Xi* (檄) was an official condemnation of the enemy and an official rallying call to fight, whereas *yi* (移) was an admonition released to the public to advise people against improper speech and behavior. As Liu Xie (465?-520? or 532?) remarked in his literary critique *The Literary Mind and the Carving of Dragons*, an imperial decree of condemnation was written to list atrocities committed by the enemy, boost soldiers' morale, win popular support and demoralize enemy troops. Therefore, it was compelling and forceful, and well-articulated, supported by ample reasoning and proofs. Where necessary, overstatement, exaggeration or even deceitful wording can be employed in such a decree. An admonition, on the other hand, was written to expose problems or vices inside the empire, alert the public to their harmful effects and demand their timely rectification. Because an admonition was issued to one's own subjects, it should be more compassionate and lenient in tone. An admonition should be factual, without pomposity or fanfare. It should get right to the heart of a problem rather than beating about the bush or even concealing the truth. A condemnation and an admonition share one thing in common: they were stern in denouncing evildoing and malpractices.

引例 Citations：

◎檄者，皦（jiǎo）也，宣露于外，皦然明白也。（刘勰《文心雕龙·檄移》）

（"檄"同"皦"，意思是说将事情、问题等公之于众，使之昭然明白。）

The character *xi* means bright and clear, as in "clear as daylight." It is meant to clarify issues to the public. (Liu Xie: *The Literary Mind and the Carving of Dragons*)

◎凡檄之大体，或述此休明，或叙彼苛虐；指天时，审人事，算强弱，角（jué）权势；标蓍龟于前验，悬鞶（pán）鉴于已然。（刘勰《文心雕龙·檄移》）

（但凡檄文，其主要特点是，或者表明我方的美好清明，或者列数敌方的苛刻残暴；指明天时，审察人事，对比双方力量强弱，衡量权势大小；根据过往经验预测敌方的失败命运，以现成事例给予敌方警告。）

A decree of condemnation is written to declare that justice is on our side and to expose the brutal nature of the enemy. It should spell out the strategic environment, compare our strengths and weaknesses with those of the enemy, and warn the enemy about its doom by citing past examples. (Liu Xie: *The Literary Mind and the Carving of Dragons*)

◎移者，易也，移风易俗，令往而民随者也。（刘勰《文心雕龙·檄移》）

（"移"同"易"，改易、转变的意思。移文的目的是移风易俗，命令所到之处，老百姓便随之改变。）

Yi (移) and *yi* (易) are two Chinese characters with almost the same sound interchangeable in this context, both meaning change. A decree of admonition aims to change improper customs and practices. Wherever such a decree reaches, people will obey it and change their customs. (Liu Xie: *The Literary Mind and the Carving of Dragons*)

洗炼 /xǐliàn/

Make Writing Succinct

精简词句，提炼要义。洗炼是一种文字干净、主旨鲜明的文学风格。"洗"指清洗矿石、去除杂质，喻指删除芜杂文字；"炼"指金属的冶炼提纯，喻指提炼文章的精义或本真性情。作为一种写作方式，它包括炼意和炼辞两个方面，较之南朝刘勰（465？—520？或532？）的"熔裁"有更明确的要求；作为一种文学风格，它要求文章的词句必须与情志理高度配合而又简明扼要。

This term means that wording should be refined to highlight the essential message. Terseness is a mark of neat and thematically explicit writing. The idea originates from the process of cleansing metal ores for the removal of impurities, or from that of smelting metals. Figuratively, it refers to an authorial effort to capture the core message by cutting out redundant wording. As a way of writing, this involves the refinement of both content and wording; it sets a more clear-cut requirement on writers than the idea of "fusion for greater brevity," which was proposed by Liu Xie (465?-520? or 532?) of the Southern Dynasties. As a literary style, it calls for full agreement between wording, aspiration, and philosophical thought, as well as for conciseness.

引例 Citations：

◎岂若澡雪灵府，洗练神宅，据道为心，依德为虑，使迹穷则义斯畅，身泰则理兼通，岂不美哉！（《宋书·顾觊之传》）

（如何比得上洗涤灵魂，修炼精神，依据道培育心志，依据德思考问题，即使行迹窘迫而道义通达，身体舒泰而事理皆通，这难道不很美好吗？）

Wouldn't it be far better to cleanse our souls, forge our character, nurture our aspiration or ponder any question under the guidance of Dao? That being the case, even if life remains tough, we will still feel morally accomplished. So long as we are in good health and understand things well, then everything is fine, isn't it? (*The History of Song of the Southern Dynasties*)

◎犹矿出金，如铅出银。超心炼冶，绝爱淄磷（lìn）。空潭泻春，古镜照神。体素储洁，乘月返真。载瞻星辰，载歌幽人。流水今日，明月前身。（司空图《二十四诗品·洗练》）

（像在矿石中炼出黄金，如从铅块里提取白银。专心反复冶炼，只为达于纯粹。如同清澈的春水直泻空潭，如同清晰的古镜映照物的神韵。体悟素朴真谛，蓄养纯洁天性，乘御皎洁月光，返归天宫仙境。瞻望天上星辰，吟唱幽居之士。清澈如同今日的春水，纯净就像明月的化身。）

This is like extracting gold from ores, or silver from chunks of lead. We smelt repeatedly for the sole purpose of attaining perfect purity. It is also like precious spring waters cascading down into an empty pool or a shining age-old mirror showing the charm of objects. We appreciate truth in all its simplicity, preserve our natural purity, and return to the celestial palace amid the beautiful moonlight. We look up at the sky full of stars, chanting in tribute to recluses of old. They are as precious as today's spring water and as pure as an incarnation of the bright moon. (Sikong Tu: Twenty-four Styles of Poetry)

◎不洗不净，不炼不纯。惟陈言之务去，独戛戛乎生新。（孙联奎《诗品臆说》）

（不淘洗就不纯净，不提炼就有杂质。只有坚决删除陈词滥调，才能生出独特的新意。）

Nothing will be clean until it is cleansed. Nothing will be pure until it is refined. Only by ridding ourselves of any banality, can we become truly original. (Sun Liankui: *A Random Interpretation of "Twenty-four Styles of Poetry"*)

戏文 /xìwén/

Southern Opera / Operatic Script

专指南戏。南戏是北宋末年至明末清初流行于浙江温州和福建沿海一带，在传统民间歌舞基础上发展起来的一种地方戏曲，与流行于北方的宋元杂剧并行，明清演变为传奇，是中国戏曲史上发展最早、最成熟、最能体现中国戏剧特质的戏曲形态。"戏文"一词也用来泛指中国传统戏曲的剧本。

This term refers to the Southern Opera. It is a type of local opera which had developed from traditional folk songs and dances and was popular in China's southeastern coastal areas from the late Northern Song Dynasty to the late Ming and early Qing dynasties. It ran parallel to *zaju* that was popular in the north at the same historical period. It later developed into the legendary drama in the Ming and Qing dynasties. As the earliest, mature operatic form, it best represents traditional Chinese opera. Hence *Xiwen* (戏文) is widely used to refer to script of traditional Chinese operas.

引例 Citations：

◎温州乐清县僧祖杰［因横行霸道］……旁观不平，惟恐其漏网也，乃撰为戏文，以广其事。(周密《癸辛杂识(zhì)别集·祖杰》)

(温州乐清县的僧人祖杰［因在地方横行霸道］……旁观者觉得不平，怕他逃脱法网，于是将他的事情编成戏文，让更多的人了解他的恶行。)

In the Southern Song Dynasty, a monk named Zujie in Yueqing County of Wenzhou rode roughshod over the locals. People resented what he did, so they compiled his evil deeds into opera scripts to make more people know about the ruffian and hoped that this would help bring him to justice. (Zhou Mi: *A Collection of My Rambling Notes from Hangzhou*)

◎宋之戏文，乃有唱念，有诨。(夏庭芝《青楼集志》)

(宋代的戏文，才有唱腔、念白和插科打诨。)

Only by the Song Dynasty did the Southern Opera consist of songs, recitation, and comic gestures and dialogues. (Xia Tingzhi: Preface to *Biographies of Courtesans*)

象外之象，景外之景

/xiàng wài zhī xiàng, jǐng wài zhī jǐng/

The Image Beyond an Image, the Scene Beyond a Scene

欣赏诗歌的过程中所产生的文本形象之外的第二艺术形象，是读者经联想产生的精神意象。前一个"象""景"指诗歌作品中直接描写的物象和景象，后一个"象""景"则是指由此引发读者多方面联想所营造出的新的意象和意境。由道家与《周易》关于"言"（语言）、"意"（思想或意义）、"象"（象征某种深意的具体形象）三者关系的学说发展而来。魏晋至唐代的诗学倡导"象外之象，景外之景"，旨在追求文本之外的精神蕴涵和意象之美。这一术语同时也表现了中华民族的艺术趣味与审美境界。

Readers of poetry create images and scenes in their minds based on what they are reading. These are the readers' imaginations based on what is depicted in the poems. The term comes from Daoist theories about the relationships between discourses, ideas or meanings, and images that symbolize profound meaning in *The Book of Changes*. From the Wei, Jin to the Tang Dynasty, poetry critics sought "the image beyond an image, the scene beyond a scene" in order to pursue the spiritual implications and the beauty of images that are beyond textual descriptions. This term gives expression to the artistic and aesthetic tastes and ideals of the Chinese nation.

引例 Citations：

◎诗家之景，如蓝田日暖，良玉生烟，可望而不可置于眉睫之前

也。象外之象，景外之景，岂容易可谈哉！（司空图《与［汪］极浦书》）

（诗歌所描写的景致，犹如蓝田蕴藏着美玉，玉的烟气在温暖的阳光中若隐若现，可以远远望见，但是不能就近清楚地观察。通过欣赏诗歌景象而产生的之外的景象，岂可容易表达出来呀！）

The imagery of poets is like the sunshine warming Lantian so that fine jades under its ground issue smoke: They can be seen from afar but not observed right before your eyes. The image beyond an image, the scene beyond a scene – are they not simply beyond words! (Sikong Tu: Letter to Wang Jipu)

◎盖诗之所以为诗者，其神在象外，其象在言外，其言在意外。（彭辂《诗集自序》）

（大概诗之所以成为诗，就在于神韵在物象之外，物象在语言之外，语言在意义之外。）

That which makes a poem a poem is a poetic appeal beyond the image, an image beyond the words and words saying things beyond their meaning. (Peng Lu: Preface to *Collected Poems of Peng Lu*)

萧散简远 /xiāosǎn-jiǎnyuǎn/
Natural, Leisurely, Simple yet Profound

指书法、诗歌、文章等艺术作品的风格天然浑成、淡泊随意，而意蕴简古高远。"萧散"指自然闲适，没有刻意繁琐的修饰，不拘泥于法度规则。作为文艺批评术语，由宋代苏轼（1037—1101）提出，对明清时期的文艺创作与批评影响较大。它以庄子（前369？—前286）的思想为基础，又融入了禅宗的思想，强调自在散淡，心中不存执念，超越一切秩序与法度的羁绊，无往而不适，追求作品的疏朗、散淡、自由之美和合乎天然之趣。

This concept refers to those calligraphic works, poems, essays, and other literary and artistic works that are natural, leisurely and simple in style but have profound implications. A natural and leisurely style rejects excessive embellishment and is not bound by any particular forms. Created by Su Shi (1037 – 1101) in the Song Dynasty as a term of literary and art criticism, this concept had great influence on literary and artistic works in the Ming and Qing dynasties. Based on the thought of Zhuangzi (369 ?- 286 BC) and including the thinking of the Chan Sect, this concept stresses the need to be leisurely and simple and the need to avoid being opinionated, to break free from the fetters of rules and regulations and to take things as they come to ensure that an artistic work embodies the beauty of leisure, simplicity, freedom, and naturalness.

引例 Citations：

◎予尝论书，以谓钟、王之迹，萧散简远，妙在笔画之外。至唐颜、柳，始集古今笔法而尽发之，极书之变，天下翕然以为宗师，而钟、王之法益微。至于诗亦然。(苏轼《书黄子思诗集后》)

(我曾经谈论书法，认为钟繇(yóu)、王羲之的书法，萧散简远，其妙处在笔画之外。到了唐代颜真卿、柳公权，集成古今的运笔方法而极力加以发挥，可以说穷尽了书法的变化，天下人一致推他们为宗师，钟繇、王羲之的书法影响反而越来越弱了。诗的创作也是这样。)

I once talked about calligraphy, and I said that the calligraphic works of Zhong You and Wang Xizhi were natural, leisurely, simple, yet profound, and their artistic appeal went far beyond the calligraphic works themselves. In the Tang Dynasty, Yan Zhenqing and Liu Gongquan drew on all the calligraphic styles of previous times to develop their own calligraphic styles. It is fair to say that Yan and Liu reached the zenith of calligraphic art, and they were unanimously regarded as the great calligraphic masters. In contrast, the influence of Zhong You and Wang Xizhi is on the decline. The same is true with poetry. (Su Shi: Postscript to *Selected Poems of Huang Zisi*)

◎诗至玄晖语益工，然萧散自得之趣，亦复少减，渐有唐风矣。（唐庚《书〈三谢诗〉后》）

（诗歌发展到谢朓（tiǎo），语句更加工整，但是自然闲适、悠然自得的趣味也随之减少了，逐渐有唐人作品的特点了。）

Xie Tiao's poems were more neatly done than his predecessors', but as a result such poems became less natural and leisurely, and one begins to see a distinctive feature of Tang poems in them. (Tang Geng: Postscript to *Poems of Xie Lingyun, Xie Huilian, and Xie Tiao*)

小收煞 /xiǎoshōushā/
Midpoint Conclusion

指戏剧上半场最后一出收场戏。明末清初曲论家李渔（1611—1680）提出这一术语，包含戏剧上半场收束的要求和技巧：既要让上半场结构相对完整，完成基本人物、事件的交代，不中断一个连续事件；又要展开主要冲突，为下半场埋下伏笔，给观众留下悬念。多场戏、长篇说书也经常运用这一收束技巧，让观众或听众得以暂时满足或是对下面的剧情产生期待。

This term, first coined by the late Ming to early Qing drama theorist Li Yu (1611 - 1680), refers to the last scene of the first half of a play. It includes the requirement for and techniques of concluding the first half of the play. Besides the structural completeness of this section, all the relevant characters and events should have appeared by now or been duly introduced, and no ongoing event should be interrupted without a proper reason. Meanwhile, main conflicts should have unfolded, leaving clues to be uncovered later and keeping the audience in suspense. A serial drama, performed in multiple installments, as well as extra long folklore, often uses this withdrawal technique to temporarily satisfy the audience's curiosity or keep them guessing what is to come next.

引例 Citations：

◎上半部之末出，暂摄情形，略收锣鼓，名为小收煞。宜紧，忌宽；宜热，忌冷。（李渔《闲情偶寄·词曲部·格局》）

（上半场的最后一出戏结束之时，要暂时收束剧情，稍稍止住锣鼓，这叫做小收煞。剧情应当紧凑而不拖沓，场景应当热闹而不冷清。）

Toward the end of a play's first half, plot development should be suspended and the beating of gongs and drums ceased for the moment. This is what is called "midpoint conclusion." At such a juncture, the plot should be well-knit rather than drawn out, and the atmosphere lively rather than cheerless. (Li Yu: *Occasional Notes with Leisure Motions*)

◎但为子辖（yóu）妾者，玉胜而下，尚四五人，不特场上不可演，即此记之后，亦收煞不尽，不能不举此遗彼矣。（祁彪佳《远山堂曲品·玉香》）

（作为主人公子辖的妾的，除了玉胜，还有四五个，这些妾不只是在场上不能全部表演，即使这折戏之后，情节也难以全部收束，因此在剧情安排中就会出现突出有些妾而不管其他妾的情况。）

Ziyou, the main character in the Ming Dynasty opera *Fragrant Jade*, has Yusheng and four or five other concubines. These women cannot play out their roles during this scene, and even at the end it is hardly possible to cover every one. Thus, while some of them are given prominence, the rest look irrelevant. (Qi Biaojia: *Commentaries on Ming-dynasty Drama from Yuanshan Studio*)

小说 /xiǎoshuō/

Fiction

以人物形象刻画为中心，通过完整的故事情节和环境描写来反映社会生活的一种文学体式。人物、情节、环境是小说的三要素。

按照篇幅及容量，小说可分为长篇、中篇、短篇。中国古典小说，按照所表现的内容，可分为神怪小说、历史演义小说、英雄传奇小说、世情小说等几大类；按照体制可分为笔记体、传奇体、话本体、章回体等；按照语言形式，可分为文言小说和白话小说。中国古典小说经过了不同的发展阶段，有着鲜明的时代特点：先秦两汉时期的神话传说、史传文学，以及诸子散文中的寓言故事等，是中国古代小说的源头；魏晋南北朝时期出现的文人笔记小说，是中国古代小说的雏形；唐代传奇标志着古典小说的正式形成；宋、元出现的话本小说，为小说的成熟奠定了坚实的基础；明清小说标志着中国古典小说发展的高峰，出现了《三国演义》《水浒传》《西游记》《红楼梦》等古典名著。"五四"新文化运动之后，现代白话小说创作大量涌现，传播着现代的科学与民主精神。

Fiction is a literary genre primarily concerned with depicting characters to tell a complete story about social life within a setting. Fiction has three main elements, namely, characters, a plot, and a setting. Depending on the length, fiction can be divided into novels, novellas, and short stories. In terms of content, traditional Chinese fiction can be divided into the following broad categories: fantasy stories of gods and spirits, historical fiction, heroic legendary tales, and stories about human relations and social mores. In terms of genre, traditional Chinese fiction is divided into literary sketches, legendary tales, story-tellers' prompt-books, and chapter-based novels. In terms of language, there is fiction in the classical language and vernacular fiction. Traditional Chinese fiction has evolved through different stages, with distinctive features for each period. The myths, legends and historical biographies of the pre-Qin and Han dynasties, and the fables in the works of the earlier Chinese thinkers were the sources of traditional Chinese fiction. The literary sketches by men of letters in the Wei, Jin, Northern and Southern dynasties were embryonic forms of traditional fiction. The legendary tales of the Tang Dynasty marked the eventual emergence of Chinese fiction. The story-tellers' prompt-books in the Song and Yuan dynasties laid the foundation that allowed traditional fiction to reach maturity. The novels of the Ming and Qing dynasties marked the peak in the development of pre-modern fiction. That period is famous for producing great Chinese classical novels, namely, *Romance of the Three Kingdoms*, *Journey to the West*, *Outlaws of the Marsh* and *Dream of the Red Chamber*. During and after the New Culture Movement and the May 4th Movement around 1919, a large amount of modern vernacular fiction appeared, bringing forth a message of science and democracy of the modern age.

引例 Citations：

◎若其小说家合丛残小语，近取譬论，以作短书，治身理家，有可观之辞。(《昭明文选》卷三十一李善注引桓谭《新论》)

（像那些小说家将零散的论述整合起来，用身边发生的事情打比方进行述说劝诫，所写文章都不长，其中论述个人修身和治理家庭的内容，有不少可看的地方。）

Those writers of stories put together scattered statements. Drawing on what happens around them, they make up parables, writing short pieces. The parts about how to improve one's character and keep good family life are worth reading. (Huan Tan: *New Treatise*, as cited in *Selections of Refined Literature Compiled by Prince Zhaoming*, Vol. 31 Li Shan's Note)

◎小说，正史之余也。(笑花主人《〈今古奇观〉序》)

（小说，是正史之外的一种文学形式。）

Fiction is a literary supplement to formal historical accounts. (Xiaohuazhuren: Foreword to *Strange Tales New and Old*)

小篆 /xiǎozhuàn/
Lesser Seal Script / Small Seal Script

由大篆改造而成的一种字体。秦始皇（前259—前210）统一中国后，令丞相李斯（？—前208）等对大篆进行简化，将小篆颁布为官定标准字体。小篆使用圆润整齐的线条，减少了异体字，便于书写和认读，汉代为隶书所取代。小篆字体修长，讲究对称，起笔不露锋毫，收笔自然下垂，笔画曲折度可以随心变化，造成多种古朴而优美的形态，一直为书法家所钟爱，成为中国书法艺术的独特形态。

Small seal script is a style of calligraphy derived from big seal script. After unifying the country, the First Emperor of Qin (259 - 210 BC) ordered Li Si (?- 208 BC), his prime minister, to simplify the big seal script that was most popular in the Western Zhou period. This simplified script was officially issued as the standard form of handwriting. Small seal script uses beautifully cursive and uniform lines, facilitating handwriting and reading by reducing the number of variant forms of Chinese characters. Characters written in this style are gracefully long and symmetrical; they feature a smooth starting stroke and a natural, final vertical one. The curvy lines vary as the calligrapher wishes, thus producing many simple yet elegant variations. Calligraphers of all ages have loved small seal script, a unique style of calligraphic art. It was replaced by clerical script in the Han Dynasty.

引例 Citations：

◎ [李] 斯作《仓颉篇》，中车府令赵高作《爰（yuán）历篇》，太史令胡毋敬作《博学篇》，皆取史籀（zhòu）大篆，或颇省改，所谓小篆者也。(许慎《说文解字·序》)

(李斯写作的《仓颉篇》，中车府令赵高写作的《爰历篇》，太史令胡毋敬写作的《博学篇》，都是借鉴最早的大篆体字书《史籀篇》，有些字稍稍加以简化和改造，这就是"小篆"。)

Cangjie written by Prime Minister Li Si, *Yuanli* written by the imperial horse-drawn carriage manager Zhao Gao, and *Broad Learning* written by the imperial astronomer Hu Wujing are all separate parts of an early school primer, and all borrow heavily from *Shizhou*, an early dictionary of Chinese big seal characters, with quite a few simplifications and transformations. Hence what we call "small seal script" today. (Xu Shen: *Explanation of Script and Elucidation of Characters*)

◎唐大历中，李阳冰篆迹殊绝，独冠古今，于是刊定《说文》，修正笔法，学者师慕，篆籀中兴。(《宋史·徐铉(xuàn)传》)

(唐大历年间，李阳冰的篆书特别奇妙，独为古今篆体书法之冠。他刊定了许慎的《说文解字》，修正了有些篆字的笔法。学篆书者仰慕而师从他，篆体书法又兴盛起来。)

During the Dali Reign period of Emperor Daizong in the Tang Dynasty, Li Yangbing's wonderfully handwritten small-seal characters crowned the world. His amended version of Xu Shen's *Explanation of Script and Elucidation of Characters* revised small-seal script in a number of ways. Learners of small-seal calligraphy admired and followed him, thus making it prosperous again. (*The History of the Song Dynasty*)

写气图貌 /xiěqì-túmào/
Depict Outward Features to Convey an Innate Liveliness

指从事文学创作时描摹事物的外在形貌，传达事物的内在气势、神韵。它强调文学创作不能仅是描摹事物的外在形貌，而要用心灵把握对象，达到物我交融的境界，着力表达事物的气势、神韵或者人对事物的内在情感，如此方能创作出优秀的作品。

This term refers to the act of depicting the outward features of an object to convey its innate character in literary writing. It stresses the need not only to reproduce in words whatever appears before one's eyes but also to capture it with one's soul, thus achieving a close communion with the object depicted. The point is to bring out the hidden impact and spirit of things, or to express a profound feeling toward them. Only thus can an excellent work of art be produced.

◎写气图貌，既随物以宛转；属（zhǔ）采附声，亦与心而徘徊。（刘勰《文心雕龙·物色》）

（描摹事物的外形特征及内在的气势、神韵，要随着景物不同而有曲折变化；安排辞藻和音律，要根据自己的内心感受而来回推敲。）

In depicting the external traits of an object and capturing its hidden momentum or spirit, it is advisable to vary one's style in accordance with circumstances; in choosing one's wording and poetic rhythm, one should mentally weigh all possibilities before deciding on the best one in response to a call from deep within. (Liu Xie: *The Literary Mind and the Carving of Dragons*)

写意 /xiěyì/

Freehand Brushwork

中国画表现手法之一。以简练恣纵的笔墨勾勒描绘物象的意态神韵，重在抒发创作主体的意兴情趣。用笔灵活，不拘工细，不求形似（与"工笔"相对）。写意看似草率随意，实则谨严而内蕴法度，不仅要求画家在创作前对物象进行深入的观察和体验，营构好画面中诸多物象的位置关系，而且还须具备精深娴熟的技法功底，才能意居笔先而神出形外。写意有小写意、大写意之分，后者多采用泼墨技法。写意对后来的戏曲创作及表演手法有较大影响。戏曲中的写意，主要通过虚拟性、程式化的动作，并融合一定的歌舞表演来呈现舞台艺术的审美意象。

Freehand brushwork is one of the traditional methods of brushwork expression in Chinese painting. Using abbreviated and willful brushwork, the artist suggests graphically the meaning and character of the object and its shape. The chief aim is to give rein to the artist's subjective state and mood.

It stresses flexibility in brushwork, unrestrained by unimportant details and rejecting naturalistic effects (in contrast with meticulous painting). This style of painting, while seemingly coarse and whimsical, is in fact highly conscious of, and strictly consistent with, standards of artistic creation. Besides demanding close observation and experience of natural objects prior to painting, such as that the various forms within the picture will be laid out appropriately, it also demands solid technical proficiency in order that the artistic intent be formed in imagination before taking shape in painting. Freehand brushwork is divided into greater freehand and lesser freehand, with the former often employing the ink-splashing technique. It had a significant influence on the production of operas and the development of acting techniques in later ages. The freehand style in Chinese-style opera is shown through consciously artificial, stylized motions, accompanied by singing and dancing, to present images artistically on the stage.

引例 Citations：

◎僧仲仁⋯⋯以墨晕作梅，如花影然，别成一家，所谓写意者也。（夏文彦《图绘宝鉴》卷三）

（僧人仲仁⋯⋯通过渲染墨晕来画梅花，仿佛花影一般，这种画法自成一家，称得上是写意高手。）

By applying washes without lines, the Buddhist monk Zhongren painted plum blossoms which looked like florid shadows, thus creating a distinctive style of his own. This is what is meant by freehand brushwork! (Xia Wenyan: *The Precious Mirror of Painting*)

◎世以画蔬果、花草随手点簇者，谓之写意；细笔钩染者，谓之写生。（方薰《山静居画论》卷下）

（世人将随手点染而画出蔬菜、瓜果、花草的称作"写意"，将用细致工整的笔法钩描实物的称作"写生"。）

People describe paintings of vegetables, fruits, plants, and flowers painted according to the artist's whim, with dots here and there, "freehand brushwork," whereas they see paintings in the detailed style as "naturalistic drawings." (Fang Xun: *On Painting in the Quiet Mountain Studio*)

信言不美，美言不信

/xìn yán bù měi, měi yán bù xìn/

Trustworthy Words May Not Be Fine-sounding; Fine-sounding Words May Not Be Trustworthy.

可信的话并不漂亮，漂亮的话多不可信。老子鉴于当时社会风气与文风的浮华不实，倡导返朴归真与自然平淡的生活方式和文学风格。魏晋时代，文人崇尚自然素朴，反对虚浮华丽的创作风气，出现了像陶渊明（365或372或376—427）这样伟大的诗人，文艺创作也倡导真实自然的思想与风格。自此之后，中国古代文艺以素朴自然为最高的审美境界。

To address the extravagance in social mores and in the style of writing of his time, Laozi advocated simple and natural lifestyles and literary presentations. During the Wei and Jin dynasties, men of letters valued natural and simple literary styles and were opposed to extravagant and superficial styles. This line of thought led to the emergence of great poets like Tao Yuanming (365 or 372 or 376-427), and shaped literary writings to reflect direct thoughts and natural expressions. Subsequently, ancient Chinese literature and art took simplicity and naturalness as the highest aesthetic standards.

引例 Citations：

◎信言不美，美言不信。善者不辩，辩者不善。(《老子·八十一章》)（可信的话并不漂亮，漂亮的话多不可信。善良的人往往不能能言善辩，能言善辩的人往往不善良。）

Trustworthy words may not be fine-sounding; fine-sounding words may not be trustworthy. A kind-hearted person may not be an eloquent speaker; a glib person is often not kind. (*Laozi*)

◎老子疾伪，故称"美言不信"，而五千精妙，则非弃美矣。(刘勰《文心雕龙·情采》)

（老子憎恶虚伪矫饰，所以他认为"漂亮的话多不可信"。但他自己写的《道德经》五千言，思想深刻而文笔优美，可见他并没有摒弃文章之美。）

Laozi detested pretense, so he said, "Flowery rhetoric words may not be trustworthy." However, the 5,000-word *Dao De Jing* (another name of *Laozi*) he wrote is not only profound in ideas but reads beautifully. That means he was not opposed to writings using fine words. (Liu Xie: *The Literary Mind and the Carving of Dragons*)

行书 /xíngshū/
Running Script

介于草书和楷书之间的一种书法艺术形态。它保留了隶书的基本结构，以自然连笔、书写流畅便捷、容易辨识为主要特征。一般认为行书起源于东汉刘德升，盛行于魏晋。行书有"行进"和"行云流水"的意思，它没有固定的形态和写法，不属于一种独立的字体，适合于任何书写工具，不同人的书写各有特色。东晋王羲之（303—361，一作307—365，又作321—379）的《兰亭集序》、颜真卿（708—784）的《祭侄季明文稿》、苏轼（1037—1101）的《寒食诗帖》是三大行书法帖典范，风格鲜明，具有极高的审美价值。

Running script is a calligraphic form between cursive script and regular script. A Chinese character written in the style of running script retains the basic structure of characters written in official script. Running script features smoothly-linked strokes, and the characters written in this style are easy to recognize. Generally, people believe that running script was created by Liu Desheng of the Eastern Han Dynasty and became popular in the Wei and Jin eras. This writing style reminds one of drifting clouds and flowing water. It has no fixed arrangement for the radicals of a character and can be executed with any writing tools. The same characters written in this style by different people are different in appearance. The best-known masterpieces in this style are Wang Xizhi's (303-361, or 307-365, 321-379) "Preface to the Collection of Poems Composed at the Orchid Pavilion," Yan Zhenqing's (708-784) "Draft Elegy to Nephew Jiming," and Su Shi's (1037-1101) "The Cold Food Observance." They are distinctive in style and have great aesthetic value.

引例 Citations：

◎行书者，后汉颍川刘德升所作也。即正书之小伪（é），务从简易，相间流行，故谓之"行书"。（张怀瓘（guàn）《书断》卷上）

（行书，是后汉颍川郡的刘德升创造的书写方法。也就是对楷书稍加改变，致力于简单方便，书写时时不时像流水一样行进，所以叫做"行书"。）

Running script was a writing form created by Liu Desheng from Yingchuan in the Eastern Han Dynasty. It is a variation of regular script, easy and convenient to write. Since writing the script sometimes resembles running water, hence the name running script. (Zhang Huaiguan: *Commentary on Calligraphy*)

◎所谓"行"者，即真书之少纵略，后简易相间而行，如云行水流，秾纤间出。非真非草，离方遁圆，乃楷隶之捷也。（宋曹《书法约言·论行书》）

（所谓行书，就是在楷书基础上稍稍自由简略一些，其后简省笔画，不时出现连笔而行，如行云流水一样，笔道粗细相间。它既不是楷书也不是草书，字形既不方也不圆，是楷书和隶书基础上的一种快捷书体。）

Running script is a freer and more concise form of regular script. Later on, strokes of some characters were sometimes linked to make writing easy and simple, looking like drifting clouds and running water. The thickness of strokes of characters keeps changing, sometimes thick, and sometimes thin.

It is neither regular script nor cursive script. The form of each character is neither square nor round. It is a quickly-written calligraphic form based on regular script and official script. (Song Cao: *Comments on Different Styles of Script*)

兴 /xìng/

Evocation

　　主要指由外物触发内心情感而产生的审美感受和心理状态。作为美学范畴的"兴"接受了"兴观群怨"之"兴（譬喻）"与"赋比兴"之"兴（六义之一）"的双重影响而兼有两者的含义。从欣赏的角度来看，孔子（前551—前479）所提出的"兴观群怨"之"兴"，注重读诗而引发的心理感受和教育功能，并非纯粹的文学理论；从创作的角度来看，"兴"是《诗经》"六义"（风、雅、颂、赋、比、兴）之一，一般说来，前三者为《诗经》的内容与体裁分类，后三者为《诗经》的创作手法。"兴"的基本特征为：由相类似的事物引发开来，运用想象与联想，达成譬喻，由此及彼，将所要表达的意义蕴含在形象中，使诗歌的韵味更加含蓄、深邃。"兴"将诗歌的发端与联想完整地融为一体，使人在鉴赏中回味无穷，是中国古代诗歌创作的特有手法。"兴"起初与"比"结合紧密，魏晋南北朝时它的蕴含和审美特征逐渐获得独立的发展，成为与"比兴"分立的诗学范畴，"兴"更注重外物对内心的感发触动。

This term refers to the state of mind in which external things evoke one's inner feelings, thus creating aesthetic appreciation. As an aesthetic term, evocation means both stimulation and association. In artistic appreciation, Confucius (551 - 479 BC) used evocation to refer to the psychological effect and educational function of reading poetry, and it was not meant to be a literary term only. In artistic creation, evocation means association, which is among the six poetic forms, namely, ballad, narrative, analogy, association, court hymns, and eulogy, as described in *The Book of Songs*. The first three refer to the content and subtypes of classic Chinese poetry, whereas the latter three elements are creative means employed by *The Book of Songs*. Evocation is defined by the use of similar or relevant things to create a metaphor which, by virtue of imagination and association, conveys a message through imagery and highlights the nuances of poetry. Evocation arouses one's imagination through reading a poem, making such experience an enjoyable one. It is a rhetorical means frequently used in classical Chinese poetry. At first, evocation was closely linked to analogy. Its implication and aesthetic properties started to grow independently in the Wei, Jin and Southern and Northern Dynasties period, and finally became a poetic term different from analogy and association. Evocation focuses on the impact of external things on one's emotions.

引例 Citations：

◎兴于诗，立于礼，成于乐（yuè）。（《论语·泰伯》）

（以诗感发意志，以礼规范行为，以乐成就人格。）

One uses poetry to evoke volition, rituals and etiquette to regulate behavior and music to shape one's character. (*The Analects*)

◎兴者，起也。取譬引类，起发己心。《诗》文诸举草木鸟兽以见意者，皆兴辞也。（《毛诗序》孔颖达正义引郑众语）

（兴，就是起意。借相类似的事物取譬喻，引发自己的情感、心志。《诗经》文本中列举草木鸟兽以表现作者情感、心志的情况，都是"兴"一类的词句。）

Evocation means using certain things in the outer world to arouse one's emotions and aspirations. *The Book of Songs*, for example, cites trees, grass, birds and animals to evoke such feelings. (Zheng Zhong, as quoted in Kong Yingda: Correct Meaning of "Introductions to *Mao's Version of The Book of Songs*")

◎《诗》有六义，其四为兴。兴者，因事发端（duān），托物喻意，随时成咏。（王闿运《诗法一首示黄生》）

（《诗经》有六义，第四为兴。兴，就是依凭事物而感发，借事物寄托自己的意旨，随时吟诵成诗。）

The *Book of Songs* contains six genres: ballads, narratives, analogies, associations, court hymns, and eulogies. The fourth one, namely "association," means that the poet makes use of things from the outer world to voice his feelings and volition, thus creating a poem. (Wang Kaiyun: *A Poem Written to Show Mr. Huang How to Write Poetry*)

兴观群怨 /xìng-guān-qún-yuàn/
Stimulation, Contemplation, Communication, and Criticism

孔子（前551 — 前479）所提出的《诗经》的四种主要功能，实际也是对文学基本功能与价值的高度概括。"兴"是指通过作品的欣赏引发联想，激发欣赏者对于社会人生的思考与志趣提升；"观"是通过作品认识自然与社会人生的各种状况，透视政治得失；"群"是围绕作品与别人展开讨论，交流思想感情；"怨"是表达对社会时政的不满，宣泄内心的情感。这四种功能有着内在的联系，涉及文学的审美功能、认识功能与教育功能。后世学者对此不断有新的阐发。

According to Confucius (551-479 BC), *The Book of Songs* served these four purposes, which summarize the basic functions and values of literature. "Stimulation" means that the appreciation of literary works arouses imagination, stimulates reflection on society and life, and inspires aspirations and interests. "Contemplation" means that reading leads to understanding nature, society, life, and politics. "Communication" means that reading encourages discussion with others, and exchange of thoughts and feelings.

"Criticism" means learning how to critically express oneself about state affairs and voice inner feelings. These four functions are closely associated and involve the aesthetic, cognitive, and educational functions of literature. Later scholars have continued to make original contributions to the study of these themes.

引例 Citations：

◎《诗》可以兴，可以观，可以群，可以怨；迩之事父，远之事君；多识于鸟、兽、草、木之名。(《论语·阳货》)

(《诗经》可以感发志向，引发思考，认识世界，可以交流思想感情，表达不满情绪。在家可以用它来侍奉父母，出外可以用它来侍奉国君，还可以从中学到鸟兽草木等众多事物的知识。)

The Book of Songs stimulates the mind, inspires contemplation, enables one to understand society, exchange feelings and thoughts with others, and express resentment. The book guides one on how to support and wait on one's parents at home and how to serve one's sovereign in public life. One can also learn about birds, beasts, and plants from the book. (*The Analects*)

◎ 于所兴而可观，其兴也深；于所观而可兴，其观也审；以其群者而怨，怨愈不忘；以其怨者而群，群乃益挚。(王夫之《姜斋诗话》卷一)

(经过作者感兴后的作品又具备认识价值，那么这种感兴一定深刻；经过认识又能够激发情感的，那么这种认识一定真实明察；因为聚在一起而产生某种怨恨，那么这种怨恨更加使人难忘；因为某种怨恨而聚成群体，这样的群体一定会更加紧密。)

If works created on the basis of the author's understanding have the value of cognition, his understanding must have been profound. If his feelings are based on recognition, his observation must have been sharp. If certain resentment arises from discussions among a group of people, it must be unforgettable. If a group of people have come together because they share certain resentment, they must be closely knit. (Wang Fuzhi: *Desultory Remarks on Poetry from Ginger Studio*)

兴寄 /xìngjì/

Xingji (Association and Inner Sustenance)

运用比兴、寄托等艺术手法，使诗歌情感蕴藉、内涵深厚、寄托感慨。由初唐时代的陈子昂（659—700）首次提出。"兴"是由外物触发而兴发情感，"寄"是寄托某种寓意。兴寄最初是指诗人的感兴要有寓意，达到托物言志的目的；后来引申为诗歌要有赞美或讽刺的寓意。兴寄这一术语继承了先秦时代感物起兴的诗歌传统，强调诗歌的感兴之中要有深沉的寄托，是比兴理论的重要发展，对于盛唐诗歌摆脱齐梁时代诗歌追求华彩而摒弃寄托的创作态度、推动唐诗健康发展有很大作用。

The term means the use of analogy, association, and inner sustenance in writing a poem to give implicit expression to one's sentiments, thus enabling the poem to convey a subtle message. The term was first used by the Tang-dynasty poet Chen Zi'ang (659-700). *Xing* (兴) means the development of inner feelings invoked by external objects, and *ji* (寄) means finding sustenance in them. Later it was extended to mean that poetry should be written to convey a message of praise or satire. The term carried on the pre-Qin poetical tradition of creating inspiration by writing about a subject and stressed that while depicting sentiments in poetry, the poet should find sustenance in it. The term represented an important development of the theory of analogy and association. It played a major role in ensuring that poets in the prime of the Tang Dynasty broke away from the poetic style of the Qi and Liang of the Southern Dynasties, which pursued ornate language instead of inner sustenance, thus enabling Tang poetry to develop in a healthy way.

引例 Citations：

◎仆尝暇时观齐梁间诗，彩丽竞繁而兴寄都绝。每以永叹，思古人常恐逶迤颓靡、风雅不作，以耿耿也。（陈子昂《修竹篇（并序）》）

（我曾经在闲暇时读齐梁时期的诗歌，这些诗辞藻堆砌、竞相华丽，但是兴寄的味道一点儿都没有。我常为此长叹，推想古人经常担心诗风渐至颓废华靡，《诗经》的风雅传统不再振兴，心中定会耿耿不平。）

When I read the poems of the Qi and Liang of the Southern Dynasties in my leisure time, I found them full of ornate rhetoric heaped together without sustenance. I often feel resigned as I can well imagine that the ancients were always concerned about poetry becoming decadent and the tradition of objectively reflecting reality as shown in *The Book of Songs* getting lost. (Chen Zi'ang: "The Bamboo" with a Preface)

◎仆尝病兴寄之作埋（yīn）郁于世，辞有枝叶，荡而成风，益用慨然。（柳宗元《答贡士沈起书》）

（我曾经担忧那些有兴寄特色的作品被埋没掉，文章追求浮华枝叶，恣纵成为风尚，这个时候更需要作品有感慨和意味。）

I was concerned that the works based on association and inner sustenance would get lost and that writings with only elaborate rhetoric would prevail. We really need works that have substance. (Liu Zongyuan: Letter to Scholar Shen Qi)

兴趣 /xìngqù/
Xingqu (Charm)

"兴"中所蕴含的趣或者是"兴"发时心物交会所产生的趣（情趣、意趣等）。是诗歌中所蕴含的、读者通过欣赏而获得的特定的审美趣味。南宋诗论家严羽（？—1264）在《沧浪诗话》中倡导诗歌的感染力，反对直接说理，主张让读者在品读和感悟中得到愉悦和满足。这一术语后来成为评价诗歌的重要标准，明清诗学也受到积极影响。

The term refers to charm inherent in an inspiration, or charm created when the object or scene depicted in a poem is appreciated. It is a type of aesthetic enjoyment contained in a poem which is gained through the reader's act of appreciation. In *Canglang's Criticism on Poetry*, Yan Yu (?-1264), a poetry critic of the Southern Song Dynasty, voiced his love for poetry's emotional charm and argued against direct expression of an idea in poetry. He stressed the need to enable readers to gain insight and satisfaction in a natural way through personal reflection and contemplation. This term later became an important criterion for evaluating poetry, exerting a strong influence on the poetry theories of the Ming and Qing dynasties.

引例 Citations：

◎诗者，吟咏情性也。盛唐诸人惟在兴趣，羚羊挂角，无迹可求。（严羽《沧浪诗话·诗辨》）

（诗歌吟咏的是本性真情。盛唐诗人的诗作特别着意兴趣，如同羚羊晚上将角挂在树上睡觉，没有任何痕迹可寻。）

One should write poetry only to express one's true sentiments and personality. In their poems, Tang-dynasty poets made particular efforts to inspire meaning, charm, and emotion. Their style is like an antelope hooking its horns onto a tree when sleeping at night, so that its trace cannot be found. (Yan Yu: *Canglang's Criticism on Poetry*)

◎古诗多在兴趣，微辞隐义，有足感人。而宋人多好以诗议论。夫以诗议论，即奚不为文而为诗哉？（屠隆《文论》）

（古代诗作多注重审美情趣的传达，用词含蓄而寓意隐微，足以感染读者。而宋代诗人大多借诗歌来论事说理。用诗歌论事说理，那为何不写成文章而非要写成诗呢？）

Classical poems mostly focused on inspiring meaning, charm, and emotion through hints with subtle wording and implied meanings, and that is why they moved readers. Poets during the Song Dynasty, however, tended to use poetry to comment on public affairs or make arguments. If that was what they wanted to achieve, why didn't they write essays instead of poems? (Tu Long: *On Essay Writing*)

兴象 /xìngxiàng/

Xingxiang (Inspiring Imagery)

文学作品中能够生发深远意旨和审美情境的物象，是创作者主观情感与客观景象完美融合而产生的一种艺术境界。"兴"指作者偶然生发的创作冲动，"象"则是指作者在作品中所借助的外在的具体物象。"兴象"是唐代诗论家殷璠（fán）在《河岳英灵集序》中用来品评盛唐诗人作品的用语，后来演变成诗歌评论的"兴象观"，用以衡量作品境界的高下。

Inspiring imagery is an artistic achievement of profound literary significance and with great aesthetic taste, obtained through the perfect blending of an author's feelings with an objective situation or scenery. *Xing* (兴) is an impromptu inspiration of the author, and *xiang* (象) a material object he borrows from the external world in his writing. Tang-dynasty poetry critic Yin Fan first used the term "inspiring imagery" in his "Preface to *A Collection of Poems by Distinguished Poets*" in commenting on the works of poets in the golden period of the Tang Dynasty. It later became a standard for assessing the merit of a poetic work.

引例 Citations：

◎既多兴象，复备风骨。（殷璠《河岳英灵集》卷三）

（诗人的作品既有许多兴象，又具备了风骨之美。）

These poets' works feature both inspiring imagery, as well as *fenggu* (class and integrity). (Yin Fan: *A Collection of Poems by Distinguished Poets*)

◎作诗大要不过二端：体格声调、兴象风神而已。（胡应麟《诗薮·内编五》）

（作诗大体上有两个方面：体制与声律，兴象与气韵。）

Poetry has two basic aspects: one includes form, rhythm, and rhyme; the other includes imagery and charm. (Hu Yinglin: *An In-depth Exploration of Poetry*)

性灵 /xìnglíng/

Xingling (Inner Self)

本指相对于客观外物的人的心灵世界，包括性情、才智两个方面。南北朝时期，"性灵"成为文学创作与文学批评术语，主要指与社会伦理、政治教化与传统创作观念相对的个体的精神才智与性情气质，强调文艺应该发自并表现人的性灵。明清时期，随着个性伸张与思想解放，袁宏道（1568—1610）、袁枚（1716—1798）等著名文士用"性灵"倡导文学应该直抒胸臆，表现内心真实的思想情感、兴趣见解，强调创作中的精神个性和艺术个性，反对宋明理学、传统创作观念以及复古思潮对于人性与文学的束缚，并因此成为文学创作上的一个重要流派。

The term refers to an individual's inner mind vis-à-vis the outside world, which consists of two aspects, namely, temperament and talent. During the Southern and Northern Dynasties, *xingling* (inner self) became widely used in literary writing and criticism. It refers to the combination of a writer's temperament and talent, other than his social ethics, political beliefs, and literary traditions; and it stresses that literature is inspired by traits of individuality and should give expression to them. During the Ming and Qing dynasties, along with the trend of giving free rein to individuality and shaking off intellectual straitjacket, renowned scholars such as Yuan Hongdao (1568-1610) and Yuan Mei (1716-1798) advocated giving full expression to one's inner self, namely, one's thoughts, sentiment, emotion and views. They underscored the role of intellectual and artistic individuality in literary creation as opposed to the rigid School of Principle of the earlier Song and Ming dynasties, literary dogma and blind belief in classicism which constrained people from expressing human nature and inhabited literary creativity. The Xingling School thus became an important school in literary creation.

引例 **Citations:**

◎惟人参（sān）之，性灵所钟，是谓三才。为五行之秀，实天地之心。心生而言立，言立而文明，自然之道也。（刘勰《文心雕龙·原道》）

（只有人身上钟聚了性情才智，可以与天地并称为"三才"。人是天地万物中最杰出的种类，实际是天地的核心与灵魂。心灵活动产生语言，语言表达出来就形成文章，这是自然规律。）

Temperament and talent are found only in man, constituting his inner self. One of the three elements of existence along with heaven and earth, man stands out among all species and is the essence and soul of the world. In the natural course of events, the need to express man's inner self leads to the emergence of language, which in turn gives rise to literary creation. (Liu Xie: *The Literary Mind and the Carving of Dragons*)

◎大都独抒性灵，不拘格套，非从自己胸臆流出，不肯下笔。（袁宏道《叙小修诗》）

（[他的诗]大都抒发自己真实独特的性情，不拘泥于任何格式套路。只要不是出自本心，绝不肯下笔。）

Most of his poems express his inner self, without being constrained by any particular regulations or formulas. He would not commit to paper anything not flowing naturally from his inner world. (Yuan Hongdao: Preface to Xiaoxiu's Poetry)

◎自三百篇至今日，凡诗之传者，都是性灵，不关堆垛。（袁枚《随园诗话》卷五）

（从《诗经》到今日，凡是能够广泛流传的诗歌，都是因为表达了自己的性灵，与堆砌辞藻和典故没有关系。）

Ever since *The Book of Songs* was written, all those poems which have remained popular were created to give full expression to the authors' inner self, instead of being loaded with clichés and classical references. (Yuan Mei: *Suiyuan Remarks on Poetry*)

雄浑 /xiónghún/

Powerfulness

指雄健有力、浑厚自然的艺术风格与审美气象。"雄"侧重指作品的气力;"浑"兼有浑厚、浑融、浑然诸义,侧重指作品的风格、气象。道家认为"道"具有浑然天成的特点,"雄浑"即渊源于此。雄浑的形成,并非出于人为的故意安排,而是以作品蓄积的内在气力为基础,由内向外、自然生发的浑融雄阔的艺术风格。雄浑不能勉强得来,它与作者自身的修养、气质密切相关。就作品而言,语言的组织、词汇的选择、意象的呈现等诸多要素趋向于崇高宏伟,与阔大雄奇的思想意识浑融无间,从总体上表现为雄浑的审美风貌。

This term, which literally means power and splendor, refers to a natural and powerful artistic style and aesthetic taste. In Daoist terms, the Way features the great and vast power of nature, hence the term. Powerfulness is not deliberately created by the author. Rather, it is a majestic, forceful style of artistic expression flowing naturally from the inner strength built up in a work of art itself. Powerfulness cannot be achieved artificially; it has a great deal to do with an author's disposition and self-cultivation. Such a work has a powerful style in terms of wording, syntactic structure or presentation of imagery. Giving full expression to the author's emotions, it creates a powerful artistic impact.

引例 Citations:

◎ 大用外腓(féi),真体内充。返虚入浑,积健为雄。(司空图《二十四诗品·雄浑》)

(大道呈现于外显得雄浑阔大,真实的本体则充满于内。唯有返回虚静,内心才能到达浑然之境;积蓄精神力量,笔力才能雄放豪健。)

The grand appearance is an external manifestation of Dao, while the true vitality permeates itself internally. Reverting to a tranquil void, one may gain fullness and amass inner strength, and he will produce powerful works. (Sikong Tu: Twenty-four Styles of Poetry)

◎大力无敌为雄，元气未分曰浑。（杨廷芝《〈二十四诗品〉浅解》）

（力量刚健而无可匹敌为"雄"，元气浑融而不可区分为"浑"。）

Powerfulness means invincible power and indivisible mass of vital energy. (Yang Tingzhi: *A Shallow Interpretation of Sikong Tu's Twenty-four Styles of Poetry*)

虚静 /xūjìng/
Void and Peace

　　排除一切欲望与理性思维的干扰，达到心灵的纯净与安宁。由道家老庄最先提出，荀子（前313？—前238）也用它说明专心致志所达到的一种精神状态。由于这种心境与文艺审美中无物无我、无知无欲的心理特性相通，因此，古代思想家与文艺批评家也用"虚静"来说明文艺活动中的审美心理。这一术语强调文艺创作中的心灵自由，认为它是达到审美最高境界的重要前提。

Void and peace mean that all distractions, such as desires and rational thoughts, should be dispelled to attain peace and purity of the soul. The idea of void and peace was first proposed by Laozi and Zhuangzi (369?-286 BC), the founders of Daoism, and then used by Xunzi (313?-238 BC) to refer to a state of mental concentration. Such a state of mind is similar to the psychological conditions in appreciation of works of literature and art, which are characterized by being totally free from the awareness of oneself and the outside world, and free from any urge and desire. Therefore, thinkers and literary critics of earlier times used this term to explain the state of mind in literary and artistic creation and appreciation. It stressed the need for spiritual freedom in artistic creation, suggesting that this is an important precondition for reaching the highest level of aesthetic appreciation.

引例 Citations:

◎致虚极，守静笃。(《老子·十六章》)

（达到虚空境界，没有任何杂念；坚守安宁心境，不受外物干扰。）

When one attains the state of void and peace, his mind becomes peaceful and free of any distractions. He can withstand the temptations of the outside world. (*Laozi*)

◎是以陶钧文思，贵在虚静，疏瀹（yuè）五藏（zàng），澡雪精神。(刘勰《文心雕龙·神思》)

（因此构思文章，最重要的是虚静，不受外物干扰，身体舒泰如同五脏贯通了一样，精神洁净如同洗洁过一样。）

In conceiving an essay, one should strive for a mental state of quiet emptiness and not let oneself be bothered by external interferences, and be relaxed and at ease just like all his internal organs are put in perfect comfort and his spirits refreshed by a thorough wash. (Liu Xie: *The Literary Mind and the Carving of Dragons*)

玄览 /xuánlǎn/

Xuanlan (Pure-minded Contemplation)

原指在深远虚净的心境下览知万物，是老子提出的认识"道"的一种方法。老子认为，只有摒弃一切杂念与成见，保持内心明澈如镜，才能静观万物，从而认识"道"，体会其精要。后世文艺评论家因为"玄览"所主张的心境与文艺创作及鉴赏所要求的审美心境相契合，遂用为文艺思想的重要术语，以说明文艺创作与鉴赏时应具有的超越一切欲望与功利的特殊心境。

This term was first used by Laozi as a way to understand Dao. He believed that one cannot understand Dao by calmly observing everything unless one abandons all distracting thoughts and biases, and keeps one's mind as clear as a mirror. Later literary critics believed that the state of mind as required for *xuanlan* has similarities with the state of mind required for literary writing and appreciation, thus they made it an important term to mean one's state of mind must transcend all desires and personal gains in literary writing and appreciation.

引例 Citations：

◎涤除玄览，能无疵乎？(《老子·十章》)

（涤除一切杂念，在深远虚静的心境下观照一切，就没有瑕疵了吗？）

Is it for sure that there will be no flaws when one cleanses away all distracting thoughts and watches the world with a clear, peaceful mind? (*Laozi*)

◎伫中区以玄览，颐情志于典坟。(陆机《文赋》)

（久立于天地间以深远虚静的心境观照一切，在典籍的阅读中颐养性情、培养志向。）

Standing between heaven and earth and watching the world with a clear, peaceful mind, the writer enriches and improves himself through reading great works of the past. (Lu Ji: The Art of Writing)

玄言诗 /xuányánshī/
Metaphysical Poetry

一种以阐发老庄、佛教和《周易》哲理为主要内容的诗歌流派，起于西晋末年而盛行于东晋，其主要特点是以玄理入诗，代表诗人有孙绰（ 314 — 371 ）、许询（ 314 — 361 ）、庾亮（ 289 — 340 ）、桓温（312—373）等。魏晋时期社会动荡，士大夫专心老庄与佛学，贵玄理，尚清谈，以此全身远祸。到西晋后期，玄谈之风逐步影响到诗歌创作，形成玄言诗，后玄言诗与山水诗相融合。

This term refers to a poetic style that chiefly explicated Laozi, Zhuangzi (369?-286 BC), Buddhism, and *The Book of Changes*. Metaphysical poetry emerged at the end of the Western Jin Dynasty and flourished during the subsequent Eastern Jin Dynasty. Represented by Sun Chuo (314-371), Xu Xun (314-361), Yu Liang (289-340), and Huan Wen (312-373), this genre featured the expounding of abstruse and metaphysical thinking in poetry. During the turbulent years of the Wei and Jin dynasties, scholars stayed away from politics and focused on the study of Laozi, Zhuangzi, and Buddhism to explore abstruse and philosophical ideas unrelated to current social developments. By the end of the Western Jin Dynasty, this rarefied discourse found its way into writing, creating the metaphysical style of poetry, which later merged with landscape poetry.

引例 Citation：

◎ 自中朝贵玄，江左称盛，因谈余气，流成文体，是以世极迍邅（zhūnzhān），而辞意夷泰。诗必柱下之旨归，赋乃漆园之义疏。（刘勰《文心雕龙·时序》）

（自从西晋崇尚玄学，到东晋风气更盛，因袭清谈风气，逐渐形成新的文风。因此，虽然时势极其艰难，而文章的辞意却显得平和宽缓。诗歌必定以老庄为宗旨，辞赋也成了老庄的注解。）

In the Western Jin Dynasty, discourse of metaphysics was hot, which became even more popular during the Eastern Jin Dynasty, giving rise to a new literary style. Consequently, despite the tumultuous times, writers composed literary works characterized by detachment and aloofness. Poetry invariably illustrated the ideas of Laozi and Zhuangzi, and prose-poetry became commentaries on these two thinkers. (Liu Xie: *The Literary Mind and the Carving of Dragons*)

选体 /《Xuǎn》tǐ, xuǎntǐ/

Xuanti Poetry / Poetry in Prince Zhaoming's Favorite Style

主要指南朝梁昭明太子萧统（501 — 531）《文选》中所收汉魏以来的五言古诗。但这一概念后来超越了单纯的诗歌体式而兼具时代特征与诗歌风格等含义。在体式上，"选体"是与乐府、歌行、律绝并列的概念，在古人眼光中，它几乎就是五言古诗的代名词，是诗家创作五古的范式；在风格上，"选体"有典雅、翰藻、新创三个主要特征；从时代看，"选体"接续风骚，历跨汉魏、晋宋、齐梁。唐代以后，文论家多用"选体"这一术语来评诗、论诗。但"选体"派强调模仿古人，为此受到后来一些锐意创新的文人的批评。

This refers mainly to the five-character-a-line poems of the Han and Wei dynasties in *Selections of Refined Literature* compiled by Xiao Tong (501 - 531), Crown Prince Zhaoming of the Liang Dynasty during the Southern Dynasties. Later, this term meant not just a specific type of poetry, but also both the prevailing poetic features of an era and general poetic style. Poems of this style were regarded as in the same rank as *yuefu* (乐府) poetry, which were folk songs and ballads collected and compiled by the Han government office in charge of musical preservation, or any poetic imitation equally suitable for musical composition, as well as *gexing* (歌行), which were odes to events or physical objects in free-verse form, and *lüjüe* (律绝), or poetry with fixed patterns. To poetic critics in later generations, *xuanti* (选体) poetry was synonymous with five-character poetry and was a standard way to write poems with five characters per line. In terms of style, it is elegant, richly colorful, and innovative. This type of poetry inherited the poetic tradition all the way from *The Book of Songs* and *Odes of Chu* to the Han and Wei dynasties, the Jin Dynasty, and the Song, Qi, and Liang during the Southern Dynasties. From the Tang Dynasty onward, many literary critics used the term "*xuanti* poetry" as a standard in their comments on poetry. This poetic style was criticized later by some creative-minded poets for its excessive emphasis on following the classical tradition.

引例 Citations：

◎五言诗，三百五篇中间（jiàn）有之，逮汉魏苏、李、曹、刘之作，号为《选》体。（刘克庄《林子显（xiǎn）》）

（五言诗在《诗经》中只是间或出现，到汉魏时期苏武、李陵、曹操、刘桢等人的创作［才得以定形，又因《文选》收录，故而］被称为"《文选》体"。）

Five-character-a-line poems were found occasionally in *The Book of Songs*. By the Han and Wei dynasties, Su Wu, Li Ling, Cao Cao, and Liu Zhen had written more five-character-a-line poems and established the style. These poems were collected in *Selections of Refined Literature* and therefore the style is known as the *xuanti* style. (Liu Kezhuang: Preface to *A Collection of Poems by Lin Zixian*)

◎昭明选古诗，人遂以其所选者为"古诗"，因而名古诗曰"选体"。唐人之古诗曰"唐选"。呜呼！非惟古诗亡，几并古诗之名而亡之矣。（钟惺《诗归·序》）

（昭明太子选古诗，后人于是把他所选的诗称为古诗，因此就称古诗为"选体"。唐代人创作的古诗叫做"唐选"。可惜啊！不仅古诗消亡了，就连"古诗"这一名称也跟着消亡了。）

Prince Zhaoming selected ancient poems, which people of later generations would call "ancient poems." They were also known as *xuanti* poetry or poetry in Prince Zhaoming's favorite style. The works by Tang-dynasty poets were called Tang *xuanti* poetry. But now, alas, ancient poetry has become extinct; even the term itself is sadly forgotten. (Zhong Xing: Preface to *The Purport of Poetic Creation*)

雅俗 /yǎsú/

Highbrow and Lowbrow

　　指文艺作品品味的雅正与通俗、高尚与低俗。是文艺批评中评论作品品味高下的一对范畴。"雅"指作品的品味高雅正统，符合主流的意识形态；"俗"多指流行于大众与民间的世俗审美标准。从文艺创作上说，高雅文艺优美精良，但人工雕琢的痕迹较重；而通俗文艺源自民间，自然清新，质朴粗放。唐以后，不少文人从通俗文艺中汲取养分，通俗文艺逐渐增多，丰富了社会文艺生活，推动了文艺形态的丰富和发展。

Highbrow and lowbrow, a dichotomy in literary criticism, refer to two kinds of literary and artistic works, namely, the refined versus the popular, and the lofty versus the vulgar. Highbrow describes works that are elegant and reflect what conforms with mainstream ideology, whereas lowbrow-art forms tend to meet popular aesthetic standard. From the perspective of art creation, highbrow art may be exquisite, but often appears affected, whereas lowbrow art, which has a folk origin, is natural, refreshing, unaffected, and unconstrained. From the Tang Dynasty onward, it became a trend for men of letters to borrow the best from popular art, thus further spurring the growth of lowbrow art, enriching cultural life and leading to more diversified artistic expressions.

引例 Citations：

◎子曰："恶紫之夺朱也，恶郑声之乱雅乐也，恶利口之覆邦家者。"（《论语·阳货》）

（孔子说："我厌恶用紫色取代红色，厌恶用郑国的音乐扰乱雅正的音乐，憎恶伶牙俐齿而使国家倾覆的人。"）

Confucius said, "I detest replacing red with purple and interfering refined classical music with the music of the State of Zheng. I loathe those who overthrow the state with their glib tongues." (*The Analects*)

◎是以绘事图色，文辞尽情，色糅而犬马殊形，情交而雅俗异势。（刘勰《文心雕龙·定势》）

（因此绘画要讲究色彩，写文章要尽力表现思想感情。调配不同的色彩，所画出的狗和马形状才有区别；思想感情有了交错融合，文章的雅俗才显出不同的体势。）

The art of painting requires masterful use of colors, while the art of writing entails effective expression of thoughts and emotions. One needs to blend different colors in order to depict the different shapes of dogs and horses. Only writings that integrate thoughts and emotions demonstrate their highbrow or lowbrow qualities. (Liu Xie: *The Literary Mind and the Carving of Dragons*)

雅乐 /yǎyuè/
Fine Music

典雅纯正的音乐。是古代帝王祭祀天地、祖先，举行朝贺、宫廷宴享及其他重大庆典活动时所用的音乐。"雅乐"多歌颂朝廷功德，音乐中正平和，歌词典雅纯正，其奏唱、伴舞都有明确的礼仪规范。历代朝廷都将雅乐作为推行教化、感化民风的重要手段。雅乐作为宫廷音乐，有保守的一面，但在实际历史发展中也注意吸收民间歌舞、异域歌舞的成分而不断创新，因而代表着不同时代的音乐最高水准。唐以后雅乐传入日本、韩国、越南等国，成为这些国家的乐舞文化的重要组成部分。

The term refers to a kind of classical music in China. Noble and pure, it was the music used by kings in ancient times when worshipping heaven, earth, and ancestors, receiving congratulations from other quarters of the world, or holding feasts and major ceremonial activities. Chinese classical music often eulogized the royal court's accomplishments; its melodies were tranquil and stately, its wording elegant and tasteful, and its performance of song and dance followed explicit codes of etiquette. Rulers of all dynasties used this kind of music as an effective means to instruct their people and promote civic virtue. As a courtly tradition, the music was necessarily conservative. However, throughout history the assimilation of elements of folk song and dance, as well as the music and dance of foreign lands, inevitably led to innovation. Thus, it maintained throughout the ages the highest levels of musical excellence. After the Tang Dynasty, this kind of music spread to other Asian countries such as Japan, Korea, and Vietnam, becoming a constituent part of their musical culture.

引例 Citations：

◎子曰："恶紫之夺朱也，恶郑声之乱雅乐也，恶利口之覆邦家者也。"（《论语·阳货》）

（孔子说："我厌恶用紫色取代红色，厌恶用郑国的音乐扰乱雅正的音乐，憎恶伶牙俐齿而使国家倾覆的人。"）

Confucius said, "I detest replacing red with purple and interfering refined classical music with the music of the State of Zheng. I loathe those who overthrow the state with their glib tongues." (*The Analects*)

◎是时，河间献王有雅材，亦以为治道非礼乐不成，因献所集雅乐。（《汉书·礼乐志》）

（当时，河间献王有很高的才能，他也认为治国之道如果没有礼乐就不完备，于是就把他所收集的雅乐献给了朝廷。）

At the time, Liu De, Prince Xian of Hejian, was an exceptionally talented man, and he believed that music and ceremony were essential to the proper governing of the state. As a result he donated all the documents of classical music he had collected to the court. (*The History of the Han Dynasty*)

◎荀勖（xù）善解音声，时论谓之闇（ān）解。遂调律吕，正雅乐。
（刘义庆《世说新语·术解》）

（荀勖善于辨音，时人认为他有音乐天赋。于是朝廷让他负责调整音律、校定雅乐。）

Xun Xu had a sensitive ear for musical tones. Some, recognizing his musical gift, recommended him for a position overseeing musical rules and revising classical music. (Liu Yiqing: *A New Account of Tales of the World*)

言之无文，行而不远

/yán zhī wú wén, xíng ér bù yuǎn/

Lackluster Wording Never Travels Far.

语言如果缺乏文采和技巧，就不可能流传广泛久远。孔子（前551—前479）原话的意思是说，在外交场合，使臣须要擅长辞令，讲究语言技巧，才能达成目标、建立功业。进而引申出，一种思想如果想久远传播，就必须借助于有章法、有文采的书面文字。南朝刘勰（465？—520？或532？）在《文心雕龙》中征引了孔子的话，一方面充分肯定文辞的功效，另一方面是为了强调文章形式与技巧的重要性。该语阐明了语文对于明道经世的工具性作用，提升了文艺批评在思想文化史上的地位。

Lackluster writing or speech never travels far. What Confucius (551-479 BC) meant when he said this is that, in foreign relations, a diplomat should be eloquent and persuasive to achieve goals and become meritorious. Likewise, if an idea is to spread far or be remembered for long, it must be put to paper by rules of writing and with beautiful wording. In *The Literary Mind and the Carving of Dragons*, Liu Xie (465?-520? or 532?) of the Southern Dynasties cited these words of Confucius to uphold the importance of diction and to stress the importance of an essay's layout and technique. This term highlights the instrumental role of writing in explaining and being useful to the world, thus raising the status of literary criticism in the history of thought and culture.

◎仲尼曰："志有之：'言以足志，文以足言。'不言，谁知其志？言
之无文，行而不远。"（《左传·襄公二十五年》）

（孔子说："古书上记载：'言语用以表达意愿，文采和技巧是为了实
现表达意愿的功能。'不说话，有谁能知道他的意愿？语言如果缺
乏文采和技巧，就不可能流传广泛久远。"）

Confucius said: "According to ancient sources, 'Language is used to express
wishes, and eloquence and literary skill perform an expressive function.' If he
doesn't speak, who knows how he views anything? Even if he does, lackluster
writing or speech will not travel far." (*Zuo's Commentary on The Spring and
Autumn Annals*)

◎言以文远，诚哉斯验。心术既形，英华乃赡。（刘勰《文心雕龙·情
采》）

（语言要讲究文采和技巧才能流传广泛久远，这的确已经得到了证
验。如果懂得了如何表现情志，就可以自如展现丰富的文采。）

Beautiful wording with literary grace spreads far and wide. This has been
proved sufficiently true. Once we know how to express our feelings and
aspirations, we will be able to display our literary talent with ease. (Liu Xie:
The Literary Mind and the Carving of Dragons)

扬州八怪 /Yángzhōu bāguài/
The Magical Eight Painters of Yangzhou

　　清代康熙（1662—1722）到乾隆（1736—1795）年间，活跃于
扬州一带的八位画家，因其个性独特、画风怪诞，被称为"八怪"。
一般指汪士慎（1686—1762？）、李鱓（shàn，1686—1762）、金农
（1687—1763）、黄慎（1687—1768后）、高翔（1688—1753）、郑

燮（1693—1765）、李方膺（1695—1754）、罗聘（1733—1799）等八人，亦有其他说法。他们多为失意官吏或无功名的文人，借书画表现心中不平，作画不拘成法，反对正统画风，在题画诗、书法、篆刻创作领域锐意创新，成就卓著，被当时人视为"偏师""怪物"，"扬州八怪"由此而得名。他们对近代画家如陈师曾（1876—1923）、齐白石（1864—1957）等产生了很大影响。

These were the eight outstanding artists active in the Yangzhou area during Qing Emperors Kangxi's (1662-1722) and Qianlong's (1736-1795) reigns. They boasted unique personalities and magical styles of painting. Their names are: Wang Shishen (1686-1762?), Li Shan (1686-1762), Jin Nong (1687-1763), Huang Shen (1687-1768?), Gao Xiang (1688-1753), Zheng Xie (1693-1765), Li Fangying (1695-1754) and Luo Pin (1733-1799) (a slightly different list of names also exists). They were mostly officials who had fallen from favor or scholars who had failed to accomplish what they aspired to achieve, and therefore found an outlet for their pent-up anger through painting and calligraphy. Disdaining conventional ways of painting, they created novel styles of their own, breaking new ground in the fields of calligraphy-in-painting, pure calligraphy, and seal cutting. For their unique accomplishments, they were called "wayward geniuses" and "weirdoes" by their contemporaries. Their more honorable title was "The Magical Eight Painters of Yangzhou." They exerted a profound influence on modern period painters such as Qi Baishi (1864-1957) and Chen Shizeng (1876-1923).

引例 Citations：

◎掀天揭地之文，震电惊雷之字，呵神骂鬼之谈，无古无今之画，原不在寻常眼孔中也。（《郑板桥集·乱兰乱竹乱石与汪希林》）

（揭开天地奥秘的文章，如惊雷暴雨一般的文字，呵斥怒骂鬼神的言论，自古及今未曾有过的画作，寻常人眼里原本就看不到的。）

Articles which unravel the mysteries of heaven and earth, writing that triggers thunder and rainstorms, invectives unleashed against evil spirits, and paintings that defy all established rules – all these things are hardly noticed by ordinary people. (*Collected Works of Zheng Banqiao*)

◎所惜同时并举，另出偏师，怪以八名，画非一体。(汪鋆(jūn)《扬州画苑录》卷二)

(可惜的是，他们于同一时期兴起，师法与主流画风不合，虽以"八怪"扬名，但他们的画作并没有形成统一风格。)

It is a pity that the eight men who emerged in the same period, with their styles of painting distinct from the mainstream style of the time, did not have a unified means of expression, despite their renown as "The Magical Eight." (Wang Jun: *Biographies of Painters of Yangzhou*)

养气 /yǎngqì/
Cultivate *Qi*

涵养道德精神、调养身心健康以达到良好的心态，从而创作出优秀的文艺作品。这一术语具有多重蕴涵：其一，先秦孟子(前372？—前289)强调君子应善于培养道德精神的"浩然之气"。其二，东汉王充(27—97？)在《论衡》中有《养气篇》，专门从养生角度提倡"养气"。其三，南朝刘勰(465？—520？或532？)《文心雕龙·养气》，汲取上述思想，主张在从事文艺创作的初始阶段，要保持良好的身体状态和从容自由的心态，不应过度消耗精神。后来"养气"成为文艺心理学的重要术语。

This term suggests cultivating one's moral spirit and improving one's physical and mental well-being to achieve the best state of mind in order to write excellent works. "Cultivating *qi* (气)" has three implications: 1) in the pre-Qin period Mencius (372?-289 BC) emphasized that the virtuous and the capable should foster a "noble spirit" conducive to moral cultivation; 2) *A Comparative Study of Different Schools of Learning* by Wang Chong (27-97?) of the Eastern Han Dynasty has a chapter entitled "Treatise on Cultivating

Qi," which emphasizes *qi* cultivation primarily in regards to maintaining good health; 3) Liu Xie (465?-520? or 532?) of the Southern Dynasties, in *The Literary Mind and the Carving of Dragons*, drew upon the foregoing ideas and suggested maintaining good physical condition and a free, composed mental state in the initial phase of literary creation, while opposing excessive mental exertion. "Cultivating *qi*" subsequently became an important term in the lexicon of literary psychology.

引例 Citations：

◎我知言，我善养吾浩然之气。(《孟子·公孙丑上》)

(我能够察知各种言辞的真意，善于培养自己的刚强正直之气。)

I can perceive the true meaning of various statements, and I am good at self-cultivating righteousness. (*Mencius*)

◎是以吐纳文艺，务在节宣，清和其心，调畅其气；烦而即舍，勿使壅滞。(刘勰《文心雕龙·养气》)

(因此从事写作必须学会节制和疏导，让内心纯净平和，将气调理顺畅，内心烦乱时就应停止，不要让思路滞涩。)

Hence, when engaging in writing one must learn how to constrain and regulate oneself, keep one's mind pure and peaceful, and modulate one's mental vitality and activities. One should stop writing when upset so as not to disrupt one's train of thinking. (Liu Xie: *The Literary Mind and the Carving of Dragons*)

一画 /yīhuà/

All Forms of Painting as Multiplied from a Single Stroke / Oneness in Painting

字面义指绘画用的线条，实际指绘画艺术的根本法则，亦为宇宙一切事物生成发展的普遍法则。由清代画家石涛（1641—1718？）提出，其具体含义今人有不同理解。石涛借鉴老子学说及禅宗的理论（或说取自伏羲从阴阳一画创制八卦，进而创建文明世界），认为宇宙万物都生成于原始的"一"，画家笔下的有形万物，亦由"一"创生并贯之以"一"。在石涛那里，"一"指"无"，绘画就是从"无"创生有形物象的过程；"一"又指"道"，既是绘画之"道"，又是宇宙万物之"道"，两者相通合一；"一"还是蕴含、贯通于各种绘画手法的普遍法则，画家笔下的每一笔、每一根线条都体现着这一普遍法则。"一画论"包含"一"与"道"、与"无"、与"有"、与"多"等多重关系的概括，有着丰富的哲学意蕴和艺术思想。这一术语后来成为中国传统美学思想、画论的重要范畴。

While this literally means "lines employed in painting," it is used to refer to the fundamental rules guiding the art of painting and, furthermore, to the universal laws of the formation and development of everything in the universe. This notion was first put forward by the Qing-dynasty painter Shi Tao (1641 - 1718 ?), though his ideas were controversial among contemporary scholars and artists. Shi, drawing inspiration from Daoist philosophy and Chan theory, and perhaps from Fuxi's use of a single line to symbolize yin and yang as a unitary whole in creating the eight trigrams (eight combinations of three whole or broken lines formerly used in divination), held that all things in the universe derive from a single oneness. All tangible things under a painter's brush, likewise, forever have that oneness at their core. For him, oneness means naught. Painting is thus a process of generating tangible objects from nothing. This is also the ultimate Dao – a combination of the way of painting with that of all things in the universe. As well, oneness is a set of broadly applicable rules present throughout the process of painting.

Each stroke or line reflects these rules. The oneness in painting theory encompasses multiple relationships between oneness on the one hand, and the Dao, nothingness, tangibility, and multiplicity on the other. It is rich in philosophical implication and artistic significance. This term later became an important part of traditional Chinese aesthetic thought and painting theory.

引例 Citations：

◎一画者，众有之本，万象之根，见用于神，藏用于人，而世人不知。（石涛《画语录·一画章》）

（"一画"是一切事物和现象生成发展的根本，用"心"体悟可以观照到它，它就隐藏在人的心中并为人所用，但世人对此并不了解。）

Oneness in painting is the foundation of all things and phenomena in their formation and development. We can perceive it if we are willing to experience it with our soul. It inheres in our souls though we do not quite understand it. (Shi Tao: *On the Principle and Techniques of Painting*)

◎受之于远，得之最近；识之于近，役之于远。一画者，字画下手之浅近功夫也；变画者，用笔用墨之浅近法度也。（石涛《画语录·运腕章》）

（领悟宇宙的普遍法则，须从身边最近的事物入手；在细微浅近的笔画之间，把握宇宙人生之道。"一画"是字画最粗浅的入门功夫；而它的千变万化，也是运笔用墨最基本的法度。）

To feel the universal laws of the nature needs to focus on the things at hand. Capture the essence of life and the universe. Oneness in painting is the most basic skill of painting and calligraphy; its numerous variations are a most basic measure, too, for the execution of brush and ink. (Shi Tao: *On the Principle and Techniques of Painting*)

以形媚道 /yǐxíng-mèidào/

Natural Shapes Adapting to Dao

　　山水以其外在形貌与"道"亲近、契合。南朝画家宗炳（375—443）在《画山水序》中发挥孔子（前551—前479）"仁者乐（yào）山，智者乐水"的思想，认为山水不仅向人类竞相展示了大自然的造化之功，也向人类婉转展示了宇宙天地的变化规律，因而为有德行的人所喜爱。这一术语表现出六朝人的山水审美观念。

Mountains and rivers accord with Dao by way of their shapes. Zong Bing (375‑443), a painter of Song of the Southern Dynasties, in his "On the Creation of Landscape Paintings" expanded on a saying by Confucius (551‑479 BC) – "A virtuous man loves mountains and a wise man loves water." Zong held that mountains and rivers not only displayed their natural splendor to humanity, but also demonstrated the natural law of changes. Therefore, they were loved by men of virtue. This term shows the aesthetic view of people in the period of the Six Dynasties.

引例 Citations：

◎知者乐水，仁者乐山；知者动，仁者静；知者乐，仁者寿。(《论语·雍也》)

（有智慧的人喜爱水，有德行的人喜爱山；有智慧的人好动，有德行的人好静。有智慧的人快乐，有德行的人长寿。）

Confucius said, "A wise man loves water, a virtuous man loves mountains. A wise man is active; a virtuous man stays peaceful in mind. A wise man is happy; a virtuous man enjoys longevity." (*The Analects*)

◎夫圣人以神法道，而贤者通；山水以形媚道，而仁者乐（yào）。不亦几（jī）乎？（宗炳《画山水序》）

（圣人精神上效法道，而德才杰出的人可以通达于道；山水以其自然形质婉转契合道，使仁者对之喜爱。这难道不是很微妙吗？）

Sages follow Dao with their spirit. Men of virtue and talent may comprehend and practice Dao. Mountains and rivers conform to Dao through their natural shapes. That is why they are loved by benevolent people. Isn't this subtle and profound? (Zong Bing: On the Creation of Landscape Paintings)

以形写神 /yǐxíng-xiěshén/
Capture the Spirit Beyond Form

画家通过刻画外形来表现其内在精神。东晋画家顾恺之（345？—409）强调形与神的对应关系，他既重视外形的刻画，同时倡导由外形进而表现对象内在的精神气质，认为表现精神气质是绘画创作的最高要求。同时要求画者捕捉到最能代表对象内在精神的外形特征。这一见解对后世文艺创作影响很大。

Painters depict physical appearances to reveal the essence. Gu Kaizhi (345?-409), a painter of the Eastern Jin Dynasty, lays great emphasis on the correspondence between the essence and physical forms: He depicts the appearance of objects in great detail, which embodies their spiritual disposition. He believes this is the highest requirement of painting. He urges painters to capture those outward features that best reveal the spiritual attributes of the objects depicted. This view has exerted a great influence on later artistic endeavors.

引例 Citation：

◎凡生人，亡（wú）有手揖眼视而前亡所对者。以形写神，而空其实对，荃生之用乖，传神之趋失矣。（顾恺之《魏晋胜流画赞》）

（大凡活人，若面前没有人，他不会无缘无故地对着作揖。绘画是通过形体来表现其内在精神的，如果没有实实在在的对象，那就背离了绘画用来描摹物象的功用，也丧失了用来表现物象内在精神的宗旨。）

A living person will not look ahead and make a bow without any reason, unless there is someone in front of him. Painting shows the essence of something by depicting its physical form and features. Lack of concrete objects can make a painting deviate from its function of portraying images and lose the goal of manifesting an object's innermost spirit. (Gu Kaizhi: In Praise of Renowned Paintings of the Wei and Jin Dynasties)

以意逆志 /yǐyì-nìzhì/
Interpret a Writing from One's Own Perspective

依据自己的理解去解读文学作品中的意思。这说的是正确阅读文学作品的方法，由战国时期思想家孟子（前372？—前289）提出。孟子这个观点是针对如何正确理解《诗经》作品而发，后来被广泛引申为对诗歌乃至其他一切文学作品的阐释方法。这一观点主张，读者在阅读文学作品时，要结合自己的生活经验和思考，去领会、推测作者在作品中所寄寓的情感，从而理解作品的内容和主旨。这一观念发展为中国古代文学批评中的鉴赏理论。

This term describes an appropriate approach to reading literary works by understanding the work from one's own perspective. It was put forth by Mencius (372? - 289 BC), a thinker in the Warring States Period, when he talked about how to correctly understand *The Book of Songs*. Since then, this concept, extended to become hermeneutic, has been applied broadly to poetry and all other literary works. This point of view emphasizes that readers should activate their own personal experiences and reflective thinking when reading literary works so as to grasp or infer the sentiments that authors try to convey through their work, thus becoming able to understand its content and main themes. This viewpoint has evolved into a theory for artistic appreciation in ancient Chinese literary criticism.

◎ 故说诗者，不以文害辞，不以辞害志。以意逆志，是为得之。
（《孟子·万章上》）

（解说诗的人，不拘泥于文字而误解词句，不拘泥于个别词句而误
解作品的完整意思。能以自己的切身体会去推测作者的本意，这才
是懂得读诗的正确方法。）

When reading a poem, one should not be confined by its words as to
misread the lines, nor should one be confined by the lines as to misread its
main meaning. Only by using one's own experiences in getting to know the
intention of the poet can one appropriately appreciate the poem. (*Mencius*)

义法 /yìfǎ/
Yi Fa (Guidelines for Writing Good Prose)

清代方苞（1668 — 1749）提出的关于文章写作的方法，包括文
章的思想内容及形式结构、剪裁取舍等方面的规范要求。源于《春
秋》《史记》等史传文章的结撰方法，"义法"是将这些经典的写作
方法推广为文章写作的典范。"义"指文章的意蕴和事理，重在"言
有物"，即文章的思想内容要充实、有意义；"法"指文章的组织结
构和写作技法，重在"言有序"，即语言得当、有条理次序。"义"
为根本，"法"随"义"而变化，根据"义"的表达需要而选择灵活
多样的写作技法，在叙事之中寓褒贬论断。义法论是清代桐城派古
文理论的起点和基础。

Yi fa refers to the guidelines and criteria for prose writing advocated by Fang
Bao（1668 - 1749）of the Qing Dynasty, which concerns content, structure,
and editing. He held up the structural composition of the historical texts *The
Spring and Autumn Annals* and *Records of the Historian* as examples of fine

prose, and popularized them. *Yi* (义) refers to content and meaningfulness, with an emphasis on substance and logic; *fa* (法) refers to structure and writing techniques, with an emphasis on appropriate language and sequence. *Yi* is primary and *fa* adjusts accordingly to express the content in a flexible and varied way, so as to ensure that the author's opinion is clearly stated and the argument is powerful. The concept of *yi fa* is the cornerstone for the prose-writing theory of the Tongcheng School of the Qing Dynasty.

引例 Citations：

◎孔子明王道，干（gān）七十余君，莫能用，故西观周室，论史记旧闻，兴于鲁而次《春秋》。上记隐，下至哀之获麟，约其辞文，去其烦重（chóng），以制义法。(《史记·十二诸侯年表》)

（孔子懂得以仁政治理天下，他用王道学说拜谒了七十多个君主，但都不被采用。因此，他西行去观览周王室的典藏，详列、评论历史记载及过去的传闻，按鲁国历史顺序编成《春秋》。上起鲁隐公元年，下至鲁哀公捕获麒麟之年，简省《春秋》的文辞，删除其中繁琐重复的记载，以此制定了史书编撰的义理和规范。）

Confucius understood the need to rule with benevolence, and took this message to over seventy different rulers, but no one heeded him. So he went westward to the Court of Zhou to consult its archives. There he carefully went through the documents and compiled the historical accounts and ancient stories of the State of Lu into *The Spring and Autumn Annals* in chronological order. He started from the first year of the reign of Duke Yin of Lu, and finished with the year in which Duke Ai of Lu caught a *qilin*, a legendary animal. He condensed the texts, eliminated repetitions and redundancies, and thus laid out the guidelines for writing historical annals. (*Records of the Historian*)

◎《春秋》之制义法，自太史公发之，而后之深于文者亦具焉。义即《易》之所谓"言有物"也，法即《易》之所谓"言有序"也。义以为经而法纬之，然后为成体之文。（方苞《又书〈货殖传〉后》）

（《春秋》所制定的义理和规范，自从司马迁加以阐发以来，后代擅长写文章的人也都具备了"义法"。"义"就是《周易》所说的"文章或言论得有内容","法"就是《周易》所说的"文章或言论得有条理和次序"。以内容为经，以条理和次序为纬，然后就能写出体式完整的文章。)

The example set by *The Spring and Autumn Annals* was later commented on by Sima Qian, and since then, all who wrote good prose have followed these guidelines. *Yi* is described in *The Book of Changes* as "texts and speech should be meaningful," and *fa*, "texts and speeches should be logical and orderly." These are like woof and web, and only then can a good text be written. (Fang Bao: On Rereading "Profit from Trade" in *Records of the Historian*)

艺术 /yìshù/

Art

原指儒家六艺及各种方术，后引申指艺术创作与审美活动。儒家的"六艺"指礼、乐、射、御、书、数等六种用以培养君子人格的教育内容，包括后世意义上的艺术；有时也指《诗》《书》《礼》《乐》《易》《春秋》六部经书。庄子（前369？—前286）则强调技与艺相通，是一种体悟道的融身心为一体的创作活动。儒家、道家与佛教关于艺术的思想，是中国艺术的内在精神与方法。中国艺术追求艺术与人生的统一、感知与体验的结合、技艺与人格的融会等，以意境为旨归。近代西方艺术学传入中国后，艺术成为人类主观精神与物态化作品相结合的技艺与创作，成为专门的学科，涵盖各类艺术。现在的艺术概念是传统艺术内涵与现代西方艺术学的有机融合。

Originally, the term referred to six forms of classical arts and various crafts, but it later extended to include artistic creation and aesthetic appreciation.

The six forms of arts as defined by Confucianism are rituals, music, archery, charioteering, writing and mathematics. These constituted the basic requirements for cultivating a man of virtue. These six arts also included what later generations deemed as arts. Sometimes, the term also meant the six classics, namely, *The Book of Songs*, *The Book of History*, *The Book of Rites*, *The Book of Music*, *The Book of Changes*, and *The Spring and Autumn Annals*. Zhuangzi (369 ?- 286 BC), on his part, emphasized the connection between crafts and arts, regarding them as physical and mental creative activities that help one gain insight into Dao. The various ideas about arts put forward by Confucian, Daoist, and Buddhist scholars defined the nature and method of Chinese arts, which seek unity between artwork and real life, fusion of senses and experiences, and integration of techniques and personality, with achieving artistic conception as the ultimate aim. Since the introduction of Western art theories in modern China, arts have become an independent discipline covering all types of arts created with skill and innovation. The concept of arts today incorporate both traditional Chinese and contemporary Western notions of arts.

引例 Citations：

◎子曰："志于道，据于德，依于仁，游于艺。"（《论语·述而》）

（孔子说："有志于行道，执守于美德，依从于仁义，游学于礼、乐、射、御、书、数六艺之间。"）

Confucius said, "One should follow Dao, adhere to virtues, embrace benevolence, and pursue freely the six arts of rituals, music, archery, charioteering, writing, and mathematics." (*The Analects*)

◎ "蓺（yì）"谓书、数、射、御，"术"谓医、方、卜、筮。（《后汉书·伏湛传》李贤注）

（"艺"指的是六书、算术、射击、驾驶车马等基本技能，"术"指的是医术、方技、卜卦、占筮等专门之学。）

Arts refer to such basic skills as writing, mathematics, archery, and charioteering. Crafts refer to such professions as medicine, fortune-telling, divination, and necromancy. (*The History of the Later Han Dynasty*)

◎艺术之兴，由来尚矣。先王以是决犹豫，定吉凶，审存亡，省祸福。(《晋书·艺术传序》)

（方术的兴起，有着久远的历史。古时的帝王通过方术来决断犹疑，判定吉凶，审度存亡，省察祸福。）

Fortune-telling has a long history. In ancient times, kings used fortune-telling to make decisions, weigh consequences, foresee fate, and judge outcomes. (*The History of the Jin Dynasty*)

议对 /yìduì/
Commentary and Proposal

　　古代文体名称，用于臣下向帝王讨论政事、提出意见或对策。"议"用于臣下与皇帝讨论、分析政事，陈述不同意见和建议；"对"主要指对策，用于回答皇帝所提的问题。《文心雕龙·议对》将二者放在同一篇讨论，实际涵盖了所有的政论文体。南朝刘勰（465？—520？或532？）认为政论文写作的关键在于：全面掌握古今典章政制和重要事例，发现和提出有意义的问题，客观、合理分析问题，提出可行观点或对策，不能不顾事实而徒然表现文辞。刘勰以政论文的实际内容和效果为本，首先强调作者的见识、才能、态度，推崇那些既懂行又善辩、能够平息争议解决复杂问题的通才。刘勰的上述见解对于今天的政论文、学术论文及其他议论文写作都具有指导作用。

In ancient times, commentaries and proposals were submitted by officials to emperors to discuss state affairs and offer solutions. The term *yi* (议 commentary) refers to an official discussion and analysis of state affairs with the emperor to air one's views, often different from that held by the emperor and other officials, and propose solutions. The term *dui* (对 proposal) refers to the act of proposing strategies and answering the emperor's questions. These two terms are discussed together in the "Commentary and Proposal" section of *The Literary Mind and the Carving of Dragons*. The general term "commentary and proposal" encompasses all types of official writing. According to Liu Xie (465?-520? or 532?) of the Southern Dynasties, to produce a good piece of official writing, one should have a good knowledge of ancient and current institutions as well as codes of law and major examples, identify problems, objectively and logically analyze them, and propose feasible solutions. Such writing should not be pompous in style or ignore facts. Liu Xie stressed that commentaries and proposals should be based on solid facts and result-oriented and that one who wrote them should have vision and talent. He admired those who were knowledgeable and persuasive and could solve difficult problems. His views on writing official documents are still of value today when it comes to writing government documents, academic papers and commentaries.

引例 Citations：

◎ "周爰谘谋"，是谓为议。议之言宜，审事宜也。(刘勰《文心雕龙·议对》)

(《诗经》说"多方咨询商讨"，这就是所谓"议"。"议"的意思是适宜，研究事情怎样做才算合宜。)

It is mentioned in *The Book of Songs* that "discussions are carried out by many different parties." Such activities, also known as "commentaries" (*yi*), should aim to handle matters properly. (Liu Xie: *The Literary Mind and the Carving of Dragons*)

◎ 文以辨洁为能，不以繁缛为巧；事以明核为美，不以深隐为奇：此纲领之大要也。(刘勰《文心雕龙·议对》)

(语言运用以简洁明了为能事，不以繁富华丽为技巧；事理分析以明晰可靠为美妙，不以深奥隐晦为新奇：这就是议论文写作的基本要领了。)

A piece of writing which is concise and clear, not pompous and oblique is to be commended. An analysis of an issue, to be deemed admirable and illuminating, should be made in a clear and reliable way, and it should not be ambiguous and abstruse. This is a key requirement for writing a commentary. (Liu Xie: *The Literary Mind and the Carving of Dragons*)

意不称物，文不逮意
/yì bù chèn wù, wén bù dài yì/

Ideas Cannot Match Actual Things and Words Cannot Fully Express Ideas.

人的心意或文章的构意不能完全反映事物的情状，而文章的语言或文辞又无法完全表达内心的想法。这是西晋陆机（261—303）《文赋》中对创作心理的描述和分析，具体所指是：由外物激发的意念或创作想法丰富而不明确，作者难以完全把握由外物所激发的全部心意，所捕捉到的可能只是其中一部分；而语言又难以将它们完全表达出来，更不可能穷尽由外物激发或与外物关联的全部意蕴。在认识及实践领域，主体对外物产生明确的认识或意愿，语言能够比较明确地记录认识并表达意愿，而文学创作则常常存在词不达意、言不尽意的难题。这也表明文学阐释较之学术经典解释具有更大的空间。陆机揭示了文学创作与接受的特征，推动了文学自觉。

This happens when inner thoughts or a written text's general idea cannot fully reflect the actual state of things, and when diction cannot fully express inner thoughts. It is a description and analysis of the psychology of writing by Lu Ji (261-303) of the Western Jin Dynasty in his literary theoretic work, "The Art of Writing." Specifically, inner thoughts or creative ideas triggered by external things can be diverse yet ambiguous and the author grasps only some of these.

Language, too, has difficulty in expressing them fully, not to mention all the implications triggered by or related to external things. In the domain of everyday human cognition and practice, language can, by and large, clearly record the subject's thoughts and express his wishes with regard to external things. But in literary creation, words often fail to do so. This also explains why literary interpretation enjoys greater latitude than purely academic interpretation. Lu Ji revealed this essential characteristic of literary creation and reception, thus promoting the development of literature under its own standards.

引例 Citation：

◎恒患意不称物，文不逮意，盖非知之难，能之难也。（陆机《文赋》）

（自己经常苦于人的心意或文章构意不能完全反映事物的情状，而语言或文章的文辞又无法完全表达内心的想法。大概这个问题，认识它并不难，解决它却很难。）

Inner thoughts or an article's general idea cannot fully reflect the actual state of things, and diction cannot fully express inner thoughts – a predicament I often find myself in. It is far easier to recognize this problem than solve it. (Lu Ji: The Art of Writing)

意境 /yìjìng/

Aesthetic Conception

指文艺作品所描绘的景象与所表现的思想情感高度融合而形成的审美境界。"境"本指疆界、边界，汉末魏晋时期佛教传入中国，认为现实世界皆为空幻，唯有心灵感知才是真实的存在，"境"被认为是人的心灵感知所能达到的界域。作为文艺术语，"境"有多重含义。"意境"由唐代著名诗人王昌龄（？—756？）提出，侧重指文艺作品中主观感知到的物象与精神蕴涵相统一所达到的审美高度，其特点是"取意造境""思与境偕"。相对于"意象"，"意境"更突出文艺作品的精神蕴涵与美感的高级形态，它拓展了作品情与景、虚与实、心与物等概念的应用，提升了文艺作品及审美活动的层次。后经过历代丰富发展，"意境"成为评价文艺作品水准的重要概念，是历代经典作品层累的结果，也是优秀文艺作品必须具备的重要特征。"意境"这一术语也是外来思想文化与中华本土思想融合的典范。

The term refers to a state where the scene described in a literary or artistic work reflects the sense and sensibility intended. *Jing* (境) originally meant perimeter or boundary. With the introduction of Buddhism into China during the late Han, Wei and Jin dynasties, the idea gained popularity that the physical world was but an illusion, and that only the mind was real in existence. So *jing* came to be seen as a realm that could be attained by having sensibilities of the mind. As a literary and artistic term, *jing* has several meanings. The term *yijing* (意境) was originally put forward by renowned Tang poet Wang Changling (?-756?). It describes an intense aesthetic experience in which one's perception of an object reaches a realm of perfect union with the implication denoted by the object. Aesthetic appreciation in the mind is characterized by "projecting meaning into a scene" and "blending sentiment with scenery." In contrast with the term *yixiang* (意象 image), *yijing* fully reveals the implication and the heightened aesthetic sense that an artistic work is intended to deliver. The concept is extended to include other notions such as sentiment and scene, actual and implied meanings, or mind and object. It also raises literary and artistic works to a new realm of aesthetic appreciation. After evolving through several dynasties, this concept developed into an important criterion to judge the quality of a literary or artistic work, representing an accomplishment drawing on classical writings through ages. It has also become a hallmark for all outstanding literary and artistic works. The term also represents a perfect union between foreign thoughts and culture and those typically Chinese.

引例 Citations：

◎诗有三境：一曰物境，二曰情境，三曰意境。物境一：欲为山水诗，则张泉石云峰之境，极丽绝秀者，神之于心，处身于境，视境于心，莹然掌中，然后用思，了然境象，故得形似。情境二：娱乐愁怨，皆张于意而处于身，然后驰思，深得其情。意境三：亦张之于意而思之于心，则得其真矣。（王昌龄《诗格·诗有三境》）

（诗歌有三种境：一是物境，二是情境，三是意境。第一，物境：想作山水诗，就要尽所能扩大你对泉石、高耸入云的山峰的观察，将其中极秀丽的景色及神韵印之于心，置身其间，再于内心审视所得到的物境，直至如同在手掌上观察一样真切，然后进行构思，对所要描绘的具体物象了然于心，所以能得形似。第二，情境：欢乐、悲愁、哀怨等情绪，都要尽量扩大你对它们的认识，切身感受，然后构思，就能将这些情感深刻地表现出来。第三，意境：也同样需要扩大你对它的认识，在内心反复思索，然后就能得到意境的本真。）

A poem accomplishes aesthetic conception in three ways. The first is through objects, the second is through sentiments, and the third is through an imagined scene. 1) Through objects: If you want to write poems about landscape, you need to observe intensely springs and creeks, rocks and towering peaks, imprint their extraordinary beauty and charm on your memory, put yourself in the scene created in your mind, and view in your mind's eye the image you obtain until you can see it as vividly as if it were right on your palm. By then, you can start to think about writing the poem. A deep appreciation of the scene and its objects is instrumental in achieving a true poetic image. 2) Through sentiments: Sentiments such as happiness, pleasure, sorrow, and anger should be allowed to develop in your mind. You should experience them personally to fully grasp the nature of these emotions. This will enable you to express them in a profound way. 3) Through an imagined scene: This requires you to reach aesthetic appreciation by reflecting it in your mind time and again. Then you can capture the genuine nature of an idea. (Wang Changling: *Rules of Poetry*)

◎作诗之妙，全在意境融彻，出音声之外，乃得真味。（朱承爵《存余堂诗话》）

（作诗的妙处，全在于意境的浑融相通，超出声音之上，才能品味诗歌的本真韵味。）

A beautifully composed poem is one in which the blending of image and concept is such that it transcends that of sound and music. Only then can one savor the real charm of poetry. (Zhu Chengjue: *Commentaries on Poetry from Cunyutang Study*)

◎盖诗之格调有尽，吾人之意境日出而不穷。（周炳曾《〈道援堂诗集〉序》）

（大概是诗的体制、声律是有限的，而我们这些诗人的意境却每天有新创，无穷无尽。）

Poems might have limited verse forms and rhythmic patterns, but we poets are capable of creating fresh ideas every day, all the time. (Zhou Bingzeng: Preface to *Collection of Poems from Daoyuantang Study*)

意象 /yìxiàng/
Yixiang (Imagery)

文学作品中表达作者主观情感和独特意境的典型物象。"意"指作者的思想情感；"象"是外在的具体物象，是寄寓了作者思想情感的艺术形象。在文学创作中，"意象"多指取自大自然中能够寄托情思的物象。"意象"强调文学作品的思想内容与形象之美的和谐生成，是一种成熟的文艺形态。

Imagery refers to a typical image in literary works, which embodies the author's subjective feelings and unique artistic conceptions. *Yi* (意) literally means an author's feelings and thoughts, and *xiang* (象) refers to the image of a material object in the external world, an artistic image reflecting the author's thoughts and feelings. In literary creation, imagery often refers to those images in nature with which an author's feelings and thoughts are associated. Emphasizing the harmonious relationship between beauty in both form and content, it is a mature state of literary creation.

引例 Citations：

◎窥意象而运斤。（刘勰《文心雕龙·神思》）

（探寻心中的意象而构思运笔。）

An author explores the imagery in his mind, conceives a work, and writes it down. (Liu Xie: *The Literary Mind and the Carving of Dragons*)

◎意象欲出，造化已奇。（司空图《二十四诗品·缜密》）

（诗歌的意象浑欲浮现，大自然是这般奇妙。）

What a wonderful state of nature it is when the imagery of a poem is about to emerge! (Sikong Tu: Twenty-four Styles of Poetry)

意兴 /yìxìng/

Inspirational Appreciation

"兴"中所蕴含的意或者"兴"发时心物交会所产生的意（意义、趣味等）。是作者通过对景物感受到某种意趣、意味等之后直接创作出富有一定含义的艺术形象。这一术语主张作者将思想情感自然而然地融入对于描写对象的感受之中，并通过艺术形象和审美情趣传达出来，从而激发读者的联想，产生更丰富的领悟。

The term refers to the meaning implicit in an inspiration, or meaning and charm generated when poetic emotion encounters an external object or scene. It is an artistic image an author creates when appreciating the beauty and charm intrinsic in an object or scene. According to this term, an author should incorporate his sentiments and thoughts into the object or scene depicted to convey them through artistic images and aesthetic appreciation. This will spark the reader's imagination and thus enable him to gain a deeper appreciation of a poem.

引例 Citations：

◎凡诗，物色兼意下为好。若有物色，无意兴，虽巧亦无处用之。（王昌龄《诗格·论文意》）

（但凡诗歌，景物描写、意义与趣味兼备最好。如果只注重景物描写，缺少意兴，描写技巧再高超也用处不大。）

A good poem instills meaning and inspiration in its description of scenery and imagery. If a poem only describes scenery and fails to inspire people, no matter how eloquent the description may be, it will have little appeal. (Wang Changling: *Rules of Poetry*)

◎南朝人尚词而病于理，本朝人尚理而病于意兴，唐人尚意兴而理在其中，汉魏之诗，词、理、意兴无迹可求。（严羽《沧浪诗话·诗评》）

（南朝诗人追求辞藻而说理不足；本朝诗人崇尚说理，作品缺乏意兴；唐代诗人注重意兴同时蕴含道理；汉魏诗歌的文辞、道理和意兴自然融合在一起而不露痕迹。）

Poets of the Southern Dynasties were good at using rhetoric but weak in logic. The poets of our Song Dynasty champion logic but are weak in creating inspirational ideas. Poets of the Tang Dynasty gave equal weight to both meaning and inspiration, with logic implicit in both. The poems of the Han and Wei dynasties blended the choice of words, logic, and the inspiration imperceptibly. (Yan Yu: *Canglang's Criticism on Poetry*)

因革 /yīngé/

Inheritance and Innovation

　　既有所继承又有所创革。"因"是继承、沿袭，"革"是革新、改变。这一思想可溯源到孔子（前551—前479）。在孔子看来，夏商周三代礼制都是在前代基础上根据当时的历史条件有所损益的。所谓"损益"就蕴含了因革的观念。汉代扬雄（前53—公元18）对"因革"作了比较系统的阐发。这一思想后来被南朝刘勰（465？—520？或532？）用于文论，进而衍生出"通变"概念。"因革""通变"体现的都是继承与创新的对立统一，强调基于历史与传统的变化，在继承前人经验、成果的基础上进行创新，既不是泥古不化，也不是追新逐异。不仅是文艺创作，其他如学术发展乃至国家治理，皆同此理。

This term highlights the relationship between inheritance and innovation. *Yin* (因) implies inheritance or adoption, whereas *ge* (革) means reform or innovation. The whole notion can be traced back to Confucius (551-479 BC). In his view, the Xia, Shang and Zhou dynasties had all modified their respective codes of etiquette in accordance with their own circumstances and on the basis of a previous era's established rules. "Modified" here implies the idea of innovation grounded in inheritance. Yang Xiong (53 BC-AD 18) of the Han Dynasty expounded this idea more systematically. This concept was later used by Liu Xie (465?-520? or 532?) of the Southern Dynasties in literary criticism, giving rise to the notion of "continuity and change." All these ideas reflect a unity of opposites, stressing constant change in history and tradition, favoring innovation grounded in past experience and achievements, as well as avoiding either unquestioning adherence to convention or blind pursuit of novelty. Besides literary and artistic creation, the concept above is also applicable to academic research and even the governance of a country.

引例 Citations：

◎子曰："殷因于夏礼，所损益，可知也；周因于殷礼，所损益，可

知也。其或继周者，虽百世可知也。"（《论语·为政》）

（孔子说："殷商沿袭夏朝的礼仪制度，所废除或所增加的，是可以知道的；周朝沿袭殷商的礼仪制度，所废除或所增加的，也是可以知道的。那么，假定有继承周朝而当政的人，就是以后一百代，也是可以预先知道的。"）

Confucius said: "The Shang Dynasty inherited the Xia Dynasty's codes of etiquette with abridgements and additions, which can be known. The Zhou Dynasty followed the Shang's codes of etiquette with abridgements and additions, which can also be known. Therefore, if there should be a successor to the Zhou Dynasty, even a hundred generations from now, its codes of etiquette could be foretold." (*The Analects*)

◎夫道有因有循，有革有化。因而循之，与道神之；革而化之，与时宜之。故因而能革，天道乃得；革而能因，天道乃驯。……故知因而不知革，物失其则；知革而不知因，物失其均。（扬雄《太玄·玄莹》）

（道的运行法则既有继承又有变革。只有懂得继承，才能穷尽道的神奇；只有懂得变革，才能与当世合宜。所以懂得有继承又有变革，才能领悟道的运行法则；懂得有变革又有继承，道的运行法则才能为人所用。……所以只懂得继承不懂得变革，就不能深刻把握万物的普遍法则；只懂得变革不懂得继承，就不能深刻把握万物之间的平衡规律。）

The operation of Dao involves inheritance and continuity, and innovation and change. Only through inheritance and continuity can we fully explore the mystery of Dao. Only through innovation and change can we meet the needs of our times. Thus, respecting tradition while pursuing innovation helps us understand the laws of Dao, and pursuing innovation while respecting tradition helps us apply the laws of Dao... Therefore, if we overemphasize tradition to the neglect of innovation, we will fail to fully understand universal laws; if we focus on innovation at the expense of tradition, we will fail to master the rules of equilibrium. (Yang Xiong: *Supreme Mystery*)

◎古来辞人，异代接武，莫不参（sān）伍以相变，因革以为功。物色尽而情有余者，晓会通也。（刘勰《文心雕龙·物色》）

（自古以来的文人作家，历代前后相继，无不靠着错综变化、有继承又有革新而收到成效。景物有穷尽而情思写不尽，就是因为他们懂得融会和变通。）

Ever since ancient times, writers from generation to generation have made remarkable achievements, through inheritance, change, and innovation, in accordance with circumstances. Scenes have limits, but human feelings linger on due to our ability to integrate and accommodate. (Liu Xie: *The Literary Mind and the Carving of Dragons*)

音 /yīn/

Musical Sounds

指音乐，是由心中情感触动而发出的有节奏和韵律的声音。古人常以"音"与"声"相对：凡自然物所发声音叫做"声"，由人的内心情感触动而发出的声音叫做"音"；单一的声响叫做"声"，不同"声"的比配叫做"音"，不同的"音"组成有节奏的曲调叫做"乐"。古人认为，"音"发自人的内心，一国或一个地区的音乐往往反映该国或地区的民心民意和世风世情，由此儒家提出了文艺反映政治得失及具有社会教化功能的理论主张。

Musical sounds, or simply music, are artistically rhythmical sounds flowing forth from one's stirring emotions. Ancient Chinese often made a distinction between musical sounds and plain sounds. Sounds created by a natural environment are plain sounds, while those created when emotions well up in one's heart is music. A single sound is called *sheng* (声), different sounds that come together are called *yin* (音); when these sounds beautifully fit together, they are called music (*yue* 乐). Ancient Chinese believed that musical sounds derive from one's inner motions, and that the music of a country or a region reflects the popular sentiments and the social mores there. Hence Confucian scholars believed that art and literature demonstrate both virtues and flaws in a country's governance and therefore play the role of moral education.

引例 Citations：

◎凡音者，生人心者也。情动于中，故形于声，声成文，谓之音。
(《礼记·乐记》)

（大凡音乐都产生于人的内心。情感在心中激荡，所以表现为各种声音。声音组合成曲调，就叫做音乐。）

All music is born in people's minds. As people's inner emotions surge, they turn into sound. When sound is formed into a pattern, music is created. (*The Book of Rites*)

◎音，声也。生于心，有节于外，谓之音。(许慎《说文解字·音部》)
（音是声音的一种。产生于内心，有节奏地表现出来后，叫做音乐。）

Music is a particular kind of sounds. What flows forth from the heart in a rhythmical pattern is music. (Xu Shen: *Explanation of Script and Elucidation of Characters*)

隐显 /yǐnxiǎn/
Concealment and Revelation

　　"隐"指隐讳含藏，"显"指鲜明显扬。作为文艺术语，它们指诗文创作过程中，有些事理须要隐讳含藏，有些事理须要鲜明显扬，体现在语义和文辞上，则或含蓄或显豁，理想的艺术境界是隐显有度。文辞含蓄，语义隐讳，并不是晦涩难懂，而是耐人寻味；

文辞明白，语义显豁，也不是直白外露，而是明确清楚。从普遍意义来讲，"隐"与"显"并不是非此即彼的对立关系，而是可以互相转变流动的辩证关系，其间体现"道"的变化。

"Concealment" refers to keeping things hidden, whereas "revelation" means making things abundantly clear. As an artistic and literary term, this pair of opposites refers to a creative process in which some things need to be hidden and others abundantly clear. When applied to semantics or rhetoric, it refers to subtle or explicit modes of expression. An ideal work of art is marked by a proper balance between concealment and revelation. Understatement or hidden meaning does not mean being cryptic, but rather being profound in significance. On the other hand, plainness of wording or conspicuousness of meaning does not mean sheer transparency, but rather clarity. Generally speaking, concealment and revelation are not mutually exclusive. They are instead interchangeable and feature two-way dialectic mobility, revealing Dao in constant change.

引例 Citations：

◎四象精义以曲隐，五例微辞以婉晦，此隐义以藏用也。故知繁略殊形，隐显异术，抑引随时，变通适会，征之周孔，则文有师矣。（刘勰《文心雕龙·征圣》）

（《周易》中的四种卦象，其道理精深而曲折隐晦，《春秋》中的五种记事条例，其文辞细微而婉转含蓄，这是用含蓄隐微的意义来暗含文章作用的例子。因此可知繁和简有不同的面貌，隐与显有不同的表达方法，或压缩或加以发挥要根据当时的要求，写作上的变化要适应不同的情况，用周公、孔子的言论来检验，那么写文章就有了师法了。）

In *The Book of Changes*, there is mention of four divinatory symbols which are of profound and intricate meanings. Recorded in *The Spring and Autumn Annals* are five essential requirements of writing, which are themselves artful and subtle. Both of these examples illustrate the function of a piece of writing by resorting to the subtle nuances of meaning. Thus, it can be seen that simplicity and complexity have different outward features, and concealment and revelation have different modes of expression. Authors should curtail or expand the contents of their writing depending on circumstances, adapting to a variety of situations. Good writing is achievable by testing it against the teachings of the Duke of Zhou and Confucius. (Liu Xie: *The Literary Mind and the Carving of Dragons*)

◎窃惟《中庸》一篇，圣贤之渊源也，体用隐显，成己成物备矣。（张栻(shì)《跋〈中庸集解〉》）

（我个人认为《中庸》这一篇文章，是圣贤思想的本源，它的本体、作用或含蓄或显扬，成就自己、成就外物的方法都齐备了。）

I personally believe that the essay titled "The Doctrine of the Mean" is the source of sagely thought. It conceals or reveals its essence and functions in accord with circumstances, resulting in accomplishment for self and other. (Zhang Shi: Postscript to *Collected Explanations of and Commentaries on The Doctrine of the Mean*)

隐秀 /yǐnxiù/

Latent Sentiment and Evident Beauty

诗歌与文章既隐含丰富的思想感情，又有秀美的名言佳句。出自《文心雕龙》篇名。"隐"是隐含，指在叙事或写景中隐含超出事、景之外的意义，能引发读者的无限联想；"秀"是秀美，指一篇之中应该有能凸显这一意义的精妙词句。二者密不可分，共同构成优秀文学作品的审美特征。后来也作为诗文写作的一种修辞手法。

This term means that prose and poetry may contain latent sentiments and thoughts, as well as expressions and sentences that present an apparent sense of beauty. "Latent sentiment and evident beauty" first appeared as the title of a chapter in *The Literary Mind and the Carving of Dragons*. There, "latent sentiment" means what lies beyond events and landscapes in a narrative or a description, triggering imaginations on the part of the reader. On the other hand, "evident beauty" refers to the kind of beauty created by expressions and sentences in a piece of writing, which bring out that latent meaning. The latent and the apparent qualities are inseparable, constituting an aesthetic feature of good literary works. Later, this term developed into a rhetorical device in writing prose and poetry.

引例 Citations:

◎是以文之英蕤，有秀有隐。隐也者，文外之重旨者也；秀也者，篇中之独拔者也。（刘勰《文心雕龙·隐秀》）

（因此优秀的文章要兼具"秀"和"隐"。所谓"隐"，就是指文章在语言之外隐含有多重意蕴；所谓"秀"，则是有既彰显主旨又独到突出的秀美词句。）

Thus, an excellent piece of writing should have both beautiful in language and a message hidden between the lines. The former refers to beautiful sentences and expressions that accentuate the message of the writing while the latter represents the multiple significance that lies beyond the text. (Liu Xie: *The Literary Mind and the Carving of Dragons*)

◎情在词外曰隐，状溢目前曰秀。（张戒《岁寒堂诗话》卷上引刘勰语）

（思想感情隐含于语言背后叫做"隐"，寄寓思想感情的景象鲜活地展现在读者眼前叫做"秀"。）

Latency happens when feelings and thoughts are hidden between the lines of a literary work. Evident beauty occurs when messages of sentiment and feelings are vividly portrayed by the images the author creates. (Zhang Jie: *Notes on Poetry Written in the Pine and Cypress Studio*)

隐逸诗 /yǐnyìshī/

Recluse Poetry

指归隐山林、田园的文人，以山林、田园生活为创作题材并寄寓个人志趣情怀的诗歌。古代有些文人，因不屑于做官或对当时的社会政治不满，转而归隐山林、田园，成为隐士。他们常常借描摹山水、田园等自然景物来表达高蹈遗世的精神旨趣。其中，陶渊明（365或372或376—427）被称为"古今隐逸诗人之宗"。唐宋以后，很多文人士大夫从陶渊明的生活方式中受到启发，在山林、田园生活中寻求心灵安顿，于是产生了有隐逸倾向的诗歌作品。

Recluse poetry refers to poems written by literary figures who retreated to the remote mountains or countryside and expressed their sentiments through depicting this kind of life. Some Chinese scholars in the old days, having disdain for taking official position or were dissatisfied with political reality of the day, chose to live in seclusion in mountains and forests or in the countryside. They expressed their pursuit of a state of mind that transcended the worldly through depicting images of mountains, rivers, and other natural scenes. Tao Yuanming (365 or 372 or 376 - 427) is regarded as the forerunner of this genre. Inspired by his recluse lifestyle, many learned men in the post-Tang and Song period also sought solace and peace of mind in the mountains and countryside, thus giving rise to recluse poetry.

引例 Citation：

◎其源出于应璩（qú），又协左思风力。文体省净，殆无长（zhàng）语。笃意真古，辞兴婉惬。每观其文，想其人德……古今隐逸诗人之宗也。（钟嵘《诗品》卷中）

（［陶诗］源于应璩，又兼有左思的风骨。陶诗简洁纯净，基本没有什么多余的词句。诗人致力于传达真淳古朴的观念，文词用兴寄手法而委婉恰切。每每读到他的诗文，都会想起他的形貌和品德……真是古今隐逸诗人中的第一人啊！）

While inspired by Ying Qu's work, Tao Yuanming's poems also inherited Zuo Si's powerful expression. His style is simple and lucid, and there are no redundant words in his poems. He devoted himself to expressing simple and unsophisticated ideas by means of association in mild, appropriate language. When we read his works, we see in them a man with noble character... He was truly the most distinguished of the recluse poets ever produced! (Zhong Rong: *The Critique of Poetry*)

永明体 /Yǒngmíng tǐ/
The Yongming Poetic Style

南朝齐武帝永明年间（483—493）出现的、以讲求声韵对偶为主要特征的诗歌风格。也称"新体诗"（与汉魏以来的"古体诗"相对而言）。代表人物是谢朓（tiǎo，464—499）、沈约（441—513）和王融（467—493）。"永明体"标志着诗人已经熟练掌握声韵对偶的规律并自觉运用于诗歌创作，增加了诗歌的形式美感与艺术表现力，为近体诗的产生奠定了基础。不足的是，"永明体"过于受声韵拘束，内容有所削弱,受到当时一些诗论家的批评，在新变中也蕴藏了危机。

Poems of this style first emerged during the reign of Emperor Wu of Qi of the Southern Dynasties. That period, lasting from 483 to 493, assumed the regal title of Yongming, hence the name of this poetic style. Yongming poems featured metrical structure and parallelism. They were also known as the "new poetry," as opposed to the "old poetry" of the Han Dynasty and the Wei period. Xie Tiao (464-499), Shen Yue (441-513), and Wang Rong (467-493) were leading poets of the Yongming style. This style was marked by a poet's deft use of metrical structure and parallelism, thus enhancing the stylistic beauty and artistic expressiveness of poetry. It laid the foundation for the emergence of the "early modern" poetry, or regulated verse. However, the Yongming poetic style was weakened by an excessive emphasis on tonal patterns at the cost of content, drawing criticism of some poetry critics of the time. The style was thus burdened by this inherent risk in its quest for innovation.

引例 Citation：

◎永明末，盛为文章，吴兴沈约、陈郡谢朓、琅琊王融以气类相推毂，汝南周颙（yóng）善识声韵。约等文皆用宫商，以平上去入为四声，以此制韵，不可增减，世呼为"永明体"。(《南齐书·陆厥传》)

（永明末年，文学创作大盛，吴兴人沈约、陈郡人谢朓、琅琊人王融等以共同的志趣相互推举，汝南人周颙精通声韵。沈约等人的创作都讲求音律，以平声、上声、去声、入声为四声，以此来创制韵律，不能随意增加或减少，世人称之为"永明体"。）

Literary writing flourished towards the end of the Yongming period. Shen Yue from Wuxing, Xie Tiao from Chenjun, and Wang Rong from Langya, encouraged and praised each other out of their shared artistic aspirations. Zhou Yong from Runan was well versed in metrical patterning. The poems by Shen Yue and the others were very strict about the use of metrical schemes, namely, the level tone, the rising tone, the falling-rising tone, and the falling tone, and departure from the strict use of such metrical schemes was forbidden. This particular style of poetic creation became known as the Yongming style. (*The History of Qi of the Southern Dynasties*)

咏史诗 /yǒngshǐshī/

Poetry on History

以历史事件或历史人物等作为创作题材并借以抒写诗人情志、感悟的诗歌。史实、史识与史情紧密结合是其主要特点。咏史诗多

以"述古""怀古""览古""感古""古兴""读史""咏史"等为题，
也有直接以被描写的历史人物、历史事件为标题的。

Poetry on history refers to poems written to convey a poet's sentiments by reflecting on historical events or historical figures. A poem on history touched on historical events and expressed the poet's historical insight as well as his emotional attachment to history. Such poems recounted, relived, revived, interpreted, or chanted about history. Some poets used historical figures or events as titles for such poems.

引例 Citation：

◎怀古者，见古迹，思古人其事。无他，兴亡贤愚而已。（方回《瀛
奎律髓》卷三）

（怀古之作，是诗人见到古迹，于是追思古人的往事。不为别的，
不过是抒写对历史兴亡和古人贤愚的看法与感悟罢了。）

Poems on history are written when poets see historical sites that take their minds to the past. In these poems, poets reflect on the rise and fall of past dynasties as well as the wisdom and folly of historical figures. (Fang Hui: *The Best Regulated Poems of the Tang and Song Dynasties*)

优人 /yōurén/
Entertainers

古代具有说唱、舞蹈、戏谑等表演才能的艺人，宋元以后也指
称戏曲演员。又称倡优、俳优、优伶等。最初是宫廷贵族为娱乐目
的而供养的小群体，宋元以后随着城市发展而出现专业艺人团队。
在重政教、轻审美的古代，优人社会地位低下。司马迁（前145或
前135？—？）《史记·滑稽列传》肯定优人对君王的劝谏作用，这
也成为后世评价名优的一个重要尺度以及艺人的自觉追求。

Entertainers, known as *youren* (优人), or *changyou* (倡优), *paiyou* (俳优), or *youling* (优伶), were folk artists who performed story-telling, dancing, acrobatics, and comedy. After the Song and Yuan dynasties, they also performed in operas. Initially formed as small groups of entertainers sponsored by court aristocrats for entertainment, they evolved into professional performing troupes as cities grew in size after the Song and Yuan dynasties. In old China when ideological and ethical principles were valued to the neglect of entertainment, entertainers were low in social status. Sima Qian (145 or 135 ?-? BC), in the "Biographies of Jesters" section of his *Records of the Historian*, praised entertainers for boldly giving moral advice to rulers. This practice later became a major criterion for commenting on entertainers, and it also became a conscious choice of aspiring entertainers.

引例 Citations：

◎今吴王淫于乐而忘其百姓，乱民功，逆天时；信谗喜优，憎辅远弼。(《国语·越语下》)

(现在吴王沉湎声色，忘记百姓，扰乱百姓农事，违反天时；相信谗言，喜欢优人，憎恨疏远那些敢于直谏的辅弼大臣。)

The King of Wu indulges himself in pleasure making and forgets all about the common folk. He meddles in farming by violating the laws governing the cycle of seasons, trusts slanderers, relishes the company of entertainers; he just does not want to hear candid advice from his ministers and keep them alienated. (*Discourses on Governance of the States*)

◎及优旃(zhān)之讽漆城，优孟之谏葬马，并谲辞饰说，抑止昏暴。(刘勰《文心雕龙·谐隐》)

(还有秦代有位叫旃的优人劝阻秦二世在城墙上刷漆，楚国有位叫孟的优人劝阻楚庄王厚葬爱马，他们都是用含蓄委婉的话，来劝阻君王昏庸暴戾的行为。)

A Qin-dynasty entertainer called Zhan advised the Second Emperor of Qin against painting city walls, and an entertainer of the State of Chu named Meng asked King Zhuang of Chu not to bury his beloved steed extravagantly.

Both of them tried to stop their rulers from acting in a fatuous and self-indulgent way. (Liu Xie: *The Literary Mind and the Carving of Dragons*)

有德者必有言 /yǒu dé zhě bì yǒu yán/
Virtuous People Are Sure to Produce Fine Writing.

品德高尚的人一定有著述或妙文传世。儒家认为作家的人品（道德修养）与作品（文章价值）往往有内在的联系，品德高尚的人文章自然高妙，而善写文章的人却未必道德高尚，以此提出作家著述应以传播道德为使命，道德文章要相互统一。但后世儒家文士有时过于强调文章的道德作用与作家个人品德对文章的影响从而忽视了文学自身的创作特点与价值。

Virtuous people are sure to write fine works which will be passed on to later generations. According to Confucianism, the moral character of a writer determines the value of his work, virtuous people would naturally write well, but those who wrote well might not necessarily be virtuous. Therefore, authors should write to disseminate moral values; virtue and writings should be consistent. However, later Confucian scholars sometimes overemphasized the influence that ethics and the authors' moral character had on their writings to the neglect of the characteristics and values of literary creation per se.

引例 Citations：

◎子曰："有德者必有言，有言者不必有德。"（《论语·宪问》）

（孔子说："道德高尚的人，一定有名言传世；有名言传世的人，不一定道德高尚。"）

Confucius said, "Virtuous people are sure to have good writings or words to pass on to later generations, but it is not always true the other way round." (*The Analects*)

◎丈夫处世，怀宝挺秀。辨雕万物，智周宇宙。立德何隐，含道必授。（刘勰《文心雕龙·诸子》）

（大丈夫活在世上，应该身怀才能，超群出众，雄辩的文辞可以摹写万物，周全的智慧可以穷尽宇宙奥秘。何须隐藏自己立德的志向，掌握了道就一定要广泛传授。）

A man of character should possess exceptional capability and his eloquent expressions should portray everything truthfully. His great wisdom should enable him to explain all things under heaven. He does not need to hide his aspirations to serve as a model of virtue. If he has come to a good understanding of Dao, he surely will disseminate it extensively. (Liu Xie: *The Literary Mind and the Carving of Dragons*)

有我之境 / 无我之境

/yǒu wǒ zhī jìng / wú wǒ zhī jìng/

Scene Involving the Self / Scene Not Involving the Self

近代学者王国维（1877 — 1927）从物我关系的角度所概括和总结的中国古典诗词的两种审美境界。王国维在其著名的文学理论著作《人间词话》中提出了"境界"概念，认为只有营造出境界的诗词才是上乘之作。王国维不仅把它视为诗词的创作原则，也把它当作批评标准，用"境界"论述诗词的演变，评价作者的得失、作品的优劣、词品的高低。围绕"境界"，他又提出了若干命题，"有我之境，无我之境"就是其中最为重要的一对术语。"有我之境"，就是词作者将自己的主观感情融入文学形象之中，使得文学形象带有强烈的感情色彩；"无我之境"并不是没有感情的融入，只是这种感情冲淡平和，也可以说是作者的情感表达与文学形象形成了契合。在王氏看来，"无我之境"无需刻意雕琢，巧然天成，是艺术追求的最高境界。"境界"说既是王国维文艺批评的出发点，又是其文艺思想的总归宿。

This term refers to the dual character of aesthetic appreciation of classic Chinese poetry highlighted by the early modern scholar Wang Guowei (1877-1927), from the perspective of the relationship between the self and the external world. In his renowned literary theoretic work *Poetic Remarks in the Human World*, Wang put forward the notion of *jingjie* (visionary world), arguing that only poetry written to invoke such a state can be deemed excellent work. He regarded this notion not only as a creative principle of poetry but also a criterion for poetry criticism. Besides, he used it to recount the evolution of poetry and to evaluate the taste or merit of a poem and its author. He also raised many propositions concerning the visionary world. Of these, the most important is the binary term "scene involving the self / scene not involving the self." "Scene involving the self" means that the author incorporates personal feelings into the literary image he creates, thus imbuing it with a tremendous emotional force. "Scene not involving the self," on the other hand, does not mean a lack of emotion; rather, the author tempers this emotional force by exercising restraint and achieving a perfect harmony between personal feelings with literary imagery. To him, "without the self in it" is a perfectly natural state of creation, without any need for fabrication or alteration; therefore, it represents the highest level of artistic excellence. Overall, this term marks the starting point of Wang's literary criticism and the final destination of his literary thought.

引例 Citations：

◎境非独谓景物也。喜怒哀乐，亦人心中之一境界。故能写真景物、真感情者，谓之有境界，否则谓之无境界。（王国维《人间词话》）

（境界并不是仅指景物，喜怒哀乐等情感也是人心中的一种境界。所以能够描写真切的景物、真实的情感的作品，就被称为有境界，否则就称为没有境界。）

What constitutes "the visionary world" is not only scene but also feelings of joy, anger and sorrow lying deep in one's heart. Therefore, a literary work which contains true feeling as well as authentic scenery has created a visionary world, otherwise it has not. (Wang Guowei: *Poetic Remarks in the Human World*)

◎有有我之境，有无我之境。……有我之境，以我观物，故物皆著我之色彩。无我之境，以物观物，故不知何者为我，何者为物。古人为词，写有我之境者为多，然未始不能写无我之境，此在豪杰之士能自树立耳。（王国维《人间词话》）

（有有我之境，也有无我之境。……有我之境，用我的眼光来观察自然景物，所以景物都笼罩上了我的情感色彩。无我之境，用自然的眼光和心态来观察景物，所以就分不清哪里是我、哪里是景物了。古人写词，能够写出有我之境的人比较多，但并不意味着无我之境就无法达到，这在才华杰出的词人那里正是使其能独树一帜的地方。）

Poetry can be created with or without an "author" in it... In the former case, the poet beholds natural scene from a personal perspective, coating everything he sees with a subjective color. In the latter case, however, the poet observes external objects and scenery as if he were part of nature, thus eliminating the division between him and his surroundings. Many old-time poets were able to write good poetry with the self in it, but that does not mean that poetry without the self in it is unachievable. Truly talented poets distinguish themselves from the common run exactly in this aspect. (Wang Guowei: *Poetic Remarks in the Human World*)

元和体 /Yuánhé tǐ/
The Yuanhe Style of Poetry

指唐宪宗元和年间（806—820）开始流行的诗歌体式及风格。有广狭二义：广义的理解指元和以来的各种新体诗文，一般认为元和以后流行的新的文风、诗风，是由韩愈（768—824）、元稹（779—831）、白居易（772—846）、张籍（767？—830？）等元和年间的著名作家开创的；狭义的理解则是指元稹、白居易诗歌中的长篇排律和中短篇杂体诗。元稹、白居易的诗歌注重叙事，如《连昌宫词》《长恨歌》《琵琶行》都是长篇叙事诗的代表作；其次是注重诗歌形式的通俗化，具体说就是诗的语言明白晓畅，容易为读者理解记忆；注意诗歌与音乐的结合，韵律的优美和谐，便于唱诵。

This term refers to the poetic style most popular during the rule of Emperor Xianzong (806-820) of the Tang Dynasty under the reign title of Yuanhe. It can be understood either broadly or narrowly. In a broad sense, the Yuanhe style of poetry refers to all new forms of verse prevalent from the Yuanhe era onward, created by famed Yuanhe-era writers such as Han Yu (768-824), Yuan Zhen (779-831), Bai Juyi (772-846), and Zhang Ji (767?-830?). In a narrow sense, it refers to lengthy regulated verse and shorter poems of mixed metrical schemes in poetic composition of the works of Yuan Zhen and Bai Juyi. Both poets paid careful attention to the narrative function of poetry. For example, "A Song of the Lianchang Palace," "A Song of Unending Sorrow," and "A Song of the Pipa Player" are all representative of lengthy narrative poetry. They also pursued a more popular style of poetry, using vernacular language which was intelligible and easy to remember for ordinary readers. Moreover, they tried to combine poetry and music, making their works rhythmically beautiful and harmonious, thus suitable for chanting or singing.

引例 Citations：

◎元和已后，为文笔则学奇诡于韩愈，学苦涩于樊宗师；歌行则学流荡于张籍；诗草则学矫激于孟郊，学浅切于白居易，学淫靡于元稹，俱名为"元和体"。（李肇《唐国史补》卷下）

（元和以后，写文章的人学韩愈的奇特怪异，学樊宗师的晦涩生僻；写歌行体长诗的人则学张籍的放荡不羁；写诗的人则学孟郊的奇异偏激，学白居易的浅易切当，学元稹的浮华艳丽，这些当时都称之为"元和体"。）

Since the Yuanhe era, essay writers have come to imitate Han Yu's oddity and Fan Zongshi's opaqueness; writers of long poetic songs have taken fancy to Zhang Ji's bold, uninhibited ways; and poets embraced Meng Jiao's strangeness and extremity, Bai Juyi's intelligibility and aptness, and Yuan Zhen's pomposity and flamboyance. All this constitutes what is known as the "Yuanhe style." (Li Zhao: *A Supplement to Liu Su's Dynastic History*)

◎［元］稹聪警绝人，年少有才名，与太原白居易友善，工为诗，善状咏风态物色，当时言诗者称元白焉。自衣冠士子，至闾阎下俚，悉传讽之，号为"元和体"。(《旧唐书·元稹传》)

（元稹聪慧过人，年少时就有才名，与太原人白居易是好友，他们都擅长写诗，善于描摹歌咏事物的形态景色，当时谈论诗歌的人都会提及元白。从士大夫、儒林学子到市井百姓，都在流传歌咏他们的诗，称之为"元和体"。）

Yuan Zhen was unusually talented and achieved renown at a very young age. He and Bai Juyi, a native of Taiyuan were good friends. Both of them were remarkable at writing poetry, depicting and extolling things in all colors and forms. All lovers of poetry at the time would mention Yuan Zhen and Bai Juyi together. Everybody, whether they were scholar-officials, students or ordinary people, was found chanting their poetry, calling it "Yuanhe-style poetry." (*The Old Tang History*)

元杂剧 /Yuán zájù/
Zaju of the Yuan Dynasty

是元代代表性戏剧种类。其前身为宋代北方杂剧，它以北方民间流行的俚俗表演形式为基础，吸收了金代诸宫调、院本的表演特点和舞台经验，经元初关汉卿等戏剧名家完善定型，最终形成了独特的戏剧表演形式。元杂剧通常一本四折，每折由同一宫调的曲子

组成套曲，主角正旦或正末主唱。元杂剧剧情完整，在人物形象塑
造方面更加生动立体，人物的念白科介等戏曲表现手法更加丰富。
元大都经济发达，市井繁荣，文人与艺人联系密切，也助推了元杂
剧创作的兴盛。元代末年，元杂剧衰落，至明代，逐渐被其他戏曲
形式取代。

Zaju, a unique dramatic genre of the Yuan Dynasty, grew out of the
northern *zaju* of the earlier Song Dynasty. Originally drawing on popular
local performing styles of the north, it later absorbed *zhugongdiao,* a kind of
song-speech drama with mixed modes of musical tunes, as well as scores /
scripts performed in brothels by courtesans of the Jin Dynasty. Well-
known playwrights like Guan Hanqing in the early Yuan period refined and
formalized these various styles into this unique dramatic genre. *Zaju* is made
up of four acts, each with sets of songs starting from the same *gongdiao* note,
and sung by the principal female or male performers. The *gongdiao* note
changes with each act. The plots are complete and well-constructed, while the
lively and interesting characters rely on a rich repertoire of dramatic gestures
and expressions. Dadu, capital of the Yuan Dynasty, was a prosperous center
of economic activity where scholars and performers mingled well, which
encouraged the rapid growth of the *zaju* genre. However, the style declined
together with the Yuan Dynasty and by the following Ming Dynasty, it had
been replaced by other operatic and performing genres.

引例 Citations：

◎乐音与政通，而伎剧亦随时所尚而变。近代，教坊院本之外，再
变而为杂剧。（胡祗（zhī）遹（yù）《赠宋氏序》）

（音乐与国家治理的好坏相通，而戏剧也随着时代的审美观念和趣
味而变化。近代，教坊在院本之外，又变化出杂剧。）

Music follows the trends of political governance, and dramas too change with
the preferences of the times. The scripts used in brothels later evolved into
zaju. (Hu Zhiyu: Text Presented to the Entertainer Song)

◎唐时有传奇，皆文人所编，犹野史也，但资谐笑耳。宋之戏文，

乃有唱念，有诨。金则院本、杂剧合而为一。至我朝，乃分院本、杂剧而为二。（夏庭芝《青楼集志》）

（唐代有传奇，都是文人编写的，就像野史那样，只是用作谈资取笑罢了。宋代的戏文，才有唱腔、念白和插科打诨。金代时院本和杂剧是合在一起的。到了本朝，才将院本、杂剧分成两种。）

In the Tang period, there were legendary tales like unofficial histories written by scholars often for entertainment and light conversation. Only by the Song Dynasty did the Southern Opera consist of songs, recitation, and comic gestures and dialogues. In the Jin, brothel scripts and *zaju* were combined. In our dynasty, the two are separated into distinct forms. (Xia Tingzhi: Preface to *Biographies of Courtesans*)

怨刺 /yuàncì/
Resentment and Sting

用文学形式表达对社会不公的不满及对统治者的讽刺劝谏。特指《诗经》中对时政和统治者进行批判和讽喻，表达诗人心中强烈怨愤与不平的诗作。汉代学者认为《诗经》中的"怨"是有节制的宣泄，"刺"则是积极意义上的规劝，因此将二者合成一个文学批评术语，肯定这类作品所具有的现实意义。唐宋以后，此术语有激烈批判和强烈怨恨的意味，不过核心内涵仍以向往政治清明、社会和谐为旨归。

This term means using a literary form to express resentment towards social injustice and satirize and admonish those in power. It especially refers to the poems in *The Book of Songs*, in which poets criticized and satirized the politics and the ruling class of the time to vent their indignation and resentment. Scholars in the Han Dynasty considered resentment in *The Book of Songs* as controlled venting and the satiric sting constructive admonishment.

They therefore combined the two into a term of literary criticism with positive implication. After the Tang and Song dynasties, the term gained a connotation of intense criticism and indignation. However, the essential meaning was still a yearning for good governance and social harmony.

引例 Citation：

◎周道始缺，怨刺之诗起。王泽既竭，而诗不能作。(《汉书·礼乐志》)

(在周代仁义之道遭到破坏之后，开始出现表达不满之情和讽劝之意的诗歌。当帝王对百姓的恩德完全失去之后，人们就不再用诗歌表达心声了。)

When the benevolent way of ruling in the Zhou Dynasty was abandoned, there appeared poems that expressed resentment towards those in power and satirized or admonished them. When the king no longer cared for the general public, people stopped using poems to express what they had in mind. (*The History of the Han Dynasty*)

院本 /yuànběn/

Jin Opera / Scripts Used by Courtesans

有广狭二义：广义指流行于金代的一种戏曲形式，狭义指这种戏曲演唱用的脚本。因多在行院(hángyuàn)演出，故称院本。元代初年仍然流行，目前无独立完整的作品传世，其艺术特点可大致归纳为：篇幅较短，结构简单，多调笑语言及滑稽动作表演，主要角色是副净和副末，继承了唐代参军戏、宋代杂剧的戏谑手法。金院本直接影响了元杂剧的演出形式。

In a broad sense, the term means a style of traditional opera popular in the Jin Dynasty. In a narrow sense, it refers to the scores and librettos used in this type of drama, which was performed mainly in *hangyuan* (行院), or brothels, hence the name. This genre was very popular in the early Jin Dynasty but no separate, complete works have come down to us today. The format is as follows: short acts, simple plots, humorous language and comic gestures. The main performer *fujing* (副净) provides the humor while the supporting performer *fumo* (副末) provides comic backup. The form inherited a great deal from the Tang-dynasty two-person comic banter of *canjunxi* (参军戏), and Song-dynasty *zaju* comedy. The brothel scores had a great influence on the development of the later Yuan *zaju* or opera.

引例 Citation：

◎金有院本、杂剧、诸宫调。院本、杂剧，其实一也。国朝院本、杂剧，始厘而二之。（陶宗仪《南村辍耕录》卷二十五）

（金代有院本、杂剧、诸宫调。院本、杂剧，实际是一回事。到了我们元朝，院本、杂剧才分为两种。）

In the Jin Dynasty, there were scores used by courtesans, *zaju* and *zhugongdiao*, a kind of song-speech drama with mixed modes of tunes. In fact the scores and *zaju* were the same thing. They were not divided into two separate genres until the Yuan Dynasty. (Tao Zongyi : *Stories by Master Nancun*)

乐 /yuè/

Yue (Music)

古代六艺之一，常与"礼"并称。相较于各种外在的礼法规范，音乐最能感动人的内心并对人的言行产生影响。但并不是所有的音乐都属于儒家所说的"乐"的范畴。"乐"应能有助于人的性情处于平和中正的状态，使人的言行自觉符合礼的要求，从而实现人与人之间的和谐共处。"乐"常与其他礼仪形式配合运用，是维系人伦秩序、移风易俗的重要手段。

Yue (乐) is one of the six arts of ancient times, often mentioned together with *li* (礼 rites / social norms). In contrast to external rules and rites, music touches the emotions and thus can affect human behavior. However, not all music counts as the Confucian *yue* which must have the effect of making the listener calm and measured so as to willingly behave in accordance with social norms, and thus engage harmoniously with others. *Yue* is often associated with other forms of ceremonial actions; it is one important way of maintaining proper human relations and encouraging better social practices and customs.

引例 Citations：

◎乐也者，和之不可变者也；礼也者，理之不可易者也。乐合同，礼别异。礼乐之统，管乎人心矣。(《荀子·乐论》)

(没有一种东西能替代乐来促成社会的和谐，也没有一种东西能替代礼来分别社会的伦理差等。乐使人们相互和谐，礼使人们分别差等。礼和乐一起管控人心的各个方面。)

Nothing can replace music for creating social harmony, and nothing can replace rites for determining ethical social differences. Music brings people together in harmony; rites establish roles and relationships. Together they direct human morality. (*Xunzi*)

◎子曰："恶紫之夺朱也，恶郑声之乱雅乐也，恶利口之覆邦家者。"(《论语·阳货》)

(孔子说："我厌恶用紫色取代红色，厌恶用郑国的音乐扰乱雅正的音乐，憎恶伶牙俐齿而使国家倾覆的人。")

Confucius said, "I detest replacing red with purple and interfering refined classical music with the music of the State of Zheng. I loathe those who overthrow the state with their glib tongues." (*The Analects*)

乐教 /yuèjiào/

Music Education

中国古代借助音乐实施政治教化的方式，与"诗教"相配合。先秦儒家总结周代的音乐教育成果，认为音乐可以移风易俗，感化人心，培养人格，并由此建构了儒家关于音乐及音乐教育的一套完整的理论体系。后"乐教"和"诗教"都是官方教育的重要科目，成为中国古代礼乐文明的重要组成部分。

In ancient China, music, together with poetry, was a way to conduct political education. Reviewing music education in the Zhou Dynasty, the Confucian scholars before the Qin-dynasty unification of China at the time concluded that music could transform social and cultural practices, stir up one's inner emotions, and cultivate a good character. On this basis, they developed a comprehensive Confucian theory of music and music education. Subsequently, both "music education" and "poetry education" became important subjects in the official school system, forming a key part of early Chinese ritual and music culture.

引例 Citations：

◎乐也者，圣人之所乐也。而可以善民心，其感人深，其移风易俗，故先王著其教焉。(《礼记·乐记》)

（音乐是圣人所喜爱的。它可以使人心向善，感人至深，能够移风易俗，因此先王非常注重其教化功能。）

Music is what sages take delight in. It can cultivate goodness, move the people and transform social mores. That is why the past kings valued its role of education. (*The Book of Rites*)

◎夫声乐之入人也深，其化人也速。(《荀子·乐论》)

（音乐能够深深打动人心，让人迅速得到感化。）

Music touches people profoundly; its transformative power is rapid. (*Xunzi*)

韵 /yùn/

Rhyme / Charm

主要含义有二：其一，作为文体形式的组成要素，指清雅、和谐、动听的声音之美。"韵"最先指构成汉语字音的要素之一。诗、词、曲等文体讲究押韵，被称为韵文。韵文讲求韵的位置安排和合理组合，节奏参差而和谐，能充分体现汉语的韵律美。其二，作为文艺范畴，主要指文艺作品中飘逸流动的精神气质和清远淡雅的意味。常组合成"气韵""风韵""神韵"等词语，广泛运用于画论、书论、乐论中。"韵"与"气"皆可指能意会不能言传的艺术感受，但是"韵"更侧重于温柔含蓄及清雅灵动。

This term has two meanings. Firstly, as a stylistic term in writing, it represents a combination of elegant, concordant, and melodious sounds. Rhyme originally was one of the factors contributing to the correct pronunciation of Chinese characters. Rhyme is important for poetry, including *ci* poetry, and ballad verses. In such writings, attention is placed on where rhyming should take place in a poetic line, whether rhymes actually match well, and rhythms' harmonious variations, thus showing the rhythmical beauty of the Chinese language. Secondly, as a literary term, it means charm, suggesting natural fluidity and elegant simplicity. It is often used together with other Chinese characters to mean vivid charm, graceful appeal, or creative verve. Nuanced beauty is widely used in commentaries on painting, calligraphy and musical composition. Charm and vividness both refer to an indescribable appeal a piece of artistic writing emanates, but the former is more about aspects such as tenderness, implications, elegance and natural flow of such a work.

引例 Citations：

◎六法者何？一气韵生动是也，二骨法用笔是也，三应物象形是也，四随类赋彩是也，五经营位置是也，六传移模写是也。（谢赫《古画品录》）

（绘画的六个法则是什么呢？其一是作品要充满生气，富有神韵；其二是运笔能自如呈现各种线条变化；其三是造型要顺应对象外形特征；其四是要根据对象特征进行着色；其五是构图要合理搭配，呈现整体效果；其六是要临摹佳作以传承前人画技。）

There are six rules for painting. A painting should be full of vitality and artistic appeal; the painting brush should be used in such a way as to make changes in lines natural; the image painted should suit the appearance of the painted object; coloring should suit the features of the object portrayed; the painting should be well structured to present an overall visual effect; and masterpieces of past painters should be copied to draw inspiration from them. (Xie He: *An Appraisal of Ancient Paintings*)

◎乍读渊明诗，颇似枯淡，久久有味。东坡晚年酷好之，谓李杜不及也。此无他，韵胜而已。（陈善《扪虱新话·陶渊明杜子美韩退之诗》）

（初读陶渊明的诗，好像很枯燥平淡，读久了就有味道了。苏轼晚年最喜爱陶诗，认为李白、杜甫的诗都比不上。这没有其他原因，就是在"韵"方面胜出罢了。）

I found Tao Yuanming's poems boring when I first read them. Only after a more thorough reading did I recognize their charm. In his old age, Su Shi loved Tao's poems most, believing that even Li Bai or Du Fu was no match for him. What attracted him was the distinctive appeal of charm in Tao's poems. (Chen Shan: *Daring Remarks on Literature*)

◎读古人诗，须观其气韵。气者，气味也；韵者，态度风致也。如对名花，其可爱处，必在形色之外。（方东树《昭昧詹言》卷一）

（读古人的诗，应该观察其气韵。气，就是气味；韵，就是态度风致。如同欣赏名花，名花可爱的地方，一定在形状颜色之外。）

When reading ancient people's poems, one needs to watch for their spirit and charm. Spirit means a poet's charisma, whereas charm reflects his style and grace. It is like admiring a fine flower, when one comes to learn that its loveliness lies beyond mere color or form. (Fang Dongshu: *Rambling Words to Expose the Secrets of Poetry Writing*)

章表 /zhāngbiǎo/

Memorial of Gratitude or Petition

古代文体名称，是臣下感谢皇帝恩宠或向皇帝有所请求的文书。"章"用于谢恩，"表"用于陈请。两者从文体上说差别不大。南朝刘勰（465？—520？或532？）在《文心雕龙》中对写作章表提出的理想标准是：表意明确而不肤浅，陈述与分析既精练又充实，合乎礼仪规范和文字规范。

This is an ancient style of official communication, through which a high-ranking official expressed his gratitude or presented a petition to the emperor. *Zhang*, or memorial of gratitude, and *biao*, or memorial of petition, differed little in style. Liu Xie (465?-520? or 532?) of the Southern Dynasties observed in his literary critique *The Literary Mind and the Carving of Dragons* that an ideal piece of writing should convey its essential message in a clear and in-depth way, state or analyze a case succinctly and thoroughly, and obey rules of ritual propriety and standards of writing.

引例 Citations：

◎秦初定制，改书曰奏。汉定礼仪，则有四品：一曰章，二曰奏，三曰表，四曰议。章以谢恩，奏以按劾，表以陈请，议以执异。（刘勰《文心雕龙·章表》）

（秦初设定制度，将上书改称上奏。汉朝设定礼制，将上书分为章、奏、表、议四种，"章"用于谢恩，"奏"用于检举弹劾，"表"用于陈述请求，"议"用于提出不同看法。）

It was officially decided at the beginning of the Qin Dynasty that a letter to the emperor should be renamed as a "memorial to the throne." In the Han Dynasty, this form of writing was divided into four sub-types by the court: *zhang*, memorial of gratitude, *zou*, memorial of impeachment, *biao*, memorial of petition, and *yi*, memorial of dissent. (Liu Xie: *The Literary Mind and the Carving of Dragons*)

◎原夫章表之为用也，所以对扬王庭，昭明心曲。既其身文，且亦国华。章以造阙，风矩应明；表以致禁，骨采宜耀。循名课实，以文为本者也。（刘勰《文心雕龙·章表》）

（推究章表本来的功用，在于回报和颂扬朝廷恩德，表明内心衷曲。既要体现自身的文采，也要显示国家的荣耀。章是要送到朝廷的，风格和表达都要显明；表也是要进入宫廷的，骨力和文采也要出色。按照章表的名称来考察其实质，要以文采鲜明为其要旨。）

Memorials of gratitude or petition are intended to express gratitude to and extol the imperial court for the love and care it has shown to its subjects, or to present one's true feelings. Such memorials should both demonstrate the authors' literary talent and honor the empire. As these memorials are to be submitted to the court, they should be well-structured and eloquent in style. A memorial of gratitude or of petition should be explicit in wording. (Liu Xie: *The Literary Mind and the Carving of Dragons*)

章句 /zhāngjù/

Textual Components / Annotation Work

　　主要含义有二：其一，汉语诗文中字词、句、段、篇的统称。南朝刘勰（465？—520？或532？）《文心雕龙》重点从写作角度探讨围绕文章主题遣词造句、安排段落、形成篇章的一般原则与方法。刘勰在强调立意高的前提下要求章句精雕细琢，启示后人在写作中自觉揣摩文法，总结经验，展开文学批评和理论探讨。其二，为古代一种注释体著作名称，意思是分章析句，主要对儒家经典文本划分段落，解释其中的字词并串讲大意。如东汉王逸的《楚辞章句》、南宋朱熹（1130—1200）的《大学章句》《中庸章句》等。

This term has two meanings. First, it means words, sentences, paragraphs, or an entire text. In his literary critique, *The Literary Mind and the Carving of Dragons*, Liu Xie (465?-520? or 532?) of the Southern Dynasties discussed the general principles and rules governing the wording, syntax, paragraphs arrangement and text composition in writing. While stressing the importance of writing for a worthy goal, he also called for meticulous depiction in terms of wording and textual composition. This provided a source of inspiration to writers of later generations to improve grammar, practice literary criticism and launch theoretical discussions on writing. Second, this term also means an ancient annotative work showing how to divide a text into paragraphs and analyze syntax. Such works discuss paragraph arrangement in the Confucian classics, explain the meanings of words and expressions, and offer a general interpretation of the text. Typical examples are *Annotations on Odes of Chu* by Wang Yi of the Eastern Han Dynasty, as well as *Annotations on The Great Learning* and *Annotations on The Doctrine of the Mean* by Zhu Xi (1130-1200) of the Southern Song Dynasty.

引例 Citations：

◎空守章句，但诵师言，施之世务，殆无一可。(颜之推《颜氏家训·勉学》)

(空守着书卷，只会背诵老师的话，如果用之处理实际事务，只怕一点儿也派不上用场。)

If one can only recite words and sentences taught by the teacher, what he has learned is of little value in handling matters in real life. (Yan Zhitui: *Admonitions for the Yan Clan*)

◎夫人之立言，因字而生句，积句而成章，积章而成篇。篇之彪炳，章无疵也；章之明靡，句无玷也；句之清英，字不妄也：振本而末从，知一而万毕矣。(刘勰《文心雕龙·章句》)

(人们从事写作，总是由字词组成句子，由句子组成段落，由段落组成篇章。要想整篇文章绽放光彩，必须保证每个段落都没有缺陷；要想每个段落明白细密，必须保证每个句子都没有缺陷；要想每个句子清新优美，每个字词就不能乱用。树的根干摇动了枝叶一定跟着颤动，懂得这个基本道理，就能写好一切文章了。)

When writing, one starts with words and sentences; then he proceeds to build paragraphs, until a full text is composed. To make a piece of writing a good one, one should see that each paragraph is without flaws; to make each paragraph clear and well-organized, one should ensure that each sentence has no flaws; to make each sentence refreshing and beautiful, one should make careful use of each word or expression. It is just like when the roots and stem of a tree are shaken, all the branches and leaves will tremble. Once this rule is observed, it will be easy to compose a good piece of writing. (Liu Xie: *The Literary Mind and the Carving of Dragons*)

诏策 /zhàocè/
Imperial Edicts

古代文体名称，是帝王向臣下宣示旨意的文书。"诏"即诏书，是皇帝颁发的训诫或命令；"策"即策书，是帝王对臣下进行封赏、任免官爵的文书。南朝刘勰（465？—520？或532？）在《文心雕龙·诏策》中论述了帝王对臣下、上级对下级所使用的各类文体。他认为这类公文具有最大的权威性、影响力和垂范作用，封赏嘉奖类文书应当如星月生辉、雨露滋润般亲民，训诫责罚类文书则应当如霹雳之威、秋霜之烈。其基本写作要求是态度明确，交代周到，合乎制度、情理、事实及文字规范，措辞上追求典雅、庄重、适度。

Imperial edicts consist of *zhao* (诏) and *ce* (策). *Zhao* were orders made by an emperor while *ce* were issued by the emperor to confer commendation on officials and appoint and dismiss them. Liu Xie (465?-520? or 532?) of the Southern Dynasties discussed in his literary critique *The Literary Mind and the Carving of Dragons* various types of official documents used by the

中华思想文化术语
文艺卷

emperor to his ministers and those used by higher-ranking officials to lower-ranking ones. Liu Xie pointed out that these types of official documents were highly authoritative and influential, setting rules for the whole nation to follow. Conferring commendations were like "the moon and shining stars" or "timely rain and dew," showing the emperor's loving care for his subjects. Reprimands and punishments, on the other hand, showed his "thunderous rage" or the "chill of autumn frost." These kinds of official documents should be clear-cut in stand, well thought of, based on laws and rules as well as common sense and facts, and correct in wording and syntax. Such official documents should be solemn in tone and refined and moderate in style.

引例 Citations：

◎王幸受诏策，通经术，知诸侯名誉不当出竟。(《汉书·淮阳宪王刘钦传》)

（王有幸接受诏书册封，通晓儒家经术，知道以诸侯的名分不应当离开国境。）

The prince was honored to receive an edict from His Majesty giving him this title. Well versed in Confucian classics, he knew that as a subject prince he was not supposed to leave his designated territory. (*The History of the Han Dynasty*)

◎皇帝御宇，其言也神。渊嘿（mò）黼（fǔ）扆（yǐ），而响盈四表，唯诏策乎！(刘勰《文心雕龙·诏策》)

（皇帝统治着天下，他的话是神圣的。帝王威严地端坐在御座上，他的号令却能够传遍四方，只有诏策才具有这种功效吧！）

The emperor reigns over the land. His word is sacred. Sitting solemnly in his throne, he is able to have his orders delivered across the country. Only imperial edicts have such power! (Liu Xie: *The Literary Mind and the Carving of Dragons*)

正声 /zhèngshēng/

Proper Music / Finest Poetry

　　原为中国古代音乐概念，主要含义有二：其一，指儒家与官方倡导的典雅、纯正的音乐；有时也指五正声，即宫、商、角、徵、羽五音。其二，因儒家认为《诗经》的音乐体制与思想内容最为纯正典雅，是"正声"的典范，故后世用"正声"转指在内容与意境上纯正典雅、堪为典范的诗歌作品。如明代高棅（bǐng，1350—1423）编选的《唐诗正声》，就是通过精选唐诗各体的代表性作品，试图为后人确立诗歌写作的正宗轨范。

It is originally a term in ancient Chinese music. It has two meanings: 1) The refined and pure music encouraged by Confucian scholars and official circles; sometimes it was also a general term for the five notes of ancient music *gong, shang, jue, zhi,* and *yu.* 2) Examples of the finest poems and songs. Confucian scholars believed that the content and music of *The Book of Songs* were the best and most refined, and thus were set as the models for *zhengsheng,* or the finest poetry. Gao Bing (1350-1423) of the Ming Dynasty named his collection of carefully selected Tang poems *A Selection of Finest Tang Poems* in an effort to present the finest and purest examples of different styles of Tang poetry for later generations.

引例 Citations：

◎凡奸声感人而逆气应之，逆气成象而淫乐兴焉。正声感人而顺气应之，顺气成象而和乐兴焉。（《礼记·乐记》）

（凡是邪恶的音乐作用于人，人自身的不正之气就会被激发而荒淫享乐就产生了。凡是纯正的音乐作用于人，人自身的和顺之气就会被激发而和谐安乐就产生了。）

Vicious music affects people by arousing their negative instincts, so licentiousness and degeneracy surface. Pure music moves people and stimulates their decent and amiable and obedient impulses, therefore harmony and peace prevail. (*The Book of Rites*)

◎ 正声何微茫，哀怨起骚人。（李白《古风》其一）

（为何《诗经》那样雅正的诗风非常微弱，而屈原的作品呈现出新的
哀怨？）

Why are the refined notes as in *The Book of Songs* remote and weak, while in
Li Sao Qu Yuan created a new sorrowful style? (Li Bai: A Poem in Ancient
Style)

正始体 /Zhèngshǐ tǐ/
The Zhengshi Literary Style

指三国曹魏后期的文学风格。因始于魏齐王曹芳（232—274）
正始（240—249）年间，故名。这一时期的政治现实极其严酷，正
始文人因此以哲学眼光来看待、思考更为广阔的人生和宇宙问题。
深刻的理性思考和强烈的人生悲哀，构成了正始文学最基本的特
点。正始文学的主要特征是崇尚老庄，以玄理入诗，呈现出浓厚
的哲理色彩。当时作家主要有两派：一派是以何晏（？—249）、王
弼（226—249）为代表，开两晋"玄言诗"之先河；另一派是以嵇
康（223—262，或224—263）、阮籍（210—263）为代表，继承建
安文学传统，其作品有深厚的思想感情、鲜明的时代特色和个性特
点，因而成就较大。

The term refers to the literary style of the final years of the State of Wei in
the Three Kingdoms period. It emerged in the Zhengshi era (240–249)
under the reign of Cao Fang (232-274), also known as Prince Qi of Wei.
Facing the harsh prevailing political conditions, literary figures of the era
viewed life and the world in a broader and philosophical context, and
profound and rational analysis as well as penetrating depiction of human
tragedies were underlying features of their writings. Reverence for Laozi and

Zhuangzi was a key feature of this literary style, with poetry, in particular, being abstruse and philosophical in terms of message. The Zhengshi style had two schools. One was represented by He Yan (?-249) and Wang Bi (226-249), whose works heralded the Jin-dynasty metaphysical poetry. The other school, represented by literary figures like Ji Kang (223-262 or 224-263) and Ruan Ji (210-263), was more influential. Building on the Jian'an literary tradition, they conveyed in their writings profound thought and emotions, and gave vivid expression to social life at the time with intense individual characteristics.

引例 Citation：

◎及正始明道，诗杂仙心，何晏之徒，率多浮浅。唯嵇志清峻，阮旨遥深，故能标焉。（刘勰《文心雕龙·明诗》）

（到了正始年间，盛行道家思想，诗歌夹杂出尘求仙的内容。何晏等人的作品大都比较浅薄。只有嵇康的诗有清远高峻的情志，阮籍的诗表现出深远意旨，所以他们能高出同时代人。）

By the Zhengshi era, Daoism was popular and, as a result, poetry reflected people's desire to reach the immortal world. Works by He Yan and his followers were for the most part superficial. Only Ji Kang expressed lofty ideals, and Ruan Ji showed depth and insight in his poetry; they thus stood out among the writers of that age. (Liu Xie: *The Literary Mind and the Carving of Dragons*)

郑声 /zhèngshēng/

The Music of the State of Zheng

指与"雅乐"相对的民间通俗音乐。原指春秋战国时期郑、卫地区的音乐，又称"郑卫之音"。较之雅乐的庄重、大气、规范，郑声曲调自由、富于形式变化，歌词内容多写男女之情。孔子（前

551—前479）认为这些作品放纵个人情感，思想不够纯正，有损礼乐教化，应该加以排斥。后世学者多以"郑声"指代低俗文艺，亦有学者认为它们应该属于民歌等通俗文艺范畴，是艺术创新的源头及对高雅艺术的一种补充。

This refers to popular folk music in history, as opposed to formal ceremonial music. The term, originally "the music of Zheng and Wei," referred to music from the states of Zheng and Wei during the Spring and Autumn and the Warring States periods. Unlike stately, grand and highly structured classical music, the music of Zheng featured free-flowing melodies and a wealth of variations, with lyrics that often spoke of the love between men and women. Confucius (551 - 479 BC) felt that works of this sort gave free rein to personal emotions and lacked purity in ways of thinking, that they were not conducive to educating people through etiquette and music, and should therefore not be permitted. Many scholars subsequently used "the music of Zheng" to refer to lowbrow arts, but others considered these tunes to be folk songs which were a form of popular culture, a source of artistic creation and a complement to highbrow arts.

引例 Citations：

◎放郑声，远佞人。郑声淫，佞人殆。(《论语·卫灵公》)

（抛弃郑国的音乐，远离花言巧语的小人。郑国的音乐淫靡，花言巧语的小人危险。）

Cast aside the music of Zheng, and keep your distance from smooth-talking petty men. The music of Zheng is seductive, and smooth-talking petty men are dangerous. (*The Analects*)

◎《韶》响难追，郑声易启。岂惟观乐？于焉识礼。(刘勰《文心雕龙·乐府》)

（虞舜时的《韶》乐难以企及，而淫靡俗乐却很容易流行。难道季札当年只是为了想听鲁国的音乐？他是想通过音乐了解礼的兴衰啊。）

Classical music from the era of Yu and Shun is hard to grasp, whereas the crass and seductive music (of Zheng) can easily become popular. Do you think Jizha only wanted to listen to the music of the State of Lu? He wanted to understand, through music, the decline of rites and etiquette. (Liu Xie: *The Literary Mind and the Carving of Dragons*)

知音 /zhīyīn/
Resonance and Empathy

　　体会和理解文艺作品的意蕴与作者的思想感情。原指音乐欣赏中的知己，后经魏晋南北朝时期文艺批评家的阐释，用来泛指文艺鉴赏中的心心相印、互相理解。"知音"作为文学批评的核心概念，涉及文艺创作与鉴赏中的个体差异与共性等诸多问题，有着丰富的精神蕴涵，与西方的读者反应批评理论、接受美学、解释学等基本思想有一致之处。

The term is about appreciating and understanding the ideas in literary and artistic works and the thoughts of their authors. The original meaning was feeling a sense of resonance with music. It was later extended by literary critics in the Wei, Jin, and Southern and Northern dynasties to mean resonance or empathy between writers / artists and their readers / viewers. As a core concept in literary criticism, it touches upon both general and particular issues in artistic creation and appreciation, involves rich intellectual implications, and meshes with the audience's response in Western criticism, receptive aesthetics, and hermeneutics.

引例 Citations：

◎是故不知声者不可与言音，不知音者不可与言乐，知乐则几于礼矣。(《礼记·乐记》)

（不懂自然声音的人无法与其谈论音律，不懂音律的人无法与其谈论音乐，通晓音乐的人也就接近懂得礼了。）

Talking about melody with someone who has no ear for natural sounds would be a waste of time, and so would discussing music with someone who knows nothing about melody. One who knows music is close to understanding social norms. (*The Book of Rites*)

◎知音其难哉！音实难知，知实难逢，逢其知音，千载其一乎！（刘勰《文心雕龙·知音》）

（理解音乐是多么困难啊！音乐实在难于理解，理解音乐的人很难遇到，要遇到理解音乐的人，恐怕是千年一遇呀！）

It is such a challenge to understand music! Since music is so hard to understand, it is difficult to find people who can appreciate it. It may take a thousand years to find someone who understands music! (Liu Xie: *The Literary Mind and the Carving of Dragons*)

直寻 /zhíxún/
Direct Quest

诗人即兴而感，直接抒写。这是南朝钟嵘（？—518？）《诗品》中针对诗歌过多使用典故的现象提出的创作主张，他汲取了道家的自然思想，通过考察前人的优秀诗篇，提炼出一种新的诗歌创作方式——"直寻"，即直接描写所感知事物，直接抒发内心情感并创造出情景契合的审美意象。明清时期诗学的"性灵说"受到其影响。

A poet should directly express his thoughts and sentiments when he is inspired. This is a concept for writing poems proposed by poetry critic Zhong Rong (?-518?) of the Southern Dynasties in his work *The Critique of Poetry* as a reaction to the excessive use of allusions and quotes from earlier works.

Inspired by naturalist ideas of Daoism and by his own reading of the fine works of earlier poets, he developed a new form of poetic creation which he named "direct quest." By this, he meant directly describing matters that one senses and learns about, directly expressing one's inner feelings, and creating aesthetic images in which the sensibilities match up with current realities. The theory of inner self used in Ming- and Qing-dynasty poetics was influenced by this idea.

引例 **Citations**：

◎观古今胜语，多非补假，皆由直寻。（钟嵘《诗品》卷中）

（综观古今名篇佳句，大都不是借用前人诗句或使用典故，而是直接从自身体验中寻求而得。）

A comprehensive survey of the best-known works of ancient and current poets shows that most of the poets did not borrow favored lines or literary allusions from their predecessors, but directly sought inspirations from their personal experiences. (Zhong Rong: *The Critique of Poetry*)

◎我手写我口，古岂能拘牵！（黄遵宪《杂感》其二）

（我写出的都是我想说的话，怎能受古人的文字拘束牵制！）

I write what I want to say,
Not to be constrained by old writing styles. (Huang Zunxian: Random Thoughts)

咫尺有万里之势 /zhǐchǐ yǒu wànlǐ zhī shì/
Power of Landscape Within Inches

著名的山水画大师在咫尺见方的画幅上可以描画出辽远广阔的景致。这种艺术描绘方式，并不是事无巨细地全部照搬，而是融合了创作者的艺术素养，展现出创作者的心灵与胸襟，对于素材则删繁就简，由约而博，由近而远。"咫尺有万里之势"后也用于诗歌批评。这个术语中，最重要的是"势"，体现在诗歌、绘画等创作方面，即注重炼意构思，使作品具备艺术张力和强大的表现力，整体气势动人，不拘泥于一字一笔。要达到这种艺术境界，不能只依靠临摹和模仿，而要亲身阅历，开拓眼界，感知造化神奇，超越尘俗。

Masters of landscape painting are able to depict natural scenery which has vast breadth and distance on an inches-wide scroll. The artist does not just copy a scenery, but rather creates a work of art which integrates his artistic accomplishments and displays his heart and mind. The artist omits superfluous details and brings close a distant landscape with a broad perspective. This idea also applies to poetry criticism. Its most important element is "power," which means that general layout and core message give poems, paintings, and other works of art a dramatic effect, expressiveness and appeal, rather than paying excessive attention to detail. To achieve this, artists should not merely duplicate or imitate a landscape; they should personally experience it, expand their horizons, feel the natural wonders and transcend worldly concerns.

引例 Citations：

◎［萧贲（bì）］雅性精密，后来难尚。含毫命素，动必依真，尝画团扇，上为山川，咫尺之内，而瞻万里之遥；方寸之中，乃辨千寻之峻。（姚最《续画品》）

（萧贲作画非常精致细密，后人很难比得上。他构思作画铺设绢素的时候，一笔一画必然依据真实情况，他曾经在团扇上画山水，一尺见方的画幅上，竟然能看到万里远的景致；一寸大小的画面上，可以辨明几千寻高的峻山。）

Xiao Bi paints carefully and meticulously, and later generations can hardly match him. When he paints on silk, he executes every stroke precisely in accordance with the real scenery. He once painted on a dainty round fan a landscape on which you can see the scenery of hundreds of miles into the distance. In the painting, mountains which are thousands of feet high can be discerned within a square-inch space. (Yao Zui: *A Sequel to the Criticism of Painting*)

◎论画者曰"咫尺有万里之势",一"势"字宜着眼。若不论势,则缩万里于咫尺,直是《广舆记》前一天下图耳。五言绝句,以此为落想时第一义。唯盛唐人能得其妙。如:"君家住何处?妾住在横塘。停船暂借问,或恐是同乡。"墨气所射,四表无穷,无字处皆其意也。(王夫之《姜斋诗话》卷二)

(论画的人说"一尺有万里的气势",其中一个"势"字应该抓住。如果不讲"势",就是把万里江山缩进一尺里,只不过是《广舆记》前面的一张天下地图而已。五言绝句,以这为构思的第一要义。唯有盛唐时期的诗人能够掌握奥妙。比如"君家住何处?妾住在横塘。停船暂借问,或恐是同乡",笔墨气势发散,向四方无限辐射,就是没有字的地方也满是情意。)

Critics say that a landscape painting can appear to be stretching ten thousand *li* on a very small piece of paper. The key point here is whether an overwhelming impact can be achieved. Without such impact, even if a vast landscape is squeezed into an extremely limited space, the result will be just another all-inclusive map of the country easily available in *The Geography Guidebook*. A five-character quatrain, which is supposed to present a big picture in extremely few words, puts the creation of power above all else. Only poets in the golden years of the Tang Dynasty can truly understand this marvel. For example, between poetic lines such as "May I ask where you live, stranger? I live in Hengtang not far from here. Let's halt our boats and ask more about each other, for after all we might be folks from the same hometown," a tremendous poetic impact keeps hovering even though details are omitted. So much affection is conveyed where no words are actually said. (Wang Fuzhi: *Desultory Remarks on Poetry from Ginger Studio*)

至乐无乐 /zhìlè-wúlè/

Utmost Happiness Lies in Not Aware of the Happiness.

至高的快乐是内心祥和而超越乐与不乐的判断。庄子（前369？—前286）认为，快乐应该依从于自己的本心，如果以世俗观念为判断依据，可能会背离生命的本质；如果为情感和欲望所驱使，可能会伴随失落与伤害。快乐与否的判断实际上源于对利害得失的判断，而利害得失是相对的、可变的，因此，忘却得失利害、没有了快乐意念才是"至乐"的境界。"至乐无乐"说体现出中国古代文人学士通达的心性、自由多元的人生价值观，激发了他们反思、批判与超越的精神。

Utmost happiness is an inner peace that transcends any judgment as to whether we are happy or not. Zhuangzi (369?-286 BC) held that happiness should be dictated solely by the heart. If we measure happiness against a worldly criterion, we may lose sight of life's essential purpose. If we are driven by emotions and base desires, harm and loss may be the result. Our happiness in fact depends on our judgment of loss or gain. However, loss or gain is relative and subject to change. Only when we totally forget this question can we attain utmost happiness. This term reflects the spiritual magnanimity and the open, pluralistic worldview of ancient Chinese scholars, while urging them to greater effort at self-reflection, criticism, and transcendence.

引例 Citations：

◎果有乐无有哉？吾以无为诚乐矣，又俗之所大苦也。故曰："至乐无乐，至誉无誉。"（《庄子·至乐》）

（世间果真是存在快乐呢，还是不存在呢？我认为没有快乐与不快乐的意识才是真正的快乐，而这又是世人为之大感苦恼的事情。所以说："至高的快乐是无需感到快乐，最高的荣誉是无需众人赞誉。"）

Is there happiness or not in this world of ours? My belief is that utmost happiness lies in not even being aware of it. However, this very thought is exactly what agonizes us all. Hence the maxim: "Utmost happiness is when we do not strive for it, and highest praise consists in having no need for praise." (*Zhuangzi*)

◎孔子曰:"请问游是。"老聃曰:"夫得是,至美至乐也,得至美而游乎至乐,谓之至人。"(《庄子·田子方》)

(孔子说:"请问游心于万物的本原状态是怎样的情景?"老聃说:"达到这样的境界,就领略到极致的美,畅游于极致的快乐中,达到这种人生境界的人就称为'至人'。")

When Confucius asked: "When the heart roams free between heaven and earth, what will the scene look like?" Laozi answered: "Once a person has reached that realm, he will be able to savor beauty at its best and bask in extreme happiness. Such a person is known as a 'man of the highest order.'" (*Zhuangzi*)

治世之音 /zhìshìzhīyīn/
Music of an Age of Good Order

　　指太平时代的音乐。儒家认为,音乐与社会政治相互联通,音乐能反映一个国家的政治盛衰得失及社会风俗的变化。乐教能促使政治清明,社会秩序稳定;反过来,太平时代政治开明、和美,其音乐、诗歌作品一定充满祥和欢乐。"治世之音"也被用来指《诗经》中的某些美颂之作。

Confucian scholars believed that music interacts with both society and its political evolution; it also reflects the rise and decline of a state's political strength and changes of social customs. Music education fosters good governance and social stability. In an age of peace and stability with enlightened governance and harmony, its music and poetry are characterized by serenity and joyfulness. "Music of an age of good order" also refers to some eulogies in *The Book of Songs*.

引例 Citation：

◎凡音者，生人心者也。情动于中，故形于声。声成文，谓之音。是故治世之音安以乐，其政和。(《礼记·乐记》)

（大凡音乐都产生于人的内心。情感在心中激荡，所以表现为各种声音。声音组合成曲调，就叫做音乐。所以，太平时代的音乐祥和欢乐，这是因为政治宽和的缘故。）

All music is born in people's minds. As people's inner emotions surge, they turn into sound. When sound is formed into a pattern, music is created. The music of an age of good order is filled with peace and joyfulness thanks to the harmonious political atmosphere of the time. (*The Book of Rites*)

诸宫调 /zhūgōngdiào/
Song-speech Drama

一种源于北宋、流行于金元的说唱艺术。同一宫调的多首曲子，可组成一个套曲，诸宫调则是不同宫调的多个套曲的组合。其表演形式是唱完一个宫调的套曲，即换韵演唱另一个宫调的套曲。在套曲与套曲的演唱间隙，表演者通过说白来叙述情节，衔接前后。套曲之间，有时也夹有单曲小令。诸宫调对于元杂剧的成型与发展影响较大。董解(jiè)元创作的《西厢记诸宫调》是存世最完整的诸宫调作品，代表了金代戏曲的最高水平。

The term refers to a form of theatrical performance combining song and speech popular in the Jin and Yuan periods. The drama is composed of sets of songs. Each set of songs is composed of the same mode of music, or *gongdiao*. During the performance, one set of songs is followed by another set of songs. Between them, the performer adds spoken narrative to explain the story and string the plot together. Sometimes single ditties are added. The genre had a marked influence on the development of Yuan *zaju* or opera. The *zhugongdiao* version of *Romance of the Western Chamber* by Dong Jieyuan is the most intact extant *zhugongdiao* drama, and represents the best of Jin Dynasty opera.

引例 Citations：

◎长短句中，作滑稽无赖语，起于至和。嘉祐之前，犹未盛也。熙、丰、元祐间，宛州张山人以诙谐独步京师，时出一两解。泽州孔三传（chuán）者，首创诸宫调古传，士大夫皆能诵之。（王灼《碧鸡漫志》卷二）

（词作中，使用滑稽逗笑的语言，是从至和年间开始的。嘉祐之前，还不兴盛。熙宁、元丰和元祐年间，宛州张山人的诙谐表演在京城无人能比，时不时地就作一两首。泽州孔三传，首创用诸宫调演绎古代传奇故事，士大夫都能吟诵。）

The use of humorous and comic language in *ci* poems began in the Zhihe era (1054) of the Song Dynasty, but did not become widespread until the Jiayou era (1056 - 1063). During the Xining, Yuanfeng and Yuanyou periods (1068 - 1093), the comic performances of Zhang Shanren of Yanzhou were the best in the capital, and he would often make up verses of his own. It was Kong Sanchuan of Zezhou who first used *zhugongdiao* to tell the legendary tales of ancient times, and most literati could recite the lines and hum the tunes. (Wang Zhuo: *Musings from Biji Lane*)

◎说唱诸宫调，昨汴京有孔三传，编成传奇灵怪，入曲说唱；今杭城有女流熊保保，及后辈女童皆效此，说唱亦精。（吴自牧《梦粱录》卷二十"妓乐"）

（用诸宫调说唱，以前汴京有个孔三传，自编了一些传奇故事和有关

神灵鬼怪的话本，配合乐曲说唱；现在杭州女艺人熊保保以及后辈
女童都模仿他，她们的说唱技艺也很精湛。）

In the capital Bianjing, there was Kong Sanchuan who wrote dramas based on legendary tales and stories of gods and spirits, which he then combined with music to perform in *zhugongdiao* song-speech style. Today, Xiong Baobao, a female performer in Hangzhou, and other younger women who imitated him, also perform exquisitely. (Wu Zimu: *Notes of Past Dreams*)

主文而谲谏 /zhǔ wén ér jué jiàn/
Admonition Through Tactful Wording

　　诗歌在歌咏的同时以含蓄委婉的方式对执政者进行讽谏。"文"
指有文采的歌咏；"谲"义为曲折变化，意思是不要直陈执政者的
过失；"谏"就是规劝、谏诫。出自《毛诗序》。最初由儒家总结
《诗经》的表达手法而提出，后来用为一切文艺作品应当遵循的标
准。它的核心思想是，诗歌可以对执政者进行劝谏、讽刺，但要以
含蓄委婉的言辞、比兴譬喻的方式寄托对执政者的批评以及对现实
的不满。这一命题是儒家政治伦理在文学批评领域的具体表现。

This term shows that poetry should indirectly and mildly advise a ruler against wrongdoing. The critic should resort mainly to tactful and sensitive wording, trying not to appear blunt or offensive when admonishing the ruler. The term first appeared in the "Introductions to *Mao's Version of The Book of Songs*"; it was created by Confucian scholars in summarizing the various means of expression in *The Book of Songs*. Later, it became a criterion for measuring all works of art and literature. The core message is that, while poetry can be used to criticize or satirize a ruler and also to show discontent with social reality, a mild or indirect way should be employed, namely analogy, association, simile, and metaphor. This view is a manifestation of Confucian political ethics in the field of literary criticism.

引例 Citation：

◎上以风化下，下以风刺上。主文而谲谏，言之者无罪，闻之者足
以戒，故曰风。(《毛诗序》)

(执政者用风诗教化百姓，百姓也用风诗讥刺执政者，用富于文采
的诗歌对执政者含蓄委婉地进行劝讽，歌咏的人不会因此获罪，听
闻诗歌的人足以引起警诫，所以将这类诗称作"风"。)

Rulers use *feng* (ballads) to cultivate the people and the people use them to
ridicule the rulers. So long as a critic advises the monarch mildly and through
beautiful poetry, he will not be found guilty and the monarch he criticizes
will become more careful in making decisions. These poems are called *feng*.
(Introductions to *Mao's Version of The Book of Songs*)

祝盟 /zhùméng/

Benediction and Vow of Allegiance

　　古代文体名称。"祝"指祝辞，是祭祀时对神赞美、向神祷祝
并求得神灵福佑的文辞；"盟"指盟辞，是结盟时以神为证所立的
誓约。它们的共同点都是以向神祷请的方式表达意愿和承诺。南朝
刘勰（465？—520？或532？）认为，祷神的祝辞应该诚恳质朴，
不能华丽夸饰；"盟"的目的是订立盟誓，使神明知晓自己的意愿
和承诺，强调结盟的意义和彼此同进退、共存亡的意愿，因此立辞
应当坦诚恳切，以感恩神灵的美好话语加强誓约各方的感情联系。
刘勰指出，誓约最终取决于各方的诚信而不是神灵，但美好的祝盟
文字有助于培育君子的德行。

Zhu or benediction is a short essay written to pay tribute to gods and seek
their blessing. *Meng* or a vow of allegiance is made by allies to gods. They both
express a wish and a commitment to gods. According to Liu Xie (465 ?- 520 ?

or 532?) of the Southern Dynasties, a *zhu* should be sincere in tone and plain in wording, without any pomposity or fanfare. A *meng*, as a vow of allegiance, is intended to let gods know the commitment of rulers to entering into an alliance and sharing weal and woe. Therefore, a *meng* should be candid and sincere and reinforce solidarity between the allies through a prayer to gods. The success of entering into an alliance, said Liu Xie, depends ultimately on the sincerity of all the parties involved, not on gods. But a beautifully written *zhu* or *meng* will help to foster trust in and noble character among the people involved.

引例 Citations：

◎ 天地定位，祀遍群神。六宗既禋（yīn），三望咸秩。甘雨和风，是生黍稷。兆民所仰，美报兴焉。牺盛（chéng）惟馨，本于明德；祝史陈信，资乎文辞。（刘勰《文心雕龙·祝盟》）

（天地的位置确定以后，人们祭祀各种神祇，对天地四时的祭祀已经完成，对山、河、海的遥祭也次第进行，于是有和风甘雨，帮助谷物生长。万民信仰神力，用上好祭品酬报神灵。供奉的祭品固然要无比馨香，而根本在于彰显神明的功德；主持祭祀的祝史向神灵表达心意，这就需要借助于祝辞。）

After the positions of heaven and earth were determined, people began offering sacrifices to gods. The prayers to heaven, earth and the four seasons were offered, and tributes were being paid to distant mountains, rivers and sea. As a result, mild winds and precious rain helped crops to grow. People all had faith in divine power; they offered their best sacrifices to repay gods for their blessings. The best food would be offered to gods in reverence. The master of sacrificial ceremonies would naturally use *zhu* (benedictions) to express people's sincere wish. (Liu Xie: *The Literary Mind and the Carving of Dragons*)

◎ 故知信不由衷，盟无益也。（刘勰《文心雕龙·祝盟》）

（由此可见，誓约如果不能出自真心，订立的誓约也毫无意义。）

It can thus be seen that a *meng* or a vow of allegiance made without sincerity would be meaningless. (Liu Xie: *The Literary Mind and the Carving of Dragons*)

◎然非辞之难，处辞为难。后之君子，宜在殷鉴，忠信可矣，无恃神焉。（刘勰《文心雕龙·祝盟》）

（誓约的文辞不难写，难在遵守约定。后世君子应当以背弃誓约的有关史实为鉴戒，恪守忠信的原则才行，不要依赖于神灵。）

It is not difficult to write a vow of allegiance. The hard part is honoring it. People in later generations should learn the past lessons of breaking vows of allegiance. One should remain true to one's word and not rely on the grace of the gods. (Liu Xie: *The Literary Mind and the Carving of Dragons*)

转益多师 /zhuǎnyì-duōshī/
Learn from Many Masters, and Form Your Own Style

尽可能博采众长，以丰富自己的文艺创作。"转益"意为辗转自益，只要对自己创作有益的东西都应该加以学习吸收；"多师"谓广泛师法，不必专主一家。出自唐代诗人杜甫（712—770）《戏为六绝句》。它包含相互联系的两个方面：其一，尽可能广泛学习、师法古人或时贤的创作经验，博采众长，兼收并蓄。其二，在无所不师的同时既有继承也要有所批判。只有这样，才能合乎或接近《诗经》的风雅传统，形成自己的艺术风格。后来这一术语的使用范围由诗歌创作而扩展至文学艺术等各个领域。

The expression means to learn widely from others so as to enrich one's own artistic creation. *Zhuanyi* (转益) means to learn and absorb everything that can further one's creativity; *duoshi* (多师) means to learn from many teachers. This comes from "Six Playful Quatrains" by Du Fu (712-770) of the Tang Dynasty. There are two related meanings in this term: 1) learn from the experience and skills of all masters, past and present; and 2) while learning and carrying on the best, also be discerning, so as to approach or conform to the traditions of meaning and form as expressed in *The Book of Songs*, and then develop one's own poetic style. The expression later came to include not just poetry but also literature and art.

引例 Citations：

◎ 未及前贤更勿疑，递相祖述复先谁？别裁伪体亲风雅，转益多师是汝师。(杜甫《戏为六绝句》其六)

(浅薄之辈不及前贤这点不必怀疑，代代继承前人为何区分谁先谁后？甄别去除猥杂不纯的诗歌而直接亲近《诗经》的风雅传统，多方师法、博采众长，才是你真正有益的老师。)

Superficial men are clearly not the equal of past masters; why would one mind who was the first to pass on the tradition? Discard the poorly written and learn from *The Book of Songs*. And learning from many past masters means you've found the right teacher. (Du Fu: Six Playful Quatrains)

◎ 昔昌黎《进学》，马、扬上并《盘》《诰》。杜陵论文，卢、骆譬之江河。同工异曲，转益多师，明示轨躅 (zhuó)，无区畺畛 (jiāngzhěn)。(陈塘《答吴子述书》，见缪荃孙《艺风堂杂钞》卷五)

(过去韩愈写《进学解》，把司马相如、扬雄的作品与古代的《尚书》相提并论。杜甫谈论诗文创作，把卢照邻、骆宾王的创作比作江河奔流。韩愈、杜甫的论述对象虽然不同，思路却是一致的，都强调博采众长、多方师法，给后人明确指示了文学创作的法则，不应自我封闭、自我设限。)

In his work "Progress in Learning," Han Yu compared the writings of Sima Xiangru and Yang Xiong to *The Book of History*. In his commentary on poetry composition, Du Fu likened the works of Lu Zhaolin and Luo Binwang to rapidly flowing rivers. Han and Du were writing for different readers, but both believed in the value of learning from many teachers, and advised writers and poets not to close themselves off from multiple influences. (Chen Yong: Reply to Wu Zishu)

滋味 /zīwèi/

Nuanced Flavor

　　诗歌中能够使欣赏者反复回味的意蕴，实即诗歌美感。南朝诗论家钟嵘（？—518？）在《诗品》中提出，五言诗歌创作应重视内容与形式的配合，使欣赏者在品读中产生无穷的回味。后来"滋味"也指从事文艺创作时的一种趣味。

This term refers to an effect that allows lasting satisfaction and rewarding in poetry appreciation, which is a particular sense of beauty offered by poetry. In the Southern Dynasties, poetry critic Zhong Rong (?- 518 ?) proposed in *The Critique of Poetry* that in writing five-character-per-line poems, one should pay special attention to the combination of form and content, so that readers could enjoy a poem with inexhaustible delight. Later, nuanced flavor also came to refer to a kind of taste in literary and artistic creation.

引例 Citations：

◎五言居文词之要，是众作之有滋味者也。（钟嵘《诗品》卷上）

（五言诗在各种诗体中居于首位，是众多作品中最有审美意味的。）

Five-character-per-line poems constitute the most important poetic form and are most richly imbued with nuanced flavors. (Zhong Rong: *The Critique of Poetry*)

◎至于陶冶性灵，从容讽谏，入其滋味，亦乐事也。（颜之推《颜氏家训·文章》）

（至于文章可以陶冶心灵，从容巧妙地讽谏帝王，使读者感受到一种审美意味。这也是一大快事。）

A literary work cultivates the mind, implicitly satirizes or criticizes a monarch, and enables the reader to obtain a sense of aesthetic appreciation. Reading such works gives one great delight. (Yan Zhitui: *Admonitions for the Yan Clan*)

紫之夺朱 /zǐzhīduózhū/

Purple Prevailing over Red

指社会生活与文学艺术等领域以邪乱正、真伪混淆的现象。朱指红色，古人认为是正色，而紫色则看作杂色，"夺"是胜过的意思。孔子（前551—前479）对于在春秋时期出现邪正不分、淫靡的音乐取代雅正音乐的现象十分反感，提出要加以正本清源、拨乱反正。南朝刘勰（465？—520？或532？）借此批评有的作者在文章写作上背离了儒家经典，迎合人们的猎奇心理。后世以此倡导、确立儒家的文学标准与规范。

This refers to evil prevailing over good and falsehood being mistaken for truth in literature and art as well as in social life. It is red, not purple, that was viewed as a truly proper color by the ancient Chinese. Confucius (551 - 479 BC), upset by the loss of judgment over good and evil, and by the fact that vulgar music was taking the place of refined classical music in the Spring and Autumn Period, called for dispelling confusion and putting things in the right order. With this in mind, Liu Xie (465 ?- 520 ? or 532 ?) of the Southern Dynasties criticized some writers for abandoning Confucian teachings and catering to vulgar tastes. Scholars of later generations used this notion to reaffirm Confucian criteria and norms for literary creation.

引例 Citations：

◎子曰："恶紫之夺朱也，恶郑声之乱雅乐也，恶利口之覆邦家者。"（《论语·阳货》）

（孔子说："我厌恶用紫色取代红色，厌恶用郑国的音乐扰乱雅正的音乐，憎恶伶牙俐齿而使国家倾覆的人。"）

Confucius said, "I detest replacing red with purple and interfering refined classical music with the music of the State of Zheng. I loathe those who overthrow the state with their glib tongues." (*The Analects*)

◎辞为肌肤，志实骨髓。雅丽黼黻（fǔfú），淫巧朱紫。（刘勰《文心雕龙·体性》）

（文辞好比文章的肌肤，作者的思想感情才是文章的骨髓。高雅的文章犹如上古礼服所绣的花纹那样华丽庄重，过分追求辞藻与技巧则如同杂色搅乱了正色。）

Rhetoric is like the skin of an essay; the writer's thoughts and feelings are its marrow. A piece of elegant writing is like the embroidery on a ceremonial gown in ancient times – magnificent and dignified. Excessive focus on rhetoric and technique, however, is no different from an abnormal color taking the place of a truly proper one. (Liu Xie: *The Literary Mind and the Carving of Dragons*)

自然英旨 /zìrán-yīngzhǐ/
Charm of Spontaneity

在诗歌创作中不假雕饰地呈现自然万物之美和人的真情实感。"英旨"本义是美好的滋味，用为文学术语，指诗歌美妙的内容和意境。南朝钟嵘（？—518？）在《诗品》中，要求诗人用自己的语言直接抒写思想感情，反对借用前人的诗句来吟咏自己的情志，批评五言诗创作中过度讲究辞藻和声律，认为符合"自然英旨"的创作才是最为珍贵的诗歌作品。后世文论中的"自然""天真"等词传承了上述内涵。

This term means poetry creation should present the unembellished beauty of nature and the genuine sentiments of human beings. The original meaning of *yingzhi* (英旨) is good taste. Used as a literary term, however, it refers to charming content and aesthetic conception in poetry. In *The Critique of Poetry*, Zhong Rong (?-518?) of the Southern Dynasties called on poets to express their thoughts and sentiments in their own words and opposed borrowing expressions from ancient poets. He criticized the excessive attention to ornate language and tonal rhythms in the writing of five-character-per-line poetry. He maintained that spontaneously created poems of good taste were most valuable. The expressions "natural" and "simple and unaffected" in later literary criticisms contain Zhong Rong's ideas.

引例 Citations：

◎近任昉、王元长等，词不贵奇，竞须新事，尔来作者，寖（jìn）以成俗。遂乃句无虚语，语无虚字；拘挛补衲，蠹文已甚。但自然英旨，罕值其人。（钟嵘《诗品》卷中）

（近来的文人任昉、王融等，不注重语言创新，争相使用各种无人用过的典故，此后的作者逐渐形成了这样的习惯。于是没有不用典故的句子，没有无来历的字词；典故与自己的文字勉强牵合拼贴，对作品破坏严重。几乎很少有诗人能够写出不假雕饰地呈现自然美和真情实感的作品。）

Ren Fang, Wang Rong and some other writers of recent times have given no attention to linguistic innovation yet vied with each other for using literary allusions that no one else has ever employed. Subsequent writers have turned this practice into a habit. And so, all sentences must contain allusions, and every word and expression has to be traceable to some sources. Allusions are clumsily tacked onto the authors' own words, severely damaging their works. There are few poets capable of producing works that display the pristine beauty of nature or their genuine sentiments. (Zhong Rong: *The Critique of Poetry*)

◎所示书教及诗赋杂文，观之熟矣。大略如行云流水，初无定质，但常行于所当行，常止于所不可不止，文理自然，姿态横生。（苏轼《答谢民师书》）

（你给我看的信和诗赋杂文，我阅读得很熟了。大致都像飘动着的云和流动着的水一样，本来没有固定的形态，经常行进在应当行进

的地方，经常停止于不得不停止的地方，文章条理自然，姿态多变
而不受拘束。）

I have read with great interest the letters, poems, and essays you have sent to me. Broadly speaking, these articles are like floating clouds and flowing water; they have no fixed form or structure, and drift to where they should or stop when they have to. The articles are written in a natural way and have changing and unrestricted styles. (Su Shi: A Letter of Reply to Xie Minshi)

总集 /zǒngjí/
General Collection / Anthology

汇集多人诗文作品的集子（与汇集某一作家诗文作品的"别集"相对）。总集的体例，从内容角度看，有"全集式"总集与"选集式"总集；按照收录时代范围，可分为通代总集和断代总集；按所收录作品的文体，可分为专辑同一文体的总集和汇集各种文体作品的总集。总集中最有代表性的为南朝梁昭明太子萧统（501—531）及文士共同编选的《文选》。《文选》选录先秦至梁初各类文体700余篇文学作品，以内容与文采并茂为收录标准，不收经、史、子类文章（仅收史传中的少量序、论、赞），反映出当时人们的文学观念，对于后世文学发展影响深远。

Zongji (总集) is a collection of various authors' poems and proses (distinct from *bieji* 〔别集〕, a collection of a particular author's literary works). In terms of content, an anthology could be either comprehensive or limited in selection. Chronically, an anthology can be a general collection spanning written history, or a general collection from one dynasty. In terms of the genre of collected works, it can be divided into collections of a specific genre and collections of various genres. The most representative anthology is *Selections of Refined Literature* compiled and edited jointly by Xiao Tong (501-

531, Crown Prince Zhaoming of the Liang Dynasty during the Southern Dynasties) and his literary advisors. *Selections of Refined Literature* consists of more than 700 outstanding literary pieces of various genres from pre-Qin through the early Liang. It does not include any work that belongs to the categories of *jing* (经 Confucian classics), *shi* (史 history), or *zi* (子 thoughts of ancient scholars and schools), but does include a small number of prefaces, commentaries, and eulogies from *shi*. *Selections of Refined Literature* reflects the literary trend of the time and exerted a far-reaching impact on the development of Chinese literature in the years to come.

引例 Citations：

◎总集者，以建安之后，辞赋转繁，众家之集，日以滋广，晋代挚虞……合而编之，谓为《流别》。(《隋书·经籍志》)

(总集之由来，是因为汉建安之后，辞赋创作数量繁多，各家的文集，日益增广。于是晋朝的挚虞……把它们合编在一起，称之为《流别》。)

An anthology was compiled because a large number of works of *ci* (辞) and *fu* (赋) were created, and different collections of various authors were widespread. They were put together under the title of *Literary Trends and Schools* by Zhi Yu of the Jin Dynasty. (*The History of the Sui Dynasty*)

◎总集盖源于《尚书》、《诗》三百篇，洎(jì)王逸《楚词》、挚虞《流别》后，日兴纷出，其义例可得而言。(马其昶《〈桐城古文集略〉序》)

(总集大体源于《尚书》《诗经》，及至王逸编选《楚辞》、挚虞编选《流别》之后，纷纷面世，它的主旨和体例才可以论说清楚。)

The form of anthology originated from *The Book of History* and *The Book of Songs*. After *Annotations on Odes of Chu* and *Literary Trends and Schools* were compiled and edited by Wang Yi and Zhi Yu respectively, various anthologies began to appear, and became clear in themes and formats. (Ma Qichang: Preface to *Selected Classic Works of the Tongcheng School*)

奏启 /zòuqǐ/

Memorial or Statement to Present One's View to the Emperor

　　古代文体名称，是臣下向帝王言事、提出意见的文书。"奏"的意思是"进言"，臣下向皇帝论述政事、报告下情并明确提出意见；"启"的意思是"开启、敞开"，向皇帝坦诚提出看法。"奏"讲求明辨通达，文辞质朴；"启"兼有奏、表两种文体的功用，篇幅简短，略有文采。南朝刘勰（465？—520？或532？）认为，奏启是为口头进言准备的文本，主要用来向皇帝报告紧急事变、弹劾过失、陈述政事、表达政见等，因此较之章表，要求更加客观严谨，要言不烦，少有主观情绪。这对今天的公文写作仍有指导意义。

This genre of writing was used by officials to report important matters or present personal views to the emperor. *Zou* (奏) here means "a reminder to the throne," i.e., a statement of an administrative matter plus a clear-cut view on how to handle it. *Qi* (启) here means "a candid view on state business." The former should be prudent, insightful and plain in style, whereas the latter, functioning as both a memorial and a petition, should be brief and unassuming in style. Liu Xie (465 ?-520 ? or 532 ?) of the Southern Dynasties observed that this kind of writing was prepared for making an oral presentation to the emperor. It reported an urgent situation, exposed wrongdoers, expressed one's views on governance issues, and proposed ways to handle them. Therefore, unlike a memorial of gratitude or petition, a memorial to present one's view to the emperor should be objective, discreet and succinct, and unaffected by one's own mood. This observation still holds true for writing official communications today.

引例 Citations：

◎夫奏之为笔，固以明允笃诚为本，辨析疏通为首。强志足以成务，博见足以穷理，酌古御今，治繁总要。此其体也。（刘勰《文心雕龙·奏启》）

（"奏"这种文体，本就应以明白允实、忠厚诚实为根本，以明辨分析、疏通畅达为首要任务。要以坚定的意志来达成目标，要有广博的见识以穷究事理，借鉴历史经验来解决当下问题，抓住要领来处理繁杂事务。这就是写作奏书的大致要求。）

Zou or memorial to the emperor should be objective, candid and truthful. Its primary purpose is to fully clarify and analyze an issue. One who writes a memorial to the emperor should do so with firm resolve to reach a worthy goal. He should be highly knowledgeable so that he can explore an issue thoroughly, draw on past experience to solve the problem at hand, and identify key factors in addressing a multitude of issues. These are the basic elements that are important for writing a good memorial. (Liu Xie: *The Literary Mind and the Carving of Dragons*)

◎ 自晋来盛启，用兼表奏。陈政言事，既奏之异条；让爵谢恩，亦表之别干。必敛饬入规，促其音节，辨要轻清，文而不侈，亦启之大略也。（刘勰《文心雕龙·奏启》）

（晋代以来，"启"的运用相当普遍，兼有表和奏的功能。就用于陈述政见、讨论国事说，"启"是"奏"的分支；就用于辞让封爵、感谢恩典方面说，"启"是"表"的枝干。"启"一定要行文严谨，合乎法度，音节短促，论辩简要，行文轻快，有文采而不浮夸，写作"启"的要领大致如此。）

The use of *qi* or memorial to present one's views has remained quite common since the Jin Dynasty. As far as the articulation of views and the discussion of state affairs are concerned, such memorials are a sub-type of general memorials (*zou*) submitted to the emperor. Such memorials may also be submitted to decline a title of nobility or express gratitude for an honor conferred by the emperor. In this sense, they are a sub-type of general memorials (*biao*) submitted to the emperor. In writing a memorial to present a candid view, one should be careful about wording and comply with laws and regulations. The memorial should be short in sense groups, highlight key facts and arguments and be persuasive in style. It should be eloquent but not flamboyant. These are the basic rules for writing a good memorial to present one's views. (Liu Xie: *The Literary Mind and the Carving of Dragons*)

尊碑贬帖 /zūnbēi-biǎntiè/

Praising Stone Inscriptions while Belittling Copying from Stone Rubbings

推崇碑刻书法，贬抑单纯摹仿名家帖书。它是一种书法思潮，也是追求自然多变、推崇个性与创新的书论主张。阮元（1764—1849）反对独尊二王、以学帖为法的悠久传统，指出帖书和碑刻书体各有所长。包世臣（1775—1855）详论碑刻书体的特点，有以其优点补帖书之不足的意思。康有为（1858—1927）指出帖书辗转相传、失却原貌是尊碑的客观原因，碑刻能够呈现书体的阶段性变化和历史多样性。康有为认为书论"可著圣道，可发王制，可洞人理，可穷物变"，应该立足现状考察历史，穷则思变，其维新变法思想在此初露端倪。

This term means to advocate stone-borne calligraphy while deprecating hand-copied script in mere imitation of famed calligraphers. It reflects a calligraphic trend toward natural variation and individual creativity. Ruan Yuan (1764-1849), for example, opposed the age-old tradition of lauding master calligraphers Wang Xizhi and Wang Xianzhi alone and honoring the practice of learning calligraphy only by copying an exemplary sample preserved on paper. He held that stone-borne calligraphy, like hand-copied script, had its own distinctive merits. Bao Shichen (1775-1855) elaborated further on the features of stone-borne calligraphy, stating that it made up for the inadequacies in paper-borne calligraphy. Kang Youwei (1858-1927) saw the loss of original form when paper-borne copies passed from hand to hand over generations as justification for favoring stone-borne calligraphy. Calligraphy on stones, he maintained, could show its change and variety over different historical periods. He said that commentaries on calligraphy "helped to highlight the ways of the sages, urge the renewal of monarchical institutions, gain insight into human nature, and explore the laws of change for all things in the universe." Calligraphy should inspire a re-examination of history on the basis of present-day conditions and prepare people for drastic reform.

引例 Citations：

◎是故短笺长卷，意态挥洒，则帖擅其长；界格方严，法书深刻，则碑据其胜。（阮元《北碑南帖论》）

（因此无论是短笺还是长卷，随心挥洒笔墨，是帖书的长处；若论结构方正严谨而又下笔深沉有力，则是碑刻的长处。）

Therefore, whether in the form of a brief note or a long scroll, free and uninhibited execution is the merit of paper-borne calligraphy. On the other hand, stone-borne calligraphy boasts structural rigor and discipline marked by deep, powerful execution. (Ruan Yuan: On Stone-borne Calligraphy in the North and Paper-borne Calligraphy in the South)

◎今日欲尊帖学，则翻之已坏，不得不尊碑。（康有为《广艺舟双楫·尊碑》）

（今人想要尊崇帖学，但书帖因辗转翻刻而原貌已被破坏，从而不得不转而推尊碑体书法。）

Many of our contemporaries honor the practice of emulating paper-borne calligraphy. However, calligraphy on that medium has lost its genuineness passing through generations, hence the shift to stone-borne calligraphy. (Kang Youwei: *A Further Elaboration on the Techniques of Writing and Calligraphy*)

附录 Appendices

中国历史年代简表
A Brief Chronology of Chinese History

远古时代 Prehistory		
夏 Xia Dynasty		c. 2070 - 1600 BC
商 Shang Dynasty		1600 - 1046 BC
周 Zhou Dynasty	西周 Western Zhou Dynasty	1046 - 771 BC
	东周 Eastern Zhou Dynasty 春秋时代 Spring and Autumn Period 战国时代 Warring States Period	770 - 256 BC 770 - 476 BC 475 - 221 BC
秦 Qin Dynasty		221 - 206 BC
汉 Han Dynasty	西汉 Western Han Dynasty	206 BC-AD 25
	东汉 Eastern Han Dynasty	25 - 220
三国 Three Kingdoms	魏 Kingdom of Wei	220 - 265
	蜀 Kingdom of Shu	221 - 263
	吴 Kingdom of Wu	222 - 280
晋 Jin Dynasty	西晋 Western Jin Dynasty	265 - 317
	东晋 Eastern Jin Dynasty 十六国 Sixteen States*	317 - 420 304 - 439
南北朝 Southern and Northern Dynasties	南朝 Southern Dynasties	宋 Song Dynasty	420 - 479
		齐 Qi Dynasty	479 - 502
		梁 Liang Dynasty	502 - 557
		陈 Chen Dynasty	557 - 589
	北朝 Northern Dynasties	北魏 Northern Wei Dynasty	386 - 534
		东魏 Eastern Wei Dynasty 北齐 Northern Qi Dynasty	534 - 550 550 - 577
		西魏 Western Wei Dynasty 北周 Northern Zhou Dynasty	535 - 556 557 - 581

隋 Sui Dynasty		581 - 618
唐 Tang Dynasty		618 - 907
五代十国 Five Dynasties and Ten States	后梁 Later Liang Dynasty	907 - 923
	后唐 Later Tang Dynasty	923 - 936
	后晋 Later Jin Dynasty	936 - 947
	后汉 Later Han Dynasty	947 - 950
	后周 Later Zhou Dynasty	951 - 960
	十国 Ten States**	902 - 979
宋 Song Dynasty	北宋 Northern Song Dynasty	960 - 1127
	南宋 Southern Song Dynasty	1127 - 1279
辽 Liao Dynasty		907 - 1125
西夏 Western Xia Dynasty		1038 - 1227
金 Jin Dynasty		1115 - 1234
元 Yuan Dynasty		1206 - 1368
明 Ming Dynasty		1368 - 1644
清 Qing Dynasty		1616 - 1911
中华民国 Republic of China		1912 - 1949

中华人民共和国1949年10月1日成立

People's Republic of China, founded on October 1, 1949

*"十六国"指东晋时期在我国北方等地建立的十六个地方割据政权，包括：汉（前赵）、成（成汉）、前凉、后赵（魏）、前燕、前秦、后燕、后秦、西秦、后凉、南凉、南燕、西凉、北凉、北燕、夏。

The "Sixteen States" refers to a series of local regimes established in the northern area and other regions of China during the Eastern Jin Dynasty, including Han (Former Zhao), Cheng (Cheng Han), Former Liang, Later Zhao (Wei), Former Yan, Former Qin, Later Yan, Later Qin, Western Qin, Later Liang, Southern Liang, Southern Yan, Western Liang, Northern Liang, Northern Yan, and Xia.

**"十国"指五代时期先后存在的十个地方割据政权，包括：吴、前蜀、吴越、楚、闽、南汉、荆南（南平）、后蜀、南唐、北汉。

The "Ten States" refers to the ten local regimes established during the Five Dynasties period, including Wu, Former Shu, Wuyue, Chu, Min, Southern Han, Jingnan (also Nanping), Later Shu, Southern Tang, and Northern Han.

人名索引

Index of Names

著作名索引
Index of Cited Works

H

J

评韩柳诗 / 苏轼 A Critique of Poems by Han Yu and Liu Zongyuan 188

Q

R

S

X

Y

Z

术语条目笔画索引

Concepts Listed in Order of Number of Strokes

图书在版编目（CIP）数据

中华思想文化术语．文艺卷：汉英对照 /《中华思想文化术语》编委会编．——北京：外语教学与研究出版社，2021.5（2024.10重印）
ISBN 978-7-5213-2543-0

Ⅰ. ①中… Ⅱ. ①中… Ⅲ. ①中华文化－术语－汉、英②中华文化－术语－汉、英 Ⅳ. ①B2-61②K203-61

中国版本图书馆 CIP 数据核字 (2021) 第 059240 号

出 版 人　王　芳
责任编辑　刘　佳
项目编辑　赵璞玉
责任校对　刘虹艳
装帧设计　李　高
出版发行　外语教学与研究出版社
社　　址　北京市西三环北路 19 号（100089）
网　　址　https://www.fltrp.com
印　　刷　北京盛通印刷股份有限公司
开　　本　880×1230　1/32
印　　张　18
版　　次　2021 年 5 月第 1 版 2024 年 10 月第 5 次印刷
书　　号　ISBN 978-7-5213-2543-0
定　　价　138.00 元

如有图书采购需求，图书内容或印刷装订等问题，侵权、盗版书籍等线索，请拨打以下电话或关注官方服务号：
客服电话：400 898 7008
官方服务号：微信搜索并关注公众号"外研社官方服务号"
外研社购书网址：https://fltrp.tmall.com

物料号：325430001